Kaplan Publishing are constantly fi
ways to make a difference to your s
exciting online resources really do
different to students looking for exam success.

C000185871

This book comes with free MyKaplan online resources so that you can study anytime, anywhere. This free online resource is not sold separately and is included in the price of the book.

Having purchased this book, you have access to the following online study materials:

CONTENT	ACCA (including FFA,FAB,FMA)		FIA (excluding FFA,FAB,FMA)	
	Text	Kit	Text	Kit
iPaper version of the book	✓	✓	✓	✓
Interactive electronic version of the book	✓			
Check Your Understanding Test with instant answers	✓			
Material updates	✓	✓	✓	✓
Latest official ACCA exam questions*		✓		
Extra question assistance using the signpost icon**		✓		
Timed questions with an online tutor debrief using clock icon*		✓		
Interim assessment including questions and answers	✓		✓	
Technical answers	✓	✓	✓	✓

* Excludes F1, F2, F3, F4, FAB, FMA and FFA; for all other papers includes a selection of questions, as released by ACCA
** For ACCA P1-P7 only

How to access your online resources

Kaplan Financial students will already have a MyKaplan account and these extra resources will be available to you online. You do not need to register again, as this process was completed when you enrolled. If you are having problems accessing online materials, please ask your course administrator.

If you are already a registered MyKaplan user go to www.MyKaplan.co.uk and log in. Select the 'add a book' feature and enter the ISBN number of this book and the unique pass key at the bottom of this card. Then click 'finished' or 'add another book'. You may add as many books as you have purchased from this screen.

If you purchased through Kaplan Flexible Learning or via the Kaplan Publishing website you will automatically receive an e-mail invitation to MyKaplan. Please register your details using this email to gain access to your content. If you do not receive the e-mail or book content, please contact Kaplan Flexible Learning.

If you are a new MyKaplan user register at www.MyKaplan.co.uk and click on the link contained in the email we sent you to activate your account. Then select the 'add a book' feature, enter the ISBN number of this book and the unique pass key at the bottom of this card. Then click 'finished' or 'add another book'.

Your Code and Information

This code can only be used once for the registration of one book online. This registration and your online content will expire when the final sittings for the examinations covered by this book have taken place. Please allow one hour from the time you submit your book details for us to process your request.

Please scratch the film to access your MyKaplan code.

Please be aware that this code is case-sensitive and you will need to include the dashes within the passcode, but not when entering the ISBN. For further technical support, please visit www.MyKaplan.co.uk

Professional Examinations

Paper F7

Financial Reporting

EXAM KIT

September 2016 – June 2017
Applicable for computer-based exams and
paper-based exams

KAPLAN

PUBLISHING

British Library Cataloguing-in-Publication Data

A catalogue record for this book is available from the British Library.

Published by:

Kaplan Publishing UK

Unit 2 The Business Centre

Molly Millar's Lane

Wokingham

Berkshire

RG41 2QZ

ISBN: 978-1-78415-696-1

Acknowledgements

The past ACCA examination questions are the copyright of the Association of Chartered Certified Accountants. The original answers to the questions from June 1994 onwards were produced by the examiners themselves and have been adapted by Kaplan Publishing.

We are grateful to the Chartered Institute of Management Accountants and the Institute of Chartered Accountants in England and Wales for permission to reproduce past examination questions. The answers have been prepared by Kaplan Publishing.

CONTENTS

Section

Key features in this edition

In addition to providing a wide ranging bank of exam standard questions, we have also included in this edition:

- An analysis of all of the recent examination papers.

- Paper specific information.

- Our recommended approach to make your revision for this particular subject as effective as possible. This includes step by step guidance on how best to use our Kaplan material (Complete text, pocket notes and exam kit) at this stage in your studies.

- Enhanced tutorial answers packed with specific key answer tips, technical tutorial notes and exam technique tips from our experienced tutors.

- Complementary online resources including full tutor debriefs and question assistance to point you in the right direction when you get stuck.

You will find a wealth of other resources to help you with your studies on the following sites:

www.mykaplan.co.uk

www.kaplan-exam-tips.com

www.accaglobal.com/students/

Quality and accuracy are of the utmost importance to us so if you spot an error in any of our products, please send an email to mykaplanreporting@kaplan.com with full details, or follow the link to the feedback form in MyKaplan.

Our Quality Co-ordinator will work with our technical team to verify the error and take action to ensure it is corrected in future editions.

KAPLAN PUBLISHING

INDEX TO QUESTIONS AND ANSWERS

INTRODUCTION

Following the revised exam format, and the addition of *IFRS 15 Revenue from contracts with customers,* many of the previous ACCA exam questions within this kit have been adapted to reflect updated standards, and the revised exam format. If changed in any way from the original version, whether due to updates in the IFRSs or due to changes in exam format, this is indicated in the end column of the index below with the mark *(A).*

The specimen paper is included at the end of the kit.

KEY TO THE INDEX

PAPER ENHANCEMENTS

We have added the following enhancements to the answers in this exam kit:

Key answer tips

All answers include key answer tips to help your understanding of each question.

Tutorial note

All answers include more tutorial notes to explain some of the technical points in more detail.

Top tutor tips

For selected questions, we 'walk through the answer' giving guidance on how to approach the questions with helpful 'tips from a top tutor', together with technical tutor notes.

These answers are indicated with the 'footsteps' icon in the index.

ONLINE ENHANCEMENTS

 Timed question with Online tutor debrief

For selected questions, we recommend that they are to be completed in full exam conditions (i.e. properly timed in a closed book environment).

In addition to the examiner's technical answer, enhanced with key answer tips and tutorial notes in this exam kit, online you can find an answer debrief by a top tutor that:

- works through the question in full

- points out how to approach the question

- how to ensure that the easy marks are obtained as quickly as possible, and

- emphasises how to tackle exam questions and exam technique.

These questions are indicated with the 'clock' icon in the index.

 Online question assistance

Have you ever looked at a question and not know where to start, or got stuck part way through?

For selected questions, we have produced 'Online question assistance' offering different levels of guidance, such as:

- ensuring that you understand the question requirements fully, highlighting key terms and the meaning of the verbs used

- how to read the question proactively, with knowledge of the requirements, to identify the topic areas covered

- assessing the detail content of the question body, pointing out key information and explaining why it is important

- help in devising a plan of attack

With this assistance, you should then be able to attempt your answer confident that you know what is expected of you.

These questions are indicated with the 'signpost' icon in the index.

Online question enhancements and answer debriefs will be available on MyKaplan at:

www.MyKaplan.co.uk

BUSINESS COMBINATIONS

ANALYSING FINANCIAL STATEMENTS

ANALYSIS OF PAST EXAM PAPERS

The table summarises the key topics that have been tested in F7 exams to date. A much wider range of topics will now be examined following the introduction of multiple choice questions. The information from June 2015 onwards only relates to constructed response questions.

	Jun 11	Dec 11	Jun 12	Dec 12	Jun 13	Dec 13	Jun 14	Specimen 14	Dec 14	Jun 15	Sep/Dec 15
Group financial statements											
Consolidated statement of profit or loss and other comprehensive income	✓			✓			✓	✓		✓	
Consolidated statement of financial position		✓	✓		✓			✓			✓
Consolidated P/L and SFP						✓			✓		
Associates		✓	✓	✓				✓			
Non-group financial statements											
From trial balance	✓	✓	✓	✓	✓	✓	✓	✓	✓	✓	✓
Redraft											
Statement of changes in equity	✓	✓	✓	✓			✓			✓	✓
Statement of cash flows	✓	✓	✓	✓	✓			✓	✓		
Performance appraisal											
Ratios				✓			✓	✓	✓	✓	✓
Framework/IFRS											
IASB Framework	✓		✓	✓	✓	✓		✓	✓		
Accounting principles/ substance						✓		✓	✓		
Not for profit/specialised entities								✓	✓		
IAS 2									✓		
IAS 8				✓			✓	✓	✓		
IAS 10								✓			
IAS 12								✓	✓		
IAS 16				✓	✓	✓	✓	✓	✓		
IAS 17						✓		✓	✓		
IAS 20				✓			✓				
IAS 23											
IAS 32/IAS 39/IFRS 7/IFRS 9		✓						✓	✓		
IAS 33	✓							✓	✓		
IAS 36			✓		✓			✓	✓		
IAS 37		✓		✓		✓	✓	✓	✓		
IAS 38								✓			
IAS 40											
IAS 41								✓			
IFRS 5					✓				✓		
IFRS 13											
IFRS 15									✓		

EXAM TECHNIQUE

It is suggested that you take time at the beginning of the exam to read the questions and examination requirements carefully, and begin planning your answers.

- **Divide the remaining time** you spend on questions in proportion to the marks on offer. For example, if you spent 15 minutes reading the paper and planning your answers, there would be 1.8 minutes available per mark in the examination.

  Whatever happens, always keep your eye on the clock and **do not over run on any part of any question!**

However you plan to use your exam time, you should:

- take time to accurately insert the objective question responses into the answer grid

- ensure for all questions that the requirement has been fully understood and determine the process necessary to answer the question; and

- for long questions (also referred to as Constructed Response questions) properly consider how to structure the response and lay it out so as to articulate the answer clearly.

- If you **get completely stuck** with a question:
  - leave space in your answer book, and
  - **return to it later.**

- Stick to the question and **tailor your answer** to what you are asked.
  - pay particular attention to the verbs in the question.

- You should do everything you can to make things easy for the marker.

  The marker will find it easier to identify the points you have made if your **answers are legible**.

- **Written questions:**

  Your answer should have:
  - a clear structure
  - a brief introduction, a main section and a conclusion.

  It is better to write a little about a lot of different points than a great deal about one or two points.

- **Computations:**

  It is essential to include all your workings in your answers.

  Many computational questions require the use of a standard format:

  e.g. statement of profit or loss and other comprehensive income, statement of financial position and statement of cash flow.

  Be sure you know these formats thoroughly before the exam and use the layouts that you see in the answers given in this book and in model answers.

- **Objective test and objective case questions:**

  Decide whether you want to attempt these at the start of the exam or at the end.

  No credit for workings will be given in these questions; the answers will either be correct (2 marks) or incorrect (0 marks).

  Read the question carefully, as the alternative answer choices will be given based on common mistakes that could be made in attempting the question.

PAPER SPECIFIC INFORMATION

THE EXAM

FORMAT OF THE EXAM

The exam will be in **THREE sections**, and will be a mix of narrative and computational answers. Section A will be 15 objective test questions, each worth 2 marks. Section B will consist of 3 objective case questions, each worth 10 marks and containing 5 questions. Section C will consist of two 20 mark questions

		Number of marks
Section A:	Fifteen 2-mark objective test questions	30
Section B:	Thee 10-mark objective case questions	30
Section C:	Two 20-mark constructed response questions, covering the interpretation and preparation of financial statements for a single entity or a group	40
		100

Total time allowed: 3 hours 15 minutes

Note that:

- The F7 will have both a discursive and computational element. The questions will therefore include a mix of calculation-based and explanations-based questions.

- There is likely to be a longer discussion element within section C.

- This exam kit contains questions which could appear in either a computer-based exam (CBE) or paper-based exams. In the paper-based exam, all objective questions will be multiple-choice, with candidates selecting the correct answer from 4 options. In the computer-based exam, the objective questions will be in a variety of formats, which can be seen in this exam kit.

PASS MARK

The pass mark for all ACCA Qualification examination papers is 50%.

KAPLAN GUIDANCE

As all questions are compulsory, there are no decisions to be made about choice of questions, other than in which order you would like to tackle them.

Therefore, in relation to F7, we recommend that you take the following approach with your time:

- **Write down** on the question paper next to the mark allocation **the amount of time you should spend on each part.** Do this for each part of every question.

- **Decide the order** in which you think you will attempt each question:

  This is a personal choice and you have time on the revision phase to try out different approaches, for example, if you sit mock exams.

  A common approach is to tackle the section A first, so they are out of the way and dealt with. Others may prefer to tackle section C first, as they will take longer than the individual questions in sections A and B.

- **Always read the requirement** first as this enables you to **focus on the detail of the question with the specific task in mind**.

  For computational questions:

  Highlight key numbers/information and key words in the question, scribble notes to yourself to remember key points in your answer. Jot down proformas required if applicable.

  For multiple choice questions:

  Read the question extremely carefully. All of the choices given are likely to be potential answers people could get if one or more errors are made, so take your time on these.

  For longer questions:

  Spot the easy marks to be gained in a question and parts which can be performed independently of the rest of the question. For example laying out basic proformas correctly, answer written elements not related to the scenario etc.

  Make sure that you do these parts first when you tackle the question.

  Don't go overboard in terms of planning time on any one question – you need a good measure of the whole paper and a plan for all of the questions at the end of the 15 minutes.

  With your plan of attack in mind, **start answering your chosen section** with your plan to hand, as soon as you are allowed to start.

 Always keep your eye on the clock and do not over run on any part of any question!

DETAILED SYLLABUS

The detailed syllabus and study guide written by the ACCA can be found at:

www.accaglobal.com/students/

KAPLAN'S RECOMMENDED REVISION APPROACH

QUESTION PRACTICE IS THE KEY TO SUCCESS

Success in professional examinations relies upon you acquiring a firm grasp of the required knowledge at the tuition phase. In order to be able to do the questions, knowledge is essential.

However, the difference between success and failure often hinges on your exam technique on the day and making the most of the revision phase of your studies.

The **Kaplan complete text** is the starting point, designed to provide the underpinning knowledge to tackle all questions. However, in the revision phase, pouring over text books is not the answer.

Kaplan Online knowledge check tests help you consolidate your knowledge and understanding and are a useful tool to check whether you can remember key topic areas.

Kaplan pocket notes are designed to help you quickly revise a topic area, however you then need to practice questions. There is a need to progress to full exam standard questions as soon as possible, and to tie your exam technique and technical knowledge together.

The importance of question practice cannot be over-emphasised.

The recommended approach below is designed by expert tutors in the field, in conjunction with their knowledge of the examiner and their recent real exams.

The approach taken for the fundamental papers is to revise by topic area.

You need to practice as many questions as possible in the time you have left.

OUR AIM

Our aim is to get you to the stage where you can attempt exam standard questions confidently, to time, in a closed book environment, with no supplementary help (i.e. to simulate the real examination experience).

Practising your exam technique on exam standard examination questions, in timed conditions, is also vitally important for you to assess your progress and identify areas of weakness that may need more attention in the final run up to the examination.

In order to achieve this we recognise that initially you may feel the need to practice some questions with open book help and exceed the required time.

The approach below shows you which questions you should use to build up to coping with exam standard question practice, and references to the sources of information available should you need to revisit a topic area in more detail.

Remember that in the real examination, all you have to do is:

- attempt all questions required by the exam

- only spend the allotted time on each question, and

- get them at least 50% right!

Try and practice this approach on every question you attempt from now to the real exam.

Previously, the exam format meant that students were able to attempt some form of 'question spotting' as there were three large topic areas. Following the introduction of multiple choice questions, this will no longer be the case and to pass F7, students will need to understand information from the wide range of topics across the syllabus.

EXAMINER COMMENTS

We have included some of the examiners comments to the examination questions in this kit for you to see the main pitfalls that students fall into with regard to technical content.

However, too many times in the general section of the report, the examiner comments that students had failed due to:

- 'misallocation of time'

- 'running out of time' and

- showing signs of 'spending too much time on an earlier question and clearly rushing the answer to a subsequent question'.

Good exam technique is vital.

THE KAPLAN PAPER F7 REVISION PLAN

Stage 1: Assess areas of strengths and weaknesses

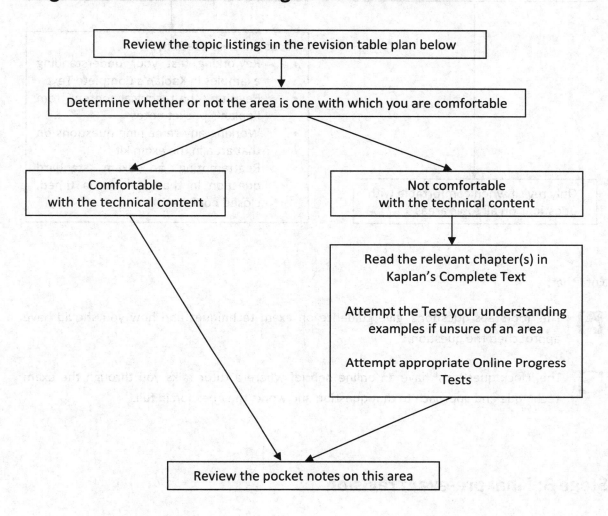

Stage 2: Practice questions

Follow the order of revision of topics as recommended in the revision table plan below and attempt the questions in the order suggested.

Try to avoid referring to text books and notes and the model answer until you have completed your attempt.

Try to answer the question in the allotted time.

Review your attempt with the model answer and assess how much of the answer you achieved in the allocated exam time.

Fill in the self-assessment box below and decide on your best course of action.

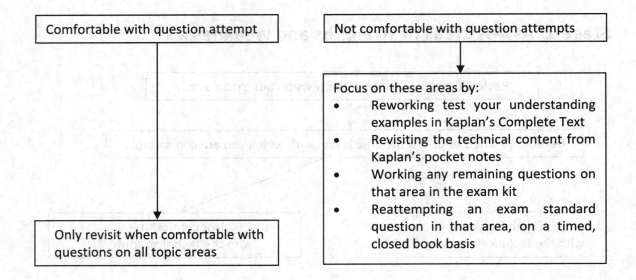

Comfortable with question attempt	Not comfortable with question attempts
	Focus on these areas by: • Reworking test your understanding examples in Kaplan's Complete Text • Revisiting the technical content from Kaplan's pocket notes • Working any remaining questions on that area in the exam kit • Reattempting an exam standard question in that area, on a timed, closed book basis
Only revisit when comfortable with questions on all topic areas	

Note that:

 The 'footsteps questions' give guidance on exam techniques and how you should have approached the question.

 The 'clock questions' have an online debrief where a tutor talks you through the exam technique and approach to that question and works the question in full.

Stage 3: Final pre-exam revision

We recommend that you **attempt at least one three hour mock examination** containing a set of previously unseen exam standard questions.

It is important that you get a feel for the breadth of coverage of a real exam without advanced knowledge of the topic areas covered – just as you will expect to see on the real exam day.

Ideally this mock should be sat in timed, closed book, real exam conditions and could be:

• a mock examination offered by your tuition provider, and/or

• the specimen paper in the back of this exam kit, and/or

• the last released examination paper (available shortly afterwards on MyKaplan with 'enhanced walk through answers' and a full 'tutor debrief').

KAPLAN'S DETAILED REVISION PLAN

Topic	Complete Text Chapter	Pocket note Chapter	Questions to attempt	Tutor guidance	Date attempted	Self assessment
Consolidated statement of financial position	17/19	17/19	141-150 316-320 374, 375 379, 384, 389	Practice the Kaplan 5 working approach. Ensure you get the easy marks available in the question from adding the parent and subsidiary assets and liabilities together.		
Consolidated statement of profit or loss and other comprehensive income	18/19	18/19	151-154 156-162 321-325 376, 378, 380 383, 386	Watch the dates carefully – is there a mid-year acquisition? If so you have to time apportion the subsidiary company results when adding the parent and subsidiary together.		
Consolidated statement of profit or loss and other comprehensive income and statement of financial position			373 377 385 387	Set up your proformas first and get the easy marks by adding the parent and subsidiary results together – then complete the 5 standard statement of financial position workings before moving on to complete the statement of profit or loss.		
Disposals of subsidiaries	20	20	182-185 330	Ensure you familiarise yourself with the workings related to calculating a profit/loss on disposal.		

Topic	Complete Text Chapter	Pocket note Chapter	Questions to attempt	Tutor guidance	Date attempted	Self assessment
Accounting standards:						
Non-current assets (IAS 16, IAS 38, IAS 40, IFRS 5, IAS 20)	2	2	1-6, 8-13 15-22 31-36 221-230 236-245	Be clear on initial recognition rules and subsequent measurement for PPE, intangible assets and investment properties. Ensure you understand how to deal with assets held for sale.		
IAS 23	2	2	7, 14 231-235	Ensure you know the definition of borrowing costs at the 3 recognition and 2 derecognition criteria.		
IAS 36	4	4	23-29 246-250	Learn the impairment test proforma and the cash generating unit write down rules.		
Framework	6/7	6/7	37-58	Learn the key definitions and be able to apply them to various standards		
IAS 2, IAS 8, IAS 41, IFRS 13	8	8	59-62 69-75 256-265	Each standard is relatively small, but it is key that you learn definitions and the specific rules relating to each.		
IAS 17	9	9	76-86 266-275	Be sure you can identify the differences between an operating and a finance lease.		

Topic	Complete Text Chapter	Pocket note Chapter	Questions to attempt	Tutor guidance	Date attempted	Self assessment
IAS 32/IFRS 7/IFRS 9	10	10	87-96 276-285	Amortised cost is the core area of financial liabilities here. Make sure you can deal with loans issued at a discount & redeemed at a premium. You will also need an awareness of the categories of financial asset in accordance with IFRS 9 and the accounting treatment for them.		
IAS 21	11	11	97-101 286-288	Examine the initial and subsequent treatment, in addition to the rules for unsettled transactions.		
IFRS 15	12	12	102-114 291-300	The different revenue scenarios should be looked at, in particular where revenue is recognised over time.		
IAS 12	13	13	115-118 289-290	Learn the definition of a temporary difference and practice its application.		
IAS 33	14	14	119-128 301-305	Learn the formula and apply to share issues.		
IAS 37	12	12	129-130 132-134 306-312	For IAS 37 the recognition rules are very clear – learn the 3 recognition rules.		
IAS 10	12	12	131, 135-136 313-315	Learn the differences between adjusting and non-adjusting events.		

Topic	Complete Text Chapter	Pocket note Chapter	Questions to attempt	Tutor guidance	Date attempted	Self assessment
Preparation of individual company financial statements	1, 23	1	351-367	You have to learn the accounting standards examinable first and then apply your knowledge to these recommended questions.		
Ratio interpretation	20	20	186-210 331-340 390-400	Learn the ratio calculations and practice identifying where you pull the information for the formula out of the financial statements.		
Statement of cash flows	22	22	211-220 341-350 368-372	Learn the proforma. Start with calculations in questions 201, 203, and 204 before moving on to analysing cash flows in 221 and 226.		

TECHNICAL UPDATE

IAS 21 THE EFFECTS OF CHANGES IN FOREIGN EXCHANGE RATES

IAS 21 The Effects of Changes in Foreign Exchange Rates is a new addition to the F7 syllabus. Students should study the complete text for further detail regarding this, but the key points are as follows:

Initial transactions should be translated at the historic rate at the date of the transaction.

When the transaction is settled (cash paid or received), the amount is retranslated at the date of payment. Any gain or loss on retranslation is taken to the statement of profit or loss.

For transactions that remain unsettled at the reporting date, monetary items should be retranslated at the closing rate, with gains or losses being taken to the statement of profit or loss. Non-monetary items should not be retranslated.

DISPOSAL OF SUBSIDIARIES

The disposal of a subsidiary is now examinable within F7. Students must be able to calculate the profit on disposal in the individual parent's financial statements in addition to the consolidated financial statements. A student should refer to the complete text for more detail, but the workings for each are shown below.

Parent's individual financial statements:

	$
Sales proceeds	X
Carrying amount of investment	(X)
Gain/loss to parent	X

Consolidated financial statements:

	$
Sales proceeds	X
Less: Carrying amount of goodwill at disposal	(X)
Less: Net assets at disposal	(X)
Add: Non-controlling interest at disposal	X
Gain/loss on disposal	X

It should be noted that disposals of subsidiaries will not be examined within a constructed response question.

GROUP INTERPRETATION QUESTIONS

Whilst group accounting and interpretations questions have both been on the F7 syllabus for many years, interpretations questions have traditionally focused on individual entities. From September 2016 onwards, interpretations questions may involve elements associated with group accounting.

This can involve adjusting a set of financial statements for an acquisition or disposal of a subsidiary, as well as making some adjustments which relate to group accounting.

Interpretations are likely to include a discussion of the fact that one year contains a subsidiary when the other does not. Consideration should also be given to any transactions between the group companies, particularly on any transactions which may not be at market value.

Section 1

OBJECTIVE TEST QUESTIONS – SECTION A

The objective test questions in this kit contain question types which will only appear in a computer-based exam, but these still provides valuable practice for all students whichever version of the exam they are taking. Students attempting a paper-based exam will only be examined on multiple-choice objective test questions, selecting the correct option from 4 choices.

CONCEPTUAL FRAMEWORK/INTERNATIONAL FINANCIAL REPORTING STANDARDS

1   IAS 16 *Property, Plant and Equipment* requires an asset to be measured at cost on its original recognition in the financial statements. EW used its own staff, assisted by contractors when required, to construct a new warehouse for its own use.

Identify whether the costs listed below should be capitalised or expensed.

	Capitalise	Expense
Clearance of the site prior to work commencing		
Professional surveyors' fees for managing the construction work		
EW's own staff wages for time spent working on the construction		
An allocation of EW's administration costs, based on EW staff time spent		

2   On 1 July 20X4, Experimenter opened a chemical reprocessing plant. The plant was due to be active for five years until 30 June 20X9, when it would be decommissioned. At 1 July 20X4, the costs of decommissioning the plant were estimated to be $4 million in 5 years time. The company considers that a discount rate of 12% is appropriate for the calculation of a present value, and the discount factor at 12% for Year 5 is 0.567.

What is the total charge to the statement of profit or loss in respect of the decommissioning for the year ended 30 June 20X5?

A $453,600

B $725,760

C $800,000

D $2,268,000

3 An entity purchased property for $6 million on 1 July 20X3. The value of the land was $1 million and the buildings $5 million. The expected life of the building was 50 years and its residual value nil. On 30 June 20X5 the property was revalued to $7 million (land $1.24 million, buildings $5.76 million). On 30 June 20X7, the property was sold for $6.8 million.

What is the gain on disposal of the property that would be reported in the statement of profit or loss for the year to 30 June 20X7?

A   Gain $40,000

B   Loss $200,000

C   Gain $1,000,000

D   Gain $1,240,000

4 A manufacturing entity receives a grant of $1m to purchase a machine on 1 January 20X3. The grant will be repayable if the company sells the asset within 4 years, which it does not intend to do. The asset has a useful life of 5 years.

What is the deferred income liability balance at 30 June 20X3?

$_____'000

5 On 1 January 20X1, Sty Co received $1m from the local government on the condition that they employ at least 100 staff each year for the next 4 years. Due to an economic downturn and reduced consumer demand, on 1 January 20X2, Sty no longer needed to employ any more staff and the conditions of the grant required full repayment.

What should be recorded in the financial statements on 1 January 20X2?

A   Reduce deferred income balance by $750,000

B   Reduce deferred income by $750,000 and recognise a loss of $250,000

C   Reduce deferred income by $1,000,000

D   Reduce deferred income by $1,000,000 and a gain of $250,000

6 **Which of the following properties owned by Scoop Co would be classified as an investment property?**

A   A stately home used for executive training but which is no longer required and is now being held for resale

B   Purchased land for investment potential. Planning permission has not been obtained for building construction of any kind

C   A new office building used as its head office, purchased specifically in order to exploit its capital gains potential

D   A property that has been leased out under a finance lease

7 An entity has the following loan finance in place during the year:

$1 million of 6% loan finance; $2 million of 8% loan finance

It constructed a new factory which cost $600,000 and this was funded out of the existing loan finance. The factory took 8 months to complete.

To the nearest thousand, what borrowing costs should be capitalised?

A $44,000

B $29,000

C $28,000

D $24,000

8 **Which of the following statements is correct?**

Statement 1: If the revaluation model is used for property, plant and equipment, revaluations must subsequently be made with sufficient regularity to ensure that the carrying amount does not differ materially from the fair value at each reporting date.

Statement 2: When an item of property, plant and equipment is revalued, there is no requirement that the entire class of assets to which the item belongs must be revalued.

	Statement 1	Statement 2
True		
False		

9 **Which TWO of the following items should be capitalised within the initial carrying amount of an item of plant?**

A Cost of transporting the plant to the factory

B Cost of installing a new power supply required to operate the plant

C A deduction to reflect the estimated realisable value

D Cost of a three-year maintenance agreement

E Cost of a three-week training course for staff to operate the plant

10   Tibet acquired a new office building on 1 October 20X4. Its initial carrying amount consisted of:

	$000
Land	2,000
Building structure	10,000
Air conditioning system	4,000
	16,000

The estimated lives of the building structure and air conditioning system are 25 years and 10 years respectively.

When the air conditioning system is due for replacement, it is estimated that the old system will be dismantled and sold for $500,000.

Depreciation is time apportioned where appropriate.

At what amount will the office building be shown in Tibet's statement of financial position as at 31 March 20X5?

A   15,625

B   15,250

C   15,585

D   15,600

11   The following trial balance extract relates to a property which is owned by Veeton as at 1 April 20X4:

	Dr	Cr
	$000	$000
Property at cost (20 year original life)	12,000	
Accumulated depreciation as at 1 April 20X4		3,600

On 1 October 20X4, following a sustained increase in property prices, Veeton revalued its property to $10.8 million.

What will be the depreciation charge in Veeton's statement of profit or loss for the year ended 31 March 20X5?

A $540,000

B $570,000

C $700,000

D $800,000

12   Which TWO of the following statements about IAS 20 *Accounting for Government Grants and Disclosure of Government Assistance* are true?

    A   A government grant related to the purchase of an asset must be deducted from the carrying amount of the asset in the statement of financial position.

    B   A government grant related to the purchase of an asset should be recognised in profit or loss over the life of the asset.

    C   Free marketing advice provided by a government department is excluded from the definition of government grants.

    D   Any required repayment of a government grant received in an earlier reporting period is treated as prior period adjustment.

13   Smithson Co purchased a new building with a 50 year life for $10 million on 1 January 20X3. On 30 June 20X5, Smithson Co moved out of the building and rented it out to third parties. Smithson Co uses the fair value model for investment properties. At 30 June 20X5 the fair value of the property was $11 million and at 31 December 20X5 it was $11.5 million.

What is the total net amount to be recorded in the statement of profit or loss in respect of the office for the year ended 31 December 20X5?

    A   Income $400,000

    B   Income $500,000

    C   Income $1,900,000

    D   Income $2,000,000

14   Gilbert Co entered took out a $7.5 million 10% loan on 1 January 20X6 to build a new warehouse during the year. Construction for the warehouse began on 1 February and was completed on 30 November. As not all the funds were needed immediately, Gilbert Co invested $2 million in 4.5% bonds from 1 January to 1 May.

What is the total interest to be capitalised in respect of the warehouse?

$_____ '000

15   Croft Co acquired a building on 1 January 20X3 for $8 million. The building had a 40 year life and Croft Co immediately rented it to a third party on a 2 year lease for $300,000 a year. At 31 December 20X3, the fair value of the property was estimated at $9 million with costs to sell estimated at $200,000.

If Croft Co uses the fair value model for investment properties, what total income should be recorded in the statement of profit or loss for the year ended 31 December 20X3?

$_____ '000

16 **Which of the following CANNOT be recognised as an intangible non-current asset in GHK's consolidated statement of financial position at 30 September 20X1?**

A GHK spent $132,000 developing a new type of product. In June 20X1 management worried that it would be too expensive to fund. The finances to complete the project came from a cash injection from a benefactor received in November 20X1.

B GHK purchased a subsidiary during the year. During the fair value exercise, it was found that the subsidiary had a brand name with an estimated value of $50,000, but was not recognised by the subsidiary as it was internally generated.

C GHK purchased a brand name from a competitor on 1 November 20X0, for $65,000.

D GHK spent $21,000 during the year on the development of a new product, after management concluded it would be viable in November 20X0. The product is being launched on the market on 1 December 20X1 and is expected to be profitable.

17 **Which of the following could be classified as development expenditure in M's statement of financial position as at 31 March 20Y0 according to IAS 38 *Intangible Assets?***

A $120,000 spent on developing a prototype and testing a new type of propulsion system. The project needs further work on it as the system is currently not viable.

B A payment of $50,000 to a local university's engineering faculty to research new environmentally friendly building techniques.

C $35,000 developing an electric bicycle. This is near completion and the product will be launched soon. As this project is first of its kind it is expected to make a loss.

D $65,000 developing a special type of new packaging for a new energy efficient light bulb. The packaging is expected to reduce M's distribution costs by $35,000 a year.

18 **Which TWO of the following factors is a reason why key staff cannot be capitalised as an intangible asset by an entity?**

A They do not provide expected future economic benefits

B They cannot be controlled by an entity

C Their value cannot be measured reliably

D They are not separable from the business as a whole

19 Amco Co carries out research and development. In the year ended 30 June 20X5, Amco incurred costs in relation to project X of $750,000. These were incurred at the same amount each month up to 30 April 20X5, when the project was completed. The product produced by the project went on sale from 31 May 20X5

The project had been confirmed as feasible on 1 January 20X5, and the product produced by the project was expected to have a useful life of five years.

What is the carrying amount of the development expenditure asset as at 30 June 20X5?

A $295,000

B $725,000

C $300,000

D $0

20   Sybil Co has acquired a subsidiary Basil in the current year.

Basil has a brand which has been reliably valued by Sybil at $500,000, and a customer list which Sybil has been unable to value.

Which of these describes how Sybil should treat these intangible assets of Basil in their consolidated Financial Statements?

A   They should be included in goodwill.

B   The brand should be capitalised as a separate intangible, whereas the customer list should be included within goodwill.

C   Both the brand and the customer list should be capitalised as separate intangibles.

D   The customer list should be capitalised as a separate intangible, whereas the brand should be included within goodwill.

21   Dempsey's year end is 30 September 20X4. Dempsey commenced the development stage of a new pharmaceutical drug on 1 January 20X4. $40,000 per month was incurred until the project was completed on 30 June 20X4 when the drug went into immediate production. The directors became confident of the project's success on 1 March 20X4. The drug has an estimated life span of five years; time apportionment is used by Dempsey where applicable.

What amount will Dempsey charge to profit or loss for development costs, including any amortisation, for the year ended 30 September 20X4?

A $12,000

B $98,667

C $48,000

D $88,000

22   **Which of the following statements relating to intangible assets is true?**

A   All intangible assets must be carried at amortised cost or at an impaired amount; they cannot be revalued upwards.

B   The development of a new process which is not expected to increase sales revenues may still be recognised as an intangible asset.

C   Expenditure on the prototype of a new engine cannot be classified as an intangible asset because the prototype has been assembled and has physical substance.

D   Impairment losses for a cash generating unit are first applied to goodwill and then to other intangible assets before being applied to tangible assets.

The following information is to be used for questions 23 and 24.

A division of a company has the following balances in its financial statements:

Goodwill	$700,000
Plant	$950,000
Property	$2,300,000
Intangibles	$800,000
Other net assets	$430,000

Following a period of losses, the recoverable amount of the division is deemed to be $4 million. A recent valuation of the building showed that the building has a market value of $2.5 million. The other net assets are at their recoverable amount. The company uses the cost model for valuing property, plant and equipment.

23   To the nearest thousand, what is the balance on property following the impairment review?

    A $2,300,000

    B $2,500,000

    C $2,027,000

    D $1,776,000

24   To the nearest thousand, what is the balance on plant following the impairment review?

    A $862,000

    B $837,000

    C $689,000

    D $261,000

25   A vehicle was involved in an accident exactly halfway through the year. The vehicle cost $10,000 and had a remaining life of 10 years at the start of the year. Following the accident, the expected present value of cash flows associated with the vehicle was $3,400 and the fair value less costs to sell was $6,500.

    What is the recoverable amount of the vehicle following the accident?

    $_____

26   The net assets of Fyngle, a cash generating unit (CGU), are:

	$
Property, plant and equipment	200,000
Allocated goodwill	50,000
Product patent	20,000
Net current assets (at net realisable value)	30,000
	———
	300,000
	———

As a result of adverse publicity, Fyngle has a recoverable amount of only $200,000.

What would be the value of Fyngle's property, plant and equipment after the allocation of the impairment loss?

A $154,545

B $170,000

C $160,000

D $133,333

27   **Which of the following is NOT an indicator of impairment?**

A   Advances in the technological environment in which an asset is employed have an adverse impact on its future use.

B   An increase in interest rates which increases the discount rate an entity uses.

C   The carrying amount of an entity's net assets is higher than the entity's number of shares in issue multiplied by its share price.

D   The estimated net realisable value of inventory has been reduced due to fire damage although this value is greater than its carrying amount.

28   Riley acquired a non-current asset on 1 October 20X9 at a cost of $100,000 which had a useful economic life of ten years and a nil residual value. The asset had been correctly depreciated up to 30 September 20Y4. At that date the asset was damaged and an impairment review was performed. On 30 September 20Y4, the fair value of the asset less costs to sell was $30,000 and the expected future cash flows were $8,500 per annum for the next five years. The current cost of capital is 10% and a five year annuity of $1 per annum at 10% would have a present value of $3.79

What amount would be charged to profit or loss for the impairment of this asset for the year ended 30 September 20Y4?

$_____

29 Metric owns an item of plant which has a carrying amount of $248,000 as at 1 April 20X4. It is being depreciated at 12.5% per annum on a reducing balance basis.

The plant is used to manufacture a specific product which has been suffering a slow decline in sales. Metric has estimated that the plant will be retired from use on 31 March 20X7.

The estimated net cash flows from the use of the plant and their present values are:

	Net cash flows	Present values
	$	$
Year to 31 March 20X5	120,000	109,200
Year to 31 March 20X6	80,000	66,400
Year to 31 March 20X7	52,000	39,000
	252,000	214,600

On 1 April 20X5, Metric had an alternative offer from a rival to purchase the plant for $200,000.

At what value should the plant appear in Metric's statement of financial position as at 31 March 20X5?

$_____

30 As at 30 September 20X3 Dune's property in its statement of financial position was:

Property at cost (useful life 15 years) $45 million

Accumulated depreciation $6 million

On 1 April 20X4, Dune decided to sell the property. The property is being marketed by a property agent at a price of $42 million, which was considered a reasonably achievable price at that date. The expected costs to sell have been agreed at $1 million. Recent market transactions suggest that actual selling prices achieved for this type of property in the current market conditions are 10% less than the price at which they are marketed.

At 30 September 20X4 the property has not been sold.

At what amount should the property be reported in Dune's statement of financial position as at 30 September 20X4?

A $36 million

B $37.5 million

C $36.8 million

D $42 million

31 BN has an asset that was classed as held for sale at 31 March 20X2. The asset had a carrying amount of $900 and a fair value of $800. The cost of disposal was estimated to be $50.

According to IFRS 5 *Non-current Assets Held for Sale and Discontinued Operations*, which value should be used for the asset as at 31 March 20X2?

A $750

B $800

C $850

D $900

32 **According to IFRS 5 Non-current Assets Held for Sale and Discontinued Operations which of the following relate to the criteria for an asset held for sale?**

(i)   Available for immediate sale in its present condition

(ii)   Sale is highly probable

(iii)   The sale is expected to be completed within the next month

(iv)   A reasonable price has been set

A   All of the above

B   (i), (ii) and (iii)

C   (i), (ii) and (iv)

D   (ii), (iii) and (iv)

33 **According to IFRS 5 *Non-current Assets Held for Sale and Discontinued Operations* which of the following amounts in respect of a discontinued operation must be shown on the face of the statement of profit or loss?**

	Shown on the face of the statement of profit or loss	Not shown
Revenue		
Gross profit		
Profit after tax		

34 Rural Co has the following two lines of business that have been disposed of in the year:

Sector X operated in Country A. Rural Co has no other operations in Country A, and Country A made up 0.5% of the total revenue of Rural Co.

Sector Y operated in the same country as the Rural Co head office. It produced a different item from the other parts of total Co, and this item contributed 10% of the total revenue of Rural Co

Which of these Sectors, if any, should be disclosed as a discontinued operation in the current year?

	Discontinued operation Yes/No
Sector X	
Sector Y	

35 **What is the primary reason why discontinued operations are presented separately within financial statements?**

A   To show an accurate valuation of the business

B   To enhance the predictive nature of financial statements

C   To make the financial statements easier to understand

D   So the financial statements are verifiable

36 At 1 April 20X4, Tilly owned a property with a carrying amount of $800,000 which had a remaining estimated life of 16 years. The property had not been revalued. On 1 October 20X4, Tilly decided to sell the property and correctly classified it as being 'held-for-sale'. A property agent reported that the property's fair value less costs to sell at 1 October 20X4 was expected to be $790,500 which had not changed at 31 March 20X5.

What should be the carrying amount of the property in Tilly's statement of financial position as at 31 March 20X5?

A $775,000

B $790,500

C $765,000

D $750,000

37 **Which one of the following gives the best description of the objectives of financial statements as set out by the International Accounting Standards Board's (IASB) *The Conceptual Framework for Financial Reporting*?**

A   To fairly present the financial position and performance of an enterprise

B   To fairly present the financial position, performance and changes in financial position of an enterprise

C   To provide information about the financial position and performance of an enterprise that is useful to a wide range of users in making economic decisions

D   To provide information about the financial position, performance and changes in financial position of an enterprise that is useful to a wide range of users in making economic decisions

38 **The IASB's *The Conceptual Framework for Financial Reporting* defines a liability as:**

A   an amount owed to another entity

B   a present obligation arising as a result of past events, the settlement of which is expected to result in an outflow of economic benefits

C   expenditure that has been incurred but not yet charged to the statement of profit or loss

D   an obligation that may arise in the future

39 The IASB's *The Conceptual Framework for Financial Reporting* lists two fundamental qualitative characteristics of financial statements, relevance and faithful representation.

Place the qualities listed alongside the appropriate qualitative characteristic.

	Faithful representation	**Relevance**
Completeness		
Predictive value		
Neutrality		

40 The IASB's *The Conceptual Framework for Financial Reporting* identifies qualitative characteristics of financial statements.

Which TWO of the following characteristics are NOT fundamental qualitative characteristics according to the IASB's *The Conceptual Framework for Financial Reporting*?

A Relevance

B Reliability

C Faithful representation

D Comparability

41 **Match the element to the correct definition according to The IASB's *The Conceptual Framework for Financial Reporting*?**

Element	Definition
Expense	A resource controlled by the entity as a result of past events and from which future economic benefits are expected to flow to the entity.
Liability	The residual interest in the assets of the entity after deducting all its liabilities.
Asset	A present obligation of the entity arising from past events, the settlement of which is expected to result in an outflow from the entity of resources embodying economic benefits.
Equity	Decrease in economic benefits during the accounting period in the form of outflows or depletions of assets or incurrences of liabilities.

42 **Which of the following explains the value that relevant information contains?**

A Instructive value

B Fair value

C Confirmatory value

D Approximate value

43 Which of the following is an example of following the principle of faithful representation?

    A   Showing finance lease payments as a rent expense

    B   Being prudent by recording the entire amount of a convertible loan as a liability

    C   Recording the future payments under an operating lease as a long-term liability

    D   Recording a sale and repurchase transaction with a bank as a loan rather than a sale

44 The *Conceptual Framework for Financial Reporting* defines an asset as:

    A   A resource controlled by an entity which is capable of generating independent cash flows

    B   A resource controlled by an entity as a result of past events, from which future economic benefits are expected

    C   A resource owned by an entity as a result of past events, from which future economic benefits are expected

    D   A resource capable of generating income for the entity

45 Which of the following criteria need to be satisfied in order for an item to be recognised?

    (i)   It meets the definition of an element of the financial statements

    (ii)   It is probable that future economic benefits will flow to or from the enterprise

    (iii)   It is certain that future economic benefits will flow to or from the enterprise

    (iv)   The item has a cost or value

    (v)   The item has a cost or value that can be reliably measured

    A   (i), (ii) and (v)

    B   (i), (iii) and (v)

    C   (i), (ii) and (iv)

    D   (i), (iii) and (iv)

46 Which description defines information that is relevant to users of financial information?

    A   Information that is free from error, bias and is a faithful representation of events

    B   Information that has been prudently prepared

    C   Information that is comparable from one period to the next

    D   Information that influences the decisions of users

47 Which description is most representative of the accounting framework used under IFRS?

	True	False
It is a principles-based framework		
It is a legal obligation		

48 Which is NOT a likely advantage of the global harmonisation of accounting standards?

A   Greater comparability between different firms

B   Greater ease for preparing consolidated financial statements

C   Easier for large international accounting firms

D   Greater compatibility with legal systems

49 Which THREE of the following are advantages of applying a principles-based framework of accounting rather than a rules-based framework?

A   It avoids 'fire-fighting', where standards are developed in responses to specific problems as they arise

B   It allows preparers and auditors to deal with complex transactions which may not be specifically covered by an accounting standard

C   Principles-based standards are thought to be harder to circumvent

D   A set of rules is given which attempts to cover every eventuality

E   It is easier to prove non-compliance

50 Which of the following is NOT a purpose of the IASB's Conceptual Framework?

A   To assist the IASB in the preparation and review of IFRS

B   To assist auditors in forming an opinion on whether financial statements comply with IFRS

C   To assist in determining the treatment of items not covered by an existing IFRS

D   To be authoritative where a specific IFRS conflicts with the Conceptual Framework

51 Financial statements represent transactions in words and numbers. To be useful, financial information must represent faithfully these transactions in terms of how they are reported.

Which of the following accounting treatments would be an example of faithful representation?

A   Charging the rental payments for an item of plant to the statement of profit or loss where the rental agreement meets the criteria for a finance lease

B   Including a convertible loan note in equity on the basis that the holders are likely to choose the equity option on conversion

C   Derecognising factored trade receivables sold without recourse

D   Treating redeemable preference shares as equity

52   Faithful representation is a fundamental characteristic of useful information within the IASB's *Conceptual framework for financial reporting*.

Which of the following treatments applies the principle of faithful representation?

A   Reporting a transaction based on its legal status rather than its economic substance.

B   Excluding a subsidiary from consolidation because its activities are not compatible with those of the rest of the group.

C   Recording the whole of the net proceeds from the issue of a loan note which is potentially convertible to equity shares as debt (liability).

D   Allocating part of the sales proceeds of a motor vehicle to interest received even though it was sold with 0% (interest free) finance.

53   The IASB's *Conceptual framework* for financial reporting defines recognition as the process of incorporating in the financial statements an item which meets the definition of an element and satisfies certain criteria.

Which of the following elements should be recognised in the financial statements of an entity in the manner described?

A   As a non-current liability: a provision for possible hurricane damage to property for a company located in an area which experiences a high incidence of hurricanes.

B   In equity: irredeemable preference shares.

C   As a trade receivable: an amount of $10,000 due from a customer which has been sold (factored) to a finance company with no recourse to the seller.

D   In revenue: the whole of the proceeds from the sale of an item of manufactured plant which has to be maintained by the seller for three years as part of the sale agreement.

54   Increasingly the IASB is requiring or allowing current cost to be used in many areas of financial reporting.

Drexler acquired an item of plant on 1 October 20X2 at a cost of $500,000. It has an expected life of five years (straight-line depreciation) and an estimated residual value of 10% of its historical cost or current cost as appropriate. As at 30 September 20X4, the manufacturer of the plant still makes the same item of plant and its current price is $600,000.

What is the correct carrying amount to be shown in the statement of financial position of Drexler as at 30 September 20X4 under historical cost and current cost?

	Historical cost $	Current cost $
A	320,000	600,000
B	320,000	384,000
C	300,000	600,000
D	300,000	384,000

55 Tynan's year end is 30 September 20X4 and a number of potential liabilities have been identified.

Which TWO of the following should Tynan recognise as liabilities as at 30 September 20X4?

A   The signing of a non-cancellable contract in September 20X4 to supply goods in the following year on which, due to a pricing error, a loss will be made.

B   The cost of a reorganisation which was approved by the board in August 20X4 but has not yet been implemented, communicated to interested parties or announced publicly.

C   An amount of deferred tax relating to the gain on the revaluation of a property during the current year. Tynan has no intention of selling the property in the foreseeable future.

D   The balance on the warranty provision which relates to products for which there are no outstanding claims and whose warranties had expired by 30 September 20X4.

56 **Which of the following items should be recognised as an asset in the statement of financial position of a company?**

A   A skilled and efficient workforce which has been very expensive to train. Some of these staff are still in the employment of the company.

B   A highly lucrative contract signed during the year which is due to commence shortly after the year end.

C   A government grant relating to the purchase of an item of plant several years ago which has a remaining life of four years.

D   A receivable from a customer which has been sold (factored) to a finance company. The finance company has full recourse to the company for any losses.

57 Comparability is identified as an enhancing qualitative characteristic in the IASB's *Conceptual framework for financial reporting*.

Which of the following does NOT improve comparability?

A   Restating the financial statements of previous years when there has been a change of accounting policy.

B   Prohibiting changes of accounting policy unless required by an IFRS or to give more relevant and reliable information.

C   Disclosing discontinued operations in financial statements.

D   Applying an entity's current accounting policy to a transaction which an entity has not engaged in before.

58 **Which of the following criticisms does NOT apply to historical cost accounts during a period of rising prices?**

A   They contain mixed values; some items are at current values, some at out of date values

B   They are difficult to verify as transactions could have happened many years ago

C   They understate assets and overstate profit

D   They overstate gearing in the statement of financial position

59 According to IAS 8 *Accounting Policies, Changes in accounting estimates and errors*, how should a material error in the previous financial reporting period be accounted for in the current period?

A By making an adjustment in the financial statements of the current period through the statement of profit or loss, and disclosing the nature of the error in a note

B By making an adjustment in the financial statements of the current period as a movement on reserves, and disclosing the nature of the error in a note

C By restating the comparative amounts for the previous period at their correct value, and disclosing the nature of the error in a note

D By restating the comparative amounts for the previous period at their correct value, but without the requirement for a disclosure of the nature of the error in a note

60 Which of the following statements regarding IFRS 13 *Fair Value Measurement* is not true?

A Level 1 inputs are likely to be used without adjustment

B Level 3 inputs are based on the best information available to market participants and are therefore regarded as providing the most reliable evidence of fair value

C Level 2 inputs may include quoted prices for similar (but not identical) assets and liabilities in active markets

D Level 1 inputs comprise quoted prices in active markets for identical assets and liabilities at the reporting date

61 Which ONE of these changes would be classified as 'a change in accounting policy' as determined by IAS 8 *Accounting Policies, Changes in Accounting Estimates and Errors*?

A Increased the allowance for irrecoverable receivables for 20X6 from 5% to 10% of outstanding debts

B Changed the method of valuing inventory from FIFO to average cost

C Changed the depreciation of plant and equipment from straight line depreciation to reducing balance depreciation

D Changed the useful economic life of its motor vehicles from six years to four years

62 In which TWO of the following situations can a change in accounting policy be made by an entity?

A If the change is required by an IFRS

B If the company thinks a new accounting policy would be easier to report

C If a new accounting policy would show more favourable results

D If a new accounting policy results in a more reliable and relevant presentation of events or transactions

63   According to the IASB's *Conceptual Framework for Financial Reporting* which of the measurement bases below can be used by an entity for measuring assets and liabilities shown in its statement of financial position?

	Can be used	Cannot be used
Historical cost		
Present value		
Realisable value		

64   Which ONE of the following statements is true about historical cost accounts in times of rising prices?

   A   Profits will be overstated and assets will be understated

   B   The asset values will be overstated

   C   Unrecognised gains will be recorded incorrectly

   D   Depreciation will be overstated

65   Which of the following concepts aims to ensure that excess dividends aren't paid in times of changing prices?

   A   Going concern

   B   Amortised cost

   C   Faithful representation

   D   Capital maintenance

66   Which of the following is a change of accounting policy under IAS 8 *Accounting Policies, Changes in Accounting Estimates and Errors*?

	Change in accounting policy	Change in accounting estimate
Classifying commission earned as revenue in the statement of profit or loss, having previously classified it as other operating income		
Revising the remaining useful life of a depreciable asset		

67   Which of the following would be a change in accounting policy in accordance with IAS 8 *Accounting Policies, Changes in Accounting Estimates and Errors*?

   A   Adjusting the financial statements of a subsidiary prior to consolidation as its accounting policies differ from those of its parent

   B   A change in reporting depreciation charges as cost of sales rather than as administrative expenses

   C   Depreciation charged on reducing balance method rather than straight line

   D   Reducing the value of inventory from cost to net realisable value due to a valid adjusting event after the reporting period

68 Isaac is a company which buys agricultural produce from wholesale suppliers for retail to the general public. It is preparing its financial statements for the year ending 30 September 20X4 and is considering its closing inventory.

In addition to IAS 2 *Inventories*, which of the following IFRSs may be relevant to determining the figure to be included in its financial statements for closing inventories?

A   IAS 10 *Events After the Reporting Period*

B   IAS 11 *Construction Contracts*

C   IAS 16 *Property, Plant and Equipment*

D   IAS 41 *Agriculture*

69 **To which of the following items does IAS 41 Agriculture apply?**

(i)   A change in fair value of a herd of animals relating to the unit price of the animals

(ii)   Logs held in a wood yard

(iii)   Farm land which is used for growing vegetables

(iv)   The cost of developing a new type of crop seed which is resistant to tropical diseases

A   All four

B   (i) only

C   (i) and (ii) only

D   (ii) and (iii) only

70 IAS 2 *Inventories* specifies expenses that should be included in year-end inventory values. These could include:

A   Marketing and selling overhead

B   Variable production overhead

C   General management overhead

D   Factory management overhead allocated to production

E   Cost of delivering raw materials to the factory

F   Abnormal increase in overhead charges caused by unusually low production levels due to the exceptionally hot weather.

Which THREE of the above are allowable by IAS 2 as expenses that should be included in the cost of finished goods inventories?

71 Neville has only two items of inventory on hand at its reporting date.

Item 1 – Materials costing $24,000 bought for processing and assembly for a customer under a 'one off' order which is expected to produce a high profit margin. Since buying this material, the cost price has fallen to $20,000.

Item 2 – A machine constructed for another customer for a contracted price of $36,000. This has recently been completed at a cost of $33,600. It has now been discovered that, in order to meet certain health and safety regulations, modifications at an extra cost of $8,400 will be required. The customer has agreed to meet half the extra cost.

What should be the total value of these two items of inventory in the statement of financial position?

$_____

72 Mario has incurred the following costs in relation to a unit of inventory:

	$
Raw materials cost	1.50
Import duties	0.40
Direct Labour	0.50
Subcontracted labour costs	0.80
Refundable sales tax	0.20
Storage costs	0.05
Production overheads (per unit)	0.25

There was a problem with the first batch of items produced, so abnormal wastage costs of 0.10 per unit have also been incurred by Mario.

At what value should Mario value this inventory in its Financial Statements?

A $3.50

B $3.45

C $3.80

D $3.70

73 On 30 September 20X4, Razor's closing inventory was counted and valued at its cost of $1 million.

Some items of inventory which had cost $210,000 had been damaged in a flood (on 15 September 20X4) and are not expected to achieve their normal selling price which is calculated to achieve a gross profit margin of 30%.

The sale of these goods will be handled by an agent who sells them at 80% of the normal selling price and charges Razor a commission of 25%.

At what value will the closing inventory of Razor be reported in its statement of financial position as at 30 September 20X4?

$_____

74 Identify whether the following items would be accounted for under IAS 41 *Agriculture* or not.

	Accounted for under IAS 41 *Agriculture*	Outside the scope of IAS 41 *Agriculture*
Dairy cattle		
Milk		
Cheese		

75 Magna owned cattle recorded in the financial statements at $10,500 on 1 January. At 31 December, the cattle has a fair value of $13,000. If Magna sold the cattle, commission of 2% would be payable.

What is the correct accounting treatment for the cattle at 31 December according to IAS 41 *Agriculture*?

A   Hold at cost of $10,500

B   Revalue to $13,000, taking gain of $2,500 to the statement of profit or loss

C   Revalue to $13,000, taking gain of $2,500 to the revaluation surplus

D   Revalue to $12,740, taking gain of $2,240 to the statement of profit or loss

76 During the year ended 30 September 20X4 Hyper entered into two lease transactions:

On 1 October 20X3, a payment $90,000 being the first of five equal annual payments of a finance lease for an item of plant. The lease has an implicit interest rate of 10% and the fair value (cost to purchase) of the leased equipment on 1 October 20X3 was $340,000.

On 1 January 20X4, a payment of $18,000 for a one-year lease of an item of equipment.

What amount in total would be charged to Hyper's statement of profit or loss for the year ended 30 September 20X4 in respect of the above transactions?

A $108,000

B $111,000

C $106,500

D $115,500

77 Z entered into a finance lease agreement on 1 November 20X2. The lease was for five years, the fair value of the asset acquired was $45,000 and the interest rate implicit in the lease was 7%. The annual payment was $10,975 in arrears.

What is the amount to be shown within non-current liabilities at 31 October 20X3?

A $27,212

B $28,802

C $37,175

D $36,407

78   HP entered into an operating lease for a machine on 1 July 20X7 with the following terms:

- three years non-cancellable lease

- 6 months rent free period from commencement

- rent of $12,000 per annum payable at $1,000 a month from month 7 onwards

- machine useful life 15 years.

What is the amount that should be charged to HP's statement of profit or loss for the year to 31 December 20X7?

$_____

79   Rabbit Co has 2 options to acquire a new machine with an estimated useful life of 6 years. It can buy it today, the 1st January 20X3 at a cash price of $100,000 or it can lease the asset under the following agreement:

- An initial payment of $13,760 will be payable straight away

- 5 further annual payments of $20,000 will be due, beginning on 1st Jan 20X3

- The interest rate implicit in the lease is 8%

If Rabbit decides to lease the asset, what will be recorded in its financial statements at the y/e 31 December 20X4 in respect of the lease liability?

	Finance cost	Non-current liability	Current liability
A	4,123	35,662	20,000
B	5,299	51,539	20,000
C	5,312	51,712	20,000
D	5,851	43,709	15,281

80   Squirrel Co enters into an operating lease contract on the 1st July 20X5 to lease an item of office equipment for 3 years. The equipment has an expected useful life of 6 years and if bought outright would cost $50,000. The original lease agreement stated that the annual lease payments were to be $10,000 per annum commencing on 30th June 20X6. Squirrel Co will pay nothing for the first year.

Select the items which will appear in the financial statements of Squirrel Co for the year ended 30th June 20X6.

Statement of profit or loss expense	Statement of financial position
3,333	Accrual
6,667	Prepayment

81 On 1st January 20X4 Badger Co entered into a lease agreement to lease an item of machinery for 4 years with rentals of $210,000 payable annually in arrears. The asset has a useful life of 5 years and at the end of the lease term legal ownership will pass to Badger Co. The fair value of the asset at the inception of the lease was $635,000 and the interest rate implicit in the lease is 12.2%. For the year ended 31st December 20X4 Badger Co has accounted for this lease as an operating lease and recorded the payment of $210,000 as an operating expense. This treatment was discovered during 20X5.

What will the adjustment to retained earnings b/fwd be?

A $5,530 credit

B $132,530 credit

C $210,000 debit

D $Nil

82 Owl Co leases an asset under a finance lease. The lease has a primary period of 5 years and a secondary period of 2 years during which a nominal rental will be payable so Owl will take this up. The asset has an estimated useful life of 6 years and a current cash value of $89,000. The present value of the minimum lease payments is $87,000.

What will the carrying amount of the asset be in Owl's statement of financial position at the end of the second year of the lease?

$_____

83 On 1 July 20X6, Sideshow sold a piece of property for $2 million and leased it back under a 5 year operating lease, paying $150,000 a year. The sale value and rentals were at the market value. The carrying amount of the property on 1 January was $1,600,000 and it had a remaining useful life of 20 years.

What entries would be made in Sideshow's statement of profit or loss for the year ended 31 December 20X6?

A   Profit on disposal of $400,000, rent expense of $150,000

B   Profit on disposal of $400,000, rent expense of $75,000

C   Profit on disposal of $440,000, depreciation expense of $40,000, rent expense of $75,000

D   Depreciation expense of 80,000, profit on disposal of $480,000, rent expense of $75,000

84 On 1 October 20X3, Fresco acquired an item of plant under a five-year finance lease agreement. The plant had a cash purchase cost of $25 million. The agreement had an implicit finance cost of 10% per annum and required an immediate deposit of $2 million and annual rentals of $6 million paid on 30 September each year for five years.

What would be the current liability for the leased plant in Fresco's statement of financial position as at 30 September 20X4?

A $19,300,000

B $4,070,000

C $5,000,000

D $3,850,000

85 The objective of IAS 17 *Leases* is to prescribe the appropriate accounting treatment and required disclosures in relation to leases.

Which TWO of the following situations would normally lead to a lease being classified as a finance lease?

A   The lease transfers ownership of the asset to the lessee by the end of the lease term

B   The lease term is for approximately half of the economic life of the asset

C   The lease assets are of a specialised nature such that only the lessee can use them without major modifications being made

D   At the inception of the lease, the present value of the minimum lease payments is 60% of what the leased asset would cost to purchase

86 On 1 January 20X4, Stark Co entered into a sale and leaseback of its property. When it was sold, the asset had a carrying amount of $6 million and a remaining life of 10 years. Stark Co sold the asset for $7 million and leased it back on a 10 year lease, paying $1 million on 31 December each year. The lease carried an implicit interest rate of 7%.

What is the total expense that should be recorded in the statement of profit or loss for the year ended 31 December 20X4?

$_____'000

87 An entity issues 3,000 convertible bonds at the start of year 1 at par. They have a three year term and a face value of $1,000 per bond. Interest is payable annually in arrears at 7% per annum. Each bond is convertible at any time up to maturity into 250 common shares. When the bonds are issued, the prevailing market interest rate for similar debt without conversion options is 9%. The relevant discount factors are shown below.

Discount factors	7%	9%
Year 1	0.933	0.914
Year 2	0.871	0.837
Year 3	0.813	0.766

How is this initially recorded between the debt and equity elements?

	Debt element	*Equity element*
A	$2,988,570	$ 11,430
B	$2,826,570	$173,430
C	$528,570	$2,471,430
D	$3,000,000	$Nil

88 Viking issues $100,000 5% loan notes on 1 January 20X4, incurring issue costs of $3,000. These loan notes are redeemable at a premium, meaning that the effective rate of interest is 8% per annum.

What is the finance cost to be shown in the statement of profit or loss for the year ended 31 December 20X5?

A $8,240

B $7,981

C $7,760

D $8,000

89 For a debt investment to be held under amortised cost, it must pass two tests. One of these is the contractual cash flow characteristics test.

What is the other test which must be passed?

A   The business model test

B   The amortised cost test

C   The fair value test

D   The purchase agreement test

90 **What is the default classification for an equity investment?**

A   Fair value through profit or loss

B   Fair value through other comprehensive income

C   Amortised cost

D   Net proceeds

91 ABC Co purchased 10,000 shares on 1 September 20X4, making the election to use the alternative treatment under IFRS 9. The shares cost $3.50 each. Transaction costs associated with the purchase were $500.

At 31 December 20X4, the shares are trading at $4.50 each.

What is the gain to be recognised on these shares for the year ended 31 December 20X4?

$_____

92 DEF Co has purchased an investment of 15,000 shares on 1 August 20X6 at a cost of $6.50 each. Transaction costs on the purchase amounted to $1,500.

As at the year end 30 September 20X6, these shares are now worth $7.75 each.

Select the correct gain and the place it will be recorded

Gain
17,250
18,750

Where recorded
Other Comprehensive Income
Statement of profit or loss

93 **For which category of financial instruments are transaction costs excluded from the initial value, and instead expensed to profit or loss?**

    A   Financial Liabilities at amortised cost

    B   Financial Assets at fair value through profit or loss

    C   Financial Assets at fair value through other comprehensive income

    D   Financial Assets at amortised cost

94 On 1 October 20X3, Bertrand issued $10 million convertible loan notes which carry a coupon rate of 5% per annum. The loan notes are redeemable on 30 September 20X6 at par for cash or can be exchanged for equity shares. A similar loan note, without the conversion option, would have required Bertrand to pay an interest rate of 8%.

The present value of $1 receivable at the end of each year, based on discount rates of 5% and 8%, can be taken as:

	5%	8%
End of year 1	0.95	0.93
2	0.91	0.86
3	0.86	0.79

How much would be recorded in equity in relation to the loan notes?

$_____'000

95 Wonder Co issued $10 million 5% loan notes on 1 January 20X9, incurring issue costs of $400,000. The loan notes are redeemable at a premium, giving them an effective interest rate of 8%.

What expense should be recorded in relation to the loan notes for the year ended 31 December 20X9?

$_____'000

96 **For each of the financial instruments below, match them to the appropriate accounting treatment.**

Instrument		Treatment
Convertible loan notes		Fair value through profit or loss
Equity investments where the entity has an intention to hold long-term and has chosen to apply the alternative treatment		Amortised cost
Financial liability, not held for trading		Split accounting
Equity investments (default position)		Fair value through other comprehensive income

97 IAS 21 *The Effects of Changes in Foreign Exchange Rates* defines the term 'functional currency'.

Which one of the following is the correct definition of 'functional currency'?

A   The currency in which the financial statements are presented

B   The currency of the country where the reporting entity is located

C   The currency that mainly influences sales prices and operating costs

D   The currency of the primary economic environment in which an entity operates

98 Sunshine is a public limited company with a reporting date of 31 December 20X1 and a functional currency of dollars ($).On 30 June 20X1, it purchased land from overseas at a cost of 30 million dinars. The land is an item of property, plant and equipment and is measured using the cost model.

Exchange rates are as follows:

	Dinars: $1
30/6/20X1	3
31/12/20X1	2
Average rate for year-ended 31/12/20X1	2.5

The fair value of the land at 31 December 20X1 was 32 million dinars.

What is the carrying amount of the land as at 31 December 20X1?

A $10 million

B $15 million

C $12 million

D $16 million

99 **In relation to IAS 21 *The Effects of Changes in Foreign Exchange Rates*, which of the following statements are true?**

(i)   Exchange gains and losses arising on the retranslation of monetary items are recognised in other comprehensive income in the period

(ii)   Non-monetary items measured at historical cost in a foreign currency are not retranslated at the reporting date

(iii)   An intangible asset is a non-monetary item

A   All of the above

B   (ii) and (iii) only

C   (i) and (iii) only

D   (i) and (ii) only

100 An entity took out a bank loan for 12 million dinars on 1 January 20X1. It repaid 3 million dinars to the bank on 30 November 20X1. The entity has a reporting date of 31 December 20X1 and a functional currency of dollars ($). Exchange rates are as follows:

	Dinars: $1
1/1/20X1	6.0
30/11/20X1	5.0
30/12/20X1	5.6

What is the total loss arising on the above transactions in the year ended 31 December 20X1?

$_____

101 A manufacturing entity buys a machine (an item of property, plant and equipment) for 20 million dinars on 1 January 20X1. The machine is held under the cost model and was attributed a useful economic life of 20 years. The entity has a reporting date of 31 December 20X1 and a functional currency of dollars ($). Exchange rates are as follows:

	Dinars: $1
1/1/20X1	2
31/12/20X1	3
Average rate for year-ended 31/12/20X1	2.5

What is the carrying amount of the machine as at 31 December 20X1?

A $9.7 million

B $9.6 million

C $9.5 million

D $6.3 million

102 Mango sold an item of maturing inventory to a bank on 1 January 20X3 for $500,000. At this date the inventory had cost $200,000 to produce but had a fair value of $900,000, which was expected to increase over the next 3 years. At the end of 3 years, Mango have the option to repurchase the inventory at $665,000, giving an effective interest rate of 10%.

What items should be recorded in the statement of profit or loss for the year ended 31 December 20X3?

A   Revenue $500,000, cost of sales $200,000

B   Profit on disposal $300,000

C   Deferred income $500,000

D   Finance cost $50,000

103 Repro, has prepared its draft financial statements for the year ended 30 September 20X4. It has included the following transactions in revenue at the stated amounts below.

Which of these has been correctly included in revenue according to IFRS 15 *Revenue from contracts with customers*?

A   Agency sales of $250,000 on which Repro is entitled to a commission.

B   Sale proceeds of $20,000 for motor vehicles which were no longer required by Repro.

C   Sales of $150,000 on 30 September 20X4. The amount invoiced to and received from the customer was $180,000, which includes $30,000 for ongoing servicing work to be done by Repro over the next two years.

D   Sales of $200,000 on 1 October 20X3 to an established customer which (with the agreement of Repro) will be paid in full on 30 September 20X5. Repro has a cost of capital of 10%.

104 Yling entered into a contract to construct an asset for a customer on 1 January 20X4 which is expected to last 24 months. The agreed price for the contract is $5 million. At 30 September 20X4, the costs incurred on the contract were $1.6 million and the estimated remaining costs to complete were $2.4 million. On 20 September 20X4, Yling received a payment from the customer of $1.8 million which was equal to the full amount billed. Yling calculates the progress on the basis of amount billed compared to the contract price.

What amount would be reported in Yling's statement of financial position as at 30 September 20X4?

$_____

105 CN started a three-year contract to build a new university campus on 1 April 20X4. The contract had a fixed price of $90 million. CN will satisfy the performance obligation over time. CN incurred costs to 31 March 20X5 of $77 million and estimated that a further $33 million would need to be spent to complete the contract.

CN measures the progress of contracts using work completed compared to contract price. At 31 March 20X5, a surveyor valued the work completed to date at $63 million.

Select the correct amounts to be shown in revenue and cost of sales in the statement of profit or loss for the year ended 31 March 20X5?

Revenue	Cost of sales
$63 million	$77 million
$57 million	$83 million

106 Locke sells machines, and also offers installation and technical support services. The individual selling prices of each product are shown below.

Sale price of goods	$75
Installation	$25
A year's service	$50

Company X bought a machine on 1 May 20X1, and was charged a reduced price of $100.

Locke only offers discounts when customers purchase a package of products together.

According to IFRS 15 *Revenue from Contracts with Customers*, how much should be recorded in revenue for the year ended 31 December 20X1? Workings should be rounded to the nearest $.

$_____

107 **Place the following steps for recognising revenue in order in accordance with IFRS 15 *Revenue from Contracts with Customers***

Step	Correct order
Identify the separate performance obligations within a contract	
Identify the contract	
Determine the transaction price	
Recognise revenue when (or as) a performance obligation is satisfied	
Allocate the transaction price to the performance obligations in the contract	

108 BL started a contract on 1 November 20X4. The contract was scheduled to run for two years and has a sales value of $40 million. BL will satisfy the performance obligation over time.

At 31 October 20X5, the following details were obtained from BL's records:

	$m
Costs incurred to date	16
Estimated costs to completion	18
Progress at 31 October 20X5	45%

Applying IFRS 15 *Revenue from contracts with customers*, how much revenue and cost of sales should BL recognise in its statement of profit or loss for the year ended 31 October 20X5?

	Revenue	Cost of sales
A	$40 million	$15.3 million
B	$40 million	$34 million
C	$18 million	$16 million
D	$18 million	$15.3 million

109 Malik is a construction company, recognising progress based on work certified over total contract value. Malik will satisfy the performance obligation over time. The following information relates to one of its long-term contracts as at 31 May 20X4, Malik's year-end.

Contract price $200,000

Costs incurred to date $130,000

Estimated cost to complete $20,000

Invoiced to customer $120,000

Work certified to date $180,000

In the year to 31 May 20X3 Malik had recognised revenue of $60,000 and profit of $15,000 in respect of this contract.

What profit should appear in Malik's Statement of Profit or Loss as at 31 May 20X4 in respect of this contract?

$_____

110 **Which of the following items has correctly been included in Hatton's revenue for the year?**

A $2 million in relation to a fee negotiated for an advertising contract for Rees, one of Hatton's clients. Hatton acted as an agent during the deal and is entitled to 10% commission.

B $500,000 relating to a sale of specialised equipment on 31 December 20X1. The full sales value was $700,000 but $200,000 relates to servicing that Hatton will provide over the next 2 years, so Hatton has not included that in revenue this year.

C $800,000 relating to a sale of some surplus land owned by Hatton.

D $1 million in relation to a sale to a new customer on 31 December 20X1. Control passed to the customer on 31 December 20X1. The $1 million is payable on 31 December 20X3. Interest rates are 10%.

111 Sugar has entered into a long-term contract to build an asset for a customer, Hewer. Sugar will satisfy the performance obligation over time and has measured the progress towards satisfying the performance obligation at 45% at the year end.

The price of the contract is $8 million. Sugar has spent $4.5 million to date, but the estimated costs to complete are $5.5 million. To date, Hewer has paid Sugar $3 million.

What is the net liability that should be recorded in Sugar's statement of financial position?

$_____'000

112 Ratten commenced a contract to build an asset for a customer in the year ended 30 September 20X4. The contract price was agreed at $1.5m, and the total expected costs of the contract are $800,000. Ratten will satisfy the performance obligation over time.

The following figures were correctly recognised in the profit or loss account for the year ended 30 September 20X4:

	$000
Revenue	450
Cost of Sales	(240)
Profit	**210**

The following figures are also relevant in relation to this contract:

	X4	X5
	$000	$000
Costs incurred to date	325	575
Work certified to date	450	1,050

Ratten recognises progress on the basis of work certified compared to contract price.

What should be the cost of sales figure for Ratten in its Profit or Loss account for the year ended 30 September 20X5?

A $320,000

B $250,000

C $560,000

D   240,000

113 Sawyer entered into a contract to construct an asset for a customer during the year, and identified the performance obligation as one which is satisfied over time. Sawyer recognises progress towards completion using an output method, based on work certified compared to contract price. The following information is relevant to the contract.

Contract price $1,000,000

Costs incurred to date $530,000

Estimated cost to complete $170,000

Work certified to date and invoiced $600,000

What items should be recorded in Sawyer's statement of financial position?

A   Contract asset $110,000

B   Contract asset $100,000

C   Contract asset $190,000

D   Contract asset $150,000

114 Hindberg is a car retailer. On 1 April 20X4, Hindberg sold a car to Latterly on the following terms:

The selling price of the car was $25,300. Latterly paid $12,650 (half of the cost) on 1 April 20X4 and would pay the remaining $12,650 on 31 March 20X6 (two years after the sale). Hindberg's cost of capital is 10% per annum.

What is the total amount which Hindberg should credit to profit or loss in respect of this transaction in the year ended 31 March 20X5?

A $23,105

B $23,000

C $20,909

D $24,150

115 Tamsin Co's accounting records shown the following:

Income tax payable for the year $60,000

Over provision in relation to the previous year $4,500

Opening provision for deferred tax $2,600

Closing provision for deferred tax $3,200

What is the income tax expense that will be shown in the statement of profit or loss for the year?

A $54,900

B $67,700

C $65,100

D $56,100

116 The following information has been extracted from the accounting records of Clara Co:

Estimated income tax for the year ended 30 September 20X0: $75,000

Income tax paid for the year ended 30 September 20X0: $80,000

Estimated income tax for the year ended 30 September 20X1: $83,000

What figures will be shown in the statement of profit or loss for the year ended 30 September 20X1 and the statement of financial position as at that date in respect of income tax?

Statement of profit or loss	Statement of financial position

Options:

$75,000
$80,000
$83,000
$88,000

117 Hudson has the following balances included on its trial balance at 30 June 20X4

Taxation $4,000 Credit

Deferred taxation $12,000 Credit

The balance on Taxation relates to an overprovision from 30 June 20X3.

At 30 June 20X4, the directors estimate that the provision necessary for taxation on current year profits is $15,000.

The carrying amount of Hudson's non-current assets exceeds the tax written-down value by $30,000. The rate of tax is 30%.

What is the charge for taxation that will appear in the Statement of Profit or Loss for the year to 30 June 20X4?

A $23,000

B $28,000

C $8,000

D $12,000

118 Holmes has the following balances included on its trial balance at 30 June 20X4:

Taxation $7,000 Credit

Deferred taxation $16,000 Credit

The balance on Taxation relates to an overprovision from 30 June 20X3.

At 30 June 20X4, the directors estimate that the provision necessary for taxation on current year profits is $12,000. The balance on the deferred tax account needs to be increased to $23,000, which includes the impact of the increase in property valuation below.

During the year Holmes revalued its property for the first time, resulting in a gain of $10,000. The rate of tax is 30%.

What is the charge for taxation that will appear in the Statement of Profit or Loss for the year to 30 June 20X4?

A $9,000

B $12,000

C $23,000

D $1,000

119 Garfish Co had profits after tax of $3.0 million in the year ended 31 December 20X7. On 1 January 20X7, Garfish had 2.4 million ordinary shares in issue. On 1 April 20X7 Garfish made a one for two rights issue at a price of $1.40 when the market price of Garfish's shares was $2.00.

What is the basic earnings per share (to one decimal place) for the year ended 31 December 20X7, according to IAS 33 _Earnings Per Share_?

$_____

120 On 1st January 20X4, Sam Co had 3 million ordinary shares in issue. On 1st June 20X4, Sam Co made a 1 for 3 bonus issue. On 30th September 20X4, Sam Co then issued a further 1 million shares at full market price. Sam Co had profits attributable to ordinary equity holders of $2million for the year ended 31st December 20X4.

What is the basic earnings per share figure for the year ended 31st December 20X4, according to IAS 33 *Earnings Per Share*?

A $0.47

B $0.43

C $0.49

D $0.5

121 During the year, Mac made a 1 for 3 rights issue at $1.60 when the market price was $2.20. Last year's EPS was 81 cents. There were no other issues of shares during the year.

What will the restated earnings per share figure be for comparative purposes?

$_____

122 Coral Co has net profit for the year ended 30 September 20X5 of $10,500,000. Coral has had 6 million shares in issue for many years. In the current year, Coral has issued a convertible bond. It was issued at its nominal value of $2,500,000, and carries an effective interest rate of 8%. The bond is convertible in five years, with 50 shares issued for every $100 nominal of convertible bond held. Coral Co pays tax at a rate of 28%

What is the Diluted Earnings per Share figure?

A $1.77

B $1.75

C $1.48

D $1.47

123 Isco's financial statements show a profit for the year of $2million. On 1 January 20X5, Isco had 4 million shares in issue. There were 1 million outstanding options to buy shares for $3 each. For the year, the average market value of Isco's shares was $5.00.

What is Isco's diluted earnings per share for the year ended 31 December 20X5?

A $0.30

B $0.44

C $0.46

D $0.40

124 Gromit Co has the following extract from its consolidated profit or loss account:

	$000
Profit for the period	2,800
Other Comprehensive income	
Revaluation gain	500
Total Comprehensive Income	3,300
Profit for the period attributable to:	
Parent	2,250
Non-controlling Interest	550
	2,800
Total Comprehensive Income attributable to:	
Parent	2,600
Non-controlling interest	700
	3,300

What figure should be used as Earnings by Gromit in its Earnings Per Share (EPS) calculation?

$_____'000

125 **Which TWO of the following do NOT need to be removed from a company's net profit in a profit or loss account in order to calculate the earnings figure to be used in the Earnings Per Share calculation?**

A   Redeemable preference share dividends

B   Irredeemable preference share dividends

C   Profit attributable to the non-controlling interest

D   An error in expenses discovered after the financial statements have been authorised for issue

E   Ordinary dividends

126   Aqua has correctly calculated its basic earnings per share (EPS) for the current year.

Drag the items into the appropriate category

Considered within DEPS	Considered within Basic EPS

Options:

A 1 for 5 rights issue of equity shares during the year at $1.20 when the market price of the equity shares was $2.00
The issue during the year of a convertible (to equity shares) loan note
The granting during the year of directors' share options exercisable in three years' time
Equity shares issued during the year as the purchase consideration for the acquisition of a new subsidiary company

127   Many commentators believe that the trend of earnings per share (EPS) is a more reliable indicator of underlying performance than the trend of the net profit for the year.

Which of the following statements supports this view?

A   Net profit can be manipulated by the choice of accounting policies but EPS cannot be manipulated in this way.

B   EPS takes into account the additional resources made available to earn profit when new shares are issued for cash, whereas net profit does not.

C   The disclosure of a diluted EPS figure is a forecast of the trend of profit for future periods.

D   The comparative EPS is restated where a change in accounting policy affects the previous year's profits.

128   On 1 October 20X3, Hoy had $2.5 million of equity shares of 50 cents each in issue.

No new shares were issued during the year ended 30 September 20X4, but on that date there were outstanding share options to purchase 2 million equity shares at $1.20 each. The average market value of Hoy's equity shares during the year was $3 per share.

Hoy's profit after tax for the year ended 30 September 2014 was $1,550,000.

What is Hoy's diluted earnings per share for the year ended 30 September 20X4?

A $0.25

B $0.22

C $0.31

D $0.42

129 AP has the following two legal claims outstanding:

- A legal action claiming compensation of $500,000 filed against AP in March 20X4.

- A legal action taken by AP against a third party, claiming damages of $200,000 was started in January 20X3 and is nearing completion.

In both cases, it is more likely than not that the amount claimed will have to be paid.

How should AP report these legal actions in its financial statements for the year ended 31 March 20X5?

Drag the items into the appropriate category

Legal action against AP	Legal action by AP

Options:

Contingent Liability
Contingent Asset
Provision
Asset

130 **Which ONE of the following would require a provision for a liability to be created by BW at its reporting date of 31 October 20X5?**

A   The government introduced new laws on data protection which come into force on 1 January 20X6. BW's directors have agreed that this will require a large number of staff to be retrained. At 31 October 20X5, the directors were waiting on a report they had commissioned that would identify the actual training requirements.

B   At the date, BW is negotiating with its insurance provider about an insurance claim that it had filed. On 20 November 20X5, the provider agreed to pay $200,000.

C   BW makes refunds to customers for any goods returned within 30 days of sale, and has done so for many years.

D   A customer is suing BW for damages alleged to have been caused by BW's product. BW is contesting the claim and, at 31 October 20X5, the directors have been advised by BW's legal advisers it is very unlikely to lose the case.

131 Using the requirements set out in IAS 10 Events after the Reporting Period, which of the following would be classified as an adjusting event after the reporting period in financial statements ended 31 March 20X4 that were approved by the directors on 31 August 20X4?

A A reorganisation of the enterprise, proposed by a director on 31 January 20X4 and agreed by the Board on 10 July 20X4.

B A strike by the workforce which started on 1 May 20X4 and stopped all production for 10 weeks before being settled.

C The receipt of cash from a claim on an insurance policy for damage caused by a fire in a warehouse on 1 January 20X4. The claim was made in January 20X4 and the amount of the claim had not been recognised at 31 March 20X4 as it was uncertain that any money would be paid. The insurance enterprise settled with a payment of $1.5 million on 1 June 20X4.

D The enterprise had made large export sales to the USA during the year. The year-end receivables included $2 million for amounts outstanding that were due to be paid in US dollars between 1 April 20X4 and 1 July 20X4. By the time these amounts were received, the exchange rate had moved in favour.

132 Target Co is preparing its financial statements for the year ended 30 September 20X7. The company is facing a number of legal claims from its customers with regards to a faulty product sold. The total amount being claimed is $3.5 million. The company's lawyers say that the customers have an 80% chance of being successful.

Per IAS 37 Provisions, Contingent Liabilities and Contingent Assets, what amount, if any, should be recognised in respect of the above in Target Co's statement of financial position as at 30 September 20X7?

$_____

133 ABC Co has a year end of 31 December 20X4. On 15th December 20X4 the directors publicly announced their decision to close an operating unit and make a number of employees redundant. Some of the employees currently working in the unit will be transferred to other operating units within ABC.

The estimated costs of the closure are as follows:

	$000
Redundancy costs	800
Lease termination costs	200
Relocation of continuing employees to new locations	400
Retraining of continuing employees	300
	1,700

What is the closure provision that should be recognised?

A $800,000

B $1,000,000

C $1,400,000

D $1,700,000

134 On 1 October 20X3, Xplorer commenced drilling for oil from an undersea oilfield. The extraction of oil causes damage to the seabed which has a restorative cost (ignore discounting) of $10,000 per million barrels of oil extracted. Xplorer extracted 250 million barrels of oil in the year ended 30 September 20X4.

Xplorer is also required to dismantle the drilling equipment at the end of its five-year licence. This has an estimated cost of $30 million on 30 September 20X8. Xplorer's cost of capital is 8% per annum and $1 has a present value of 68 cents in five years' time.

What is the total provision (extraction plus dismantling) which Xplorer would report in its statement of financial position as at 30 September 20X4 in respect of its oil operations?

A $34,900,000

B $24,532,000

C $22,900,000

D $4,132,000

135 **Which TWO of the following events which occur after the reporting date of a company but before the financial statements are authorised for issue are classified as ADJUSTING events in accordance with IAS 10 *Events after the Reporting Period*?**

A   A change in tax rate announced after the reporting date, but affecting the current tax liability

B   The discovery of a fraud which had occurred during the year

C   The determination of the sale proceeds of an item of plant sold before the year end

D   The destruction of a factory by fire

136 Each of the following events occurred after the reporting date of 31 March 20X5, but before the financial statements were authorised for issue.

Identify whether the events would represent adjusting or non-adjusting events

	Adjusting	Non-adjusting
A public announcement in April 20X5 of a formal plan to discontinue an operation which had been approved by the board in February 20X5.		
The settlement of an insurance claim for a loss sustained in December 20X4.		

137 In a review of its provisions for the year ended 31 March 20X5, Cumla's assistant accountant has suggested the following accounting treatments:

(i)   Based on past experience, a $200,000 provision for unforeseen liabilities arising after the year end.

(ii)   The partial reversal (as a credit to the statement of profit or loss) of the accumulated depreciation provision on an item of plant because the estimate of its remaining useful life has been increased by three years.

(iii) Providing $1 million for deferred tax at 25% relating to a $4 million revaluation of property during March 20X5 even though Cumla has no intention of selling the property in the near future.

Which of the above suggested treatments of provisions is/are permitted by IFRS?

A   (i) only

B   (i) and (ii)

C   (ii) and (iii)

D   (iii) only

138   Identify whether the statements below are true or false:

	True	False
IAS 10 *Events After the Reporting Period* covers the period from the reporting date to the annual general meeting		
According to IAS 10 *Events After the Reporting Period*, any non-adjusting event should be disclosed as a note in the financial statements		

139   Fauberg Co owns a number of offices in country Y and is in the process of finishing its financial statements for the year ended 31 December 20X4. In December 20X4, country Y announced changes to health and safety regulations, meaning that Fauberg's air conditioning units will have to be replaced by 30 June 20X5.

This is estimated to cost Fauberg $500,000. Fauberg has a history of compliance with regulations and intends to do the work by June 20X5.

Which of the conditions for a provision will be met at 31 December 20X4?

	Yes/No
There is a present obligation from a past event	
A reliable estimate can be made	
There is a probable outflow of economic benefits	

140   **Which TWO of the following statements about provisions are true?**

A   Future operating losses cannot be provided for

B   Changes in provisions should be applied retrospectively, adjusting the prior year financial statements

C   Provisions should be accounted for prudently, reflecting the maximum that could possibly be paid out

D   Provisions should be discounted to present value if the effect of the time value of money is material

CONSOLIDATED FINANCIAL STATEMENTS

141 Petre owns 100% of the share capital of the following companies. The directors are unsure of whether the investments should be consolidated into the group financial statements of not.

Identify whether the following companies should be consolidated or not

	Consolidated	Not to be consolidated
Beta is a bank and its activity is so different from the engineering activities of the rest of the group that it would be meaningless to consolidate it.		
Delta is located in a country where local accounting standards are compulsory and these are not compatible with IFRS used by the rest of the group.		
Gamma is located in a country where a military coup has taken place and Petre has lost control of the investment for the foreseeable future.		

142 Tazer, a parent company, acquired Lowdown, an unincorporated entity, for $2.8 million. A fair value exercise performed on Lowdown's net assets at the date of purchase showed:

	$000
Property, plant and equipment	3,000
Identifiable intangible asset	500
Inventory	300
Trade receivables less payables	200
	4,000

How would the purchase be reflected in the consolidated statement of financial position?

A   Record the net assets at their above values and credit profit or loss with $1.2 million

B   Record the net assets at their above values and credit goodwill with $1.2 million

C   Write off the intangible asset ($500,000), record the remaining net assets at their values shown above and credit profit or loss with $700,000

D   Record the purchase as a financial asset investment at $2.8 million

143 **Which ONE of the following definitions is not included within the definition of control per IFRS 10?**

A   Having power over the investee

B   Having exposure, or rights, to variable returns from its investment with the investee

C   Having the majority of shares in the investee

D   Having the ability to use its power over the investee to affect the amount of the investor's returns

144 Pamela acquired 80% of the share capital of Samantha on 1/1/20X1. Part of the purchase consideration was to pay additional cash on 1/1/20X4 of $200,000. The applicable cost of capital is 10%.

What will the deferred consideration liability be at 31/12/20X2?

A $150,262

B $165,288

C $200,000

D $181,817

145 Philip acquired 85% of the share capital of Stanley on 1/10/20X1. The profit for the year ended 31/12/20X1 for Stanley was $36,000. Profits are deemed to accrue evenly over the year. At 31/12/20X1 Stanley's statement of financial position for Stanley showed:

Equity share capital	$200,000
Retained earnings	$180,000

What are the net assets on acquisition?

$_____ '000

146 On 30 June 20X4 GHI acquired 800,000 of JKL's 1 million shares.

GHI issued 3 shares for every four shares acquired in JKL. On 30 June the market price of a GHI share was $3.80 and the market price of a JKL share was $3.00.

GHI agreed to pay $550,000 in cash to the existing shareholders on 30 June 20X5. GHI's borrowing rate was 10% per annum.

GHI paid advisors $100,000 to advise on the acquisition.

What is the cost of investment that will be used in the goodwill calculation in the consolidated accounts of GHI?

$_____ '000

147 MNO has a 75% owned subsidiary PQR. During the year MNO sold inventory to PQR for an invoiced price of $800,000. PQR have since sold 75% of that inventory on to third parties. The sale was at a mark-up of 25% on cost to MNO. PQR is the only subsidiary of MNO.

What is the adjustment to inventory that would be included in the consolidated statement of financial position of MNO at the year-end resulting from this sale?

A $120,000

B $40,000

C $160,000

D $50,000

148 West Co has a 75% subsidiary, Land Co, and is preparing its consolidated statement of financial position as at 31 December 20X6. The carrying amount of property, plant and equipment in the two companies at that date is as follows:

West Co $300,000

Land Co $60,000

On 1 January 20X6 Land Co had transferred some property to West Co for $40,000. At the date of transfer the property, which had cost $42,000, had a carrying amount of $30,000 and a remaining useful life of five years.

What is the carrying amount of property, plant and equipment in the consolidated statement of financial position of West Co as at 31 December 20X6?

$_____ '000

149 **Which TWO of the following situations are unlikely to represent control over an investee?**

A   Owning 55% and being able to elect 4 of the 7 directors

B   Owning 51%, but the constitution requires that decisions need the unanimous consent of shareholders

C   Having currently exercisable options which would take the shareholding of the company to 55%

D   Owning 40% of the shares but having majority of voting rights within the company

E   Owning 35% of the ordinary shares and 80% of the preference shares of the company

150 **Identify if the following will be recognised as part of the cost of an investment in a subsidiary company**

	Include in cost of investment	Do not include in the cost of investment
An agreement to pay a further $30,000 if the subsidiary company achieves an operating profit of over $100,000 in the first 3 years after acquisition.		
Professional fees of $10,000 in connection with the investment		

151 Peter Co acquires 80% of the share capital of Paul Co on 1/8/X6 and is preparing its group financial statements for the year ended 31/12/X6.

How will Paul's results be included in the group statement of profit or loss?

A   80% of Paul's revenue and expenses for the year ended 31/12/X6

B   100% of Paul's revenue and expenses for the year ended 31/12/X6

C   80% of Paul's revenue and expenses for the period 1/8/X6–31/12/X6

D   100% of Paul's revenue and expenses for the period ended 1/8/X6–31/12/X6

152 **Which of the following would result in an unrealised profit within a group scenario?**

    A   A parent sells a building originally costing $800,000 to its subsidiary company for $900,000. The subsidiary still holds this asset at the date of consolidation.

    B   A parent sells a building originally costing $800,000 to its subsidiary company for $900,000. The subsidiary has sold this asset before the date of consolidation.

    C   A parent sells goods which originally cost $14,000 to its subsidiary company for $18,000. The subsidiary company has sold all of these goods at the date of consolidation.

    D   A parent sells goods which originally cost $14,000 to an associate company for $18,000. The associate company has sold all of these goods at the date of consolidation.

153 **Identify whether the following facts about impairment are true or false**

	True	False
It will always be deducted in full from the parent's retained earnings		
It will be apportioned between the parent company and the non-controlling interest (NCI) when the NCI is valued at fair value		

154 **Which one of the following is not a condition which must be met for the parent to be exempt from producing consolidated financial statements?**

    A   The activities of the subsidiary are significantly different to the rest of the group and to consolidate them would prejudice the overall group position

    B   The ultimate parent company produces consolidated financial statements that comply with IFRS and are publicly available

    C   The parent's debt or equity instruments are not traded in a public market

    D   The parent itself is a wholly owned subsidiary or a partially owned subsidiary whose owners do not object to the parent not producing consolidated financial statements

155 On 1 January 20X1, Branch purchased 75% of Leaf's 80 million shares. At this date, Leaf's retained earnings were $60 million. The consideration given for Leaf was 2 Branch shares for every 3 Leaf shares purchased, plus a cash payment of $1 per purchased share. At the date of acquisition, the value of a Branch share was $2.50.

What is the consideration paid for Branch at 1 January 20X1?

$_____ '000

156 STU has an 80% subsidiary, VWX. VWX, which has been a subsidiary of STU for the whole year, reported a profit after tax of $600,000 in its own financial statements. You ascertain the following additional matters:

At the year-end there was unrealised profit of $60,000 on sales by VWX to STU.

What is the non-controlling interest in VWX that would be reported in the consolidated statement of profit or loss and other comprehensive income of STU for the year?

$_____ '000

157 H acquired an 80% holding in S. On 1st April 20X6. From 1st April 20X6 to 31st December 20X6 S sold goods for $4.3m at a mark-up of 10% to H. H's inventory at 31st December 20X6 included $2.2m of such inventory. The statements of profit or loss for each company for year to 31st December 20X6 showed the following in respect of cost of sales:

H CO $14.7m

S CO $11.6m

Show the cost of sales figure in the consolidated statement of profit or loss for year to 31 December 20X6.

A $18,900,000

B $20,200,000

C $19,100,000

D $19,300,000

158 X CO acquired a 60% holding in Y Limited on 1 January 20X6. At this date, Y had a building with a fair value $200,000 in excess of its carrying amount, which had a remaining life of 10 years. Also, goodwill had been impaired by $55,000 in the year to 31 December 20X6. The balances on operating expenses for the year to 31 December 20X7 are shown below:

X CO $600,000

Y CO $350,000

What are consolidated operating expenses for the year to 31 December 20X7?

$_____'000

159 A CO acquired a 60% holding in B Limited on 1 July 20X6. At this date, A gave B a $500,000 8% loan. The interest on the loan has been accounted for correctly in the individual financial statements. The following totals for finance costs for the year to 31 December 20X6 in the individual financial statements are shown below.

A CO $200,000

B CO $70,000

What are consolidated finance costs for the year to 31 December 20X6?

A $215,000

B $225,000

C $230,000

D $250,000

160 Identify whether the following would impact the profit attributable to the non-controlling interest in the consolidated statement of profit or loss if the non-controlling interest is measured at fair value

	Impacts the NCI share of profit	Does not impact the NCI share
Goodwill impairment		
The parent transferring an item of inventory to the subsidiary for $10,000 greater than its carrying amount, all of which remains in the group at the year end		
The subsidiary having an item of plant with a fair value of $500,000 above its carrying amount, and a remaining life of 10 years		

161 AB has owned 80% of CD for many years. In the current year ended 30 June 20X3, AB has reported total revenues of $5.5 million, and CD of $2.1 million. AB has sold goods to CD during the year with a total value of $1 million. Half of these goods sold remain in year end inventories.

What is the consolidated revenue figure for the AB group for the year ended 30 June 20X3?

$_____'000

162 Burridge bought 30% of Allen on 1 July 20X4. Allen's statement of profit or loss for the year shows a profit of $400,000. Allen paid a dividend to Burridge of $50,000 on 1 December. At the year end, the investment in Allen was judged to have been impaired by $10,000.

What will be shown under 'Share of profit from associate' in the consolidated statement of profit or loss for the year ended 31 December 20X4?

A   Nil

B $50,000

C $60,000

D $110,000

163 Beasant bought 30% of Arnie on 1 January 20X8, when Arnie had share capital of $100,000 $1 shares and $400,000 retained earnings. Beasant paid by giving the previous owners of Arnie one Beasant share for every 3 shares bought in Arnie. At the date of acquisition, Beasant's shares had a market value of $4.50 and Arnie's had a market value of $2. At 31 December, Arnie's net assets were $460,000.

What is the value shown under 'Investment in Associate in the consolidated statement of financial position as at 31 December 20X8?

A   8,000

B $33,000

C $63,000

D $123,000

164   Identify which concept each of the following transactions is applying

	Single entity concept	Going concern concept
Removing unrealised profits on group sales		
Removing intra-group balances		

165   Identify the correct treatments for the following investments in the consolidated financial statements of the Nicol group

30% of the share capital of Hansen Co. The other 70% is owned by Lawro, another listed company, whose directors make up Hansen's board.	Subsidiary
80% of the share capital of Kennedy Co, whose activities are significantly different from the rest of the Nicol group.	Associate
30% of the share capital of Bruce Co. The Nicol group have appointed 2 of the 5 board members of Bruce Co, with the other board members coming from three other entities.	Investment

166   Badger Co acquired 30% of Eagle Co on 1 July 20X3. Badger has classified Eagle as an associate undertaking. The investment cost was $5.5 million. For the year ended 30 September 20X3, Eagle Co is reporting a net profit of $625,000.

What is the value of the associate investment in the group Statement of Financial Position of Badger Co as at 30 September 20X3?

A $5,546,875

B $5,500,000

C $6,125,000

D $5,968,750

167   Green Co is an associate undertaking of Purple Co. Purple Co owns 30% of the shares in Green Co, and has done so for many years.

During the year ended 31 December 20X4, Green Co made a net profit of $1.5 million. Green sold goods to Purple Co during the year with a value of $2 million, and half are still in Purple's inventories at year end. All the goods were sold at a margin of 30%.

Purple has recognised previous impairments in relation to its investment in Green Co of $225,000. In the current year, Purple wishes to recognise an additional impairment charge of $35,000.

What is the share of profit of associate to be shown in Purple's consolidated statement of Profit or Loss?

$_____ '000

168 Which ONE of the following statements regarding consolidated financial statements is correct?

A For consolidation, it may be acceptable to use financial statements of the subsidiary if the year-end differs from the parent by 2 months.

B For consolidation, all companies within the group must have the same year end.

C All companies within a group must have the same accounting policy in their individual financial statements.

D The profit made on all intra-group sales in the year must be removed from the consolidated financial statements.

169 An associate is an entity in which an investor has significant influence over the investee.

Which TWO of the following indicate(s) the presence of significant influence?

A The investor owns 330,000 of the 1,500,000 equity voting shares of the investee

B The investor has representation on the board of directors of the investee

C The investor is able to insist that all of the sales of the investee are made to a subsidiary of the investor

D The investor controls the votes of a majority of the board members

170 Consolidated financial statements are presented on the basis that the companies within the group are treated as if they are a single (economic) entity.

Which TWO of the following are requirements of preparing group accounts?

A All subsidiaries must adopt the accounting policies of the parent in their individual financial statements

B Subsidiaries with activities which are substantially different to the activities of other members of the group should not be consolidated

C All assets and liabilities of subsidiaries should be included at fair value

D Unrealised profits within the group must be eliminated from the consolidated financial statements

171 The Caddy group acquired 240,000 of August's 800,000 equity shares for $6 per share on 1 April 20X4. August's profit after tax for the year ended 30 September 20X4 was $400,000 and it paid an equity dividend on 20 September 20X4 of $150,000.

On the assumption that August is an associate of Caddy, what would be the carrying amount of the investment in August in the consolidated statement of financial position of Caddy as at 30 September 20X4?

A $1,455,000

B $1,500,000

C $1,515,000

D $1,395,000

172 On 1 January 20X4, Viagem acquired 80% of the equity share capital of Greca.

Extracts of their statements of profit or loss for the year ended 30 September 20X4 are:

	Viagem	Greca
	$000	$000
Revenue	64,600	38,000
Cost of sales	(51,200)	(26,000)

Sales from Viagem to Greca throughout the year ended 30 September 20X4 had consistently been $800,000 per month.

Viagem made a mark-up on cost of 25% on these sales.

Greca had $1.5 million of these goods in inventory as at 30 September 20X4.

What would be the cost of sales in Viagem's consolidated statement of profit or loss for the year ended 30 September 20X4?

$_____'000

173 Pact acquired 80% of the equity shares of Sact on 1 July 20X4, paying $3.00 for each share acquired. This represented a premium of 20% over the market price of Sact's shares at that date.

Sact's shareholders' funds (equity) as at 31 March 20X5 were:

	$	$
Equity shares of $1 each	100,000	
Retained earnings at 1 April 20X4	80,000	
Profit for the year ended 31 March 20X5	40,000	120,000
		220,000

The only fair value adjustment required to Sact's net assets on consolidation was a $20,000 increase in the value of its land.

Pact's policy is to value non-controlling interests at fair value at the date of acquisition.

For this purpose the market price of Sact's shares at that date can be deemed to be representative of the fair value of the shares held by the non-controlling interest.

What would be the carrying amount of the non-controlling interest of Sact in the consolidated statement of financial position of Pact as at 31 March 20X5?

A $54,000

B $50,000

C $56,000

D $58,000

174 Germane has a number of relationships with other companies.

In which of the following relationships is Germane necessarily the parent company?

(i)   Foll has 50,000 non-voting and 100,000 voting equity shares in issue with each share receiving the same dividend. Germane owns all of Foll's non-voting shares and 40,000 of its voting shares.

(ii)   Kipp has 1 million equity shares in issue of which Germane owns 40%. Germane also owns $800,000 out of $1 million 8% convertible loan notes issued by Kipp. These loan notes may be converted on the basis of 40 equity shares for each $100 of loan note, or they may be redeemed in cash at the option of the holder.

(iii) Germane owns 49% of the equity shares in Polly and 52% of its non-redeemable preference shares. As a result of these investments, Germane receives variable returns from Polly and has the ability to affect these returns through its power over Polly.

A   (i) only

B   (i) and (ii) only

C   (ii) and (iii) only

D   All three

175 Wilmslow acquired 80% of the equity shares of Zeta on 1 April 20X4 when Zeta's retained earnings were $200,000. During the year ended 31 March 20X5, Zeta purchased goods from Wilmslow totalling $320,000. At 31 March 20X5, one quarter of these goods were still in the inventory of Zeta. Wilmslow applies a mark-up on cost of 25% to all of its sales.

At 31 March 20X5, the retained earnings of Wilmslow and Zeta were $450,000 and $340,000 respectively.

What would be the amount of retained earnings in Wilmslow's consolidated statement of financial position as at 31 March 20X5?

$_____ '000

176 IFRS requires extensive use of fair values when recording the acquisition of a subsidiary.

Which TWO of the following comments, regarding the use of fair values on the acquisition of a subsidiary, are correct?

A   The use of fair value to record a subsidiary's acquired assets does not comply with the historical cost principle.

B   The use of fair values to record the acquisition of plant always increases consolidated post-acquisition depreciation charges compared to the corresponding charge in the subsidiary's own financial statements.

C   Cash consideration payable one year after the date of acquisition needs to be discounted to reflect its fair value.

D   When acquiring a subsidiary, the fair value of liabilities and contingent liabilities must also be considered

E   Patents must be included as part of goodwill because it is impossible to determine the fair value of an acquired patent, as, by definition, patents are unique.

177 **Identify whether the following statements are true or false**

	True	False
The profit made by a parent on the sale of goods to a subsidiary is only realised when the subsidiary sells the goods to a third party		
Eliminating intra-group unrealised profits never affects non-controlling interests		
The profit element of goods supplied by the parent to an associate and held in year-end inventory must be eliminated in full		

178 Johnson paid $1.2 million for a 30% investment in Treem's equity shares on 1 August 20X4.

Treem's profit after tax for the year ended 31 March 2015 was $750,000. On 31 March 20X5, Treem had $300,000 goods in its inventory which it had bought from Johnson in March 20X5. These had been sold by Johnson at a mark-up on cost of 20%.

Treem has not paid any dividends.

On the assumption that Treem is an associate of Johnson, what would be the carrying amount of the investment in Treem in the consolidated statement of financial position of Johnson as at 31 March 20X5?

$_____'000

179 On 1 January 20X4, Pigagem acquired 80% of the equity share capital of Streca.

Extracts of their statements of financial position for the year ended 30 September 20X4 are:

	Pigagem	Streca
	$000	$000
Receivables	64,600	38,000

At 31 December 20X4, Streca recorded a payable to Pigagem of $3 million which did not agree to Pigagem's receivable balance due to $1 million cash in transit.

What are the consolidated receivables in the consolidated statement of financial position as at 31 December 20X4?

$_____'000

180 **Identify whether the following statements are true or false**

	True	False
If a subsidiary is disposed of on the last day of the reporting period then its assets and liabilities must still be included in the consolidated statement of financial position		
The gain or loss arising on the disposal of a subsidiary in the consolidated financial statements is recorded in other comprehensive income		

181 Johanna Co acquired 100% of Sidney Co on 1 January 20X4. Johanna Co paid $5 million cash, including $200,000 professional fees. Johanna Co also agreed to pay $10 million on 1 January 20X6. Johanna Co has a cost of capital of 10%

Identify the components to be included within the calculation of goodwill for the acquisition of Sidney Co for the year ended 31 December 20X4.

Consideration		To be included in goodwill
Cash consideration of $5 million		
Cash consideration of $4.8 million		
Deferred cash consideration of $8.3 million		
Deferred cash consideration of $9.1 million		

182 The Garden group has a reporting date of 31 December 20X3. On 30 September 20X3, the group disposed of its 80% holding in the ordinary shares of Shed for $10 million in cash. It has been deemed that the disposal of Shed constitutes a discontinued operation. The following information relates to Shed:

	$m
Goodwill at disposal	2
Net assets at disposal	9
Non-controlling interest at disposal	3

What should be recorded as the 'profit (or loss) on disposal in the consolidated statement of profit or loss for the year ended 31 December 20X3?

A   Loss of $2 million

B   Profit of $2 million

C   Profit of $4 million

D   Loss of $4 million

183 Wind purchased 80% of the ordinary shares of Snow for $4 million many years ago and holds the investment in its individual statement of financial position at cost. On 30 September 20X3, Wind disposed of its shares in Snow for $10 million in cash

What is the profit arising on the disposal of the shares that will be reported in Wind's individual statement of profit or loss for the year ended 30 September 20X3?

$_____m

184 On 30 June 20X4, the Winter group disposed of its 70% holding in the ordinary shares of Spring for $9 million in cash. Winter originally purchased the shares for $6 million. At the acquisition date, the goodwill was $4.6 million. Spring's net assets at the disposal date were $5 million. The non-controlling interest in Spring at the disposal date was $3.1 million.

What is the profit arising on the disposal of Spring that will be recorded in the consolidated statement of profit or loss for the year ended 31 December 20X4?

$_____'000

185 On 30 June 20X4, the Tea group disposed of its 60% holding in the ordinary shares of Coffee for $15 million in cash. The non-controlling interest at the acquisition date was measured at its fair value of $2.2 million.

Coffee's net assets at the acquisition and the disposal date were $5 million and $8 million respectively. Goodwill arising on the acquisition of Coffee of $1 million had been fully impaired by the disposal date.

What is the profit or loss arising on the disposal of Coffee that will be recorded in the consolidated statement of profit or loss for the year ended 31 December 20X4?

A   Profit of $10.0 million

B   Profit of $9.2 million

C   Profit of $10.4 million

D   Profit of $10.2 million

INTERPRETATION OF FINANCIAL STATEMENTS

186 **Which of the following statements about a not-for-profit entity is valid?**

A   There is no requirement to calculate an earnings per share figure as it is not likely to have shareholders who need to assess its earnings performance.

B   The current value of its property is not relevant as it is not a commercial entity.

C   Interpretation of its financial performance using ratio analysis is meaningless.

D   Its financial statements will not be closely scrutinised as it does not have investors.

187 **Which of the following ratios is likely to be most relevant for a local charity?**

A   Operating profit margin

B   Current ratio

C   Earnings per share

D   Return on capital employed

188 **Identify whether each of the following is a limitation of applying ratio analysis to published financial statements or not**

	Limitation	Not a limitation
Different ways of calculating certain ratios exist		
Accounting policy choices can limit comparability between different companies		

189 The following information has been taken from Preston's financial statements:

Preston has inventory turnover of six times.

The year-end receivables collection period is 42 days.

Cost of sales for the year was $1,690,000. Credit purchases for the year were $2,150,000.

Preston's cash cycle at 31 December 20X7 was 68 days

All calculations should be made to the nearest full day, and the trading year has 365 days.

What is Preston's trade payables collection period as at 31 December 20X7?

_____ days

190 **Which TWO of the following explanations are unlikely to lead to an increase in receivables collection period?**

A   A new contract with a large customer has been won following a competitive tender

B   A large one-off credit sale has been completed just before the year end

C   The company has recently expanded into a number of high street retail units

D   Difficult economic conditions have led to some customers struggling to pay on time

E   A website has been opened in the year for trade direct to the public

191 The following extracts of the financial statements of Wiggo have been obtained:

Revenue	$980,000
Cost of sales	($530,000)
Operating expenses	($210,000)
Equity	$600,000
Loan, repayable 20X8	$300,000
Deferred tax	$44,000
Payables	$46,000

What is the return on capital employed of Wiggo?

A   24.2%

B   25.4%

C   26.7%

D   50%

192 The following extracts of the financial statements of Wiggo have been obtained:

	20X5
Inventories	$130,000
Receivables	$80,000
Cash	$10,000
Loan repayable 20X8	$90,000
Deferred tax	$14,000
Payables	$70,000
Overdraft	$34,000

What is the quick ratio of Wiggo?

_____ :1

193 **Which of the following items is unlikely to be considered a 'one-off' item which would impact the comparability of ratios?**

 A A new website selling direct to the public has meant that deliveries are now made to more diverse geographical areas, increasing delivery costs

 B A closure of a department has led to redundancies

 C Sale of surplus property leading to a profit on disposal

 D A storm in the year led to significant damage to the warehouse

194 **Which ONE of the following is not a valid reason for a decrease in gross profit margin?**

 A A major customer renewed their contract during the year following a competitive tender process

 B New plant and equipment used in the manufacturing process has been purchased in the year, which has increased the depreciation expense

 C Delivery costs to customers have risen following an increase in the rates charged by couriers

 D A national recession has led to sales prices being cut in response

195 KRL is a company which manufactures pharmaceuticals, and is investigating a proposed takeover of another entity which is based overseas.

Identify which sources of information will be available for KRL to use in relation to the acquisition

	Available to KRL to use	Not available to KRL to use
Details of the overseas country in which the target entity operates		
Recent financial statements of the entity		
Internal business plans of the takeover target		

196 Marcel Co has calculated that its current year Price Earnings (P/E) ratio is 12.6.

The sector average P/E ratio is 10.5

Which ONE of the following would be an explanation of the difference between Marcel's P/E ratio and the sector average?

 A Marcel is seen as a less risky investment than the sector average, and there is higher confidence about the future prospects of Marcel.

 B Marcel is seen as a more risky investment than the sector average, however there is higher confidence about the future prospects of Marcel.

 C Marcel is seen as a less risky investment than the sector average, however there is low confidence about the future prospects of Marcel.

 D Marcel is seen as a more risky investment than the sector average, and there is low confidence about the future prospects of Marcel.

197 **Identify whether the statements about diluted EPS below are true or false**

	True	False
It acts as a prediction of the future Earnings Per Share figure		
It discloses that Earnings Per Share could have been higher		

198 Apollo Co took out a new loan on 1st January 20X6. This loan is carries an effective interest rate of 8%. The initial proceeds of the loan are $2.5m, which is after paying issue costs of $250k. The coupon rate on the loan is 6%. Apollo must keep to an interest cover ratio of 9 times under the arrangements made with the bank.

What operating profit must be maintained by Apollo in the year ended 31st December 20X6, in order to meet the minimum interest cover ratio specified by the bank?

A $1,350,000

B $1,800,000

C $450,000

D $1,980,000

The following information is to be used for questions 199 and 200:

Rogers Co has just completed their financial statements for the year ended 30 June 20X6. They are reporting a net profit of $1,250,000 for the current year, and they have $1 million 50 cent shares in issue. The current market price of Rogers' shares is $3.50.

Rogers Co has total dividends during the year ended 30 June 20X6 of $1,500,000

---

199 **What is the Price Earnings (P/E) ratio of Rogers Co for the year ended 30 June 20X6?**

_____ times

200 **What is the Dividend Yield (to one decimal place) for the year ended 30 June 20X6?**

_____ %

201 Alco and Saleco are both food retailers. They are both showing a Return on Capital Employed (ROCE) figure of 10% for the current year. Both companies have the same financial year end. Alco has reported a net profit (based on profit before interest and tax) of 25% and Saleco has reported a net profit of 2%.

What, if any, is the difference between these two companies, even though they are showing the same ROCE calculation?

A   The companies are identical

B   Alco operates at the high end of the market, and Saleco at the lower end of

C   Alco operates at the lower end of the market, and Saleco at the high end

D   There is not enough information in the question to determine the difference

202 Identify whether each of the following is a limitation of applying ratio analysis to published financial statements or not

	Limitation	Not a limitation
Financial statements often use historic cost, meaning that inflation is not taken into account		
Complex items may not fit into any accounting standards and therefore may be omitted from the financial statements		

203 Lepchem is a pharmaceutical company which was launched in September 20X1. Lepchem have been funded through bank loans and equity investment. Lepchem's aim is to develop new pharmaceuticals which could then be sold for a high margin. So far, Lepchem have not managed to successfully develop or sell any pharmaceuticals.

Which ratio is likely to be the most relevant for Lepchem for the year to 31 December 20X1?

A   Current ratio

B   Gross profit margin

C   Operating profit margin

D   Receivables collection period

204 Identify whether the following criteria could be used to assess the performance of a not-for-profit entity

	Could be used to assess	Will not be used
The return given to investors		
The success in achieving the organisation's stated aims		
How well costs are being managed		

205 Which ONE of the following measures is likely to be the least relevant to a property management company which rents out properties to businesses?

A   Non-current asset turnover

B   Return on capital employed

C   Average rent earned

D   Inventory turnover period

206 Quartile is in the jewellery retail business which can be assumed to be highly seasonal. For the year ended 30 September 20X4, Quartile assessed its operating performance by comparing selected accounting ratios with those of its business sector average as provided by an agency. You may assume that the business sector used by the agency is an accurate representation of Quartile's business.

Which TWO of the following circumstances may invalidate the comparison of Quartile's ratios with those of the sector average?

A   In the current year, Quartile has experienced significant rising costs for its purchases

B   The sector average figures are compiled from companies whose year-end is between 1 July 20X4 and 30 September 20X4

C   Quartile does not revalue its properties, but is aware that other entities in this sector do

D   During the year, Quartile discovered an error relating to the inventory count at 30 September 20X3. This error was correctly accounted for in the financial statements for the current year ended 30 September 20X4

207 The following information has been taken or calculated from Fowler's financial statements for the year ended 30 September 20X4.

Fowler's cash cycle at 30 September 20X4 is 70 days. Its inventory turnover is six times.

Year-end trade payables are $230,000.

Purchases on credit for the year were $2 million.

Cost of sales for the year was $1·8 million.

What is Fowler's trade receivables collection period as at 30 September 20X4?

$_____ days

208 Trent uses the formula (trade receivables at its year end/credit sales for the year × 365) to calculate how long on average (in days) its customers take to pay.

Which TWO of the following would NOT affect the correctness of the above calculation of the average number of days a customer takes to pay?

A   Trent experiences considerable seasonal trading

B   Trent makes a number of cash sales through retail outlets

C   Revenue does not include a 15% sales tax whereas the receivables do include the tax

D   Trent factors with recourse the receivable of its largest customer

209 At 31 March 2015, Jasim had equity of $200,000 and debt of $100,000.

Which of the following transactions would increase Jasim's gearing compared to what it would have been had the transaction NOT taken place?

Gearing should be taken as debt/(debt + equity). Each transaction should be considered separately.

A   During the year a property was revalued upwards by $20,000

B   A bonus issue of equity shares of 1 for 4 was made during the year using other components of equity

C   A provision for estimated damages was reduced during the year from $21,000 to $15,000 based on the most recent legal advice

D   An asset with a fair value of $25,000 was acquired under a finance lease on 31 March 2015

210 **Which of the following current year events would explain a fall in a company's operating profit margin compared to the previous year?**

A   An increase in gearing leading to higher interest costs

B   A reduction in the allowance for uncollectible receivables

C   A decision to value inventory on the average cost basis from the first in first out (FIFO) basis. Unit prices of inventory had risen during the current year

D   A change from the amortisation of development costs being included in cost of sales to being included in administrative expenses

STATEMENT OF CASH FLOWS

211 The following information is available for the property, plant and equipment of Fry as at 30 September:

	20X4	20X3
	$000	$000
Carrying amounts	23,400	14,400

The following items were recorded during the year ended 30 September 20X4:

(i)   Depreciation charge of $2.5 million

(ii)   An item of plant, with a carrying amount of $3 million, was sold for $1.8 million

(iii) A property was revalued upwards by $2 million

(iv) Environmental provisions of $4 million relating to property, plant and equipment were capitalised during the year

What amount would be shown in Fry's statement of cash flows for purchase of property, plant and equipment for the year ended 30 September 20X4?

$_____ '000

212 At 1 October 20X4, BK had accrued interest payable of $12,000.

During the year ended 30 September 20X5, BK charged finance costs of $41,000 to its statement of profit or loss, including unwinding a discount relating to a provision stated at its present value of $150,000 at 1 October 20X4. The closing balance on accrued interest payable account at 30 September 20X5 was $15,000, and BK has a discount rate of 6%.

How much interest paid should BK show on its statement of cash flows for the year ended 30 September 20X5?

A $38,000

B $29,000

C $35,000

D $41,000

213 The following balances were extracted from N's financial statements:

Extracts from the statement of financial position as at 31 December

	20X9	20X8
	$000	$000
Deferred taxation	38	27
Current tax payable	119	106

Extract from statement of profit or loss for the year ended 31 December 20X9

	$000
Income tax expense	122

The amount of tax paid that should be included in N's statement of cash flows for the year ended 31 December 20X9 is:

$_____'000

214 **Which item would be NOT be shown in a statement of cash flow using the direct method?**

A   Cash payments to employees

B   Cash paid to suppliers

C   Cash sales

D   Finance costs

215 IAS 7 Statement of cash flows sets out the three main headings to be used in a statement of cash flows.

Which TWO of the items below would be included under the heading 'Cash flows from operating activities' according to IAS 7?

A   Tax paid

B   Purchase of investments

C   Loss on disposal of machinery

D   Purchase of equipment

216 During the year to 31st July Smartypants made a profit of $37,500 after accounting for depreciation of $2,500.

During the year non-current assets were purchased for $16,000, receivables increased by $2,000, inventories decreased by $3,600 and trade payables increased by $700.

What was the increase in cash and bank balances during the year?

A $21,300

B $30,300

C $24,900

D $26,300

217 Identify the correct treatment in the calculation of net cash from operating activities under the indirect method

	Add to profit before tax	Deduct from profit before tax
Decrease in trade receivables		
increase in inventories		
Profit on sale of non-current assets		
Depreciation		

218 Butcher Co had the following balances in its statement of financial position as at 30 June 20X0 and 20X1:

	20X0	20X1
Share capital	$150,000	$170,000
Share premium	$95,000	$105,000
10% debentures	$190,000	$170,000

How much will appear in the statement of cash flows for the year ended 30 June 20X1 under the heading 'cash flows from financing activities'?

$_____'000

219 At 1 January 20X0 Casey Co had property, plant and equipment with a carrying amount of $180,000. In the year ended 31 December 20X0 the company disposed of assets with a carrying amount of $60,000 for $50,000. The company revalued a building from $75,000 to $100,000 and charged depreciation for the year of $20,000. At the end of the year, the carrying amount of property, plant and equipment was $250,000.

How much will be reported in the statement of cash flows for the year ended 31 December 20X0 under the heading 'cash flows from investing activities'?

A $75,000 outflow

B $125,000 outflow

C $135,000 outflow

D $50,000 inflow

220 At 1 January 20X0 Casey Co had government grants held in deferred income of $900,000. During the year, Casey Co released $100,000 to the statement of profit or loss. At 31 December 20X0, the remaining deferred income balance was $1,100,000.

Select the TWO amounts to be included in the statement of cash flows for Casey Co.

Amortisation of government grant	Receipt of grant
Increase of 100,000 to cash generated from operations	Cash received from grant $300,000 in investing activities
Decrease of 100,000 to cash generated from operations	Cash received from grant $100,000 in investing activities

Section 2

OBJECTIVE CASE QUESTIONS – SECTION B

CONCEPTUAL FRAMEWORK/INTERNATIONAL FINANCIAL REPORTING STANDARDS

The following scenario relates to questions 221–225

This objective test case question contains question types which will only appear in a computer-based exam, but this question provides valuable practice for all students whichever version of the exam they are taking.

Flightline is an airline which treats its aircraft as complex non-current assets, accounted for under the historical cost model. The cost and other details of an aircraft are:

	$000	*Estimated life*
Interior cabin fittings – installed 1 April 20X5	25,000	5 years
Engine - installed 1 April 20X5	9,000	36,000 flying hours

In the year ended 31 March 20X9, the aircraft flew for 1,200 hours for the six months to 30 September 20X8.

On 1 October 20X8 the aircraft suffered a 'bird strike' accident which damaged the engine beyond repair. This was replaced by a new engine 1 with a life of 36,000 hours at cost of $10.8 million.

Flightline's year end is 31 March 20X9.

---

221 What is the depreciation to be charged in respect of the engine for the 6 month period to 1 October 20X8?

$_____000

222 Which of the following explains the correct accounting treatment in relation to the engine?

A   Write off engine 1, capitalise the new engine 1 and depreciate over 24,000 hours

B   Treat the $10.8 million as a repair to engine 1 and continue to depreciate the engine as in the first 6 months

C   Capitalise $6 million to replace engine 1, expense the other $4.8 million

D   Write off engine 1, capitalise the new engine 1 and depreciate over 36,000 hours

223 A wing was also damaged, but was repaired at a cost of $3 million. The accident also caused cosmetic damage to the exterior of the aircraft which required repainting at a cost of $2 million.

Identify the correct treatment for the $3 million repair costs to engine 2 and the $2 million repainting of the aircraft

	Capitalise	Expense
$3 million repair of the wing		
$2 million repainting of the exterior		

224 As the aircraft was out of service for some weeks due to the accident, Flightline took the opportunity to upgrade its cabin facilities at a cost of $4.5 million. This did not increase the estimated remaining life of the cabin fittings, but the improved facilities enabled Flightline to substantially increase the air fares on this aircraft.

What is the carrying amount of the cabin fittings as at 31 March 20X9?

A $8,600,000

B $8,000,000

C $5,000,000

D $7,250,000

225 The 'bird strike' accident represents an indication of impairment.

Which of the following statements regarding impairments is true?

A Annual impairment reviews are needed for complex assets

B The accident means an impairment review should be performed on all aircraft

C Any impairment on the aircraft would be expensed in the statement of profit or loss

D The aircraft will be impaired if its recoverable amount exceeds its carrying amount

---

The following scenario relates to questions 226–230

Speculate owns 2 properties and uses fair value accounting where possible.

Property A: An office building used by Speculate for administrative purposes. At 1 April 20X2 it had a $2 million carrying amount and a remaining life of 20 years. On 1 October 20X2, the property was let to a third party and reclassified as an investment property. The property had a fair value of $2.3 million at 1 October, and $2.34 million at 31 March 20X3.

Property B: Another office building sub-let to a subsidiary of Speculate. At 1 April 20X2, it had a fair value of $1.5 million which had risen to $1.65 million at 31 March 20X3.

---

226 **What is the correct treatment when Property A is reclassified as an investment property?**

A Take $350,000 gain to other comprehensive income

B Take $350,000 gain to the statement of profit or loss

C Take $400,000 gain to other comprehensive income

D Take $400,000 gain to the statement of profit or loss

---

227 Which of the following models can Speculate use to account for investment properties in its individual financial statements?

(i) Cost model

(ii) Revaluation model

(iii) Fair value model

A (i) and (ii) only

B (i) and (iii) only

C (ii) and (iii) only

D All three

228 What is the total gain for investment properties to be included in Speculate's individual statement of profit or loss for the year ended 31 March 20X3?

A $40,000

B $150,000

C $190,000

D Nil

229 In the consolidated financial statements of Speculate, how would Property B be accounted for?

A Removed as an intra-group item

B In investment properties

C Within goodwill

D In property, plant and equipment

230 What would the carrying amount of Property A be at 31 March 20X3 if Speculate used the cost model for investment properties?

A $1,950,000

B $1,900,000

C $2,185,000

D $2,182,051

The following scenario relates to questions 231–235

This objective test case question contains question types which will only appear in a computer-based exam, but this question provides valuable practice for all students whichever version of the exam they are taking.

Apex received a $10 million 6% loan on 1 April 20X7. The loan will be redeemable at a premium which means the loan has an effective finance cost of 7.5% per annum. The loan was specifically issued to finance the building of the new store.

Construction of the store commenced on 1 May 20X7 and it was completed and ready for use on 28 February 20X8, but did not open for trading until 1 April 20X8.

231   How should the loan be treated in the financial statements of Apex for the year ended 31 March 20X8?

A   Present value

B   Fair value through other comprehensive income

C   Fair value through profit or loss

D   Amortised cost

232   Which of the statements below regarding IAS 23 Borrowing Costs is correct?

A   Borrowing costs must be capitalised if they are directly attributable to qualifying assets

B   Borrowing costs may be capitalised if they are directly attributable to non-current assets

C   Borrowing costs must be capitalised if they are directly attributable to non-current assets

D   Borrowing costs may be capitalised if they are directly attributable to qualifying assets

233   How much should be recorded as finance costs in the statement of profit or loss for the year ended 31 March 20X8?

$_____000

234   How much interest should be capitalised as part of property, plant and equipment as at 31 March 20X8?

$_____000

235   Apex decided that not all of the funds raised were needed immediately and temporarily invested some of the funds in April 20X7, earning $40,000 interest.

How should the $40,000 be accounted for in the financial statements of Apex?

A   Net off the amount capitalised in property, plant and equipment

B   Taken to the statement of profit or loss as investment income

C   Taken as other comprehensive income

D   Deducted from the outstanding loan amount in the statement of financial position

The following scenario relates to questions 236–240

Shawler constructed a furnace on 1 April 20X3, causing significant environmental damage which must be repaired at the end of the asset's useful life of ten years. The present value of this is estimated to be $4 million. Shawler has a cost of capital of 8%.

On 1 October 20X3, Shawler received a government grant of $1.2 million relating to the cost of plant with a five year life. Shawler accounts for grants using deferred income.

On 1 October 20X3, Shawler also acquired land for 12 million dinars. The land was used to construct a factory during the year. Shawler's functional currency is dollars.

On 1 October 20X3 the exchange rate was 4 Dinars: $1. At 31 March 20X4 the exchange rate was 2 Dinars:$1 and the average rate for the year was 3 Dinars:$1.

236 **What is the total finance cost (to the nearest thousand) to be recorded in the statement of profit or loss in respect of the environmental damage caused by the furnace for the year ended 30 June 20X5?**

A $400,000

B $320,000

C $4,000,000

D $185,000

237 **What is the non-current liability to be shown in Shawler's statement of financial position in respect of the government grant as at 31 March 20X4?**

A $840,000

B $1,080,000

C $960,000

D $720,000

238 **What is the carrying amount of the land in the statement of financial position of Shawler as at 31 March 20X4?**

A $3,000,000

B $6,000,000

C $12,000,000

D $4,000,000

239 The costs below are the costs associated with the construction of the factory.

Which of the following can NOT be capitalised?

A Legal fees relating to the site purchase

B Health and safety training for new construction workers

C Direct labour costs associated with the construction

D Costs of site preparation

240 In the following year, it was discovered that Shawler had breached the conditions relating to the government grant and therefore the grant had to be repaid.

Which TWO of the following describe the correct accounting treatment to record the repayment of the grant?

A   Remove all deferred income balances

B   Record an expense in the statement of profit or loss

C   Increase the cost of plant

D   Make an adjustment to the prior year financial statements

The following scenario relates to questions 241–245

This question contains question types which will only appear in a computer-based exam, but this question provides valuable practice for all students whichever version of the exam they are taking.

During the year Darby started research work on a new processor chip. Darby has a past history of being particularly successful in bringing similar projects to a profitable conclusion. In addition to this, Darby spent $200,000 training staff to use new equipment.

Darby also developed a new online platform during the year, spending $100,000 a month evenly from 1 February 20X5 to 31 October 20X5. Darby was unsure of the outcome of the project, but doubts were resolved on 1 May, following successful testing. The platform launched on 1 November and was expected to last 5 years.

241 Darby's accounting assistant has read something which states that intangible assets are identifiable, non-monetary items without physical substance.

Which TWO of the following relate to items being classed as identifiable?

A   Items must have probable future economic benefits

B   Items must arise from legal or contractual rights

C   Items must have a measurable cost

D   Items must be separable

242 Identify the correct accounting treatment for items below.

	Capitalise	Expense
Training for staff		
Expenditure on processor chip		

243 How much should be recorded in Darby's statement of profit or loss for the year ended 31 December 20X5 in relation to the development of the online platform?

$_____000

244 Which of the facts relating to the online platform is correct?

(i) The online platform will be subject to annual impairment review due to the judgemental nature of the project

(ii) Once capitalised, the development costs should be held at fair value at each year-end

(iii) Depreciation on any plant used to develop the platform could be capitalised as part of the development costs

A (i) only

B (ii) and (iii) only

C (iii) only

D (i) and (ii) only

245 Darby acquired a patent with a 10 year life for $500,000 on 1 January 20X5. On 31 December 20X5, management believed that the patent was less fully utilised than expected and determined the following information as part of their impairment review:

	$000
Fair value of the asset	400
Estimated incremental costs attributable to the asset disposal	20
Value in use of the asset	480

What is the value of the impairment loss in the year ended 31 December 20X5?

A $70,000

B $30,000

C $20,000

D Nil

The following scenario relates to questions 246–250

Wilderness owns and operates an item of plant that cost $640,000 and had accumulated depreciation of $400,000 at 1 October 20X4. It is being depreciated at 12.5% per annum on cost. On 1 April 20X5 the plant was damaged when a factory vehicle collided into it.

Based on the damage, the estimated value of the plant in use is $150,000. The plant has a current disposal value of $20,000, but Wilderness has been offered a trade-in value of $180,000 if it upgrades, which Wildnerness is unlikely to do.

Wilderness also sold bottled water, and the assets in the water division are:

	$000
Brand (Quencher – see below)	7,000
Land containing spa	12,000
Purifying and bottling plant	8,000

During the year, the water became contaminated and Wilderness' reputation was affected. It is estimated that the division is worth $15 million in total.

Due to the reputational damage, the Quencher brand is now deemed to be worthless.

246 Which of the following statements regarding impairment is correct?

    A   The recoverable amount is the lower of the fair value less costs to sell and the value in use

    B   An asset is impaired if the carrying amount is higher than the recoverable amount

    C   The value in use represents the price in an arms-length transaction

    D   Impairment losses should always be taken to the statement of profit or loss

247 What is the carrying amount of Wilderness' plant immediately before the impairment?

    A $200,000

    B $150,000

    C $180,000

    D $240,000

248 What is the recoverable amount of Wilderness' plant at the date of the impairment?

    A $200,000

    B $150,000

    C $180,000

    D $20,000

249 What is the value of Mossel's bottling plant following the impairment review?

    A $8,000,000

    B $6,000,000

    C $5,500,000

    D $5,000,000

250 **Identify which of the assets below require an annual impairment review.**

(i)   Intangible assets with an indefinite life

(ii)   Land with an indefinite life

A   (i) only

B   (ii) only

C   Both (i) and (ii)

D   Neither of the assets

The following scenario relates to questions 251–255

Radar's directors made the following decisions during the year ended 31 March 20X3:

- it disposed of all of its outlets in country A

- it rebranded all of its outlets in country B to target the tourism market. The previous target market in country B had been aimed at business clients.

At a board meeting on 1 January 20X3, Pulsar's directors decided sell an item of plant, which had a carrying value of $4 million at 1 April 20X2 and a remaining life of 20 years. The plant is expected to sell for $3.9 million within 12 months.

A decision was also made to close down a regional office, which was communicated before the year-end. 50 employees would be retrained and kept within the company at a cost of $100,000; the others took redundancy and will be paid $300,000.

$75,000 is to be spent on marketing materials directing customers of the existing factory to other production facilities operated by Radar.

251 **Which of the following statements regarding discontinued operations is correct?**

A   Profit from discontinued operations is shown under other comprehensive   income

B   Profit from discontinued operations includes any gain or loss on disposal

C   Profit or loss from discontinued operations only relates to items that have already been sold or disposed by the year-end

D   Profit or loss from discontinued operations excludes any closure costs

252 **Identify whether the change in operations in countries A and B represent a discontinued operation in accordance with IFRS 5 *Non-Current Assets Held for Sale and Discontinued Operations*.**

A   Only country A represents a discontinued operation

B   Only country B represents a discontinued operation

C   Both countries will be regarded as discontinued operations

D   Neither country will be regarded as a discontinued operation

253   At what value should the plant be held at 31 March 20X3 according to IFRS 5 *Non-Current Assets Held for Sale and Discontinued Operations*?

A $3,800,000

B $3,900,000

C $4,000,000

D $3,850,000

254   What provision should be recorded in relation to the office closure?

A $300,000

B $475,000

C $375,000

D $400,000

255   On 30 June 20X3, before the financial statements were authorised for issue, the plant sold at a loss of $100,000 and the redundancies were settled at $50,000 more than expected.

Identify whether each item represents an adjusting or non-adjusting event according to *IAS 10 Events After the Reporting Period*.

A   Only the disposal of plant represents an adjusting event

B   Only the redundancies represent an adjusting event

C   Both the disposal of plant and redundancies represent adjusting events

D   Neither the disposal of plant or redundancies represent adjusting events

The following scenario relates to questions 256–260

This objective test case question contains question types which will only appear in a computer-based exam, but this question provides valuable practice for all students whichever version of the exam they are taking.

Tunshill has an item of plant with a five-year life. The plant is wearing well and at 1 October 20X8 the production manager believed that the plant was likely to last 5 more years.

Tunshill wishes to change its method of inventory valuation from FIFO to AVCO. The value of Tunshill's inventory at 30 September 20X9 (on the FIFO basis) is $20 million; however on the AVCO basis it would be valued at $18 million. Tunshill's inventory at 30 September 20X8 was $15 million, however on the AVCO basis it would have been reported as $13.4 million.

Tunshill also has two items of inventory that it has problems with. Item A cost $50 per unit. Tunshill has struggled to sell the item and has 2,000 units still in inventory. Tunshill has agreed a contract with a distributor who will sell the items for $55 each. To do this, the distributor will charge commission of 20%.

Item B relates to a one-off purchase of rare metal for a lucrative contract costing $80,000. No work has yet been done, but after further costs of $20,000 it will be turned into a product and sold for an agreed price of $150,000. Since buying the metal, the cost price has fallen to $50,000.

---

256 **Which TWO circumstances are outlined in IAS 8 *Accounting Policies, Changes in Accounting Estimates and Errors* as acceptable reasons to change accounting policy?**

   A   To provide greater comparison with competitors

   B   If a change results in providing more reliable and relevant information to users

   C   If required by an International Financial Reporting Standard

   D   If tax law in a country changes

   E   To show the best possible results for the investors

257 **Fill in the blanks in the sentence below with the correct option.**

   The change in useful life of the plant will be a change in accounting _____ and should be applied _____.

   Options: Policy; Estimate; Error; Retrospectively; Prospectively; Prudently

258 **Which of the options below outline the correct treatment for the change in valuation method from FIFO to AVCO?**

   A   Profit would be reduced by $400,000

   B   Profit would be reduced by $2,000,000

   C   Opening retained earnings would increase by $1,600,000

   D   Opening retained earnings would decrease by $400,000

259 **At what value should item A be included in Tunshill's statement of financial position as at 30 September 20X9?**

   $_____000

---

260 What value should item B be shown at in the statement of financial position as at 30 September 20X9?

A $50,000

B $80,000

C $130,000

D $100,000

The following scenario relates to questions 261–265

Schrute owns a herd of cattle, which produce milk. Schrute then turns this into cheese.

On 1 April 20X5, Shrute purchased a flock of sheep for $100,000, which included transaction costs of $5,000. At 31 March 20X6, the flock was valued at $120,000. Every time animals are sold there is a 5% commission fee payable to the national farming agency.

Shrute uses the historical cost model and charges all depreciation as an operating expense.

In addition to this, Shrute uses a number of items of specialised farm machinery. This machinery cost Schrute $200,000 on 1 April 20X2 and has a 10 year useful life. At 31 March 20X6, there is only one supplier who still sells this machinery and the current price of new machinery is $300,000.

261 Which of the following items held by Schrute will be accounted for under the provisions of IAS 41 *Agriculture*?

(i)   Herd of cattle

(ii) Milk

(iii) Cheese

A   (i) only

B   (ii) and (iii) only

C   (i) and (ii) only

D   All three items

262 What gain should be taken to Shrute's statement of profit or loss for the year ended 31 March 20X6 in respect of the flock of sheep?

A $14,000

B $19,000

C $20,000

D $25,000

263 Using current cost accounting, what is the value of the machinery at 31 March 20X6?

A $120,000

B $180,000

C $200,000

D $300,000

264 At 31 March 20X6, a valuations expert informed the directors of Schrute that the property owned and used by Shrute for farming had significantly increased in value. This had been decided by looking at the price per square metre at similar properties in the area and concluded that this could be used to value Schrute's farm with no adjustments necessary.

Which of the following bases describes the fair value method used to value the farm?

A   Level 1 input

B   Level 2 input

C   Level 3 input

D   Level 4 input

265 **If Schrute chooses to value the farm at the market value, which TWO of the following ratios will NOT be affected?**

A   Current ratio

B   Return on capital employed

C   Gross profit margin

D   Gearing

E   Net profit (before tax) margin

The following scenario relates to questions 266–270

This objective test case question contains question types which will only appear in a computer-based exam, but this question provides valuable practice for all students whichever version of the exam they are taking.

On 1 April 20X7, Fino entered into an agreement to lease an item of plant from the manufacturer. The lease required four annual payments in advance of $100,000 each commencing on 1 April 20X7. The plant would have a useful life of four years and would be scrapped at the end of this period. The plant would have cost $350,000 to purchase outright.

Fino has a cost of capital of 10%.

Note: For finance lease calculations, a calculation of the present value of the minimum lease payments is not required.

266 **Which of the following applies the principle of faithful representation to the above lease agreement?**

A   Recording an annual rent expense in Fino's statement of profit or loss

B   Expensing any interest on a straight-line basis over 4 years

C   Recording an asset in Fino's statement of financial position to reflect control

D   Record the $100,000 paid as a prepayment to be released over 4 years

267 **If the lease were treated as an operating lease, select the TWO items that would be recorded in Fino's financial statements for the year ended 30 September 20X7.**

A   No impact on statement of financial position

B $50,000 prepayment in statement of financial position

C $50,000 accrual in statement of financial position

D $0 expense in statement of profit or loss

E $100,000 expense in statement of profit or loss

F $50,000 expense in statement of profit or loss

268 **If the lease were treated as a finance lease, what would be the carrying amount of Fino's plant as at 30 September 20X7?**

$_____

269 **If the lease were treated as a finance lease, what interest would be charged to Fino's statement of profit or loss for the year ended 30 September 20X7?**

A $12,500

B $25,000

C $17,500

D $35,000

270 **If the lease were treated as a finance lease rather than an operating lease, identify the impact that this would have on the following ratios for Fino.**

	Increase	*Decrease*
Return on Capital Employed		
Gearing		
Interest cover		

The following scenario relates to questions 271–275

On 1 January 20X6 Lotso began a 5 year operating lease of new warehouse premises. The premises cost Lotso $100,000 a year, paid semi-annually in arrears. The first six months were rent-free so Lotso made the first payment on 31 December 20X6.

On 1 January 20X6, Lotso also entered into an agreement to lease new machinery under a 5 year finance lease. Lotso pay $300,000 on 31 December each year. The asset has a useful life of 6 years, and ownership transfers to Lotso at the end of the lease. The interest rate implicit in the lease is 6%.

If Lotso were to buy the asset outright it would cost $1,263,000.

On 1 January 20X6, Lotso sold its head office to a finance company, leasing it back on a 20 year finance lease. The carrying amount of the asset on 1 January 20X6 was $10 million. The fair value of the asset and cash received at 1 January 20X6 was $11.5 million.

271 **Which of the following would be recorded in Lotso's financial statements in respect of the warehouse premises for the year ended 31 December 20X6?**

    A $50,000 expense in statement of profit or loss

    B $90,000 expense in statement of profit or loss

    C $100,000 expense in statement of profit or loss

    D $60,000 accrual in statement of financial position

272 **What current liability (to the nearest thousand) will be recorded in Lotso's statement of financial position as at 31 December 20X6 in relation to the machinery lease?**

    A $300,000

    B $238,000

    C $801,000

    D $921,000

273 **What is the carrying amount of the machinery as at 31 December 20X6?**

    A $1,039,000

    B $1,263,000

    C $1,052,500

    D $1,010,400

274 **What is the total impact on the statement of profit or loss for the year ended 31 December 20X6 in respect of the head office?**

    A $1,500,000 income

    B $1,425,000 income

    C $75,000 income

    D   Nil

275 Identify if the statements below are true or false

Statement 1: In a sale and leaseback transaction, the asset always remains with the lessee

Statement 2: For an item to be treated as a finance lease, the lessee must legally own the item.

A   Only statement 1 is true

B   Only statement 2 is true

C   Both statements are true

D   Neither statement is true

The following scenario relates to questions 276–280

This objective test case question contains question types which will only appear in a computer-based exam, but this question provides valuable practice for all students whichever version of the exam they are taking.

On 1 September 20X3, Laidlaw factored (sold) $2 million of trade receivables to Finease. Laidlaw received an immediate payment of $1.8 million.   Any receivables not collected after four months will be sold back to Laidlaw.

On 1 October 20X2, Laidlaw sold a property which had a carrying amount of $3.5 million to a property company for its fair value $5 million. Laidlaw will rent the property for a period of five years at an annual rental of $400,000. At the end of this period, Laidlaw will be given the opportunity to repurchase the property (at its fair value) before it is put on the open market.

Laidlaw issued $10 million convertible loan notes on 1 October 20X2 that carry a nominal interest (coupon) rate of 5% per annum. A similar loan note, without the conversion option, would have required Laidlaw to pay an interest rate of 8%.

Relevant discount rates are shown below:

End of year		5%	8%
	1	0.95	0.93
	2	0.91	0.86
	3	0.86	0.79

276 Which of the following is correct regarding Laidlaw's factoring of trade receivables for the year ended 30 September 20X3?

A $200,000 should be recorded as an administrative expense for the disposal of the receivables

B   The receivables should be removed from the statement of financial position

C   This represents a 'without recourse' factoring agreement

D   The receipt of $1.8 million should be treated as a loan

277 Which TWO of the following items should be recorded in Laidlaw's statement of profit or loss for the year ended 30 September 20X3 in respect of the property sale?

A $300,000 finance cost

B $300,000 release of deferred income

C $700,000 depreciation

D $1.5 million profit on disposal

E $400,000 rent expense

278 **What amount should be recorded in equity (to the nearest thousand) in respect of the convertible loan notes issued by Laidlaw?**

$_____000

279 **Which of the following statements regarding the convertible loan notes is NOT true?**

A   The convertible loan notes will affect gearing due to the liability component being different to the equity component

B   The equity amount will remain fixed until the date of conversion

C   The liability at 30 September 20X5 will be $10 million

D   5% interest will be charged to the statement of profit or loss as a finance cost

280 **Applying the principle of split accounting to convertible loan notes is important to satisfy which of the following qualitative characteristics?**

A   Faithful representation

B   Timeliness

C   Verifiability

D   Relevance

The following scenario relates to questions 281–285

The following trial balance extract relates to Howard at 30 September 20X5:

	$000	$000
Convertible loan notes – Liability component at 1 Oct X4 (note (i))		28,508
5% loan notes (note (ii))		10,000
Equity investments (note (iii))	6,000	

The following notes are relevant:

(i)   The convertible loan notes are 8% $30 million convertible loan notes issued on 1 October 20X4 at par. An equivalent loan without the conversion would carry an interest rate of 10%. Howard's finance director correctly split the instrument into its equity and liability components at 1 October 20X4, but has done nothing else.

(ii)   The 5% loan notes were issued at par of $10 million, but Howard incurred $400,000 issue costs. The loan notes have an effective interest rate of 8%.

(iii) The equity investments relate to 1 million shares in Kapoor, an unrelated company. During the year, Kapoor paid a dividend of 10 cents per share. At 30 September 20X5 the fair value of a Kapoor share was $7.

---

281 **Which of the items included in the trial balance extract will be classified as financial instruments?**

A   Convertible loan notes and equity investments only

B   Loan notes and equity investments only

C   Convertible loan notes and loan notes only

D   All three items

282   What should the value of the liability element of the convertible loan note be at 30 September 20X5, to the nearest thousand?

A $28,508,000

B $28,389,000

C $28,959,000

D $30,000,000

283   What finance cost should be shown in the statement of profit or loss in respect of the loan notes?

A $768,000

B $800,000

C $832,000

D $500,000

284   What income should be recorded in the statement of profit or loss in relation to the equity investments?

A $600,000

B $1,100,000

C $1,600,000

D $1,000,000

285   Howard is uncertain of how to treat professional fees. In which of the following situations should professional fees NOT be capitalised as part of the asset?

A   Acquisition of a patent

B   Acquisition of property

C   Acquisition of fair value through other comprehensive income investments

D   Acquisition of fair value through profit or loss investments

The following scenario relates to questions 286–290

Vance buys and sells goods in Kromits (Kr), but has a functional currency of dollars ($).

Vance purchased goods for Kr 10,000 on 1 September 20X1. At year-end this is unpaid.

Vance sold goods on 1 September 20X1 for Kr 60,000. On 1 October Vance received Kr 30,000. The remaining Kr 30,000 is unpaid at 31 December 20X1.

Vance estimated the current year's tax at $43,000. However, Vance's assistant accountant had ignored deferred tax. At 1 January 20X1 Vance had a deferred tax liability of $130,000. At 31 December 20X1 Vance had temporary taxable differences of $360,000. Vance pays tax at 25%. All movements in deferred tax are taken to the statement of profit or loss.

Relevant exchange rates are:

1 September   Kr10:$1

1 October   Kr10.5:$1

31 December   Kr8:$1

Average rate   Kr9:$1

286 What gain or loss should be recorded in the statement of profit or loss for the year ended 31 December 20X1 in relation to the payable recorded for the purchase of goods?

A   Loss of $111

B   Gain of $111

C   Loss of $250

D   Gain of $250

287 What gain or loss should be recorded in the statement of profit or loss for the year ended 31 December 20X1 in relation to the sale of goods?

A   Loss of $607

B   Gain of $607

C   Loss of $893

D   Gain of $893

288 Which of the statements below is/are true?

Statement 1: The inventory purchased on 1 October 20X1 should be retranslated at the closing rate if the goods remain in inventory at 31 December 20X1.

Statement 2: The foreign exchange gains will be added to the revenue for the year.

A   Statement 1 is true

B   Statement 2 is true

C   Both statements are true

D   Neither statement is true

289 What will be recorded as the tax expense in the statement of profit or loss for the year ended 31 December 20X7?

    A $3,000

    B $83,000

    C $101,000

    D $113,000

290 Vance's assistant accountant has discovered that there is a debit balance on the trial balance of $3,000 relating to the over/under provision of tax from the prior year.

What impact will this have on Vance's current year financial statements?

    A   Increase the tax liability by $3,000 in the statement of financial position

    B   Decrease the tax liability by $3,000 in the statement of financial position

    C   Increase the tax expense by $3,000 in the statement of profit or loss

    D   Decrease the tax expense by $3,000 in the statement of profit or loss

---

The following scenario relates to questions 291–295

Bailey constructs buildings for customers which can take many years to complete. Bailey has three contracts in progress at 30 September, which are detailed below. All of the contracts below began in the current year.

	Contract 1	Contract 2	Contract 3
	$000	$000	$000
Price	10,000	8,000	4,000
Costs incurred to date	(6,000)	(4,000)	(500)
Costs to complete	(1,000)	(6,000)	(2,000)
Progress	80%	60%	25%
Amount billed to date	7,000	3,000	1,000

---

291 What revenue should be recorded (to the nearest thousand) in relation to contract 1?

    A $8,000,000

    B $8,571,000

    C $7,000,000

    D $2,400,000

292 What cost of sales should be recorded (to the nearest thousand) in relation to contract 2?

    A $4,200,000

    B $9,400,000

    C $5,640,000

    D $6,800,000

293 **What should be recorded in the statement of financial position (to the nearest thousand) in relation to contract 3?**

A   Nil

B $500,000 contract liability

C $125,000 contract liability

D $3,000,000 contract asset

294 Bailey's assistant accountant is unsure about how to deal with a brand new contract where the progress and overall profit cannot yet be ascertained.

Identify which of the following statements, if any, are true.

Statement 1 – Where the progress and overall profit are unknown, no contract asset or liability can be recognised.

Statement 2 – Where the progress and overall profit are unknown, revenue should be recognised to the level of recoverable costs.

A   Statement 1 is true

B   Statement 2 is true

C   Both statements are true

D   Neither statement is true

295 Bailey's assistant has also enquired about moving to change the way of measuring the progress of contracts.

Which of the following describes how the change should be applied?

A   As a change in accounting estimate, applied retrospectively

B   As a change in accounting estimate, applied prospectively

C   As a change in accounting policy, applied retrospectively

D   As a change in accounting policy, applied prospectively

The following scenario relates to questions 296–300

Creg sold and installed a large item of machinery for $800,000 on 1 November 20X7. Included within the price was a 2 year servicing contract which has a value of $240,000 and a fee for installation of $50,000.

Creg works as an agent for a number of smaller contractors, earning commission of 10%. Creg's revenue includes $6 million received from clients under these agreements with $5.4 million in cost of sales representing the amount paid to the contractors.

Creg sold a large number of vehicles to a new customer for $10 million on 1 July 20X7. The customer paid $1 million up front and agreed to pay the remaining balance on 1 July 20X8. Creg has a cost of capital of 6%.

296 How much should be recorded in Creg's revenue in its statement of profit or loss for the year ended 31 December 20X7 in relation to the large machinery sale?

    A $530,000

    B $680,000

    C $560,000

    D $580,000

297 Creg's sales director is close to selling another large machine, offering free service, therefore selling the entire machine for $560,000. Creg never sells servicing separately.

How should this discount be applied in relation to the sale of the machinery?

    A   The discount should be applied across the machine, the service and the installation

    B   The discount should be applied against the service as this is given for free

    C   The discount should be applied solely on the machinery itself

    D   The discount should be applied across the service and installation elements

298 What adjustment needs to be made to revenue in respect of the commission sales?

    A   Reduce revenue by $6 million

    B   Reduce revenue by $5.4 million

    C   Increase revenue by $600,000

    D   No adjustment is required

299 How much should initially be recorded in revenue in respect of the sale of vehicles in the statement of profit or loss for the year ended 31 December 20X7?

    A $8,491,000

    B $9,491,000

    C $9,434,000

    D $10,000,000

300 On 31 December 20X7 Creg sold some maturing goods to a bank for $3 million. The estimated value of the goods at that date was $5 million, which is expected to keep rising. Creg keeps the goods on its premises and has the option to repurchase the goods on 31 December 20X9 for $3.63 million.

Which of the following outlines the correct treatment for the maturing inventory?

A   Record a loss on disposal of $2 million in the statement of profit or loss

B   Take $3 million to revenue, disclosing the repurchase option

C   Leave the inventory in current assets, increasing in value as the goods mature

D   Treat the $3 million as a loan with 10% compound interest accruing over the 2 years

The following scenario relates to questions 301–305

The profit after tax for Barstead for the year ended 30 September 20X7 was $15 million. At 1 October 20X6 the company had in issue 36 million equity shares. On 1 January 20X7 Barstead made a fully subscribed rights issue of one new share for every four shares held at a price of $2.80 each. The market price of the equity shares of Barstead immediately before the issue was $3.80.

The profit after tax for Cabott for the year ended 30 September 20X7 was $15 million. At 1 October 20X6 the company had in issue 43.25 million equity shares and a $10 million convertible loan note which has an effective interest rate of 8%. The loan note will mature in 20X8 and will be redeemed at par or converted to equity shares on the basis of 25 shares for each $100 of loan note at the loan-note holders' option. The loan interest is tax deductible. Cabott's tax rate is 25%.

The profit after tax for Dunstan for the year ended 30 September 20X7 was $12 million. On 1 October 20X6 Dunstan had 34 million shares in issue. On 1 February 20X7 Dunstan made a market issue of 3 million shares at full price. On 1 July 20X7 Dunstan made a bonus issue of one new share for every five shares held.

301 **What is the basic earnings per share for Barstead for the year ended 30 September 20X7?**

A $0.42

B $0.35

C $0.33

D $0.35

302 **What is the diluted earnings per share for Cabott for the year ended 30 September 20X7?**

A $0.34

B $0.35

C $0.36

D $0.33

303 **What is the basic earnings per share for Dunstan for the year ended 30 September 20X7?**

A $0.26

B $0.32

C $0.28

D $0.31

304 **Which of the three companies will have to restate the prior year comparative earnings per share figure?**

A   Barstead and Cabott only

B   Barstead and Dunstan only

C   Cabott and Dunstan only

D   All three companies

305 **Which, if any, of the statements below regarding diluted earnings per share is/are correct?**

Statement 1: Diluted earnings per share is a forecast of a future trend in profit, showing the expected earnings in the next period to improve the relevance of information for users.

Statement 2: Diluted earnings per share acts as a warning to shareholders and shows how the current earnings per share could fall based on items currently in existence.

A   Only statement 1 is correct

B   Only statement 2 is correct

C   Both statements are correct

D   Neither statement is correct

The following scenario relates to questions 306–310

This objective test case question contains question types which will only appear in a computer-based exam, but this question provides valuable practice for all students whichever version of the exam they are taking.

On 7 January 20X5, Hermione was informed that it was being sued by an employee in respect of a workplace accident that took place in October 20X4. Legal advisors advise that Hermione is certain to lose the case. They have provided the following information:

Estimated pay-out	Probability of payment occurring
$1 million	30%
$2 million	60%
$3 million	10%

Hermione has sold 100,000 machines that are covered by a warranty agreement as at the reporting date. If a machine develops a major fault then the average cost to Hermione of repairing it is $100. If a machine develops a minor fault then the average cost to Hermione of repairing it is $30. It is believed that 6% of the machines under warranty will develop major faults and that 8% will develop minor faults. The time value of money can be ignored.

On 15 December 20X4, the directors of Hermione decided to restructure the business and created a detailed and formal plan. On that date, an announcement was made to the employees who were informed that they would be made redundant in March 20X5. The directors estimate that the restructuring exercise will involve the following costs:

Type of cost	$m
Redundancy payments	1.2
Staff relocation	0.8
Investment in new systems	2.0

306 **Which of the following are outlined in IAS 37 *Provisions, Contingent Liabilities and Contingent Assets* as criteria required for recognising a provision?**

(i)   An entity has a present obligation from a past event

(ii)   It is possible that an outflow of resources will be required

(iii)   A reliable estimate can be made of the amount of the obligation

A   (i), (ii) and (iii)

B   (i) and (ii) only

C   (i) and (iii) only

D   (ii) and (iii) only

307 **What amount should be recognised as a provision in respect of the workplace accident claim in the year ended 31 December 20X4?**

A   Nil

B $1.8 million

C $2 million

D $3 million

308 **What amount should be recognised as a warranty provision in the year ended 31 December 20X4?**

$_____000

309 **What amount should be recognised as a restructuring provision in the year ended 31 December 20X4?**

A $1.2 million

B $2.0 million

C $3.2 million

D $4.0 million

310 The following situations have arisen in the year ended 31 December 20X4:

Situation 1: A law was introduced in November 20X4 requiring Hermione to fit new smoke filters in its factory by February 20X5 at an estimated cost of $500,000. By the reporting date, Hermione had not fitted the smoke filters.

Statement 2: The management accountant of Hermione has reliably forecast an operating loss of $4 million for the year ended 31 December 20X5.

Which, if any, of the situations require a provision to be recognised?

A   Situation 1 only

B   Situation 2 only

C   Both situations

D   Neither situation

The following scenario relates to questions 311–315

This objective test case question contains question types which will only appear in a computer-based exam, but this question provides valuable practice for all students whichever version of the exam they are taking.

Promoill's financial statements for the year ended 30 September 20X8 were authorised for issue by its directors on 6 November 20X8 and the AGM (annual general meeting) will be held on 6 December 20X8.

On 1 October 20X7, Promoil acquired an oil platform at a cost of $30 million. The estimated cost of removing the platform at the end of the asset's life on 30 September 20Y7 will be $15 million. The present value of $1 in 10 years is $0.46.

On 12 October 20X8 a fire destroyed the company's largest warehouse. The carrying amounts of the warehouse was $10 million. Promoil expects to be able to recover $9 million from its insurers and its going concern is not in doubt.

A single class of inventory held at another warehouse was valued at its cost of $460,000 and sold for $280,000 on 10 October 20X8.

311 There is no legal obligation for Promoil to remove the oil platform, but has a published environmental policy which it has a hisotry of honouring.

Which of the following is correct regarding Promoil's proposed accounting treatment?

A   No provision should be recorded as there is no legal obligation

B   Promoil should recognise a provision as there is a constructive obligation

C   No provision should be made but a contingent liability should be recorded

D   If Promoil make a provision, the present value of the costs will be expensed in the statement of profit or loss for the year to 30 September 20X8

312 **If Promoil makes the provision, what liability (to the nearest thousand) will be shown in its statement of financial position as at 30 September 20X8?**

$_____000

313 **Select the correct category for the events listed below in relation to IAS 10 *Events After the Reporting Period*.**

	Adjusting	Non-adjusting
Fire in the warehouse		
Sale of inventory		

314 On 18 November 20X8 the government announced tax changes which have the effect of increasing Promoil's deferred tax liability by $650,000 as at 30 September 20X8.

Which of the following is correct in respect of IAS 10 regarding the tax changes?

A   This is a non-adjusting event and no disclosure is required

B   This is an adjusting event

C   This is neither an adjusting or non-adjusting event

D   This is an adjusting event and the financial statements should be reissued

315 Promoil owns the whole of the equity share capital of its subsidiary Hamlet. Hamlet's statement of financial position includes a loan of $25 million that is repayable in five years' time. $15 million of this loan is secured on Hamlet's property and the remaining $10 million is guaranteed by Promoil in the event of a default by Hamlet. It is possible that Hamlet will be unable to repay the loan, but not likely.

How should this be treated in the financial statements of Promoil?

A   A contingent liability

B   A provision

C   Not included in Promoil's financial statements

D   A reduction to property, plant and equipment

CONSOLIDATED FINANCIAL STATEMENTS

The following scenario relates to questions 316–320

On 1 April 20X4 Penfold acquired 80% of Superted's equity shares in a share for share exchange. Penfold issued 2 shares for every 5 acquired in Superted. Penfold's share price on 1 April 20X4 was $5.30... The share exchange has not been accounted for.

Extracts from the individual financial statements of Penfold and Superted as at 30 September 20X4 are shown below

	Penfold	Superted
	$000	$000
Property, plant and equipment	345,000	141,000
Trade receivables	32,400	38,000
Equity shares of $1 each	170,000	15,000
Other components of equity (share premium)	6,000	2,000

(i)   During the year, Penfold traded with Superted, and had a payable of $6 million at 30 September 20X4. Superted's receivable balance differed from this due to a $2 million payment from Penfold not being received until October.

(ii)   Penfold measures the non-controlling interest at fair value. At the date of acquisition this was $7.2 million.

(iii)   Superted made a profit of $24,000 for the year ended 30 September 20X4.

(iv)   Penfold sold an item of plant to Superted on 1 April 20X4 for $25 million when its carrying amount was $20 million. It had a remaining useful life of 5 years at this date.

(v)   Penfold also owns 30% of Arnold, an unrelated company. Penfold are not able to appoint any members of the board of Arnold as the other 70% is held by another investor who is able to appoint all members of the board.

316   What will be the consolidated other components of equity as at 30 September 20X4?

A $31,440,000

B $26,640,000

C $28,640,000

D $33,440,000

317   What will be the consolidated receivables at 30 September 20X4?

A $64,400,000

B $68,400,000

C $66,400,000

D $62,400,000

318   What will be recorded as the non-controlling interest at 30 September 20X4?

A $9,600,000

B $12,000,000

C $7,200,000

D $4,800,000

319   What will be the consolidated property, plant and equipment at 30 September 20X4?

A $490,500,000

B $481,000,000

C $481,500,000

D $482,000,000

320   How should the investment in Arnold be recorded in the consolidated statement of financial position of Penfold?

A   A subsidiary

B   An associate

C   A financial instrument

D   A contingent asset

The following scenario relates to questions 321–325

On 1 October 20X4, Popper purchased 70% of the share capital of Stopper. Popper agreed to pay $6 million on 30 September 20X6. Popper has a cost of capital of 8%.

Extracts from the statements of profit or loss for the year ended 31 March 20X5 for both Popper and Stopper are shown below.

	Popper $000	Stopper $000
Cost of sales	(319,200)	(176,400)
Operating expenses	(50,610)	(33,120)

The following notes are relevant:

(i) Since acquisition, Popper sold goods to Stopper totalling $1 million per month, making a margin of 20%. At the year end, Stopper held 30% of these goods.

(ii) On acquisition, Stopper's net assets were equal to their carrying amount, with the exception of Stopper's head office, which had a fair value of $4 million in excess of its carrying amount and a remaining life at acquisition of 20 years. All depreciation is charges to operating expenses.

(iii) At 31 March 20X5, goodwill is impaired by $600,000. Goodwill impairment is included within operating expenses. Popper chooses to measure the non-controlling interest using the fair value method.

321 **What liability (to the nearest thousand) should be recorded in respect of the deferred consideration in Popper's consolidated statement of financial position as at 31 March 20X5?**

A $5,144,000

B $5,349,000

C $5,556,000

D $6,000,000

322 **What is the cost of sales figure to be included in the consolidated statement of profit or loss for the year ended 31 March 20X5?**

A $402,600,000

B $401,760,000

C $395,760,000

D $396,400,000

323 **What is the operating expenses figure to be included in the consolidated statement of profit or loss for the year ended 31 March 20X5?**

A $67,970,000

B $67,670,000

C $67,570,000

D $67,870,000

324 **Which of the following items would affect the profit attributable to the non-controlling interest?**

    A   Notes (i) and (ii) only

    B   Notes (i) and (iii) only

    C   Notes (ii) and (iii) only

    D   Notes (i), (ii) and (iii)

325 **Which, if any, of the following statements about fair values is/are correct?**

Statement 1: Popper must include all of Stopper's assets, liabilities and contingent liabilities at fair value in the consolidated financial statements

Statement 2: Professional fees associated with the acquisition of Stopper can be included within the goodwill because the non-controlling interest is measured at fair value

    A   Only statement 1 is correct

    B   Only statement 2 is correct

    C   Both statements are correct

    D   Neither statement is correct

The following scenario relates to questions 326–330

This objective test case question contains question types which will only appear in a computer-based exam, but this question provides valuable practice for all students whichever version of the exam they are taking.

On 1 January 20X5, Prunier acquired 80% of Sheringham's $2 million share capital. At this date, Sheringham had retained earnings of $4 million and a revaluation surplus of $2 million. Prunier had retained earnings of $10 million and a revaluation surplus of $5 million.

The fair value of Sheringham's net assets at acquisition were equal to their carrying amounts with the exception of Sheringham's property which had a fair value of $800,000 in excess of its carrying amount and a remaining life of 20 years.

At 31 December 20X5, Prunier and Sheringham both revalued their assets. Prunier's assets increased by a further $2 million while Sheringham's increased by $500,000. At this date, Prunier's retained earnings were $11 million and Sheringham's were $3.5 million.

326 **What will the consolidated retained earnings be at 31 December 20X5?**

    A $11,432,000

    B $10,560,000

    C $11,368,000

    D $10,568,000

327 **What will be the other comprehensive income attributable to the parent for the year ended 31 December 20X5?**

    $_____000

328 Identify whether or not the following items should be recognised as assets in the consolidated financial statements of Prunier.

	Recognise	Not to be recognised
Prunier's brand name, which was internally generated so not shown in Prunier's financial statements but has a fair value of $3 million		
A research project in progress, which was one of the main reasons Prunier purchased Sheringham and has a fair value of $2 million		
An intangible asset related to an encryption process which has now been deemed illegal. This is included within intangibles at $1.5 million.		

329 Prunier has also owned 30% of Anderson for many years, using equity accounting. During the year Prunier sold $3 million of goods to Anderson at a mark-up of 20%. Anderson has a quarter of the goods left in inventory at the year end.

What is the unrealised profit as at 31 December 20X5?

A $150,000

B $37,500

C $125,000

D $45,000

330 On 31 December 20X9, Prunier disposed of its entire holding of Sheringham for $9 million. At this date, the remaining goodwill was $1 million. The fair value of the non-controlling interest was $2.5 million and the fair value of the net assets (including the fair value adjustment) was $10.6 million.

What is the profit/loss on the disposal of Sheringham to be shown in the consolidated financial statements of Prunier?

A $100,000 loss on disposal

B $1,900,000 gain on disposal

C $5,100,000 loss on disposal

D $2,020,000 gain on disposal

INTERPRETATION OF FINANCIAL STATEMENTS

The following scenario relates to questions 331–335

This objective test case question contains question types which will only appear in a computer-based exam, but this question provides valuable practice for all students whichever version of the exam they are taking.

LOP is looking to expand overseas by acquiring a new subsidiary.

Two geographical areas have been targeted, Frontland and Sideland.

Entity A operates in Frontland and entity B operates in Sideland. Both entities are listed on their local exchanges.

Figures for entities A, B and LOP are provided below for the last trading period.

	A	B	LOP
Revenue	$160m	$300m	$500m
Gross profit margin	26%	17%	28%
Profit from operations margin	9%	11%	16%
Gearing	65%	30%	38%
Average rate of interest expensed in P/L	4%	9%	8%
P/E ratio	11.6	15.9	16.3

331 **Which one of the following statements is a realistic conclusion that could be drawn from the above information?**

    A   A appears to be benefiting from economies of scale.

    B   B has lower operating expenses than A.

    C   A has attracted a lower rate of interest on its borrowings than B because it's gearing level would suggest that is a lower risk to lenders than B.

    D   Acquisition of either entity would lead to an improvement in LOP's gross margin due to the increased revenue that would be achieved.

332 **Which TWO of the following statements are true, based on the information provided?**

    A   A would be a riskier investment than B because it has higher gearing.

    B   A would give LOP greater benefit in terms of additional borrowing capacity.

    C   The market is more confident about the future performance of B than LOP.

    D   The market is more confident about the future performance of LOP than A or B.

    E   LOP's P/E ratio would definitely fall if it acquired either A or B.

333 **Which one of the following statements concerning the use of ratio analysis to make a decision about investing in A or B is FALSE?**

    A   A and B may use different accounting standards when preparing their financial statements and this would reduce the comparability of their profit margins.

    B   A and B may target different types of customer, meaning that comparison between the two is difficult.

    C   A and B may apply different accounting policies, such as cost model v revaluation model for property, plant and equipment. This would reduce comparability of their gearing ratios.

    D   A and B are listed on different stock exchanges which reduces comparability of their P/E ratios.

334 If LOP acquired B, it has assessed that combining the two companies would lead to an overall saving in cost of sales of $5 million.

If this was taken into account, what would be the gross margin of LOP combined with B to one decimal place?

_____%

335 Your assistant has raised concerns about B, having heard that they may have treated finance leases incorrectly as operating leases.

Which, if any, of the following statements is/are true in relation to this?

Statement 1: If B has incorrectly treated the leases as operating leases, gearing will be overstated.

Statement 2: If B has incorrectly treated the leases as operating leases, the average rate of interest incurred could be inaccurate.

    A   Statement 1 is correct

    B   Statement 2 is correct

    C   Both statements are correct

    D   Neither statement is correct

The following scenario relates to questions 336–340

This objective test case question contains question types which will only appear in a computer-based exam, but this question provides valuable practice for all students whichever version of the exam they are taking.

Key figures from Franck's financial statements for the year ended 30 September 20X2 are shown below.

	$000
Revenue	9,400
Profit from operations	1,500
Share capital	15,000
Retained earnings	3,000
Loans	2,000

Franck has operated in the computer software industry for many years, gaining a reputation for steady growth. It is interested in acquiring a company, Duik, who has recently been put up for sale. Duik's results can be seen below.

	$000
Revenue	1,200
Loss from operations	(600)
Share capital	24,000
Retained losses	(1,200)
Loans (owed to parent)	4,000

336 Calculate Franck's return on capital employed (based on profit from operations) without the acquisition of Duik to one decimal place.

_____%

337 What is the combined operating margin if Franck and Duik are combined?

A   9.6%

B   19.8%

C   14.2%

D   8.5%

338 Which, if any, of the following statements is/are correct?

Statement 1: If Duik is acquired, gearing will increase

Statement 2: If Duik is acquired, return on capital employed will decrease

A   Statement 1 is correct

B   Statement 2 is correct

C   Both statements are correct

D   Neither statement is correct

339 Which of the following is NOT a factor to consider in respect of Duik being a subsidiary of another company?

A   Sales or purchases between the parent and Duik may not be at market rates

B   Duik may get the benefit of shared assets with the parent company

C   Duik's individual company financial statements may contain errors

D   Loans made from Duik's parent may carry lower interest than market rates

340 What other information is Franck NOT likely to be able to look before entering into negotiations for the acquisition of Duik?

A   A breakdown of dividends paid by Duik historically

B   Duik's statement of cash flows

C   A breakdown of Duik's upcoming projects which are in progress

D   The director's report outlining the performance for the year

STATEMENT OF CASH FLOWS

The following scenario relates to questions 341–345

This objective test case question contains question types which will only appear in a computer-based exam, but this question provides valuable practice for all students whichever version of the exam they are taking.

The assistant accountant of Cooper has started work on the statement of cash flows for the year ended 31 December 20X8, completing a draft of the cash generated from operations as shown below.

	$000
Profit from operations	3,500
Depreciation	4,600
Release of government grant	1,400
Profit on disposal of property	3,700
Increase in inventories	(400)
Decrease in trade and other receivables	(300)
Increase in trade and other payables	900
Cash generated from operations	**13,400**

In addition to this, the assistant has seen that the balance of property at 1 January 20X8 was $39.5 million and the balance at 31 December 20X8 was $29 million. There were no additions of property in the year.

There was also a deferred income balance relating to government grants of $6 million at 1 January 20X8. The closing deferred income balance was $8 million.

341 **What method has Cooper's assistant accountant used to calculate the cash generated from operations?**

A   Classification by function

B   Classification by nature

C   Indirect method

D   Direct method

342 **In relation to the calculation of cash generated from operations, select the TWO cells which contain errors made by the assistant.**

	$000
Profit from operations	3,500
Depreciation	4,600
Release of government grant	1,400
Profit on disposal of property	(3,700)
Increase in inventories	(400)
Decrease in trade and other receivables	(300)
Increase in trade and other payables	900
Cash generated from operations	6,000

343 **How much would be recorded in Cooper's statement of cash flows in relation to the sale of property?**

A $9,600,000

B $2,200,000

C $3,700,000

D $5,900,000

344 **What will be recorded as the receipt of government grants in the year?**

$_____000

345 Cooper's assistant accountant has been studying statements of cash flows and is unsure whether the information contained in the study material is true.

Which, if any, of the following statements is/are true?

Statement 1: Intangible assets will have no impact on the statement of cash flow as they have no physical substance.

Statement 2: A rights issue of shares will increase the cash flows from financing activities.

A   Statement 1 is correct

B   Statement 2 is correct

C   Both statements are correct

D   Neither statement is correct

The following scenario relates to questions 346–350

Extracts from Depay's financial statements for the year ended 30 September 20X2 are shown below.

Statement of profit or loss extract:	$000
Finance costs	(60)
Profit before tax	142
Income tax expense	(57)
Profit for the year	85

Statement of financial position extract:	20X2	20X1
	$000	$000
Retained earnings	900	940
5% loan notes	515	500
Deferred tax liability	150	125
Tax payable	30	40
Finance lease liabilities	300	310

The following information is relevant:

(i) Depay disposed of some land during the year, which had a remaining revaluation surplus at disposal of $20,000.

(ii) $40,000 of the finance costs relate to the loan notes which are repayable at a premium, making the effective rate of interest 8%. The rest relates to the finance lease liabilities.

(iii) During the year, Depay received a dividend from a subsidiary company.

(iv) Depay acquired $70,000 of new assets under finance leases during the year. Depay makes annual payments under finance leases on 30 September each year.

346 **What will be recorded in Depay's statement of cash flows under dividends paid?**

    A $145,000

    B $105,000

    C $40,000

    D $125,000

347 **What will be recorded in Depay's statement of cash flows under interest paid?**

    A   Nil

    B $15,000

    C $25,000

    D $40,000

348 What will be recorded in Depay's statement of cash flows under tax paid?

    A $32,000

    B $42,000

    C $57,000

    D $67,000

349 Where should the dividend received be shown in Depay's statement of cash flows?

    A   Operating activities

    B   Investing activities

    C   Financing activities

    D   It should not be recorded

350 How much should be shown within financing activities in respect of finance lease liabilities repaid?

    A $10,000

    B $30,000

    C $100,000

    D $80,000

Section 3

CONSTRUCTED RESPONSE QUESTIONS – SECTION C

PREPARATION OF SINGLE COMPANY FINANCIAL STATEMENTS

351 LLAMA

The following trial balance relates to Llama, a listed company, at 30 September 2007:

	$000	$000
Land and buildings – at valuation 1 October 2006 (note (i))	130,000	
Plant – at cost (note (i))	128,000	
Accumulated depreciation of plant at 1 October 2006		32,000
Investments – at fair value through profit and loss (note (i))	26,500	
Investment income		2,200
Cost of sales (note (i))	89,200	
Distribution costs	11,000	
Administrative expenses	12,500	
Loan interest paid	800	
Inventory at 30 September 2007	37,900	
Income tax (note (ii))		400
Trade receivables	35,100	
Revenue		180,400
Equity shares of 50 cents each fully paid		84,000
Retained earnings at 1 October 2006		25,500
2% loan note 2009 (note (iii))		80,000
Trade payables		34,700
Revaluation surplus (arising from land and buildings)		14,000
Deferred tax		11,200
Bank		6,600
	———	———
	471,000	471,000
	———	———

The following notes are relevant:

(i)   Llama has a policy of revaluing its land and buildings at each year end. The valuation in the trial balance includes a land element of $30 million. The estimated remaining life of the buildings at that date (1 October 2006) was 20 years. On 30 September 2007, a professional valuer valued the buildings at $92 million with no change in the value of the land. Depreciation of buildings is charged 60% to cost of sales and 20% each to distribution costs and administrative expenses.

During the year Llama manufactured an item of plant that it is using as part of its own operating capacity. The details of its cost, which is included in cost of sales in the trial balance, are:

	$000
Materials cost	6,000
Direct labour cost	4,000
Machine time cost	8,000
Directly attributable overheads	6,000

The manufacture of the plant was completed on 31 March 2007 and the plant was brought into immediate use, but its cost has not yet been capitalised.

All plant is depreciated at 12.5% per annum (time apportioned where relevant) using the reducing balance method and charged to cost of sales.

The fair value of the investments held at fair value through profit and loss at 30 September 2007 was $27.1 million.

(ii)   The balance of income tax in the trial balance represents the under/over provision of the previous year's estimate. The estimated income tax liability for the year ended 30 September 2007 is $18.7 million. At 30 September 2007 there were $40 million of taxable temporary differences. The income tax rate is 25%. **Note:** You may assume that the movement in deferred tax should be taken to the statement of profit or loss.

(iii) The 2% loan note was issued on 1 April 2007 under terms that provide for a large premium on redemption in 2009. The finance department has calculated that the effect of this is that the loan note has an effective interest rate of 6% per annum.

Required:

(a)   **A statement of profit or loss and other comprehensive income for the year ended 30 September 2007.**   **(10 marks)**

(b)   **A statement of financial position as at 30 September 2007.**   **(10 marks)**

       Note: A statement of changes in equity is not required.

                                                                    (Total: 20 marks)

352 CAVERN

The following trial balance relates to Cavern as at 30 September 2010:

	$000	$000
Equity shares of 20 cents each		51,000
8% loan note (note (i))		30,600
Retained earnings – 30 September 2009		6,600
Revaluation surplus		7,000
Land and buildings at valuation – 30 September 2009:		
Land ($7 million) and building ($36 million) (note (ii))	43,000	
Plant and equipment at cost (note (ii))	67,400	
Accumulated depreciation plant and equipment – 30 September 2009		13,400
Equity investments (note (iii))	15,800	
Inventory at 30 September 2010	19,800	
Trade receivables	29,000	
Bank		4,600
Deferred tax (note (iv))		4,000
Trade payables		21,700
Revenue		182,500
Cost of sales	128,500	
Administrative expenses	6,500	
Distribution costs	8,500	
Loan note interest paid	2,400	
Bank interest	300	
Investment income		700
Current tax (note (iv))	900	
	322,100	322,100

The following notes are relevant:

(i) The 8% loan note was issued on 1 October 2008 at its nominal (face) value of $30 million. The loan note will be redeemed on 30 September 2012 at a premium which gives the loan note an effective finance cost of 10% per annum.

(ii) Cavern revalues its land and building at the end of each accounting year. At 30 September 2010 the relevant value to be incorporated into the financial statements is $41.8 million. The building's remaining life at the beginning of the current year (1 October 2009) was 18 years. Cavern does not make an annual transfer from the revaluation surplus to retained earnings in respect of the realisation of the revaluation surplus. Ignore deferred tax on the revaluation surplus.

Plant and equipment includes an item of plant bought for $10 million on 1 October 2009 that will have a 10-year life (using straight-line depreciation with no residual value). Production using this plant involves toxic chemicals which will cause decontamination costs to be incurred at the end of its life. The present value of these costs using a discount rate of 10% at 1 October 2009 was $4 million. Cavern has not provided any amount for this future decontamination cost. All other plant and equipment is depreciated at 12.5% per annum using the reducing balance method.

No depreciation has yet been charged on any non-current asset for the year ended 30 September 2010. All depreciation is charged to cost of sales.

(iii) The equity investments had a fair value of $13.5 million on 30 September 2010. There were no acquisitions or disposals of these investments during the year ended 30 September 2010. The equity investments are recorded as fair value through profit or loss in accordance with IFRS 9 *Financial Instruments*.

(iv) A provision for income tax for the year ended 30 September 2010 of $5.6 million is required. The balance on current tax represents the under/over provision for the year ended 30 September 2009. At 30 September 2010 the tax base of Cavern's net assets was $15 million less than their carrying amounts. Changes in deferred tax should be taken to the statement of profit or loss. Cavern's tax rate is 25%.

Required:

(a) **Prepare the statement of profit or loss for Cavern for the year ended 30 September 2010.** **(11 marks)**

(b) **Prepare the statement of financial position of Cavern as at 30 September 2010.** **(9 marks)**

A statement of changes in equity is not required. **(Total: 20 marks)**

353 CANDEL *Walk in the footsteps of a top tutor*

The following trial balance relates to Candel at 30 September 2008:

	$000	$000
Leasehold property – at valuation 1 October 2007 (note (i))	50,000	
Plant and equipment – at cost (note (i))	76,600	
Plant and equipment – accumulated depreciation at 1 October 2007		24,600
Capitalised development expenditure – at 1 October 2007 (note (ii))	20,000	
Development expenditure – accumulated amortisation at 1 October 2007		6,000
Closing inventory at 30 September 2008	20,000	
Trade receivables	43,100	
Bank		1,300
Trade payables and provisions (note (iii))		23,800
Draft profit before tax		59,100
Preference dividend paid (note (iv))	800	
Research and development costs (note (ii))	8,600	
Equity shares of 25 cents each		50,000
8% redeemable preference shares of $1 each (note (iv))		20,000
Retained earnings at 1 October 2007		18,500
Deferred tax (note (v))		5,800
Leasehold property revaluation surplus at 1 October 2007		10,000
	219,100	219,100

The following notes are relevant:

(i) **Non-current assets – tangible:**

The leasehold property had a remaining life of 20 years at 1 October 2007. The company's policy is to revalue its property at each year end and at 30 September 2008 it was valued at $43 million. Ignore deferred tax on the revaluation.

On 1 October 2007 an item of plant was disposed of for $2.5 million cash. The proceeds have been treated as sales revenue by Candel. The plant is still included in the above trial balance figures at its cost of $8 million and accumulated depreciation of $4 million (to the date of disposal).

All plant is depreciated at 20% per annum using the reducing balance method.

Depreciation and amortisation of all non-current assets is charged to cost of sales.

(ii) **Non-current assets – intangible:**

In addition to the capitalised development expenditure (of $20 million), further research and development costs were incurred on a new project which commenced on 1 October 2007. The research stage of the new project lasted until 31 December 2007 and incurred $1.4 million of costs. From that date the project incurred development costs of $800,000 per month. On 1 April 2008 the directors became confident that the project would be successful and yield a profit well in excess of its costs. The project is still in development at 30 September 2008.

Capitalised development expenditure is amortised at 20% per annum using the straight-line method. All expensed research and development is charged to cost of sales.

(iii) Candel is being sued by a customer for $2 million for breach of contract over a cancelled order. Candel has obtained legal opinion that there is a 20% chance that Candel will lose the case. Accordingly Candel has provided $400,000 ($2 million × 20%) included in administrative expenses in respect of the claim. The unrecoverable legal costs of defending the action are estimated at $100,000. These have not been provided for as the legal action will not go to court until next year.

(iv) The preference shares were issued on 1 April 2008 at par. They are redeemable at a large premium which gives them an effective finance cost of 12% per annum. The finance assistant in Candel was uncertain how to deal with these. The dividend paid in the trial balance represents the debit side of the cash payment made during the year.

(v) The directors have estimated the provision for income tax for the year ended 30 September 2008 at $11.4 million. The required deferred tax provision at 30 September 2008 is $6 million.

Required:

(a) **Calculate the revised profit for the year, taking into account the items from notes (i) to (v).** **(8 marks)**

(b) **Prepare the statement of financial position as at 30 September 2008.** **(12 marks)**

Note: **Notes to the financial statements and a statement of changes in equity are not required.** **(Total: 20 marks)**

354 PRICEWELL

 Timed question with Online tutor debrief

The following trial balance relates to Pricewell at 31 March 2009:

	$000	$000
Leasehold property – at valuation 31 March 2008 (note (i))	25,200	
Plant and equipment (owned) – at cost (note (i))	46,800	
Plant and equipment (leased) – at cost (note (i))	20,000	
Accumulated depreciation at 31 March 2008:		
Owned plant and equipment		12,800
Leased plant and equipment		5,000
Finance lease payment (paid on 31 March 2009) (note (i))	6,000	
Obligations under finance lease at 1 April 2008 (note (i))		15,600
Contract with customer (note (ii))	14,300	
Inventory at 31 March 2009	28,200	
Trade receivables	33,100	
Bank	5,500	
Trade payables		33,400
Revenue (note (iii))		310,000
Cost of sales (note (iii))	234,500	
Distribution costs	19,500	
Administrative expenses	27,500	
Equity dividend paid	8,000	
Equity shares of 50 cents each		40,000
Retained earnings at 31 March 2008		44,100
Current tax (note (iv))	700	
Deferred tax (note (iv))		8,400
	469,300	469,300

The following notes are relevant:

(i) **Non-current assets:**

The 15 year leasehold property was acquired on 1 April 2007 at cost $30 million. The company policy is to revalue the property at fair value at each year end. The valuation in the trial balance of $25.2 million as at 31 March 2008 led to an impairment charge of $2.8 million which was reported in the statement of profit or loss and other comprehensive income of the previous year (i.e. year ended 31 March 2008). At 31 March 2009 the property was valued at $24.9 million.

Owned plant is depreciated at 25% per annum using the reducing balance method.

The leased plant was acquired on 1 April 2007. The rentals are $6 million per annum for four years payable in arrears on 31 March each year. The interest rate implicit in the lease is 8% per annum. Leased plant is depreciated at 25% per annum using the straight-line method.

No depreciation has yet been charged on any non-current assets for the year ended 31 March 2009. All depreciation is charged to cost of sales.

(ii)   On 1 October 2008 Pricewell entered into a contract to construct a bridge over a river. The performance obligation will be satisfied over time. The agreed price of the bridge is $50 million and construction was expected to be completed on 30 September 2010. The $14.3 million in the trial balance is:

	$000
Materials, labour and overheads	12,000
Specialist plant acquired 1 October 2008	8,000
Payment from customer	(5,700)
	14,300

The sales value of the work done at 31 March 2009 has been agreed at $22 million and the estimated cost to complete (excluding plant depreciation) is $10 million. The specialist plant will have no residual value at the end of the contract and should be depreciated on a monthly basis. Pricewell recognises progress towards satisfaction of the performance obligation on the percentage of completion basis as determined by the agreed work to date compared to the total contract price.

(iii)   Pricewell's revenue includes $8 million for goods it sold acting as an agent for Trilby. Pricewell earned a commission of 20% on these sales and remitted the difference of $6.4 million (included in cost of sales) to Trilby.

(iv)   The directors have estimated the provision for income tax for the year ended 31 March 2009 at $4.5 million. The required deferred tax provision at 31 March 2009 is $5.6 million; all adjustments to deferred tax should be taken to the statement of profit or loss. The balance of current tax in the trial balance represents the under/over provision of the income tax liability for the year ended 31 March 2008.

Required:

(a)   Prepare the statement of profit or loss and other comprehensive income for the year ended 31 March 2009.   **(10 marks)**

(b)   Prepare the statement of financial position as at 31 March 2009.   **(10 marks)**

Note: A statement of changes in equity and notes to the financial statements are not required.

                                                                                              (Total: 20 marks)

 Calculate your allowed time, allocate the time to the separate parts

355 SANDOWN

The following trial balance relates to Sandown at 30 September 2009:

	$000	$000
Revenue (note (i))		380,000
Cost of sales	246,800	
Operating expenses	55,900	
Loan interest paid (note (iii))	1,000	
Investment income		1,300
Current tax (note (iv))	2,100	
Property - at cost 1 October 2000 (note (v))	63,000	
Plant and equipment – at cost (note (v))	42,200	
Brand – at cost 1 October 2005 (note (v))	30,000	
Accumulated depreciation – 1 October 2008 – building		8,000
– plant and equipment		19,700
Accumulated amortisation – 1 October 2008 – brand		9,000
Investment property (note (iv))	26,500	
Current assets	90,500	
Trade payables		42,900
Equity shares of 20 cents each		50,000
Equity option		2,000
5% convertible loan note 2012 (note (iii))		18,440
Retained earnings at 1 October 2008		21,260
Deferred tax (note (iv))		5,400
	———	———
	558,000	558,000
	———	———

The following notes are relevant:

(i)   Sandown's revenue includes $16 million for goods sold to Pending on 1 October 2008. The terms of the sale are that Sandown will incur ongoing service and support costs of $1.2 million per annum for three years after the sale. The service performance obligation will be satisfied over time. Sandown normally makes a gross profit of 40% on such servicing and support work. Ignore the time value of money.

(ii)   The 5% convertible loan note was issued for proceeds of $20 million on 1 October 2007. It has an effective interest rate of 8% due to the value of its conversion option, and can be converted into 50 shares for every $100 owed.

(iii)   The investment property is considered to have a fair value of $29 million at 30 September 2009. Sandown uses the fair value model permitted by IAS 40 *Investment Properties* to account for investment property.

(iv)   The balance on current tax represents the under/over provision of the tax liability for the year ended 30 September 2008. The directors have estimated the liability for income tax for the year ended 30 September 2009 at $16.2 million. At 30 September 2009 the carrying amounts of Sandown's net assets were $13 million in excess of their tax base. The income tax rate of Sandown is 30%.

(vi) Non-current assets:

The property has a land element of $13 million. The building element is being depreciated on a straight-line basis.

Plant and equipment is depreciated at 40% per annum using the reducing balance method.

Sandown's brand in the trial balance relates to a product line that received bad publicity during the year. An impairment review was conducted on 1 April 2009 which concluded that the brand had a value in use of $12 million and a remaining life of only three years. However, on the same date as the impairment review, Sandown received an offer to purchase the brand for $15 million. Prior to the impairment review, it was being depreciated using the straight-line method over a 10-year life.

No depreciation/amortisation has yet been charged on any non-current asset for the year ended 30 September 2009. Depreciation, amortisation and impairment charges are all charged to cost of sales.

Required:

(a) **Prepare the statement of profit or loss for Sandown for the year ended 30 September 2009.** **(11 marks)**

(b) **Prepare the statement of financial position of Sandown as at 30 September 2009.**

(9 marks)

Notes to the financial statements are not required. A statement of changes in equity is not required. **(Total: 20 marks)**

356 HIGHWOOD

The following trial balance relates to Highwood at 31 March 2011:

	$000	$000
Equity shares of 50 cents each		6,000
Retained earnings at 1 April 2010		1,400
8% convertible loan note (note (i))		30,000
Property – at cost 1 April 2005 (land element $25m (note (ii)))	75,000	
Accumulated depreciation – 1 April 2010 – building		10,000
Current tax (note (iii))		800
Deferred tax (note (iii))		2,600
Inventory – 4 April 2011 (note (iv))	36,000	
Trade receivables	47,100	
Bank		11,500
Trade payables		24,500
Revenue		339,650
Cost of sales	207,750	
Distribution costs	27,500	
Administrative expenses (note (v))	30,700	
Loan interest paid (note (i))	2,400	
	426,450	426,450

The following notes are relevant:

(i)   The 8% $30 million convertible loan note was issued on 1 April 2010 at par. Interest is payable in arrears on 31 March each year. The loan note is redeemable at par on 31 March 2013 or convertible into equity shares at the option of the loan note holders on the basis of 30 equity shares for each $100 of loan note. Highwood's finance director has calculated that to issue an equivalent loan note without the conversion rights it would have to pay an interest rate of 10% per annum to attract investors.

Applicable discount rates are:

	8%	10%
End of year 1	0.93	0.91
2	0.86	0.83
3	0.79	0.75

(ii)   Non-current assets:

On 1 April 2010 Highwood decided to revalue its property. The market value of the property on this date was $80 million, of which $30 million related to the land. At this date the remaining estimated life of the property was 20 years. Highwood does not make a transfer to retained earnings in respect of excess depreciation on the revaluation of its assets. All depreciation is charged to cost of sales.

(iii)   Current tax represents the under/over provision of the tax liability for the year ended 31 March 2010. The required provision for income tax for the year ended 31 March 2011 is $19.4 million. The difference between the carrying amounts of the assets of Highwood (including the property revaluation in note (ii) above) and their (lower) tax base at 31 March 2011 is $27 million. Highwood's rate of income tax is 25%.

(iv)   The inventory of Highwood was not counted until 4 April 2011 due to operational reasons. At this date its value at cost was $36 million and this figure has been used in the cost of sales calculation above. Between the year end of 31 March 2011 and 4 April 2011, Highwood received a delivery of goods at a cost of $2.7 million and made sales of $7.8 million at a mark-up on cost of 30%. Neither the goods delivered nor the sales made in this period were included in Highwood's purchases (as part of cost of sales) or revenue in the above trial balance.

(v)   On 31 March 2011 Highwood factored (sold) trade receivables with a book value of $10 million to Easyfinance. Highwood received an immediate payment of $8.7 million and will pay Easyfinance 2% per month on any uncollected balances. Any of the factored receivables outstanding after six months will be refunded to Easyfinance. Highwood has derecognised the receivables and charged $1.3 million to administrative expenses. If Highwood had not factored these receivables it would have made an allowance of $600,000 against them.

Required:

(a)   **Prepare the statement of profit or loss and other comprehensive income for Highwood for the year ended 31 March 2011** (9 marks)

(b)   **Prepare the statement of changes in equity for year ended 31 March 2011** (3 marks)

(c)   **Prepare the statement of financial position as at 31 March 2011.** (8 marks)

Note: your answers and workings should be presented to the nearest $000.

(Total: 20 marks)

357 KEYSTONE

The following trial balance relates to Keystone at 30 September 2011:

	$000	$000
Revenue		377,600
Material purchases (note (i))	64,000	
Production labour (note (i))	124,000	
Factory overheads (note (i))	80,000	
Distribution costs	14,200	
Administrative expenses (note (ii))	46,400	
Finance costs	350	
Investment income		800
Leased property – at cost (note (i))	50,000	
Plant and equipment – at cost (note (i))	44,500	
Accumulated amortisation/depreciation at 1 October 2010		
– leased property		10,000
– plant and equipment		14,500
Inventory at 1 October 2010	46,700	
Trade receivables	31,150	
Trade payables		27,800
Bank		2,300
Equity shares of 20 cents each		50,000
Retained earnings at 1 October 2010		15,600
Deferred tax (note (iv))		2,700
	501,300	501,300

The following notes are relevant:

(i)   During the year Keystone manufactured an item of plant for its own use. The direct materials and labour were $3 million and $4 million respectively. Production overheads are 75% of direct labour cost and Keystone determines the final selling price for goods by adding a mark-up on total cost of 40%. These manufacturing costs are included in the relevant expense items in the trial balance. The plant was completed and put into immediate use on 1 April 2011.

All plant and equipment is depreciated at 20% per annum using the reducing balance method with time apportionment in the year of acquisition.

The directors decided to revalue the leased property in line with recent increases in market values. On 1 October 2010 an independent surveyor valued the leased property at $48 million, which the directors have accepted. The leased property was being amortised over an original life of 20 years which has not changed. Keystone does not make a transfer to retained earnings in respect of excess amortisation. The revaluation gain will create a deferred tax liability (see note (iv)).

All depreciation and amortisation is charged to cost of sales. No depreciation or amortisation has yet been charged on any non-current asset for the year ended 30 September 2011.

(ii) On 15 August 2011, Keystone's share price stood at $2.40 per share. On this date Keystone paid a dividend (included in administrative expenses) that was calculated to give a dividend yield of 4%.

(iii) The inventory at 30 September 2011 was valued at $56.6 million.

(iv) A provision for income tax for the year ended 30 September 2011 of $24.3 million is required. At 30 September 2011, the tax base of Keystone's net assets was $15 million less than their carrying amounts. This excludes the effects of the revaluation of the leased property. The income tax rate of Keystone is 30%.

Required:

(a) **Prepare the statement of profit or loss and other comprehensive income for Keystone for the year ended 30 September 2011.** **(12 marks)**

(b) **Prepare the statement of financial position for Keystone as at 30 September 2011.** **(8 marks)**

A statement of changes in equity is not required. **(Total: 20 marks)**

358 FRESCO

The following trial balance relates to Fresco at 31 March 2012:

	$000	$000
Equity shares of 50 cents each (note (i))		45,000
Share premium (note (i))		5,000
Retained earnings at 1 April 2011		5,100
Leased property (12 years) – at cost (note (ii))	48,000	
Plant and equipment – at cost (note (ii))	47,500	
Accumulated amortisation of leased property at 1 April 2011		16,000
Accumulated depreciation of plant and equipment at 1 April 2011		33,500
Inventory at 31 March 2012	25,200	
Trade receivables (note (iii))	28,500	
Bank		1,400
Deferred tax (note (iv))		3,200
Trade payables		27,300
Revenue		350,000
Cost of sales	298,700	
Lease payments (note (ii))	8,000	
Distribution costs	16,100	
Administrative expenses	26,900	
Bank interest	300	
Current tax (note (iv))	800	
Suspense account (note (i))		13,500
	———	———
	500,000	500,000
	———	———

The following notes are relevant:

(i)   The suspense account represents the corresponding credit for cash received for a fully subscribed rights issue of equity shares made on 1 January 2012. The terms of the share issue were one new share for every five held at a price of 75 cents each.

(ii)   Non-current assets:

To reflect a marked increase in property prices, Fresco decided to revalue its leased property on 1 April 2011. The Directors accepted the report of an independent surveyor who valued the leased property at $36 million on that date. Fresco has not yet recorded the revaluation. The remaining life of the leased property is eight years at the date of the revaluation. Fresco makes an annual transfer to retained profits to reflect the realisation of the revaluation surplus. In Fresco's tax jurisdiction the revaluation does not give rise to a deferred tax liability.

On 1 April 2011, Fresco acquired an item of plant under a finance lease agreement that had an implicit finance cost of 10% per annum. The lease payments in the trial balance represent an initial deposit of $2 million paid on 1 April 2011 and the first annual rental of $6 million paid on 31 March 2012. The lease agreement requires further annual payments of $6 million on 31 March each year for the next four years. Had the plant not been leased it would have cost $25 million to purchase for cash.

Plant and equipment (other than the leased plant) is depreciated at 20% per annum using the reducing balance method.

No depreciation/amortisation has yet been charged on any non-current asset for the year ended 31 March 2012. Depreciation/amortisation are charged to cost of sales.

(iii)   In March 2012, Fresco's internal audit department discovered a fraud committed by the company's credit controller who did not return from a foreign business trip. The outcome of the fraud is that $4 million of the company's trade receivables have been stolen by the credit controller and are not recoverable. Of this amount, $1 million relates to the year ended 31 March 2011 and the remainder to the current year. Fresco is not insured against this fraud.

(iv)   Fresco's income tax calculation for the year ended 31 March 2012 shows a tax refund of $2.4 million. The balance on current tax in the trial balance represents the under/over provision of the tax liability for the year ended 31 March 2011. At 31 March 2012, Fresco had taxable temporary differences of $12 million (requiring a deferred tax liability). The income tax rate of Fresco is 25%.

Required:

(a)   (i)   Prepare the statement of profit or loss for Fresco for the year ended 31 March 2012.   (8 marks)

       (ii)   Prepare the statement of changes in equity for Fresco for the year ended 31 March 2012.   (4 marks)

       (iii)   Prepare the statement of financial position of Fresco as at 31 March 2012.

                                                                                              (8 marks)

                                                                                    (Total: 20 marks)

359 QUINCY

The following trial balance relates to Quincy as at 30 September 2012:

	$000	$000
Revenue (note (i))		213,500
Cost of sales	136,800	
Distribution costs	12,500	
Administrative expenses (note (ii))	19,000	
Loan note interest and dividend paid (notes (ii) and (iii))	20,700	
Investment income		400
Equity shares of 25 cents each		60,000
6% loan note (note (ii))		25,000
Retained earnings at 1 October 2011		6,500
Plant and equipment at cost (note (iv))	83,700	
Accumulated depreciation at 1 October 2011: plant and equipment		33,700
Equity financial asset investments (note (v))	17,000	
Inventory at 30 September 2012	24,800	
Trade receivables	28,500	
Bank	2,900	
Current tax (note (vi))	1,100	
Deferred tax (note (vi))		1,200
Trade payables		6,700
	347,000	347,000

The following notes are relevant:

(i) On 1 October 2011, Quincy sold one of its products for $10 million (included in revenue in the trial balance). As part of the sale agreement, Quincy is committed to the ongoing servicing of this product until 30 September 2014 (i.e. three years from the date of sale). The value of this service has been included in the selling price of $10 million. The estimated cost to Quincy of the servicing is $600,000 per annum and Quincy's normal gross profit margin on this type of servicing is 25%. The service performance obligation will be satisfied over time. Ignore discounting.

(ii) Quincy issued a $25 million 6% loan note on 1 October 2011. Issue costs were $1 million and these have been charged to administrative expenses. The loan will be redeemed on 30 September 2014 at a premium which gives an effective interest rate on the loan of 8%.

(iii) Quincy paid an equity dividend of 8 cents per share during the year ended 30 September 2012.

(iv) Plant and equipment is depreciated at 15% per annum using the reducing balance method.

No depreciation has yet been charged for the year ended 30 September 2012. All depreciation is charged to cost of sales.

(v)   The investments had a fair value of $15.7 million as at 30 September 2012. There were no acquisitions or disposals of these investments during the year ended 30 September 2012.

(vi)   The balance on current tax represents the under/over provision of the tax liability for the year ended 30 September 2011. A provision for income tax for the year ended 30 September 2012 of $7.4 million is required. At 30 September 2012, Quincy had taxable temporary differences of $5 million, requiring a provision for deferred tax. Any deferred tax adjustment should be reported in the statement of profit or loss. The income tax rate of Quincy is 20%.

Required:

(a)   **Prepare the statement of profit or loss and other comprehensive income for Quincy for the year ended 30 September 2012.**   **(10 marks)**

(b)   **Prepare the statement of changes in equity for Quincy for the year ended 30 September 2012.**   **(2 marks)**

(c)   **Prepare the statement of financial position for Quincy as at 30 September 2012.**
                                                                                           (8 marks)

       Notes to the financial statements are not required.

                                                                                     (Total: 20 marks)

360   ATLAS

The following trial balance relates to Atlas at 31 March 2013:

	$000	$000
Equity shares of 50 cents each		50,000
Retained earnings at 1 April 2012		11,200
Land and buildings – at cost (land $10 million) (note (ii))	60,000	
Plant and equipment – at cost (note (ii))	94,500	
Accumulated depreciation at 1 April 2012: – buildings		20,000
– plant and equipment		24,500
Inventory at 31 March 2013	43,700	
Trade receivables	42,200	
Bank		6,800
Deferred tax (note (iv))		6,200
Trade payables		35,100
Revenue (note (i))		550,000
Cost of sales	411,500	
Distribution costs	21,500	
Administrative expenses	30,900	
Bank interest	700	
Current tax (note (iv))		1,200
	705,000	705,000

The following notes are relevant:

(i) Revenue includes the sale of $10 million of maturing inventory made to Xpede on 1 October 2012. The cost of the goods at the date of sale was $7 million and Atlas has an option to repurchase these goods at any time within three years of the sale at a price of $10 million plus accrued interest from the date of sale at 10% per annum. At 31 March 2013 the option had not been exercised, but it is highly likely that it will be before the date it lapses.

(ii) Non-current assets: On 1 October 2012, Atlas terminated the production of one of its product lines. From this date, the plant used to manufacture the product has been actively marketed at an advertised price of $4.2 million which is considered realistic. It is included in the trial balance at a cost of $9 million with accumulated depreciation (at 1 April 2012) of $5 million.

On 1 April 2012, the directors of Atlas decided that the financial statements would show an improved position if the land and buildings were revalued to market value. At that date, an independent valuer valued the land at $12 million and the buildings at $35 million and these valuations were accepted by the directors. The remaining life of the buildings at that date was 14 years. Atlas does not make a transfer to retained earnings for excess depreciation. Ignore deferred tax on the revaluation surplus.

Plant and equipment is depreciated at 20% per annum using the reducing balance method and time apportioned as appropriate.

All depreciation is charged to cost of sales, but none has yet been charged on any non-current asset for the year ended 31 March 2013.

(iii) At 31 March 2013, a provision is required for directors' bonuses equal to 1% of revenue for the year.

(iv) Atlas estimates that an income tax provision of $27.2 million is required for the year ended 31 March 2013 and at that date the liability to deferred tax is $9.4 million. The movement on deferred tax should be taken to profit or loss. The balance on current tax in the trial balance represents the under/over provision of the tax liability for the year ended 31 March 2012.

Required:

(i) **Prepare the statement of profit or loss and other comprehensive income for Atlas for the year ended 31 March 2013** (9 marks)

(ii) **Prepare the statement of financial position of Atlas as at 31 March 2013.**

(11 marks)

Notes to the financial statements and a statement of changes in equity are not required.

(Total: 20 marks)

361 MOBY

 Timed question with Online tutor debrief

The following trial balance relates to Moby as at 30 September 2013:

	$000	$000
Revenue		227,800
Cost of sales	164,500	
Contract to construct asset (note (i))	4,000	
Operating expenses	29,850	
Lease rental paid on 30 September 2013 (note (ii))	9,200	
Land ($12 million) and building ($48 million) at cost (note (ii))	60,000	
Leased plant at initial carrying amount (note (ii))	35,000	
Accumulated depreciation at 1 October 2012:		
building		10,000
leased plant		7,000
Inventory at 30 September 2013	56,600	
Trade receivables	38,500	
Bank		7,300
Insurance provision (note (iii))		150
Deferred tax (note (iv))		8,000
Finance lease obligation at 1 October 2012 (note (ii))		29,300
Trade payables		21,300
Equity shares of 20 cents each		27,000
Loan note (note (v))		40,000
Retained earnings at 1 October 2012		19,800
	397,650	397,650

The following notes are relevant:

(i)   During the year, Moby entered into a contract to construct an asset for a customer. The performance obligation is satisfied over time. The balance in the trial balance represents:

Cost incurred to date	$14 million
Value of contract billed (work certified) and cash received	$10 million

The contract commenced on 1 October 2012 and is for a fixed price of $25 million. The costs to complete the contract at 30 September 2013 are estimated at $6 million. Moby's policy is to measure progress based on the work certified as a percentage of the contract price.

(ii)   Non-current assets:

Moby decided to revalue its land and building, for the first time, on 1 October 2012. A qualified valuer determined the relevant revalued amounts to be $16 million for the land and $38.4 million for the building. The building's remaining life at the date of the revaluation was 16 years. This revaluation has not yet been reflected in the trial balance figures. Moby does not make a transfer from the revaluation surplus to retained earnings in respect of the realisation of the revaluation surplus. Deferred tax is applicable to the revaluation surplus at 25%.

The leased plant was acquired on 1 October 2011 under a five-year finance lease which has an implicit interest rate of 10% per annum. The rentals are $9.2 million per annum payable on 30 September each year.

No depreciation has yet been charged on any non-current asset for the year ended 30 September 2013. All depreciation is charged to cost of sales.

(iii) On 1 October 2012, Moby received a renewal quote of $400,000 from the company's property insurer. The directors were surprised at how much it had increased and believed it would be less expensive for the company to 'self-insure'. Accordingly, they charged $400,000 to operating expenses and credited the same amount to the insurance provision. During the year, the company incurred $250,000 of expenses relating to previously insured property damage which it has debited to the provision.

(iv) A provision for income tax for the year ended 30 September 2013 of $3.4 million is required. At 30 September 2013, the tax base of Moby's net assets was $24 million less than their carrying amounts. This does not include the effect of the revaluation in note (ii) above. The income tax rate of Moby is 25%.

(v) The $40 million loan note was issued at par on 1 October 2012. No interest will be paid on the loan; however, it will be redeemed on 30 September 2015 for $53,240,000 which gives an effective finance cost of 10% per annum.

Required:

(a) **Prepare the statement of profit or loss and other comprehensive income for Moby for the year ended 30 September 2013.** **(10 marks)**

(b) **Prepare the statement of financial position for Moby as at 30 September 2013.**
(10 marks)

Note: **A statement of changes in equity and notes to the financial statements are not required.**

(Total: 20 marks)

 Calculate your allowed time, allocate the time to the separate parts

362 XTOL

The following trial balance relates to Xtol at 31 March 2014:

	$000	$000
Revenue (note (i))		490,000
Cost of sales	290,600	
Distribution costs	33,500	
Administrative expenses	36,800	
Loan note interest (note (iv))	2,500	
Bank interest	900	
Land at cost (note (ii))	75,000	
Plant and equipment at cost (note (ii))	155,500	
Accumulated depreciation at 1 April 2013:		
plant and equipment		43,500
Inventory at 31 March 2014	61,000	
Trade receivables	63,000	
Trade payables		32,200
Bank		5,500
Equity shares of $1 each (note (iii))		66,000
Share premium		15,000
Retained earnings at 1 April 2013		15,200
5% convertible loan note (note (iii))		50,000
Current tax (note (iv))	3,200	
Deferred tax (note (iv))		4,600
	722,000	722,000

The following notes are relevant:

(i)   Revenue includes $20 million cash sales made through Xtol's retail outlets during the year on behalf of Francais. Xtol, acting as agent, is entitled to a commission of 10% of the selling price of these goods. By 31 March 2014, Xtol had remitted to Francais $15 million (of the $20 million sales) and recorded this amount in cost of sales.

(ii)   Plant and equipment is depreciated at 12½% per annum on the reducing balance basis. All amortisation/depreciation of non-current assets is charged to cost of sales.

(iii) On 1 April 2013, Xtol issued a 5% $50 million convertible loan note at par. Interest is payable annually in arrears on 31 March each year. The loan note is redeemable at par or convertible into equity shares at the option of the loan note holders on 31 March 2016. The interest on an equivalent loan note without the conversion rights would be 8% per annum.

The present values of $1 receivable at the end of each year, based on discount rates of 5% and 8%, are:

	5%	8%
End of year 1	0.95	0.93
2	0.91	0.86
3	0.86	0.79

(iv) The balance on current tax represents the under/over provision of the tax liability for the year ended 31 March 2013. A provision of $28 million is required for current tax for the year ended 31 March 2014 and at this date the deferred tax liability was assessed at $8.3 million.

(v) The equity shares and share premium balances in the trial balance above include a fully subscribed 1 for 5 rights issue at $1.60 per share which was made by Xtol on 1 October 2014. The market value of Xtol's shares was $2.50 on 1 October 2014.

Required:

(a) Prepare the statement of profit or loss for Xtol for the year ended 31 March 2014.

(b) Prepare the statement of financial position for Xtol as at 31 March 2014.

(c) Calculate the basic earnings per share of Xtol for the year ended 31 March 2014.

Note: Answers and workings (for parts (a) to (b)) should be presented to the nearest $1,000; a statement of changes in equity is not required.

The following mark allocation is provided as guidance for this question:

(a) 7 marks

(b) 8 marks

(c) 5 marks

(Total: 20 marks)

363 WELLMAY

The summarised draft financial statements of Wellmay are shown below.

Statement of profit or loss year ended 31 March 2007

	$000
Revenue (note (i))	4,200
Cost of sales	(2,700)
Gross profit	1,500
Operating expenses	(470)
Investment property rental income	20
Finance costs	(55)
Profit before tax	995
Income tax	(360)
Profit for the period	635

Statement of financial position as at 31 March 2007

	$000	$000
Assets		
Non-current assets		
Property, plant and equipment (note (ii))		4,200
Investment property (note (ii))		400
		4,600
Current assets		1,400
Total assets		6,000
Equity and liabilities		
Equity		
Equity shares of 50 cents each		1,200
Reserves:		
Revaluation surplus	350	
Retained earnings – At 1 April 2006	2,215	
Retained earnings – profit for the year	635	3,200
		4,400
Non-current liabilities		
8% Convertible loan note (2010) (note (iii))	600	
Deferred tax (note (iv))	180	780
Current liabilities		820
Total equity and liabilities		6,000

The following information is relevant to the draft financial statements:

(i)   Revenue includes $500,000 for the sale on 1 April 2006 of maturing goods to Westwood. The goods had a cost of $200,000 at the date of sale. Wellmay can repurchase the goods on 31 March 2008 for $605,000 (based on achieving a lender's return of 10% per annum) at which time the goods are estimated to have a value of $750,000.

(ii) **Non-current assets**

Wellmay owns two properties. One is a factory (with office accommodation) used by Wellmay as a production facility and the other is an investment property that is leased to a third party under an operating lease. Wellmay revalues all its properties to current value at the end of each year and uses the fair value model in IAS 40 Investment property. Relevant details of the fair values of the properties are:

	Factory	Investment property
	$000	$000
Valuation 31 March 2006	1,200	400
Valuation 31 March 2007	1,350	375

The valuations at 31 March 2007 have not yet been incorporated into the financial statements. Factory depreciation for the year ended 31 March 2007 of $40,000 was charged to cost of sales.

(iii) **8% Convertible loan note (2010)**

On 1 April 2006 an 8% convertible loan note with a nominal value of $600,000 was issued at par. It is redeemable on 31 March 2010 at par or it may be converted into equity shares of Wellmay on the basis of 100 new shares for each $200 of loan note. An equivalent loan note without the conversion option would have carried an interest rate of 10%. Interest of $48,000 has been paid on the loan and charged as a finance cost.

The present value of $1 receivable at the end of each year, based on discount rates of 8% and 10% are:

	8%	10%
End of year 1	0.93	0.91
2	0.86	0.83
3	0.79	0.75
4	0.73	0.68

(iv) The carrying amounts of Wellmay's net assets at 31 March 2007 are $600,000 higher than their tax base. The rate of taxation is 35%. The income tax charge of $360,000 does not include the adjustment required to the deferred tax provision which should be charged in full to the statement of profit or loss.

Required:

(a) Redraft the financial statements of Wellmay, including a statement of changes in equity, for the year ended 31 March 2007 reflecting the adjustments required by notes (i) to (iv) above. (15 marks)

(b) Explain the purpose of diluted earnings per share, and how it aids the predictive nature of financial statements. Your answer should make reference to note (iii).

A calculation of diluted earnings per share is NOT required. (5 marks)

Note: Calculations should be made to the nearest $000.

(Total: 20 marks)

364 DUNE

The following trial balance relates to Dune at 31 March 2010:

	$000	$000
Equity shares of $1 each		40,000
Other components of equity		20,000
5% loan note (note (i))		20,000
Retained earnings at 1 April 2009		38,400
Leasehold (15 years) property – at cost (note (ii))	45,000	
Plant and equipment – at cost (note (ii))	67,500	
Accumulated depreciation – 1 April 2009 – leasehold property		6,000
– plant and equipment		23,500
Investments at fair value through profit or loss (note (iii))	26,500	
Inventory at 31 March 2010	48,000	
Trade receivables	40,700	
Bank	15,500	
Deferred tax (note (iv))		6,000
Trade payables		52,000
Revenue (note (iv))		400,000
Cost of sales	294,000	
Distribution costs	26,400	
Administrative expenses (note (i))	34,200	
Dividend paid	10,000	
Loan note interest paid (six months)	500	
Bank interest	200	
Investment income		1,200
Current tax (note (iv))		1,400
	608,500	608,500

The following notes are relevant:

(i)   The 5% loan note was issued on 1 April 2009 at its nominal (face) value of $20 million. The direct costs of the issue were $500,000 and these have been charged to administrative expenses. The loan note will be redeemed on 31 March 2012 at a substantial premium. The effective finance cost of the loan note is 10% per annum.

(ii) Non-current assets:

In order to fund a new project, on 1 October 2009 the company decided to sell its leasehold property. From that date it commenced a short-term rental of an equivalent property. The leasehold property is being marketed by a property agent at a price of $40 million, which was considered a reasonably achievable price at that date. The expected costs to sell have been agreed at $500,000. Recent market transactions suggest that actual selling prices achieved for this type of property in the current market conditions are 15% less than the value at which they are marketed. At 31 March 2010 the property had not been sold.

Plant and equipment is depreciated at 15% per annum using the reducing balance method.

No depreciation/amortisation has yet been charged on any non-current asset for the year ended 31 March 2010. Depreciation, amortisation and impairment charges are all charged to cost of sales.

(iii) The investments at fair value through profit or loss had a fair value of $28 million on 31 March 2010. There were no purchases or disposals of any of these investments during the year.

(iv) A provision for income tax for the year ended 31 March 2010 of $12 million is required. The balance on current tax represents the under/over provision of the tax liability for the year ended 31 March 2009. At 31 March 2010 the tax base of Dune's net assets was $14 million less than their carrying amounts. The income tax rate of Dune is 30%.

(v) Dune has accounted for a fully subscribed rights issue of equity shares made on 1 January 2010 of one new share for every four in issue at 42 cents each, when the market value of a Dune share was 82 cents.

Required:

(a) **Prepare the statement of profit or loss for Dune for the year ended 31 March 2010, and the statement of financial position for Dune as at 31 March 2010.**

   Notes to the financial statements and a statement of changes in equity are not required.   **(15 marks)**

(b) **Using the information in note (v), calculate earnings per share for Dune for the year ended 31 March 2010. Also, calculate the re-stated figure for 2009 if the EPS figure in the original 2009 financial statements was 68c per share.**   **(5 marks)**

                                                                              (Total: 20 marks)

365 KANDY

After preparing a draft statement of profit or loss for the year ended 30 September 2014 and adding the year's profit (before any adjustments required by notes (i) to (iii) below) to retained earnings, the summarised trial balance of Kandy as at 30 September 2014 is:

	$000	$000
Equity shares of $1 each		40,000
Retained earnings as at 30 September 2014		19,500
Proceeds of 6% loan (note (i))		30,000
Land ($5 million) and buildings – at cost (note (ii))	55,000	
Plant and equipment – at cost (note (ii))	58,500	
Accumulated depreciation at 1 October 2013: buildings		20,000
plant and equipment		34,500
Current assets	68,700	
Current liabilities		38,400
Deferred tax (note (iii))		2,500
Interest payment (note (i))	1,800	
Operating lease payment	2,000	
Current tax (note (iii))		1,100
	———	———
	184,000	184,000
	———	———

The following notes are relevant:

(i)   The loan note was issued on 1 October 2013 and incurred issue costs of $1 million which were charged to profit or loss. Interest of $1.8 million ($30 million at 6%) was paid on 30 September 2014. The loan is redeemable on 30 September 2018 at a substantial premium which gives an effective interest rate of 9% per annum. No other repayments are due until 30 September 2018.

(ii) Non-current assets:

The price of property has increased significantly in recent years and on 1 October 2013, the directors decided to revalue the land and buildings. The directors accepted the report of an independent surveyor who valued the land at $8 million and the buildings at $39 million on that date. The remaining life of the buildings at 1 October 2013 was 15 years. Kandy does not make an annual transfer to retained profits to reflect the realisation of the revaluation gain; however, the revaluation will give rise to a deferred tax liability. The income tax rate of Kandy is 20%.

Plant and equipment is depreciated at 12½% per annum using the reducing balance method.

No depreciation has been charged for the year ended 30 September 2014.

(iii) A provision of $2.4 million is required for current income tax on the profit of the year to 30 September 2014. The balance on current tax in the trial balance is the under/over provision of tax for the previous year. In addition to the temporary differences relating to the information in note (ii), Kandy has further taxable temporary differences of $10 million as at 30 September 2014.

(iv) Kandy renewed an operating lease on a property on 1 October 2013. The operating lease payments represent an annual payment (in advance) of $1 million and a lease premium of $1 million. The lease is for four years and operating lease expenses should be included in cost of sales.

Required:

(a)   **Prepare a schedule of adjustments required to the retained earnings of Kandy as at 30 September 2014 as a result of the information in notes (i) to (iv) above.**

(b)   **Prepare the statement of financial position of Kandy as at 30 September 2014.**

Note: The notes to the statement of financial position are not required.

The following mark allocation is provided as guidance for this question:

(a)   **9 marks**

(b)   **11 marks**

(Total: 20 marks)

366 CLARION

The following trial balance relates to Clarion as at 31 March 2015:

	$000	$000
Equity shares of $1 each		35,000
Retained earnings – 1 April 2014		4,700
8% loan notes (note (i))		20,000
Plant and equipment at cost (note (ii))	85,000	
Accumulated depreciation plant and equipment – 1 April 2014		19,000
Investments through profit or loss – value at 1 April 2014 (note (iii))	6,000	
Inventory at 31 March 2015	11,700	
Trade receivables	20,500	
Bank		1,900
Deferred tax (note (v))		2,700
Trade payables		9,400
Environmental provision (note (ii))		4,000
Finance lease obligation (note (ii))		4,200
Revenue		132,000
Cost of sales	88,300	
Administrative expenses	8,000	
Distribution costs	7,400	
Loan note interest paid	800	
Suspense account (note (i))	5,800	
Bank interest	300	
Investment income (note (iii))		500
Current tax (note (v))		400
	233,800	233,800

The following notes are also relevant:

(i)   On 31 March 2015, one quarter of the 8% loan notes were redeemed at par and six months' outstanding loan interest was paid. The suspense account represents the debit entry corresponding to the cash payment for the capital redemption and the outstanding interest.

(ii)   Property, plant and equipment:

Included in property, plant and equipment are two major items of plant acquired on 1 April 2014:

Item 1 had a cash cost $14 million, however, the plant will cause environmental damage which will have to be rectified when it is dismantled at the end of its five year life. The present value (discounting at 8%) on 1 April 2014 of the rectification is $4 million. The environmental provision has been correctly accounted for, however, no finance cost has yet been charged on the provision.

Item 2 was plant acquired with a fair value of $8 million under a five-year finance lease. This required an initial deposit of $2.3 million and annual payments of $1.5 million on 31 March each year. The finance lease obligation in the trial balance above represents the fair value of the plant less both the deposit and the first annual payment. The lease has an implicit interest rate of 10% and the asset has been correctly capitalised in plant and equipment.

No depreciation has yet been charged on plant and equipment which should be charged to cost of sales on a straight-line basis over a five-year life (including leased plant). No plant is more than four years old.

(iii) The investments through profit or loss are those held at 31 March 2015 (after the sale below). They are carried at their fair value as at 1 April 2014, however, they had a fair value of $6.5 million on 31 March 2015. During the year an investment which had a carrying amount of $1.4 million was sold for $1.6 million. Investment income in the trial balance above includes the profit on the sale of the investment and dividends received during the year.

(v) A provision for current tax for the year ended 31 March 2015 of $3.5 million is required. The balance on current tax in the trial balance above represents the under/over provision of the tax liability for the year ended 31 March 2014. At 31 March 2015, the tax base of Clarion's net assets was $12 million less than their carrying amounts. The income tax rate of Clarion is 25%.

Required:

(a) **Prepare the statement of profit or loss for Clarion for the year ended 31 March 2015.**

(b) **Prepare the statement of financial position for Clarion as at 31 March 2015.**

(c) **Prepare extracts from the statement of cash flows for Clarion for the year ended 31 March 2015 in respect of cash flows from investing (ignore investment income) and financing activities.**

Notes to the financial statements are not required.

The following mark allocation is provided as guidance for these requirements:

(a) 8 marks

(b) 9 marks

(c) 3 marks   (Total: 20 marks)

367 MOSTON *Walk in the footsteps of a top tutor*

The following trial balance **extracts** (i.e. it is not a complete trial balance) relate to Moston as at 30 June 2015:

	$000	$000
Revenue (note (i))		113,500
Cost of sales	88,500	
Research and development costs (note (ii))	7,800	
Distribution costs	3,600	
Administrative expenses (note (iv))	6,800	
Loan note interest and dividends paid (notes (iv) and (vii))	5,000	
Investment income		300
Equity shares of $1 each (note (vii))		30,000
5% loan note (note (iv))		20,000
Retained earnings as at 1 July 2014		6,200
Revaluation surplus as at 1 July 2014		3,000
Other components of equity		9,300
Property at valuation 1 July 2014 (note (iii))	28,500	
Plant and equipment at cost (note (iii))	27,100	
Accumulated depreciation plant and equipment 1 July 2014		9,100
Financial asset equity investments at fair value 1 July 2014 (note (v))	8,800	

The following notes are relevant:

(i) Revenue includes a $3 million sale made on 1 January 2015 of maturing goods which are not biological assets. The carrying amount of these goods at the date of sale was $2 million. Moston is still in possession of the goods (but they have not been included in the inventory count) and has an unexercised option to repurchase them at any time in the next three years. In three years' time the goods are expected to be worth $5 million. The repurchase price will be the original selling price plus interest at 10% per annum from the date of sale to the date of repurchase.

(ii) Moston commenced a research and development project on 1 January 2015. It spent $1 million per month on research until 31 March 2015, at which date the project passed into the development stage. From this date it spent $1.6 million per month until the year end (30 June 2015), at which date development was completed. However, it was not until 1 May 2015 that the directors of Moston were confident that the new product would be a commercial success.

Expensed research and development costs should be charged to cost of sales.

(iii) Non-current assets:

Moston's property is carried at fair value which at 30 June 2015 was $29 million. The remaining life of the property at the beginning of the year (1 July 2014) was 15 years. Moston does not make an annual transfer to retained earnings in respect of the revaluation surplus. Ignore deferred tax on the revaluation.

Plant and equipment is depreciated at 15% per annum using the reducing balance method.

No depreciation has yet been charged on any non-current asset for the year ended 30 June 2015. All depreciation is charged to cost of sales.

(iv) The 5% loan note was issued on 1 July 2014 at its nominal value of $20 million incurring direct issue costs of $500,000 which have been charged to administrative expenses. The loan note will be redeemed after three years at a premium which gives the loan note an effective finance cost of 8% per annum. Annual interest was paid on 30 June 2015.

(v) At 30 June 2015, the financial asset equity investments had a fair value of $9.6 million. There were no acquisitions or disposals of these investments during the year.

(vi) A provision for current tax for the year ended 30 June 2015 of $1.2 million is required, together with an increase to the deferred tax provision to be charged to profit or loss of $800,000.

(vii) Moston paid a dividend of 20 cents per share on 30 March 2015, which was followed the day after by an issue of 10 million equity shares at their full market value of $1.70. The share premium on the issue was recorded in other components of equity.

Required:

(a) **Prepare the statement of profit or loss and other comprehensive income for Moston for the year ended 30 June 2015.** (11 marks)

(b) **Prepare the statement of changes in equity for Moston for the year ended 30 June 2015.** (4 marks)

(c) **Prepare extracts from the statement of cash flows for Moston for the year ended 30 June 2015 in respect of cash flows from investing and financing activities.**

(5 marks)

Note: The statement of financial position and notes to the financial statements are NOT required.

(Total: 20 marks)

368 MINSTER

Minster is a publicly listed company. Details of its financial statements for the year ended 30 September 20X6, together with a comparative statement of financial position, are:

Statement of financial position at	30 September 20X6		30 September 20X5	
	$000	$000	$000	$000
Non-current assets (note (i))				
Property, plant and equipment		1,280		940
Software		135		Nil
Investments at fair value through profit and loss		150		125
		1,565		1,065
Current assets				
Inventories	480		510	
Trade receivables	270		380	
Amounts due from construction contracts	80		55	
Bank	Nil	830	35	980
Total assets		2,395		2,045
Equity and liabilities				
Equity shares of 25 cents each		500		300
Reserves				
Share premium (note (iii))	150		85	
Revaluation surplus	60		25	
Retained earnings	950	1,160	965	1,075
		1,660		1,375
Non-current liabilities				
9% loan note	120		Nil	
Environmental provision	162		Nil	
Deferred tax	18	30	25	25
Current liabilities				
Trade payables	350		555	
Bank overdraft	25		40	
Current tax payable	60	435	50	645
Total equity and liabilities		2,395		2,045

Statement of profit or loss for the year ended 30 September 20X6

Revenue	1,397
Cost of sales	(1,110)
Gross profit	287
Operating expenses	(125)
	162
Finance costs (note (i))	(40)
Investment income and gain on investments (note (ii))	20
Profit before tax	142
Income tax expense	(57)
Profit for the year	85

The following supporting information is available:

(i) Included in property, plant and equipment is a coal mine and related plant that Minster purchased on 1 October 20X5. Legislation requires that in ten years' time (the estimated life of the mine) Minster will have to landscape the area affected by the mining. The future cost of this has been estimated and discounted at a rate of 8% to a present value of $150,000. This cost has been included in the carrying amount of the mine and, together with the unwinding of the discount, has also been treated as a provision. The unwinding of the discount is included within finance costs in the statement of profit or loss.

Other land was revalued (upward) by $35,000 during the year.

Depreciation of property, plant and equipment for the year was $255,000.

There were no disposals of property, plant and equipment during the year.

The software was purchased on 1 April 20X6 for $180,000.

(ii) The market value of the investments had increased during the year by $15,000. There have been no sales of these investments during the year.

(iii) On 1 April 20X6 there was a bonus (scrip) issue of equity shares of one for every four held utilising the share premium reserve. A further cash share issue was made on 1 June 20X6. No shares were redeemed during the year.

(iv) A dividend of 5 cents per share was paid on 1 July 20X6.

Required:

(a) **Prepare a statement of cash flows for Minster for the year to 30 September 20X6 in accordance with IAS 7 Statements of cash flows.** **(15 marks)**

(b) **Comment on Minster's cash flows from investing and financing activities. (5 marks)**

(Total: 20 marks)

369 TABBA *Walk in the footsteps of a top tutor*

The following draft financial statements relate to Tabba, a private company.

Statements of financial position as at:	30 September 20X5		30 September 20X4	
	$000	$000	$000	$000
Tangible non-current assets (note (ii))		10,600		15,800
Current assets				
Inventories	2,550		1,850	
Trade receivables	3,100		2,600	
Insurance claim (note (iii))	1,500		1,200	
Cash and bank	850	8,000	Nil	5,650
		———		———
Total assets		18,600		21,450
		———		———
Equity and liabilities				
Share capital ($1 each)		6,000		6,000
Reserves:				
Revaluation (note (ii))	nil		1,600	
Retained earnings	2,550	2,550	850	2,450
		———		———
		8,550		8,450
Non-current liabilities				
Finance lease obligations (note (ii))	2,000		1,700	
6% loan notes	800		Nil	
10% loan notes	nil		4,000	
Deferred tax	200		500	
Government grants (note (ii))	1,400	4,400	900	7,100
Current liabilities				
Bank overdraft	nil		550	
Trade payables	4,050		2,950	
Government grants (note (ii))	600		400	
Finance lease obligations (note (ii))	900		800	
Current tax payable	100	5,650	1,200	5,900
		———		———
Total equity and liabilities		18,600		21,450
		———		———

The following information is relevant:

(i)   Statement of profit or loss extract for the year ended 30 September 20X5:

	$000
Profit from operations	270
Finance cost	(260)
Interest income	40
Profit before tax	50
Net tax credit	50
Profit for the period	100

Note: The interest expense includes finance lease interest.

(ii)   The details of the tangible non-current assets are:

	Cost	Accumulated depreciation	Carrying amount
	$000	$000	$000
At 30 September 20X4	20,200	4,400	15,800
At 30 September 20X5	16,000	5,400	10,600

During the year Tabba sold its factory for its fair value $12 million and agreed to rent it back, under an operating lease, for a period of five years at $1 million per annum. At the date of sale it had a carrying amount of $7.4 million based on a previous revaluation of $8.6 million less depreciation of $1.2 million since the revaluation. The profit on the sale of the factory has been included in operating profit. The surplus on the revaluation surplus related entirely to the factory. No other disposals of non-current assets were made during the year.

Plant acquired under finance leases during the year was $1.5 million. Other purchases of plant during the year qualified for government grants of $950,000 received in the year. Release of government grants has been credited to cost of sales.

(iii) The insurance claim relates to flood damage to the company's inventories which occurred in September 20X4. The original estimate has been revised during the year. The claim is expected to be settled in the near future.

Required:

(a)   **Prepare a statement of cash flows using the indirect method for Tabba for the year ended 30 September 20X5.**   **(17 marks)**

(b)   **Comment on the cash generated from operations for Tabba for the year ended 30 September 20X5.**   **(3 marks)**

                                                                                      (Total: 20 marks)

370 COALTOWN *Walk in the footsteps of a top tutor*

 Timed question with Online tutor debrief

Coaltown is a wholesaler and retailer of office furniture. Extracts from the company's financial statements are set out below:

Statement of profit or loss and other comprehensive income for the year ended:

		31 March 2009	
		$000	$000
Revenue	– cash	12,800	
	– credit	53,000	65,800
Cost of sales			(43,800)
Gross profit			22,000
Operating expenses			(11,200)
Finance costs – loan notes		(380)	
	– overdraft	(220)	(600)
Profit before tax			10,200
Income tax expense			(3,200)
Profit for period			7,000
Other comprehensive income			
Gain on property revaluation			5,000
Total comprehensive income for the year			12,000

Statements of financial position as at 31 March:

	2009		2008	
	$000	$000	$000	$000
Assets				
Non-current assets (notes (i), (ii))				
Cost		93,500		80,000
Accumulated depreciation		(43,000)		(48,000)
		50,500		32,000
Current assets				
Inventory	5,200		4,400	
Trade receivables	7,800		2,800	
Bank	nil	13,000	700	7,900
Total assets		63,500		39,900

Equity and liabilities				
Equity shares of $1 each		16,600		6,000
Other components of equity		4,800		500
Revaluation surplus (note (ii))		6,500		2,500
Retained earnings (note (ii))		19,800		15,800
		47,700		24,800
Non-current liabilities				
10% loan notes	4,000		3,000	
Convertible loan (note (v))	Nil		2,000	
		4,000		5,000
Current liabilities				
Bank overdraft	3,600		Nil	
Trade payables	4,200		4,500	
Taxation	3,000		5,300	
Negligence claim (note (iii))	Nil		120	
Warranty provision	1,000	11,800	180	10,100
Total equity and liabilities		63,500		39,900

(i)   During the year the company redesigned its display areas in all of its outlets. The previous displays had cost $10 million and had been written down by $9 million. There was an unexpected cost of $500,000 for the removal and disposal of the old display areas.

(ii)   Also during the year the company revalued the carrying amount of its property upwards by $5 million, the accumulated depreciation on these properties of $2 million was reset to zero. All depreciation is charged to operating expenses. Coaltown makes annual reserves transfer from the revaluation surplus in respect of excess depreciation.

(iii)   In June 20X1 Charmer made an out of court settlement of a negligence claim brought about by a former employee. The dispute had been in progress for two years and Charmer had made provisions for the potential liability in each of the two previous years. The unprovided amount of the claim at the time of settlement was $30,000 and this was charged to operating expenses.

(iv)   The warranty provision relates to the future repair of goods and is charged to operating expenses.

(v)   During the year 20% of the convertible loan holders exercised their right to convert to ordinary shares. The terms of conversion were 25 ordinary shares of $1 each for each $100 of convertible loan. The remainder were repaid in cash. Ignore any transfer from other components of equity to retained earnings in respect of the redemption of the loan notes.

Required:

Prepare a statement of cash flows for Coaltown for the year ended 31 March 2009 in accordance with IAS 7 *Statement of Cash Flows* by the indirect method.

(Total: 20 marks)

 Calculate your allowed time, allocate the time to the separate parts

PAPER F7: FINANCIAL REPORTING

371 MONTY

Monty is a publicly listed company. Its financial statements for the year ended 31 March 2013 including comparatives are shown below:

Statements of profit or loss and other comprehensive income for the year ended:

	31 March 2013
	$000
Revenue	31,000
Cost of sales	(21,800)
Gross profit	9,200
Distribution costs	(3,600)
Administrative expenses	(2,200)
Finance costs – loan interest	(400)
Profit before tax	3,000
Income tax expense	(1,000)
Profit for the year	2,000
Other comprehensive income (note (i))	1,350
	3,350

Statements of financial position as at:

	31 March 2013		31 March 2012	
	$000	$000	$000	$000
Assets				
Non-current assets				
Property, plant and equipment		14,000		10,700
Deferred development expenditure		1,000		nil
		15,000		10,700
Current assets				
Inventory	3,300		3,800	
Trade receivables	2,950		2,200	
Bank	1,980	8,230	1,300	7,300
Total assets		23,230		18,000

KAPLAN PUBLISHING

Equity and liabilities

Equity

Equity shares of $1 each		7,000	7,000
Revaluation surplus		1,350	nil
Retained earnings		3,200	1,750
		11,550	8,750

Non-current liabilities

8% loan notes	4,080		4,000	
Deferred tax	1,500		800	
Finance lease obligation	1,200		900	
Government grant	200		100	
		6,980		5,800

Current liabilities

Finance lease obligation	750		600	
Trade payables	2,650		2,100	
Current tax payable	1,250		725	
Government grant	50	4,700	25	3,450
Total equity and liabilities		23,230		18,000

Notes:

(i) On 1 July 2012, Monty acquired additional plant under a finance lease that had a fair value of $1.5 million. On this date it also revalued its property upwards by $2 million and transferred $650,000 of the resulting revaluation surplus this created to deferred tax. There were no disposals of non-current assets during the period.

(ii) Depreciation of property, plant and equipment was $900,000 and amortisation of the deferred development expenditure was $200,000 for the year ended 31 March 2013.

(iii) The 8% loan notes are repayable at a premium, giving them an effective rate of 10%.

(iv) $25,000 was credited to administrative expenses in respect of government grants during the year.

Required:

Prepare a statement of cash flows for Monty for the year ended 31 March 2013, in accordance with IAS 7 *Statement of Cash Flows*, using the indirect method.

(Total: 20 marks)

372 KINGDOM

 Timed question with Online tutor debrief

Kingdom is a public listed manufacturing company. Its draft summarised financial statements for the year ended 30 September 2013 (and 2012 comparatives) are:

Statements of profit or loss and other comprehensive income for the year ended 30 September:

	2013
	$000
Revenue	44,900
Cost of sales	(31,300)
Gross profit	13,600
Distribution costs	(2,400)
Administrative expenses	(7,850)
Investment properties – rentals received	350
– fair value changes	(700)
Finance costs	(600)
Profit before taxation	2,400
Income tax	(600)
Profit for the year	1,800
Other comprehensive income	(1,300)
Total comprehensive income	500

Statements of financial position as at 30 September:

	2013		2012	
	$000	$000	$000	$000
Assets				
Non-current assets				
Property, plant and equipment		26,700		25,200
Investment properties		4,100		5,000
		30,800		30,200
Current assets				
Inventory	2,300		3,100	
Trade receivables	3,000		3,400	
Bank	nil	5,300	300	6,800
Total assets		36,100		37,000

Equity and liabilities

Equity

Equity shares of $1 each		17,200	15,000
Revaluation surplus		1,200	2,500
Retained earnings		7,700	8,700
		26,100	26,200
Non-current liabilities			
12% loan notes		5,000	5,000
Current liabilities			
Trade payables	4,200		3,900
Accrued finance costs	100		50
Bank	200		nil
Current tax payable	500	5,000	1,850	5,800
Total equity and liabilities		36,100	37,000

On 1 July 2013, Kingdom acquired a new investment property at a cost of $1.4 million. On this date, it also transferred one of its other investment properties to property, plant and equipment at its fair value of $1.6 million as it became owner-occupied on that date. Kingdom adopts the fair value model for its investment properties.

Kingdom also has a policy of revaluing its other properties (included as property, plant and equipment) to market value at the end of each year. Other comprehensive income and the revaluation surplus both relate to these properties.

Depreciation of property, plant and equipment during the year was $1.5 million. An item of plant with a carrying amount of $2.3 million was sold for $1.8 million during September 2013.

Required:

(a) **Prepare the statement of cash flows for Kingdom for the year ended 30 September 2013 in accordance with IAS *7 Statement* of Cash *Flows* using the indirect method.**

(15 marks)

(b) At a board meeting to consider the results shown by the draft financial statements, concern was expressed that, although there had been a slight increase in revenue during the current year, the profit before tax had fallen dramatically. The purchasing director commented that he was concerned about the impact of rising prices. During the year to 30 September 2013, most of Kingdom's manufacturing and operating costs have risen by an estimated 8% per annum.

Required:

Explain the causes of the fall in Kingdom's profit before tax. **(5 marks)**

(Total: 20 marks)

 Calculate your allowed time, allocate the time to the separate parts

BUSINESS COMBINATIONS

373 PREMIER *Walk in the footsteps of a top tutor*

On 1 June 2010, Premier acquired 80% of the equity share capital of Sanford. The consideration consisted of two elements: a share exchange of three shares in Premier for every five acquired shares in Sanford and $800,000 cash. The share issue has not yet been recorded by Premier. At the date of acquisition shares in Premier had a market value of $5 each. Below are the summarised draft financial statements of both companies.

Extracts from statements of profit or loss for the year ended 30 September 2010

	Premier	Sanford
	$000	$000
Revenue	92,500	45,000
Cost of sales	(70,500)	(36,000)
Gross profit	22,000	9,000
Other expenses	(12,000)	(5,100)
Profit for the year	10,000	3,900
Other comprehensive income:		
Gains on revaluation	nil	nil
Total comprehensive income	10,000	3,900

Statements of financial position as at 30 September 2010

	Premier	Sanford
Assets		
Non-current assets		
Property, plant and equipment	25,500	13,900
Investments	1,800	nil
	27,300	13,900
Current assets	12,500	2,400
Total assets	39,800	16,300
Equity and liabilities		
Equity		
Equity shares of $1 each	12,000	5,000
Other equity reserve – 30 September 2009 (note (iv))	500	nil
Retained earnings	12,300	4,500
	24,800	9,500
Liabilities		
Current liabilities	15,000	6,800
Total equity and liabilities	39,800	16,300

The following information is relevant:

(i)   At the date of acquisition, the fair values of Sanford's assets were equal to their carrying amounts with the exception of its property. This had a fair value of $1.2 million **below** its carrying amount, and had a remaining useful life of 8 years at the date of acquisition. Sanford has not incorporated this in its financial statements.

(ii)   Sales from Sanford to Premier throughout the year ended 30 September 2010 had consistently been $1 million per month. Sanford made a mark-up on cost of 25% on these sales. Premier had $2 million (at cost to Premier) of inventory that had been supplied in the post-acquisition period by Sanford as at 30 September 2010.

(iii)   Premier had a trade payable balance owing to Sanford of $350,000 as at 30 September 2010. This did not agree with the corresponding receivable in Sanford's books due to a $130,000 payment made to Sanford, which Sanford has not yet recorded.

(iv)   Premier's investments include investments in shares which at the date of acquisition were classified as fair value through other comprehensive income (FVTOCI). The investments have increased in value by $300,000 during the year. The other equity reserve relates to these investments and is based on their value as at 30 September 2009. There were no acquisitions or disposals of any of these investments during the year ended 30 September 2010.

(v)   Premier's policy is to value the non-controlling interest at fair value at the date of acquisition, deemed to be $3.5 million.

(vi)   There has been no impairment of consolidated goodwill.

Required:

(a)   **Prepare the consolidated statement of profit or loss and other comprehensive income for Premier for the year ended 30 September 2010.**   **(6 marks)**

(b)   **Prepare the consolidated statement of financial position for Premier as at 30 September 2010.**   **(14 marks)**

(Total: 20 marks)

374 PARENTIS

Parentis acquired 600 million equity shares in Offspring on 1 April 2006. The purchase consideration was made up of:

- a share exchange of one share in Parentis for two shares in Offspring

- the issue of $100 10% loan note for every 500 shares acquired; and

- a deferred cash payment of 11 cents per share acquired payable on 1 April 2007.

Parentis has only recorded the issue of the loan notes. The value of each Parentis share at the date of acquisition was 75 cents and Parentis has a cost of capital of 10% per annum.

The statement of financial positions at 31 March 2007 are shown below:

	Parentis		Offspring	
	$ million	$ million	$ million	$ million
Assets				
Property, plant and equipment (note (i))		640		340
Investments		120		Nil
Intellectual property (note (ii))		Nil		30
		760		370
Current assets (note (iii))		160		70
Total assets		920		440
Equity and liabilities				
Equity shares of 25 cents each		300		200
Retained earnings				
– 1 April 2006	210		120	
– year ended 31 March 2007	90	300	20	140
		600		340
Non-current liabilities				
10% loan notes		120		20
Current liabilities		200		80
Total equity and liabilities		920		440

The following information is relevant:

(i) At the date of acquisition the fair values of Offspring's net assets were approximately equal to their carrying amounts with the exception of its properties. These properties had a fair value of $40 million in excess of their carrying amounts which would create additional depreciation of $2 million in the post acquisition period to 31 March 2007. The fair values have not been reflected in Offspring's statement of financial position.

(ii) The intellectual property is a system of encryption designed for internet use. Offspring has been advised that government legislation (passed since acquisition) has now made this type of encryption illegal. Offspring will receive $10 million in compensation from the government.

(iii)   Offspring sold Parentis goods for $15 million in the post acquisition period. $5 million of these goods are included in the inventory of Parentis at 31 March 2007. The profit made by Offspring on these sales was $6 million.

(iv)   Parentis's policy is to value the non controlling interests using the fair value of the subsidiary's identifiable net assets, assessed as $125 million at acquisition.

Required:

Prepare the consolidated statement of financial position of Parentis as at 31 March 2007.

(Total: 20 marks)

375   **PLATEAU** *Walk in the footsteps of a top tutor*

On 1 October 2006 Plateau acquired 3 million equity shares in Savannah by an exchange of one share in Plateau for every two shares in Savannah plus $1.25 per acquired Savannah share in cash. The market price of each Plateau share at the date of acquisition was $6.

Only the cash consideration of the above investments has been recorded by Plateau. In addition $500,000 of professional costs relating to the acquisition of Savannah are also included in the cost of the investment.

The statement of financial positions of the companies at 30 September 2007 are:

	Plateau $000	Savannah $000
Non-current assets		
Property, plant and equipment	18,400	10,400
Investments in Savannah and Axle	13,250	Nil
Fair value through profit or loss investments	6,500	Nil
	38,150	10,400
Current assets		
Inventory	6,900	6,200
Trade receivables	2,800	1,300
Cash	400	200
Total assets	48,250	18,100
Equity and liabilities		
Equity shares of $1 each	10,000	4,000
Retained earnings – at 30 September 2006	16,000	6,500
– for year ended 30 September 2007	9,250	2,400
	35,250	12,900
Non-current liabilities	5,000	1,000
Current liabilities	8,000	4,200
Total equity and liabilities	48,250	18,100

The following information is relevant:

(i)   At the date of acquisition the fair values of Savannah's assets were equal to their carrying amounts with the exception of Savannah's land which had a fair value of $500,000 below its carrying amount; it was written down by this amount shortly after acquisition and has not changed in value since then.

(ii)   During the year ended 30 September 2007 Savannah sold goods to Plateau for $2.7 million. Savannah had marked up these goods by 50% on cost. Plateau had a third of the goods still in its inventory at 30 September 2007. (iii)

(iii)   Savannah's trade payable account (in the records of Plateau) of $700,000 does not agree with Plateau's trade receivable account (in the records of Savannah) due to cash in transit of $400,000 paid by Plateau.

(iv)   Plateau has a policy of valuing non-controlling interests at fair value at the date of acquisition. The fair value of the shares not owned by Plateau at acquisition was $3.25 million.

(v)   The fair value through profit or loss investments are included in Plateau's statement of financial position (above) at their fair value on 1 October 2006, but they have a fair value of $9 million at 30 September 2007.

(vi)   Plateau also acquired 30% of the 4 million equity shares of Axle at a cost of $7.50 per share in cash. Since acquisition, Axle have made profits of $5 million.

Required:

Prepare the consolidated statement of financial position for Plateau as at 30 September 2007.

(Total: 20 marks)

376 PATRONIC *Walk in the footsteps of a top tutor*

On 1 August 2007 Patronic purchased 18 million of a total of 24 million equity shares in Sardonic. The acquisition was through a share exchange of two shares in Patronic for every three shares in Sardonic. Both companies have shares with a par value of $1 each.

The market price of Patronic's shares at 1 August 2007 was $5.75 per share.

Patronic will also pay in cash on 31 July 2009 (two years after acquisition) $2.42 per acquired share of Sardonic. Patronic's cost of capital is 10% per annum.

The reserves of Sardonic on 1 April 2007 were $69 million.

Patronic has held an investment of 30% of the equity shares in Acerbic for many years. Acerbic made a profit of $6 million in the year.

The summarised statement of profit or loss for the three companies for the year ended 31 March 2008 are:

	Patronic	Sardonic
	$000	$000
Revenue	150,000	78,000
Cost of sales	(94,000)	(51,000)
Gross profit	56,000	27,000
Distribution costs	(7,400)	(3,000)
Administrative expenses	(12,500)	(6,000)
Finance costs (note (ii))	(2,000)	(900)
Profit before tax	34,100	17,100
Income tax expense	(10,400)	(3,600)
Profit for the period	23,700	13,500

The following information is relevant:

(i) The fair values of the net assets of Sardonic at the date of acquisition were equal to their carrying amounts with the exception of property and plant. Property and plant had fair values of $4.1 million and $2.4 million respectively in excess of their carrying amounts. The increase in the fair value of the property would create additional depreciation of $200,000 in the consolidated financial statements in the post acquisition period to 31 March 2008 and the plant had a remaining life of four years (straight-line depreciation) at the date of acquisition of Sardonic. All depreciation is treated as part of cost of sales.

The fair values have not been reflected in Sardonic's financial statements.

No fair value adjustments were required on the acquisition of Acerbic.

(ii) The finance costs of Patronic do not include the finance cost on the deferred consideration.

(iii) Prior to its acquisition, Sardonic had been a good customer of Patronic. In the year to 31 March 2008, Patronic sold goods at a selling price of $1.25 million per month to Sardonic both before and after its acquisition. Patronic made a profit of 20% on the cost of these sales. At 31 March 2008 Sardonic still held inventory of $3 million (at cost to Sardonic) of goods purchased in the post acquisition period from Patronic.

(iv) Patronic has a policy of valuing non-controlling interests using the fair value. An impairment test on the goodwill of Sardonic conducted on 31 March 2008 concluded that it should be written down by $2 million. The value of the investment in Acerbic was not impaired.

(v) All items are deemed to accrue evenly over the year.

Required:

(a) **Calculate the consideration paid on the acquisition of Sardonic at 1 August 2007.**

(3 marks)

(b) **Prepare the consolidated statement of profit or loss for the Patronic Group for the year ended 31 March 2008.** **(17 marks)**

(Total: 20 marks)

377 PEDANTIC

On 1 April 2008, Pedantic acquired 60% of the equity share capital of Sophistic in a share exchange of two shares in Pedantic for three shares in Sophistic. The issue of shares has not yet been recorded by Pedantic. At the date of acquisition shares in Pedantic had a market value of $6 each. Below are the summarised draft financial statements of both companies.

Statement of profit or loss for the year ended 30 September 2008

	Pedantic	Sophistic
	$000	$000
Revenue	85,000	42,000
Cost of sales	(63,000)	(32,000)
Gross profit	22,000	10,000
Operating expenses	(8,300)	(5,600)
Profit before tax	13,700	4,400
Income tax expense	(4,700)	(1,400)
Profit for the year	9,000	3,000

Statements of financial position as at 30 September 2008

	Pedantic	Sophistic
Assets		
Non-current assets		
Property, plant and equipment	40,600	12,600
Current assets	16,000	6,600
Total assets	56,600	19,200
Equity and liabilities		
Equity shares of $1 each	10,000	4,000
Retained earnings	35,400	6,500
	45,400	10,500
Non-current liabilities		
10% loan notes	3,000	4,000
Current liabilities	8,200	4,700
Total equity and liabilities	56,600	19,200

The following information is relevant:

(i)   At the date of acquisition, the fair values of Sophistic's assets were equal to their carrying amounts with the exception of an item of plant, which had a fair value of $2 million in excess of its carrying amount. It had a remaining life of five years at that date [straight-line depreciation is used]. Sophistic has not adjusted the carrying amount of its plant as a result of the fair value exercise.

(ii)   Sales from Sophistic to Pedantic in the post acquisition period were $8 million. Sophistic made a mark up on cost of 40% on these sales. Pedantic had sold $5.2 million (at cost to Pedantic) of these goods by 30 September 2008.

(iii) Other than where indicated, statement of profit or loss items are deemed to accrue evenly on a time basis.

(iv)   Sophistic's trade receivables at 30 September 2008 include $600,000 due from Pedantic which did not agree with Pedantic's corresponding trade payable. This was due to cash in transit of $200,000 from Pedantic to Sophistic. Both companies have positive bank balances.

(v)   Pedantic has a policy of accounting for any non-controlling interest at fair value. The fair value of the non-controlling interest at the acquisition date was $5.9 million. Consolidated goodwill was impaired by $1 million at 30 September 2008.

Required:

(a)   **Prepare the consolidated statement of profit or loss for Pedantic for the year ended 30 September 2008.**   **(7 marks)**

(b)   **Prepare the consolidated statement of financial position for Pedantic as at 30 September 2008.**   **(13 marks)**

                                                                            (Total: 20 marks)

378   PANDAR   *Walk in the footsteps of a top tutor*

On 1 April 2009 Pandar purchased 80% of the equity shares in Salva. On the same date Pandar acquired 40% of the 40 million equity shares in Ambra paying $2 per share.

The statement of profit or loss for the year ended 30 September 2009 are:

	Pandar	Salva	Ambra
	$000	$000	$000
Revenue	210,000	150,000	50,000
Cost of sales	(126,000)	(100,000)	(40,000)
Gross profit	84,000	50,000	10,000
Distribution costs	(11,200)	(7,000)	(5,000)
Administrative expenses	(18,300)	(9,000)	(11,000)
Investment income (interest and dividends)	9,500		
Finance costs	(1,800)	(3,000)	Nil
Profit (loss) before tax	62,200	31,000	(6,000)
Income tax (expense) relief	(15,000)	(10,000)	1,000
Profit (loss) for the year	47,200	21,000	(5,000)

The following information is relevant:

(i)   The fair values of the net assets of Salva at the date of acquisition were equal to their carrying amounts with the exception of an item of plant which had a carrying amount of $12 million and a fair value of $17 million. This plant had a remaining life of five years (straight-line depreciation) at the date of acquisition of Salva. All depreciation is charged to cost of sales.

The fair value of the plant has not been reflected in Salva's financial statements.

No fair value adjustments were required on the acquisition of the investment in Ambra.

(ii) Immediately after its acquisition of Salva, Pandar invested $50 million in an 8% loan note from Salva. All interest accruing to 30 September 2009 has been accounted for by both companies. Salva also has other loans in issue at 30 September 2009.

(iii) Salva paid a dividend of $8 million during the year.

(iv) After the acquisition, Pandar sold goods to Salva for $15 million on which Pandar made a gross profit of 20%. Salva had one third of these goods still in its inventory at 30 September 2009. Pandar also sold goods to Ambra for $6 million, making the same margin. Ambra had half of these goods still in inventory at 30 September 2009.

(v)   The non-controlling interest in Salva is to be valued at its (full) fair value at the date of acquisition.

(vi) The goodwill of Salva has been impaired by $2 million at 30 September 2009. Due to its losses, the value of Pandar's investment in Ambra has been impaired by $3 million at 30 September 2009.

(vii) All items in the above statement of profit or loss are deemed to accrue evenly over the year unless otherwise indicated.

Required:

(a)   **Calculate the carrying amount of the investment in Ambra to be included within the consolidated statement of financial position as at 30 September 2009. (4 marks)**

(b)   **Prepare the consolidated statement of profit or loss for the Pandar Group for the year ended 30 September 2009.** **(16 marks)**

(Total: 20 marks)

379   PICANT

On 1 April 2009 Picant acquired 75% of Sander's equity shares in a share exchange of three shares in Picant for every two shares in Sander. The market prices of Picant's and Sander's shares at the date of acquisition were $3.20 and $4.50 respectively.

In addition to this Picant agreed to pay a further amount on 1 April 2010 that was contingent upon the post-acquisition performance of Sander. At the date of acquisition Picant assessed the fair value of this contingent consideration at $4.2 million, but by 31 March 2010 it was clear that the actual amount to be paid would be only $2.7 million (ignore discounting). Picant has recorded the share exchange and provided for the initial estimate of $4.2 million for the contingent consideration.

On 1 October 2009 Picant also acquired 40% of the equity shares of Adler paying $4 in cash per acquired share and issuing at par one $100 7% loan note for every 50 shares acquired in Adler. This consideration has also been recorded by Picant.

Picant has no other investments.

The summarised statements of financial position of the three companies at 31 March 2010 are:

	Picant $000	Sander $000	Adler $000
Assets			
Non-current assets			
Property, plant and equipment	37,500	24,500	21,000
Investments	45,000	nil	nil
	82,500	24,500	21,000
Current assets			
Inventory	10,000	9,000	5,000
Trade receivables	6,500	1,500	3,000
Total assets	99,000	35,000	29,000
Equity			
Equity shares of $1 each	25,000	8,000	5,000
Share premium	19,800	nil	nil
Retained earnings – at 1 April 2009	16,200	16,500	15,000
– for the year ended 31 March 2010	11,000	1,000	6,000
	72,000	25,500	26,000
Non-current liabilities			
7% loan notes	14,500	2,000	nil
Current liabilities			
Contingent consideration	4,200	nil	nil
Other current liabilities	8,300	7,500	3,000
Total equity and liabilities	99,000	35,000	29,000

The following information is relevant:

(i)   At the date of acquisition the fair values of Sander's property, plant and equipment was equal to its carrying amount with the exception of Sander's factory which had a fair value of $2 million above its carrying amount. Sander has not adjusted the carrying amount of the factory as a result of the fair value exercise. This requires additional annual depreciation of $100,000 in the consolidated financial statements in the post-acquisition period.

Also at the date of acquisition, Sander had an intangible asset of $500,000 for software in its statement of financial position. Picant's directors believed the software to have no recoverable value at the date of acquisition and Sander wrote it off shortly after its acquisition.

(ii)   At 31 March 2010 Picant's current account with Sander was $3.4 million (debit). This did not agree with the equivalent balance in Sander's books due to some goods-in-transit invoiced at $1.8 million that were sent by Picant on 28 March 2010, but had not been received by Sander until after the year end. Picant sold all these goods at cost plus 50%.

(iii)   Picant's policy is to value the non-controlling interest at fair value at the date of acquisition. For this purpose Sander's share price at that date can be deemed to be representative of the fair value of the shares held by the non-controlling interest.

(iv) Impairment tests were carried out on 31 March 2010 which concluded that the value of the investment in Adler was not impaired but, due to poor trading performance, consolidated goodwill was impaired by $3.8 million.

(v) Assume all profits accrue evenly through the year.

Required:

(a) **Prepare the consolidated statement of financial position for Picant as at 31 March 2010.** **(15 marks)**

(b) At 31 March 2010 the other equity shares (60%) in Adler were owned by many separate investors. Shortly after this date Spekulate (a company unrelated to Picant) accumulated a 60% interest in Adler by buying shares from the other shareholders. In May 2010 a meeting of the board of directors of Adler was held at which Picant lost its seat on Adler's board.

Required:

Explain, with reasons, the accounting treatment Picant should adopt for its investment in Adler when it prepares its financial statements for the year ending 31 March 2011. **(5 marks)**

(Total: 20 marks)

380 PRODIGAL

On 1 October 2010 Prodigal purchased 75% of the equity shares in Sentinel. The summarised statements of profit or loss and other comprehensive income for the two companies for the year ended 31 March 2011 are:

	Prodigal	Sentinel
	$000	$000
Revenue	450,000	240,000
Cost of sales	(260,000)	(110,000)
Gross profit	190,000	130,000
Distribution costs	(23,600)	(12,000)
Administrative expenses	(27,000)	(23,000)
Finance costs	(1,500)	(1,200)
Profit before tax	137,900	93,800
Income tax expense	(48,000)	(27,800)
Profit for the year	89,900	66,000
Other comprehensive income		
Gain on revaluation of land (note (i))	2,500	1,000
Total comprehensive income	92,400	67,000

The following extracts for the equity of the companies at **1 April 2010** (before acquisition) is available:

	$000	$000
Revaluation surplus (land)	8,400	nil
Retained earnings	90,000	125,000

The following information is relevant:

(i) Prodigal's policy is to revalue the group's land to market value at the end of each accounting period. Prior to its acquisition Sentinel's land had been valued at historical cost. During the post acquisition period Sentinel's land had increased in value over its value at the date of acquisition by $1 million. Sentinel has recognised the revaluation within its own financial statements.

(ii) Immediately after the acquisition of Sentinel on 1 October 2010, Prodigal transferred an item of plant with a carrying amount of $4 million to Sentinel at an agreed value of $5 million. At this date the plant had a remaining life of two and half years. Prodigal had included the profit on this transfer as a reduction in its depreciation costs. All depreciation is charged to cost of sales.

(iii) After the acquisition Sentinel sold goods to Prodigal for $40 million. These goods had cost Sentinel $30 million. $12 million of the goods sold remained in Prodigal's closing inventory.

(iv) Prodigal's policy is to value the non-controlling interest of Sentinel at the date of acquisition at its fair value which the directors determined to be $100 million.

(v) The goodwill of Sentinel has not suffered any impairment.

(vi) All items in the above statements of comprehensive income are deemed to accrue evenly over the year unless otherwise indicated.

Required:

(i) **Prepare the consolidated statement of profit or loss and other comprehensive income of Prodigal for the year ended 31 March 2011**

(15 marks)

(ii) **Prepare extracts of the equity section (including the non-controlling interest) of the consolidated statement of financial position of Prodigal as at 31 March 2011.**

(5 marks)

Note: you are NOT required to calculate consolidated goodwill or produce the statement of changes in equity.

(Total: 20 marks)

381 PALADIN

On 1 October 2010, Paladin secured a majority equity shareholding in Saracen on the following terms:

an immediate payment of $4 per share on 1 October 2010

and a further amount deferred until 1 October 2011 of $5.4 million.

The immediate payment has been recorded in Paladin's financial statements, but the deferred payment has not been recorded. Paladin's cost of capital is 8% per annum.

On 1 February 2011, Paladin also acquired 25% of the equity shares of Augusta paying $10 million in cash. Augusta made a profit of $1.2 million for the year ended 30 September 2011.

The summarised statements of financial position of the three companies at 30 September 2011 are:

	Paladin	Saracen
Assets	$000	$000
Non-current assets		
Property, plant and equipment	40,000	31,000
Intangible assets	7,500	
Investments – Saracen (8 million shares at $4 each)	32,000	
– Augusta	10,000	nil
	———	———
	89,500	31,000
Current assets	22,000	13,700
	———	———
Total assets	111,500	44,700
	———	———
Equity and liabilities		
Equity		
Equity shares of $1 each	50,000	10,000
Retained earnings – at 1 October 2010	25,700	12,000
– for year ended 30 September 2011	9,200	6,000
	———	———
	84,900	28,000
Non-current liabilities		
Deferred tax	15,000	8,000
Current liabilities	11,600	8,700
	———	———
Total equity and liabilities	111,500	44,700
	———	———

The following information is relevant:

(i) Paladin's policy is to value the non-controlling interest at fair value at the date of acquisition. For this purpose the directors of Paladin considered a share price for Saracen of $3.50 per share to be appropriate.

(ii) At the date of acquisition, the fair values of Saracen's property, plant and equipment was equal to its carrying amount with the exception of Saracen's plant which had a fair value of $4 million above its carrying amount. At that date the plant had a remaining life of four years. Saracen uses straight-line depreciation for plant assuming a nil residual value.

Also at the date of acquisition, Paladin valued Saracen's customer relationships as an intangible asset at fair value of $3 million. Saracen has not accounted for this asset. Trading relationships with Saracen's customers last on average for six years.

(iii) At 30 September 2011, Saracen's inventory included goods bought from Paladin (at cost to Saracen) of $2.6 million. Paladin had marked up these goods by 30% on cost.

(iv) Impairment tests were carried out on 30 September 2011 which concluded that consolidated goodwill was not impaired, but, due to disappointing earnings, the value of the investment in Augusta was impaired by $2.5 million.

(v) Assume all profits accrue evenly through the year.

Required:

(a) **Prepare the consolidated statement of financial position for Paladin as at 30 September 2011.** (Total: 20 marks)

382 PYRAMID

On 1 April 2011, Pyramid acquired 80% of Square's equity shares by means of an immediate share exchange and a cash payment of 88 cents per acquired share, deferred until 1 April 2012. Pyramid has recorded the share exchange, but not the cash consideration. Pyramid's cost of capital is 10% per annum.

The summarised statements of financial position of the two companies as at 31 March 2012 are:

	Pyramid	Square
Assets	$000	$000
Non-current assets		
Property, plant and equipment	38,100	28,500
Investments – Square	24,000	
– Other equity (note (iii))	2,000	nil
	64,100	28,500
Current assets		
Inventory (note (ii))	13,900	10,400
Trade receivables (note (ii))	11,400	5,500
Bank (note (ii))	9,400	600
Total assets	98,800	45,000

Equity shares of $1 each	25,000	10,000
Share premium	17,600	nil
Retained earnings – at 1 April 2011	16,200	18,000
– for year ended 31 March 2012	14,000	8,000
	72,800	36,000
Non-current liabilities (note (i))	16,500	4,000
Current liabilities (note (ii))	9,500	5,000
Total equity and liabilities	98,800	45,000

The following information is relevant:

(i) At the date of acquisition, Pyramid conducted a fair value exercise on Square's net assets which were equal to their carrying amounts with the following exceptions:

- An item of plant had a fair value of $3 million above its carrying amount. At the date of acquisition it had a remaining life of five years. Ignore deferred tax relating to this fair value.

- Square had an unrecorded deferred tax liability of $1 million, which was unchanged as at 31 March 2012.

Pyramid's policy is to value the non-controlling interest at fair value at the date of acquisition. For this purpose a share price for Square of $3.50 each is representative of the fair value of the shares held by the non-controlling interest.

(ii) Pyramid sells goods to Square at cost plus 50%. Below is a summary of the recorded activities for the year ended 31 March 2012 and balances as at 31 March 2012:

	Pyramid	Square
	$000	$000
Sales to Square	16,000	
Purchases from Pyramid		14,500
Included in Pyramid's receivables	4,400	
Included in Square's payables		1,700

On 26 March 2012, Pyramid sold and despatched goods to Square, which Square did not record until they were received on 2 April 2012. Square's inventory was counted on 31 March 2012 and does not include any goods purchased from Pyramid.

On 27 March 2012, Square remitted to Pyramid a cash payment which was not received by Pyramid until 4 April 2012. This payment accounted for the remaining difference on the current accounts.

(iii) The other equity investments of Pyramid are carried at their fair values on 1 April 2011. At 31 March 2012, these had increased to $2.8 million.

Required:

Prepare the consolidated statement of financial position for Pyramid as at 31 March 2012. **(Total: 20 marks)**

383 VIAGEM

 Timed question with Online tutor debrief

On 1 January 2012, Viagem acquired 90% of the equity share capital of Greca in a share exchange in which Viagem issued two new shares for every three shares it acquired in Greca. Additionally, on 31 December 2012, Viagem will pay the shareholders of Greca $1.76 per share acquired. Viagem's cost of capital is 10% per annum. The deferred consideration has not yet been recorded by Viagem.

At the date of acquisition, shares in Viagem and Greca had a stock market value of $6.50 and $2.50 each, respectively.

Statements of profit or loss for the year ended 30 September 2012

	Viagem	Greca
	$000	$000
Revenue	64,600	38,000
Cost of sales	(51,200)	(26,000)
Gross profit	13,400	12,000
Distribution costs	(1,600)	(1,800)
Administrative expenses	(3,800)	(2,400)
Investment income	500	nil
Finance costs	(420)	nil
Profit before tax	8,080	7,800
Income tax expense	(2,800)	(1,600)
Profit for the year	5,280	6,200
Equity as at 1 October 2011		
Equity shares of $1 each	30,000	10,000
Retained earnings	54,000	35,000

The following information is relevant:

(i) At the date of acquisition, the fair values of Greca's assets were equal to their carrying amounts with the exception of two items:

- An item of plant had a fair value of $1.8 million above its carrying amount. The remaining life of the plant at the date of acquisition was three years. Depreciation is charged to cost of sales.

- Greca had a contingent liability which Viagem estimated to have a fair value of $450,000. This has not changed as at 30 September 2012.

Greca has not incorporated these fair value changes into its financial statements.

(ii) Viagem's policy is to value the non-controlling interest at fair value at the date of acquisition. For this purpose, Greca's share price at that date can be deemed to be representative of the fair value of the shares held by the non-controlling interest.

(iii) Sales from Viagem to Greca throughout the year ended 30 September 2012 had consistently been $800,000 per month. Viagem made a mark-up on cost of 25% on these sales. Greca had $1.5 million of these goods in inventory as at 30 September 2012.

(iv) Viagem's investment income is a dividend received from its investment in a 40% owned associate which it has held for several years. The underlying earnings for the associate for the year ended 30 September 2012 were $2 million.

(v) Although Greca has been profitable since its acquisition by Viagem, the market for Greca's products has been badly hit in recent months and Viagem has calculated that the goodwill has been impaired by $2 million as at 30 September 2012.

Required:

(a)   Calculate the consolidated goodwill at the date of acquisition of Greca.   (7 marks)

(b)   Prepare the consolidated statement of profit or loss for Viagem for the year ended 30 September 2012.   (13 marks)

(Total: 20 marks)

 Calculate your allowed time, allocate the time to the separate parts

384   PARADIGM

On 1 October 2012, Paradigm acquired 75% of Strata's equity shares by means of a share exchange of two new shares in Paradigm for every five acquired shares in Strata. In addition, Paradigm issued to the shareholders of Strata a $100 10% loan note for every 1,000 shares it acquired in Strata. Paradigm has not recorded any of the purchase consideration, although it does have other 10% loan notes already in issue.

The market value of Paradigm's shares at 1 October 2012 was $2 each.

The summarised statements of financial position of the two companies as at 31 March 2013 are:

	Paradigm	Strata
	$000	$000
Assets		
Non-current assets		
Property, plant and equipment	47,400	25,500
Financial asset: equity investments (notes (i) and (iii))	7,500	3,200
	———	———
	54,900	28,700
Current assets		
Inventory (note (ii))	20,400	8,400
Trade receivables	14,800	9,000
Bank	2,100	nil
	———	———
Total assets	92,200	46,100
	———	———

Equity and liabilities

Equity

Equity shares of $1 each		40,000	20,000
Retained earnings/(losses)	– at 1 April 2012	19,200	(4,000)
	– for year ended 31 March 2013	7,400	8,000
		66,600	24,000
Non-current liabilities			
10% loan notes		8,000	nil
Current liabilities			
Trade payables		17,600	13,000
Bank overdraft		nil	9,100
Total equity and liabilities		92,200	46,100

The following information is relevant:

(i)   At the date of acquisition, Strata produced a draft statement of profit or loss which showed it had made a net loss after tax of $2 million at that date. Paradigm accepted this figure as the basis for calculating the pre- and post-acquisition split of Strata's profit for the year ended 31 March 2013.

Also at the date of acquisition, Paradigm conducted a fair value exercise on Strata's net assets which were equal to their carrying amounts (including Strata's financial asset equity investments) with the exception of an item of plant which had a fair value of $3 million **below** its carrying amount. The plant had a remaining economic life of three years at 1 October 2012.

Paradigm's policy is to value the non-controlling interest at fair value at the date of acquisition. For this purpose, a share price for Strata of $1.20 each is representative of the fair value of the shares held by the non-controlling interest.

(ii)   Each month since acquisition, Paradigm's sales to Strata were consistently $4.6 million. Paradigm had marked these up by 15% on cost. Strata had one month's supply ($4.6 million) of these goods in inventory at 31 March 2013. Paradigm's normal mark-up (to third party customers) is 40%.

(iii)   The financial asset equity investments of Paradigm and Strata are carried at their fair values as at 1 April 2012. As at 31 March 2013, these had fair values of $7.1 million and $3.9 million respectively.

(iv)   There were no impairment losses within the group during the year ended 31 March 2013.

Required:

(a)   **Prepare the consolidated statement of financial position for Paradigm as at 31 March 2013.**   **(15 marks)**

(b)   A financial assistant has observed that the fair value exercise means that a subsidiary's net assets are included at acquisition at their fair (current) values in the consolidated statement of financial position. The assistant believes that it is inconsistent to aggregate the subsidiary's net assets with those of the parent because most of the parent's assets are carried at historical cost.

Required:

Comment on the assistant's observation and explain why the net assets of acquired subsidiaries are consolidated at acquisition at their fair values. **(5 marks)**

(Total: 20 marks)

385 POLESTAR

On 1 April 2013, Polestar acquired 75% of Southstar. Southstar had been experiencing difficult trading conditions and making significant losses. In allowing for Southstar's difficulties, Polestar made an immediate cash payment of only $1.50 per share. In addition, Polestar will pay a further amount in cash on 30 September 2014 if Southstar returns to profitability by that date. The fair value of this contingent consideration at the date of acquisition was estimated to be $1.8 million, but at 30 September 2013 in the light of continuing losses, its value was estimated at only $1.5 million. The contingent consideration has not been recorded by Polestar. Overall, the directors of Polestar expect the acquisition to be a bargain purchase leading to negative goodwill.

Below are the summarised draft financial statements of both companies.

Statements of profit or loss for the year ended 30 September 2013

	Polestar	Southstar
	$000	$000
Revenue	110,000	66,000
Cost of sales	(88,000)	(67,200)
Gross profit (loss)	22,000	(1,200)
Operating expenses	(8,500)	(4,400)
Profit (loss) before tax	13,500	(5,600)
Income tax (expense)/relief	(3,500)	1,000
Profit (loss) for the year	10,000	(4,600)

Statements of financial position as at 30 September 2013

Assets
Non-current assets

	Polestar	Southstar
Property, plant and equipment	41,000	21,000
Investments	13,500	
Current assets	19,000	4,800
Total assets	73,500	25,800

CONSTRUCTED RESPONSE QUESTIONS – SECTION C : **SECTION 3**

Equity and liabilities

Equity shares of 50 cents each	30,000	6,000
Retained earnings	28,500	12,000
	58,500	18,000
Current liabilities	15,000	7,800
Total equity and liabilities	73,500	25,800

The following information is relevant:

(i)   At the date of acquisition, the fair values of Southstar's assets were equal to their carrying amounts with the exception of a leased property. This had a fair value of $2 million above its carrying amount and a remaining lease term of 10 years at that date. All depreciation is included in cost of sales.

(ii)   Polestar transferred raw materials at their cost of $4 million to Southstar in June 2013. Southstar processed all of these materials incurring additional direct costs of $1.4 million and sold them back to Polestar in August 2013 for $9 million. At 30 September 2013 Polestar had $1.5 million of these goods still in inventory. There were no other intra-group sales.

(iii)   Polestar's policy is to value the non-controlling interest at fair value at the date of acquisition. This was deemed to be $3.6 million.

(iv)   All items in the above statements of profit or loss are deemed to accrue evenly over the year unless otherwise indicated.

Required:

(a)   **Prepare the consolidated statement of profit or loss for Polestar for the year ended 30 September 2013.**   **(11 marks)**

(b)   **Prepare the consolidated statement of financial position for Polestar as at 30 September 2013.**   **(9 marks)**

(Total: 20 marks)

KAPLAN PUBLISHING   161

386 PENKETH

On 1 October 2013, Penketh acquired 90 million of Sphere's 150 million $0.50 equity shares. As part of the consideration, Penketh will pay $1.54 cash on 30 September 2014 for each share acquired. Penketh's finance cost is 10% per annum. Sphere's share price as at 1 October 2013 was $1.25. The statements of profit or loss and other comprehensive income for the year ended 31 March 2014 are:

	Penketh	Sphere
	$000	$000
Revenue	620,000	310,000
Cost of sales	(400,000)	(150,000)
Gross profit	220,000	160,000
Distribution costs	(40,000)	(20,000)
Administrative expenses	(36,000)	(25,000)
Investment income	5,000	1,600
Finance costs	(2,000)	(5,600)
Profit before tax	147,000	111,000
Income tax expense	(45,000)	(31,000)
Profit for the year	102,000	80,000
Other comprehensive income		
Gain/(loss) on revaluation of land (note (ii))	(2,200)	1,000
Total comprehensive income for the year	99,800	81,000

The following information is relevant:

(i)   A fair value exercise on 1 October 2013 concluded that the carrying amounts of Sphere's net assets were equal to their fair values with the following exceptions:

- Plant with a remaining life of two years had a fair value of $6 million in excess of its carrying amount. Plant depreciation is charged to cost of sales.

- Penketh placed a value of $5 million on Sphere's good relationships with its customers. Penketh expected, on average, a customer relationship to last for a further five years. Amortisation is charged to administrative expenses.

(ii)   Sphere's land increased by $1 million since the acquisition.

(iii)   After the acquisition Penketh sold goods to Sphere for $20 million at a 25% mark-up. Sphere had one fifth of these goods still in inventory at 31 March 2014.

(iv)   All items accrue evenly over the year unless otherwise indicated. Penketh had retained earnings of $70 million at 1 April 2013.

(v)   Penketh measures the non-controlling interest at fair value at the date of acquisition. To calculate fair value, the share price of Sphere should be used.

Required:

(a) Calculate goodwill arising on the acquisition of Penketh as at 1 October 2013.

(5 marks)

(b) Prepare the consolidated statement of profit or loss and other comprehensive income of Penketh for the year ended 31 March 2014. **(15 marks)**

(Total: 20 marks)

387 PLASTIK

 Timed question with Online tutor debrief

On 1 January 2014, Plastik acquired 80% of the equity share capital of Subtrak. The consideration was satisfied by a share exchange of two shares in Plastik for every three acquired shares in Subtrak. At the date of acquisition, shares in Plastik and Subtrak had a market value of $3 and $2.50 each respectively. Plastik will also pay cash consideration of 27.5 cents on 1 January 2015 for each acquired share in Subtrak. Plastik has a cost of capital of 10% per annum. None of the consideration has been recorded by Plastik.

Below are the extracts from the draft financial statements of both companies.

Extracts from the statements of profit or loss and other comprehensive income for the year ended 30 September 2014

	Plastik	Subtrak
	$000	$000
Revenue	62,600	30,000
Cost of sales	(45,800)	(24,000)
Finance costs	(200)	(nil)

Statements of financial position as at 30 September 2014

Assets	Plastik	Subtrak
Non-current assets	$000	$000
Property, plant and equipment	18,700	13,900
Investments: 10% loan note from Subtrak (note (ii))	1,000	nil
	19,700	13,900
Current assets	9,000	4,000
Total assets	28,700	17,900

Equity and liabilities

Equity

Equity shares of $1 each	10,000	9,000
Revaluation surplus (note (i))	2,000	nil
Retained earnings	6,300	3,500
	18,300	12,500

Non-current liabilities

10% loan notes (note (ii))	2,500	1,000

Current liabilities

Trade payables (note (iv))	7,900	4,400
Total equity and liabilities	28,700	17,900

The following information is relevant:

(i) At the date of acquisition, the fair values of Subtrak's assets and liabilities were equal to their carrying amounts with the exception of Subtrak's property which had a fair value of $4 million above its carrying amount. For consolidation purposes, this led to an increase in depreciation charges (in cost of sales) of $100,000 in the post-acquisition period to 30 September 2014. Subtrak has not incorporated the fair value property increase into its entity financial statements.

The policy of the Plastik group is to revalue all properties to fair value at each year end. On 30 September 2014, the increase in Plastik's property has already been recorded, however, a further increase of $600,000 in the value of Subtrak's property since its value at acquisition and 30 September 2014 has not been recorded.

(ii) On 30 September 2014, Plastik accepted a $1 million 10% loan note from Subtrak.

(iii) Sales from Plastik to Subtrak throughout the year ended 30 September 2014 had consistently been $300,000 per month. Plastik made a mark-up on cost of 25% on all these sales. $600,000 (at cost to Subtrak) of Subtrak's inventory at 30 September 2014 had been supplied by Plastik in the post-acquisition period.

(iv) Plastik had a trade receivable balance owing from Subtrak of $1.2 million as at 30 September 2014. This differed to the equivalent trade payable of Subtrak due to a payment by Subtrak of $400,000 made in September 2014 which did not clear Plastik's bank account until 4 October 2014. Both companies have overdrafts rather than positive cash balances.

(v) Plastik's policy is to value the non-controlling interest at fair value at the date of acquisition. For this purpose Subtrak's share price at that date can be deemed to be representative of the fair value of the shares held by the non-controlling interest.

(vi) Assume, except where indicated otherwise, that all items of income and expenditure accrue evenly throughout the year. Subtrak's profit for the year ended 30 September 2014 was $2 million.

Required:

(a) **Prepare extracts from Plastik's consolidated statement of profit or loss for the year ended 30 September 2014, for:**

(i) revenue

(ii) cost of sales

(iii) finance costs (5 marks)

(b) **Prepare the consolidated statement of financial position for Plastik as at 30 September 2014.** (15 marks)

(Total: 20 marks)

 Calculate your allowed time, allocate the time to the separate parts

388 BYCOMB

On 1 July 2014 Bycomb acquired 80% of Cyclip's equity shares on the following terms:

- a share exchange of two shares in Bycomb for every three shares acquired in Cyclip; and

- a cash payment due on 30 June 2015 of $1.54 per share acquired (Bycomb's cost of capital is 10% per annum).

At the date of acquisition, shares in Bycomb and Cyclip had a stock market value of $3.00 and $2.50 each respectively.

Statements of profit or loss for the year ended 31 March 2015:

	Bycomb	Cyclip
	$000	$000
Revenue	24,200	10,800
Cost of sales	(17,800)	(6,800)
Gross profit	6,400	4,000
Distribution costs	(500)	(340)
Administrative expenses	(800)	(360)
Finance costs	(400)	(300)
Profit before tax	4,700	3,000
Income tax expense	(1,700)	(600)
Profit for the year	3,000	2,400

Equity in the separate financial statements of Cyclip as at **1 April 2014**:

	$000
Equity	
Equity shares of $1 each	12,000
Retained earnings	13,500

The following information is also relevant:

(i) At the date of acquisition, the fair values of Cyclip's assets were equal to their carrying amounts with the exception of an item of plant which had a fair value of $720,000 above its carrying amount. The remaining life of the plant at the date of acquisition was 18 months. Depreciation is charged to cost of sales.

(ii) On 1 April 2014, Cyclip commenced the construction of a new production facility, financing this by a bank loan. Cyclip has followed the local GAAP in the country where it operates which prohibits the capitalisation of interest. Bycomb has calculated that, in accordance with IAS 23 Borrowing Costs, interest of $100,000 (which accrued evenly throughout the year) would have been capitalised at 31 March 2015. The production facility is still under construction as at 31 March 2015.

(iii) Sales from Bycomb to Cyclip in the post-acquisition period were $3 million at a mark-up on cost of 20%. Cyclip had $420,000 of these goods in inventory as at 31 March 2015.

(iv) Bycomb's policy is to value the non-controlling interest at fair value at the date of acquisition. For this purpose Cyclip's share price at that date can be deemed to be representative of the fair value of the shares held by the non-controlling interest.

(v) On 31 March 2015, Bycomb carried out an impairment review which identified that the goodwill on the acquisition of Cyclip was impaired by $500,000. Impaired goodwill is charged to cost of sales.

Required:

(a) **Calculate the consolidated goodwill at the date of acquisition of Cyclip.**   **(6 marks)**

(b) **Prepare extracts from Bycomb's consolidated statement of profit or loss for the year ended 31 March 2015, for:**

(i) **revenue**

(ii) **cost of sales**

(iii) **finance costs**

(iv) **profit or loss attributable to the non-controlling interest.**

The following mark allocation is provided as guidance for this requirement:

(i) **1 mark**

(ii) **3 marks**

(iii) **2½ marks**

(iv) **2½ marks**   **(9 marks)**

(c) IFRS 3 *Business combinations* permits a non-controlling interest at the date of acquisition to be valued by one of two methods:

(i)   at its proportionate share of the subsidiary's identifiable net assets; or

(ii)   at its fair value (usually determined by the directors of the parent company).

Required:

Explain the difference that the accounting treatment of these alternative methods could have on the consolidated financial statements, including where consolidated goodwill may be impaired. **(5 marks)**

(Total: 20 marks)

389 PALISTAR

On 1 January 2015, Palistar acquired 75% of Stretcher's equity shares by means of an immediate share exchange of two shares in Palistar for five shares in Stretcher. The fair value of Palistar and Stretcher's shares on 1 January 2015 were $4.00 and $3.00 respectively. In addition to the share exchange, Palistar will make a cash payment of $1.32 per acquired share, deferred until 1 January 2016. Palistar has not recorded any of the consideration for Stretcher in its financial statements. Palistar's cost of capital is 10% per annum.

The summarised statements of financial position of the two companies as at 30 June 2015 are:

	Palistar	Stretcher
	$000	$000
Assets		
Non-current assets (note (ii))		
Property, plant and equipment	55,000	28,600
Financial asset equity investments (note (v))	11,500	6,000
	66,500	34,600
Current assets		
Inventory (note (iv))	17,000	15,400
Trade receivables (note (iv))	14,300	10,500
Bank	2,200	1,600
	33,500	27,500
Total assets	100,000	62,100

Equity and liabilities		
Equity		
Equity shares of $1 each	20,000	20,000
Other component of equity	4,000	nil
Retained earnings – at 1 July 2014	26,200	14,000
– for year ended 30 June 2015	24,000	10,000
	74,200	44,000
Current liabilities (note (iv))	25,800	18,100
Total equity and liabilities	100,000	62,100

The following information is relevant:

(i) Stretcher's business is seasonal and 60% of its annual profit is made in the period 1 January to 30 June each year.

(ii) At the date of acquisition, the fair value of Stretcher's net assets was equal to their carrying amounts with the following exceptions:

The fair value of Stretcher's investments was $7 million (see also note (v)).

Stretcher owned the rights to a popular mobile (cell) phone game. At the date of acquisition, a specialist valuer estimated that the rights were worth $12 million and had an estimated remaining life of five years.

(iii) Following an impairment review, consolidated goodwill is to be written down by $3 million as at 30 June 2015.

(iv) Palistar sells goods to Stretcher at cost plus 30%. Stretcher had $1.8 million of goods in its inventory at 30 June 2015 which had been supplied by Palistar. In addition, on 28 June 2015, Palistar processed the sale of $800,000 of goods to Stretcher, which Stretcher did not account for until their receipt on 2 July 2015. The in-transit reconciliation should be achieved by assuming the transaction had been recorded in the books of Stretcher before the year end. At 30 June 2015, Palistar had a trade receivable balance of $2.4 million due from Stretcher which differed to the equivalent balance in Stretcher's books due to the sale made on 28 June 2015.

(v) At 30 June 2015, the fair values of the financial asset equity investments of Palistar and Stretcher were $13.2 million and $7.9 million respectively.

(vi) Palistar's policy is to value the non-controlling interest at fair value at the date of acquisition. At 1 January 2015, this was valued at $15 million.

Required:

Prepare the consolidated statement of financial position for Palistar as at 30 June 2015.

(Total: 20 marks)

ANALYSING FINANCIAL STATEMENTS

390 HARDY   *Walk in the footsteps of a top tutor*

Hardy is a public listed manufacturing company. Its summarised financial statements for the year ended 30 September 2010 (and 2009 comparatives are:

Statements of profit or loss for the year ended 30 September:

	2010	2009
	$000	$000
Revenue	29,500	36,000
Cost of sales	(25,500)	(26,000)
Gross profit	4,000	10,000
Distribution costs	(1,050)	(800)
Administrative expenses	(4,900)	(3,900)
Investment income	50	200
Finance costs	(600)	(500)
Profit (loss) before taxation	(2,500)	5,000
Income tax (expense) relief	400	(1,500)
Profit (loss) for the year	(2,100)	3,500

Statements of financial position as at 30 September:

	2010		2009	
	$000	$000	$000	$000
Assets				
Non-current assets				
Property, plant and equipment		17,600		24,500
Investments at fair value through profit or loss		2,400		4,000
		20,000		28,500
Current assets				
Inventory and work-in-progress	2,200		1,900	
Trade receivables	2,200		2,800	
Tax asset	600		nil	
Bank	1,200	6,200	100	4,800
Total assets		26,200		33,300

Equity and liabilities			
Equity			
Equity shares of $1 each		13,000	12,000
Share premium		1,000	nil
Revaluation surplus		nil	4,500
Retained earnings		3,600	6,500
		17,600	23,000
Non-current liabilities			
Bank loan		4,000	5,000
Deferred tax		1,200	700
Current liabilities			
Trade payables	3,400		2,800
Current tax payable	nil	3,400	1,800 4,600
Total equity and liabilities		26,200	33,300

The following information has been obtained from the Chairman's Statement and the notes to the financial statements:

'Market conditions during the year ended 30 September 2010 proved very challenging due largely to difficulties in the global economy as a result of a sharp recession which has led to steep falls in share prices and property values. Hardy has not been immune from these effects and our properties have suffered impairment losses of $6 million in the year.'

The excess of these losses over previous surpluses has led to a charge to cost of sales of $1.5 million in addition to the normal depreciation charge.

'Our portfolio of investments at fair value through profit or loss has been 'marked to market' (fair valued) resulting in a loss of $1.6 million (included in administrative expenses).'

There were no additions to or disposals of non-current assets during the year.

'In response to the downturn the company has unfortunately had to make a number of employees redundant incurring severance costs of $1.3 million (included in cost of sales) and undertaken cost savings in advertising and other administrative expenses.'

'The difficulty in the credit markets has meant that the finance cost of our variable rate bank loan has increased from 4.5% to 8%. In order to help cash flows, the company made a rights issue during the year and reduced the dividend per share by 50%.'

'Despite the above events and associated costs, the Board believes the company's underlying performance has been quite resilient in these difficult times.'

Required:

Analyse and discuss the financial performance and position of Hardy as portrayed by the above financial statements and the additional information provided.

Your analysis should be supported by any SEVEN profitability, liquidity and gearing and other appropriate ratios (up to 7 marks available).

(Total: 20 marks)

391 PINTO

Pinto is a publicly listed company. The statement of cash flows of Pinto is available:

Statement of cash flows of Pinto for the year to 31 March 2008:

	$000	$000
Cash flows from operating activities		
Profit before tax		440
Depreciation		280
Loss on disposal of plant and machinery		90
Increase in warranty provision		100
Investment income		(60)
Finance costs		50
Redemption penalty costs included in administrative expenses		20
		─────
		920
Increase in inventories	(400)	
Decrease in trade receivables	60	
Increase in trade payables	360	20
	─────	─────
Cash generated from operations		940
Interest paid		(50)
Tax refund received		60
		─────
Net cash from operating activities		950
Cash flows from investing activities		
Purchase of property, plant and equipment	(1,440)	
Sale of property, plant and equipment	150	
Rental income received from investment property	40	
	─────	
Net cash used in investing activities		(1,250)
Cash flows from financing activities		
Proceeds from issue of shares	1,000	
Repayment of loan notes	(420)	
Dividends paid	(150)	
	─────	
Net cash from financing activities		430
		─────
Net increase in cash and cash equivalents		130
Cash and cash equivalents at beginning of period		(120)
		─────
Cash and cash equivalents at end of period		10
		─────

The following supporting information is available:

(i) An item of plant with a carrying amount of $240,000 was sold at a loss of $90,000 during the year. Depreciation of $280,000 was charged (to cost of sales) for property, plant and equipment in the year ended 31 March 2008.

Pinto uses the fair value model in IAS 40 *Investment Property*. There were no purchases or sales of investment property during the year.

(ii)   The 6% loan notes were redeemed early incurring a penalty payment of $20 thousand which has been charged as an administrative expense in the statement of profit or loss and other comprehensive income.

(iii) There was an issue of shares for cash on 1 October 2007.

(iv)   Pinto gives a 12 month warranty on some of the products it sells. The amounts shown in current liabilities as warranty provision are an accurate assessment, based on past experience, of the amount of claims likely to be made in respect of warranties outstanding at each year end. Warranty costs are included in cost of sales.

Required:

(a)   Comment on the cash flow management of Pinto as revealed by the statement of cash flows and the information provided by the above financial statements.

Note: Ratio analysis is not required, and will not be awarded any marks.   (15 marks)

(b)   In recent years many analysts have commented on a growing disillusionment with the usefulness and reliability of the information contained in some companies' statements of profit or loss and other comprehensive income.

Required:

Discuss the extent to which a company's statement of cash flows may be more useful and reliable than its statement of profit or loss.   (5 marks)

(Total: 20 marks)

392   HARBIN *Walk in the footsteps of a top tutor*

Shown below are the recently issued (summarised) financial statements of Harbin, a listed company, for the year ended 30 September 2007, together with comparatives for 2006 and extracts from the Chief Executive's report that accompanied their issue.

Consolidated statements of profit or loss

	2007	2006
	$000	$000
Revenue	250,000	180,000
Cost of sales	(200,000)	(150,000)
Gross profit	50,000	30,000
Operating expenses	(26,000)	(22,000)
Finance costs	(8,000)	(Nil)
Profit before tax	16,000	8,000
Income tax expense (at 25%)	(4,000)	(2,000)
Profit for the period	12,000	6,000

Consolidated statement of financial position

	2007	2006
	$000	$000
Non-current assets		
Property, plant and equipment	210,000	90,000
Goodwill	10,000	Nil
	220,000	90,000
Current assets		
Inventory	25,000	15,000
Trade receivables	13,000	8,000
Bank	nil	14,000
	38,000	37,000
Total assets	258,000	127,000
Equity and liabilities		
Equity shares of $1 each	100,000	100,000
Retained earnings	14,000	12,000
	114,000	112,000
Non-current liabilities		
8% loan notes	100,000	Nil
Current liabilities		
Bank overdraft	17,000	Nil
Trade payables	23,000	13,000
Current tax payable	4,000	2,000
	44,000	15,000
Total equity and liabilities	258,000	127,000

Extracts from the Chief Executive's report:

'Highlights of Harbin's performance for the year ended 30 September 2007:

- an increase in sales revenue of 39%

- gross profit margin up from 16.7% to 20%

- a doubling of the profit for the period.

In response to the improved position the Board paid a dividend of 10 cents per share in September 2007 an increase of 25% on the previous year.'

You have also been provided with the following further information.

On 1 October 2006 Harbin purchased the whole of the net assets of Fatima (previously a privately owned entity) for $100 million. The contribution of the purchase to Harbin's results for the year ended 30 September 2007 was:

	$000
Revenue	70,000
Cost of sales	(40,000)
Gross profit	30,000
Operating expenses	(8,000)
Profit before tax	22,000

There were no disposals of non-current assets during the year.

The following ratios have been calculated for the year ended 30 September 2006 and 2007:

	2007	2006
Return on year-end capital employed		7.1%
(profit before interest and tax over total assets less current liabilities)		
Net asset (equal to capital employed) turnover	1.2	1.6
Net profit (before tax) margin	6.4%	4.4%
Current ratio		2.5
Closing inventory holding period (in days)		37
Trade receivables' collection period (in days)		16
Trade payables' payment period (based on cost of sales) (in days)	42	32
Gearing (debt over debt plus equity)		Nil

Required:

(a) Calculate the missing ratios for 2007. (5 marks)

(b) Assess the financial performance and position of Harbin for the year ended 30 September 2007 compared to the previous year. Your answer should refer to the information in the Chief Executive's report and the impact of the purchase of the net assets of Fatima. (15 marks)

(Total: 20 marks)

393 GREENWOOD

Greenwood is a public listed company. During the year ended 31 March 2007 the directors decided to cease operations of one of its activities and put the assets of the operation up for sale (the discontinued activity has no associated liabilities). The cessation qualifies as a discontinued operation and has been accounted for accordingly.

Note: The statement of profit or loss figures down to the profit for the period from continuing operations are those of the continuing operations only.

Statement of profit or loss for the year ended 31 March

	2007	2006
	$000	$000
Revenue	27,500	21,200
Cost of sales	(19,500)	(15,000)
Gross profit	8,000	6,200
Operating expenses	(2,900)	(2,450)
	5,100	3,750
Finance costs	(600)	(250)
Profit before taxation	4,500	3,500
Income tax expense	(1,000)	(800)
Profit for the period from continuing operations	3,500	2,700
Profit/(Loss) from discontinued operations	(1,500)	320
Profit for the period	2,000	3,020
Analysis of discontinued operations		
Revenue	7,500	9,000
Cost of sales	(8,500)	(8,000)
Gross profit/(loss)	(1,000)	1,000
Operating expenses	(400)	(550)
Profit/(loss) before tax	(1,400)	450
Tax (expense)/relief	300	(130)
	(1,100)	320
Loss on measurement to fair value of disposal group	(500)	–
Tax relief on disposal group	100	–
Profit/(Loss) from discontinued operations	(1,500)	320

Statement of financial positions as at 31 March

	2007		2006	
	$000	$000	$000	$000
Non-current assets		17,500		17,600
Current assets				
Inventory	1,500		1,350	
Trade receivables	2,000		2,300	
Bank	Nil		50	
Assets held for sale (at fair value)	6,000	9,500	Nil	3,700
Total assets		27,000		21,300
Equity and liabilities				
Equity shares of $1 each		10,000		10,000
Retained earnings		4,500		2,500
		14,500		12,500
Non-current liabilities				
5% loan notes		8,000		5,000
Current liabilities				
Bank overdraft	1,150		Nil	
Trade payables	2,400		2,800	
Current tax payable	950	4,500	1,000	3,800
Total equity and liabilities		27,000		21,300

Note: The carrying amount of the assets of the discontinued operation at 31 March 2006 was $6.3 million.

Required:

Analyse the financial performance and position of Greenwood for the two years ended 31 March 2007.

Note: Your analysis should be supported by SEVEN appropriate ratios and refer to the effects of the discontinued operation.

(Total: 20 marks)

394   VICTULAR *Walk in the footsteps of a top tutor*

Victular is a public company that would like to acquire (100% of) a suitable private company. It has obtained the following draft financial statements for two companies, Grappa and Merlot. They operate in the same industry and their managements have indicated that they would be receptive to a takeover.

Statements of profit or loss for the year ended 30 September 2008

	$000	Grappa $000	$000	Merlot $000
Revenue		12,000		20,500
Cost of sales		(10,500)		(18,000)
Gross profit		1,500		2,500
Operating expenses		(240)		(500)
Finance costs – loan		(210)		(300)
– overdraft		Nil		(10)
– lease		Nil		(290)
Profit before tax		1,050		1,400
Income tax expense		(150)		(400)
Profit for the year		900		1,000
Note: Dividends paid during the year		250		700

Statements of financial position as at 30 September 2008

	$000	$000	$000	$000
Assets				
Non-current assets				
Freehold factory (note (i))		4,400		Nil
Owned plant (note (ii))		5,000		2,200
Leased plant (note (ii))		Nil		5,300
		9,400		7,500
Current assets				
Inventory	2,000		3,600	
Trade receivables	2,400		3,700	
Bank	600	5,000	Nil	7,300
Total assets		14,400		14,800
Equity and liabilities				
Equity shares of $1 each		2,000		2,000
Property revaluation surplus	900		Nil	
Retained earnings	2,600	3,500	800	800
		5,500		2,800

Non-current liabilities

Finance lease obligations (note (iii))	Nil		3,200	
7% loan notes	3,000		Nil	
10% loan notes	Nil		3,000	
Deferred tax	600		100	
Government grants	1,200	4,800	Nil	6,300

Current liabilities

Bank overdraft	Nil		1,200	
Trade payables	3,100		3,800	
Government grants	400		Nil	
Finance lease obligations (note (iii))	Nil		500	
Taxation	600	4,100	200	5,700
Total equity and liabilities		14,400		14,800

Notes

(i)   Both companies operate from similar premises.

(ii)   Additional details of the two companies' plant are:

	Grappa $000	Merlot $000
Owned plant – cost	8,000	10,000
Leased plant – original fair value	Nil	7,500

There were no disposals of plant during the year by either company.

(iii)   The interest rate implicit within Merlot's finance leases is 7.5% per annum. For the purpose of calculating ROCE and gearing, **all** finance lease obligations are treated as long-term interest bearing borrowings.

(iv)   The following ratios have been calculated for Grappa and can be taken to be correct:

Return on year end capital employed (ROCE)	14.8%
(capital employed taken as shareholders' funds plus long-term interest bearing borrowings – see note (iii) above)	
Gross profit margin	12.5%
Operating profit margin	10.5%
Current ratio	1.2:1
Closing inventory holding period	70 days
Trade receivables' collection period	73 days
Trade payables' payment period (using cost of sales)	108 days
Gearing (see note (iii) above)	35.3%

Required:

(a) Calculate for Merlot the ratios equivalent to all those given for Grappa above.

(4 marks)

(b) Assess the relative performance and financial position of Grappa and Merlot for the year ended 30 September 2008 to inform the directors of Victular in their acquisition decision.

(11 marks)

(c) Outline the problems in using ratios for comparison purposes between entities, and suggest what additional information would be useful for Victular in reaching its decision.

(5 marks)

(Total: 20 marks)

395 QUARTILE

Quartile sells jewellery through stores in retail shopping centres throughout the country. Over the last two years it has experienced declining profitability and is wondering if this is related to the sector as whole. It has recently subscribed to an agency that produces average ratios across many businesses. Below are the ratios that have been provided by the agency for Quartile's business sector based on a year end of 30 June 2012, as well as some ratios for Quartile that have already been completed.

	Sector	Quartile
Return on year-end capital employed (ROCE)	16.8%	
Net asset (total assets less current liabilities) turnover	1.4 times	
Gross profit margin	35%	
Operating profit margin	12%	
Current ratio	1.25:1	
Average inventory turnover	3 times	
Trade payables' payment period	64 days	
Debt to equity	38%	

The financial statements of Quartile for the year ended 30 September 2012 are:

Statement of profit or loss

	$000	$000
Revenue		56,000
Opening inventory	8,300	
Purchases	43,900	
	———	
	52,200	
Closing inventory	(10,200)	(42,000)
	———	———
Gross profit		14,000
Operating costs		(9,800)
Finance costs		(800)
		———
Profit before tax		3,400
Income tax expense		(1,000)
		———
Profit for the year		2,400
		———

Statement of financial position

	$000	$000
Assets		
Non-current assets		
Property and shop fittings		25,600
Deferred development expenditure		5,000
		30,600
Current assets		
Inventory	10,200	
Bank	1,000	11,200
Total assets		41,800
Equity and liabilities		
Equity		
Equity shares of $1 each		15,000
Property revaluation surplus		3,000
Retained earnings		8,600
		26,600
Non-current liabilities		
10% loan notes		8,000
Current liabilities		
Trade payables	5,400	
Current tax payable	1,800	7,200
Total equity and liabilities		41,800

Note: The deferred development expenditure relates to an investment in a process to manufacture artificial precious gems for future sale by Quartile in the retail jewellery market.

Required:

(a) **Prepare the missing ratios for Quartile.** (7 marks)

(b) **Assess the financial and operating performance of Quartile in comparison to its sector averages.** (13 marks)

(Total: 20 marks)

396 BENGAL

Bengal is a public company. Its most recent financial statements are shown below:

Statements of profit or loss for the year ended 31 March

	2011	2010
	$000	$000
Revenue	25,500	17,250
Cost of sales	(14,800)	(10,350)
Gross profit	10,700	6,900
Distribution costs	(4,800)	(3,300)
Finance costs	(650)	(100)
Profit before taxation	5,250	3,500
Income tax expense	(2,250)	(1,000)
Profit for the year	3,000	2,500

Statement of cash flows for the year ended 31 March 2011:

	$000	$000
Cash flows from operating activities:		
Profit from operations		5,900
Adjustments for:		
depreciation of non-current assets		640
increase in inventories		(1,800)
increase in receivables		(1,000)
increase in payables		650
Cash generated from operations		4,390
Finance costs paid		(650)
Income tax paid		(1,250)
Net cash from operating activities		2,490
Cash flows from investing activities:		
Purchase of property, plant and equipment	(6,740)	
Purchase of intangibles	(6,200)	
Net cash used in investing activities		(12,940)
Cash flows from financing activities:		
Issue of 8% loan note	7,000	
Equity dividends paid	(750)	
Net cash from financing activities		6,250
Net decrease in cash and cash equivalents		(4,200)
Cash and cash equivalents at beginning of period		4,000
Cash and cash equivalents at end of period		(200)

Notes

(i)   There were no disposals of non-current assets during the period; however Bengal does have some non-current assets classified as 'held for sale' at 31 March 2011.

(ii) Depreciation of property, plant and equipment for the year ended 31 March 2011 was $640,000.

A disappointed shareholder has observed that although revenue during the year has increased by 48% (8,250/17,250 × 100), profit for the year has only increased by 20% (500/2,500 × 100).

Required:

Comment on the performance (including addressing the shareholder's observation) and cash flow of Bengal for the year ended 31 March 2011.

Note: up to 5 marks are available for the calculation of appropriate ratios.

(Total: 20 marks)

397   WOODBANK

Shown below are the financial statements of Woodbank for its most recent two years:

Consolidated statements of profit or loss for the year ended 31 March:

	2014 $000	2013 $000
Revenue	150,000	110,000
Cost of sales	(117,000)	(85,800)
Gross profit	33,000	24,200
Distribution costs	(6,000)	(5,000)
Administrative expenses	(9,000)	(9,200)
Finance costs – loan note interest	(1,750)	(500)
Profit before tax	16,250	9,500
Income tax expense	(5,750)	(3,000)
Profit for the year	10,500	6,500

Statements of financial position as at 31 March:

	2014 $000	2013 $000
Assets		
Non-current assets		
Property, plant and equipment	118,000	85,000
Goodwill	30,000	nil
	148,000	85,000

Current assets		
Inventory	15,500	12,000
Trade receivables	11,000	8,000
Bank	500	5,000
	27,000	25,000
Total assets	175,000	110,000
Equity and liabilities		
Equity		
Equity shares of $1 each	80,000	80,000
Retained earnings	15,000	10,000
	95,000	90,000
Non-current liabilities		
10% loan notes	55,000	5,000
Current liabilities		
Trade payables	21,000	13,000
Current tax payable	4,000	2,000
	25,000	15,000
Total equity and liabilities	175,000	110,000

The following information is available:

(i) On 1 January 2014, Woodbank purchased the trading assets and operations of Shaw for $50 million and, on the same date, issued additional 10% loan notes to finance the purchase. Shaw was an unincorporated entity and its results (for three months from 1 January 2014 to 31 March 2014) and net assets (including goodwill not subject to any impairment) are included in Woodbank's financial statements for the year ended 31 March 2014 .There were no other purchases or sales of non-current assets during the year ended 31 March 2014.

(ii) Extracts of the results (for three months) of the previously separate business of Shaw, which are included in Woodbank's statement of profit or loss for the year ended 31 March 2014, are:

	$000
Revenue	30,000
Cost of sales	(21,000)
Gross profit	9,000
Distribution costs	(2,000)
Administrative expenses	(2,000)

(iii)   The following six ratios have been correctly calculated for Woodbank for the year ended 31 March:

	2013	2014
Return on capital employed (ROCE)	10.5%	12.0%
(profit before interest and tax/year-end total assets less current liabilities)		
Net asset (equal to capital employed) turnover	1.16 times	1.0 times
Gross profit margin	22.0%	22.0%
Profit before interest and tax margin	9.1%	12.0%
Current ratio	1.7:1	1.08:1
Gearing (debt/(debt + equity))	5.3%	36.7%

Required:

(a)   **Calculate for the year ended 31 March 2014:**

equivalent ratios to the first FOUR only for Woodbank excluding the effects of the purchase of Shaw.

Note: **Assume the capital employed for Shaw is equal to its purchase price of $50 million.**   **(4 marks)**

(b)   **Assess the comparative financial performance and position of Woodbank for the year ended 31 March 2014. Your answer should refer to the effects of the purchase of Shaw.**   **(12 marks)**

(c)   **Discuss what further information specific to the acquisition of Shaw that would allow you to make a more informed assessment of Woodbank's performance and position.**   **(4 marks)**

(Total: 20 marks)

398   HYDAN

 Timed question with Online tutor debrief

Xpand is a publicly listed company which has experienced rapid growth in recent years through the acquisition and integration of other companies. Xpand is interested in acquiring Hydan, a retailing company, which is one of several companies owned and managed by the same family, of which Lodan is the ultimate parent company.

The summarised financial statements of Hydan for the year ended 30 September 2014 are:

Statement of profit or loss

	$000
Revenue	70,000
Cost of sales	(45,000)
Gross profit	25,000
Operating costs	(7,000)
Directors' salaries	(1,000)
Profit before tax	17,000
Income tax expense	(3,000)
Profit for the year	14,000

Statement of financial position

	$000	$000
Assets		
Non-current assets		
Property, plant and equipment		32,400
Current assets		
Inventory	7,500	
Bank	100	7,600
Total assets		40,000
Equity and liabilities		
Equity		
Equity shares of $1 each		1,000
Retained earnings		18,700
		19,700
Non-current liabilities		
Directors' loan accounts (interest free)		10,000
Current liabilities		
Trade payables	7,500	
Current tax payable	2,800	10,300
Total equity and liabilities		40,000

From the above financial statements, Xpand has calculated for Hydan the ratios below for the year ended 30 September 2014. It has also obtained the equivalent ratios for the retail sector average which can be taken to represent Hydan's sector.

	Hydan	*Sector average*
Return on equity (ROE) (including directors' loan accounts)	47.1%	22.0%
Net asset turnover	2.36 times	1.67 times
Gross profit margin	35.7%	30.0%
Net profit margin	20.0%	12.0%

From enquiries made, Xpand has learned the following information:

(i) Hydan buys all of its trading inventory from another of the family companies at a price which is 10% less than the market price for such goods.

(ii) After the acquisition, Xpand would replace the existing board of directors and need to pay remuneration of $2.5 million per annum.

(iii) The directors' loan accounts would be repaid by obtaining a loan of the same amount with interest at 10% per annum.

(iv) Xpand expects the purchase price of Hydan to be $30 million.

Required:

(a) Recalculate the ratios for Hydan after making appropriate adjustments to the financial statements for notes (i) to (iv) above. For this purpose, the expected purchase price of $30 million should be taken as Hydan's equity and net assets are equal to this equity plus the loan. You may assume the changes will have no effect on taxation. **(6 marks)**

(b) In relation to the ratios calculated in (a) above, and the ratios for Hydan given in the question, comment on the performance of Hydan compared to its retail sector average. **(9 marks)**

(c) One of Xpand's directors has suggested that it would be wise to look at the Lodan group's consolidated financial statements rather than Hydan's individual financial statements.

As an adviser to Xpand, explain any concerns you would raise about basing an investment decision on the information available in Lodan's consolidated financial statements and Hydan's entity financial statements. **(5 marks)**

(Total: 20 marks)

 Calculate your allowed time, allocate the time to the separate parts

399 YOGI

Yogi is a public company and extracts from its most recent financial statements are provided below:

Statements of profit or loss for the year ended 31 March

	2015	2014
	$000	$000
Revenue	36,000	50,000
Cost of sales	(24,000)	(30,000)
Gross profit	12,000	20,000
Profit from sale of division (see note (i))	1,000	nil
Distribution costs	(3,500)	(5,300)
Administrative expenses	(4,800)	(2,900)
Finance costs	(400)	(800)
Profit before taxation	4,300	11,000
Income tax expense	(1,300)	(3,300)
Profit for the year	3,000	7,700

Statements of financial position as at 31 March

	2015		2014	
	$000	$000	$000	$000
Non-current assets				
Property, plant and equipment		16,300		19,000
Intangible – goodwill		nil		2,000
		16,300		21,000
Current assets				
Inventory	3,400		5,800	
Trade receivables	1,300		2,400	
Bank	1,500	6,200	nil	8,200
Total assets		22,500		29,200
Equity and liabilities				
Equity				
Equity shares of $1 each		10,000		10,000
Retained earnings		3,000		4,000
		13,000		14,000
Non-current liabilities				
10% loan notes		4,000		8,000
Current liabilities				
Bank overdraft	nil		1,400	
Trade payables	4,300		3,100	
Current tax payable	1,200	5,500	2,700	7,200
Total equity and liabilities		22,500		29,200

Notes

(i) On 1 April 2014, Yogi sold the net assets (including goodwill) of a separately operated division of its business for $8 million cash on which it made a profit of $1 million. This transaction required shareholder approval and, in order to secure this, the management of Yogi offered shareholders a dividend of 40 cents for each share in issue out of the proceeds of the sale. The trading results of the division which are included in the statement of profit or loss for the year ended 31 March 2014 above are:

	$000
Revenue	18,000
Cost of sales	(10,000)
Gross profit	8,000
Distribution costs	(1,000)
Administrative expenses	(1,200)
Profit before interest and tax	5,800

(ii) The following selected ratios for Yogi have been calculated for the year ended 31 March 2014 (as reported above):

Gross profit margin	40.0%
Operating profit margin	23.6%
Return on capital employed	
(profit before interest and tax/(total assets – current liabilities))	53.6%
Net asset turnover	2.27 times

Required:

(a) **Calculate the equivalent ratios for Yogi:**

(i) **for the year ended 31 March 2014, after excluding the contribution made by the division that has been sold; and**

(ii) **for the year ended 31 March 2015, excluding the profit on the sale of the division.** **(5 marks)**

(b) **Comment on the comparative financial performance and position of Yogi for the year ended 31 March 2015.** **(10 marks)**

(c) On a separate matter, you have been asked to advise on an application for a loan to build an extension to a sports club which is a not-for-profit organisation. You have been provided with the audited financial statements of the sports club for the last four years.

Required:

Identify and explain the ratios that you would calculate to assist in determining whether you would advise that the loan should be granted. **(5 marks)**

(Total: 20 marks)

400 XPAND

Xpand is a public company which has grown in recent years by acquiring established businesses. The following financial statements for two potential target companies are shown below. They operate in the same industry sector and Xpand believes their shareholders would be receptive to a takeover. An indicative price for 100% acquisition of the companies is $12 million each.

Statements of profit or loss for the year ended 30 September 2015

	Kandid	Kovert
	$000	$000
Revenue	25,000	40,000
Cost of sales	(19,000)	(32,800)
Gross profit	6,000	7,200
Distribution and administrative expenses	(1,250)	(2,300)
Finance costs	(250)	(900)
Profit before tax	4,500	4,000
Income tax expense	(900)	(1,000)
Profit for the year	3,600	3,000

Statements of financial position as at 30 September 2015

Non-current assets		
Property	nil	3,000
Owned plant	4,800	2,000
Leased plant	nil	5,300
	4,800	10,300
Current assets		
Inventory	1,600	3,400
Trade receivables	2,100	5,100
Bank	1,100	200
	4,800	8,700
Total assets	9,600	19,000
Equity and liabilities		
Equity		
Equity shares of $1 each	1,000	2,000
Property revaluation surplus	nil	900
Retained earnings	1,600	2,700
	2,600	5,600
Non-current liabilities		
Finance lease obligation	nil	4,200
5% loan notes (31 December 2016)	5,000	nil
10% loan notes (31 December 2016)	nil	5,000
	5,000	9,200
Current liabilities		
Trade payables	1,250	2,100
Finance lease obligation	nil	1,000
Taxation	750	1,100
	2,000	4,200
Total equity and liabilities	9,600	19,000

Notes

(i)   Carrying value of plant:

	Kandid	Kovert
	$000	$000
Owned plant – cost	8,000	10,000
Less government grant	(2,000)	
	────	
	6,000	
Accumulated depreciation	(1,200)	(8,000)
	────	────
	4,800	2,000
Leased plant – original fair value	nil	8,000

(ii)   The following ratios have been calculated:

	Kandid	Kovert
Return on year-end capital employed (ROCE)	62.5%	
(finance lease obligations are treated as debt)		
Net asset (taken as same figure as capital employed) turnover	3.3 times	2.5 times
Gross profit margin	24.0%	18.0%
Profit margin (before interest and tax)	19.0%	
Current ratio	2.4:1	2.1:1
Closing inventory holding period	31 days	38 days
Trade receivables' collection period	31 days	47 days
Trade payables' payment period (using cost of sales)	24 days	
Gearing (debt/(debt + equity))	65.8%	

Required:

(a)   Calculate the missing ratios for Kovert. All finance lease liabilities are treated as debt, and profit before interest and tax should be used for the calculation of return on capital employed.   **(4 marks)**

(b)   Using the above information, assess the relative performance and financial position of Kandid and Kovert for the year ended 30 September 2015 in order to assist the directors of Xpand to make an acquisition decision.   **(12 marks)**

(c)   Describe what further information may be useful to Xpand when making an acquisition decision.   **(4 marks)**

(Total: 20 marks)

401 SCHRUTE

Schrute is a group in the farming industry and owns a number of 100% owned farming subsidiaries. Its financial statements for the last two years are shown below.

Consolidated statement of profit or loss for the year ended 30 September:

	20X3 $000	20X2 $000
Revenue	94,000	68,500
Cost of sales	(46,000)	(28,000)
Gross profit	48,000	40,500
Distribution costs	(21,200)	(19,300)
Administrative expenses	(25,600)	(15,400)
Profit from operations	1,200	5,800
Investment income	0	600
Finance costs	(120)	0
Profit before tax	1,080	6,400
Taxation	(300)	(1,920)
Profit for the year	780	4,480
Attributable to:		
Shareholders of Schrute	1,580	4,480
Non-Controlling interest	(800)	–
	780	4,480

Extracts from the consolidated statement of financial position as at 30 September:

	20X3 $000	20X2 $000
Inventories	6,500	4,570
Trade receivables	17,000	15,600
Bank	610	6,000
Equity:		
Equity shares of $1 each	25,000	6,000
Retained earnings	73,500	72,500
Non-Controlling interest	510	–
Non-current liabilities:		
Loan	20,000	–

The following information is relevant:

(i) Schrute has become increasingly worried about two major areas in its business environment. Firstly, there are concerns that reliance on large supermarkets is putting pressure on cash flow, as the supermarkets demand long payment terms. Secondly, the consistent increases in fuel prices mean that delivering the produce nationally is becoming extremely expensive.

(ii) To manage this, Schrute acquired 80% of Howard on 1 October 20X2, which operates a small number of hotels. It was hoped that this would improve cash flow, as customers pay up front, and reduce the impact of further fuel price rises.

(iii) To fund this, Schrute disposed of $11 million held in investments, making a $4.5 million profit on disposal. This profit is included within administrative expenses.

(iv) Howard opened a new hotel in March 20X3. After poor reviews, Schrute Farms recruited a new marketing director in May. Following an extensive marketing campaign, online feedback improved.

(v) The following ratios have been calculated for the year ended 30 September 20X2:

Gross profit margin	59.1%
Operating profit margin	8.5%
Return on Capital Employed	7.4%
Current ratio	4.6:1
Inventory turnover period	60 days
Receivables collection period	83 days

Required:

(a) For the ratios provided above, prepare the equivalent figures for the year ended 30 September 2013. (5 marks)

(b) Analyse the performance and position of Schrute for the year ended 30 September 20X3, making specific reference to any concerns or expectations regarding future periods. (15 marks)

(Total: 20 marks)

402 PITCARN

The Pitcarn group owns a number of subsidiaries. On 31 March 20X6, the Pitcarn group sold its entire holding in Sitor. The consolidated statement of profit or loss of the Pitcarn group for 20X6 has been produced **without** the results of Sitor due to its disposal. No profit or loss on disposal has been included in the 20X6 consolidated statement of profit or loss.

Extracts from the consolidated statements of profit or loss for the Pitcarn group are below:

Statements of profit or loss (extracts) for the year ended 31 March

	20X6	20X5
	$000	$000
Revenue	86,000	99,000
Cost of sales (note (ii))	(63,400)	(67,200)
Gross profit	22,600	31,800
Other income (notes (i) and (iii))	3,400	1,500
Operating expenses	(21,300)	(23,200)
Profit from operations	4,700	10,100
Finance costs	(1,500)	(1,900)

The following notes are relevant:

(i) Sitor was based in the Pitcarn head offices, for which it pays annual rent to Pitcarn of $300,000, significantly below the cost of equivalent office space in Sitor's local area. As Sitor is no longer in the group, Pitcarn has included this income within other income. Sitor expenses rent payments in operating expenses.

(ii) Sitor sold goods totalling $8 million to Pitcarn (included in Pitcarn's cost of sales above) during the year. Pitcarn held none of these goods in inventory at 31 March 20X6. Sitor made a margin of 40% on all goods sold to Pitcarn.

(iii) Pitcarn received a dividend of $1 million from Sitor during the year, as well as recording interest of $500,000 on a loan given to Sitor in 20X3. Both of these amounts are included within Pitcarn's other income.

The following selected ratios for the Pitcarn group have been calculated for the years ended 31 March 20X5 and 31 March 20X6 from the information above.

	20X6	20X5
Gross profit margin	26.3%	32.1%
Operating margin	5.5%	10.2%
Interest cover	3.1 times	5.3 times

(iv) Sitor's individual statement of profit or loss for the year ended is shown below:

	$000
Revenue	16,000
Cost of sales	(10,400)
Gross profit	5,600
Operating expenses	(3,200)
Profit from operations	2,400
Finance costs	(900)

Required:

(a) **Calculate the equivalent ratios for the consolidated statement of profit or loss for the year ended 31 March 20X6 if Sitor had been consolidated** **(7 marks)**

(b) **Analyse the performance of the Pitcarn group for the year ended 31 March 20X6. This should also include a discussion of Sitor.** **(8 marks)**

(c) Pitcarn acquired 80% of Sitor's 10 million $1 shares on 1 April 20X1 for $20 million when Sitor had retained earnings of $3 million. Pitcarn uses the fair value method for valuing the non-controlling interest. At acquisition the fair value of the non-controlling interest was $1 million.

On 31 March 20X6, Pitcarn sold its entire shareholding in Sitor for $25 million when Sitor had retained earnings of $7 million. Goodwill had suffered no impairment since acquisition.

Calculate the gain/loss on disposal to be shown in the consolidated statement of profit or loss for the year ended 31 March 2016. **(5 marks)**

(Total: 20 marks)

Section 4

ANSWERS TO OBJECTIVE TEST QUESTIONS – SECTION A

CONCEPTUAL FRAMEWORK/INTERNATIONAL FINANCIAL REPORTING STANDARDS

1

	Capitalise	Expense
Clearance of the site prior to work commencing	X	
Professional surveyors' fees for managing the construction work	X	
EW's own staff wages for time spent working on the construction	X	
An allocation of EW's administration costs		X

The allocation of EW's administration costs would not be included as these costs are not directly incurred as a result of carrying out the construction. All of the others are costs which would not have been incurred without the related asset being built.

2   B

The cost of the decommissioning is assumed to be an obligation for the company. An amount should be included in the cost of the asset when it is first recognised (1 July 20X4).

The amount to include in the cost of the asset for decommissioning costs is the present value of the expected future decommissioning costs. The present value is calculated by multiplying the expected future cost by a discount factor, which in this case is the discount factor for Year 5 (20X9) at 12%. $4 million × 0.567 = $2.268 million.

Therefore:

Debit:	Cost of asset	$2.268 million
Credit:	Provision for decommissioning costs	$2.268 million

The asset is depreciated on a straight-line basis over five years.

In addition, the decommissioning cost should be increased to $4 million by the end of Year 5. This is done by making a finance charge each year. This is charged at the cost of capital (12%) and applied to the balance on the provision account. The finance charge for the year to 30 June 20X5 is 12% × $2.268 million = $272,160.

Debit:	Finance charge (expense)	$272,160
Credit:	Provision for decommissioning costs	$272,160

	$
Depreciation charge ($2.268 million/5 years)	453,600
Finance charge	272,160
	———
Total charge	725,760
	———

If you selected A, you have included the depreciation without the finance cost. If you selected C, you have just spread the present value of the dismantling over 5 years. If you selected D, you have expensed the whole asset value.

3 A

	Land	Buildings	Total
	$ million	$ million	$ million
At 30 June 20X5			
Carrying amount	1.00	4.80	5.80
Building depreciation = $5 million/50 years = $100,000 per year			
Revalued amount	1.24	5.76	7.00
			———
Transfer to revaluation reserve			1.20
			———
At 30 June 20X7			
Carrying amount	1.24	5.52	6.76
Building depreciation = $5.76 million/48 years = $120,000 per year			
Disposal value			6.80
			———
Gain on disposal			0.04
			———

The gain on disposal is $40,000. The $1.2 million balance on the revaluation reserve is transferred from the revaluation reserve to another reserve account (probably retained earnings) but is not reported through the statement of profit or loss for the year.

If you selected answer B, you have forgotten to record depreciation between 30 June 20X5 and 30 June 20X7. If you selected answer C, you have based the profit on the original depreciation. If you selected D, you have incorrectly transferred the remaining revaluation reserve into the statement of profit or loss.

4 $900,000

The grant should be released over the useful life, not based on the possibility of the item being repaid. Therefore the $1m should be released over 5 years, being a release of $200,000 a year. At 30 June 20X1, 6 months should be released, meaning $100,000 has been released (6/12 × $200,000). This leaves $900,000 in deferred income.

5   **B**

This is a revenue grant, and would therefore be released to the statement of profit or loss over the 4 year life. By the end of year one, $250,000 would have been credited to the statement of profit or loss, leaving $750,000 held in deferred income. At this point the amount is repaid, meaning that the deferred income is removed, as well as the $250,000 income previously recorded.

If you selected A, you have not removed the income that was released in the prior year. If you selected C, you have missed that $250,000 would have been released in the previous year. If you have chosen D, you have made errors over the deferring of the grant and that the repayment would be treated as an expense.

6   **B**

Asset A would be classed as a non-current asset held for sale under IFRS 5. Assets C and D would both be classified as Property, Plant and Equipment per IAS 16.

7   **B**

The weighted average cost of borrowing is 7.33% (($1m × 6%) + ($2m × 8%))/$3m.

Therefore the amount to be capitalised = 7.33% × $600,000 × 8/12 = $29,333.

If you selected A, you forgot to time apportion the borrowing costs for the construction period. If you selected D you have used 6% rather than the weighted average. If you selected C you have just used 7% as the average rather than calculating the weighted average.

8

	Statement 1	Statement 2
True	X	
False		X

IAS 16 states that when the revaluation model is used, revaluations should be made with sufficient regularity to ensure that the carrying value of the assets remain close to fair value. IAS 16 also states that, if one item in a class of assets is revalued, all the assets in that class must be revalued.

9   **A, B**

The maintenance and training costs should be expensed as incurred. The residual value should be taken into account for the purposes of calculating depreciation, but not for the amount to be capitalised.

10   A

Six months' depreciation is required on the building structure and air conditioning system.

	$000
Land (not depreciated)	2,000
Building structure (10,000 – (10,000/25 × 6/12))	9,800
Air conditioning system (4,000 – (3,500/10 × 6/12))	3,825
	———
	15,625
	———

11   C

Six months' depreciation to the date of the revaluation will be $300,000 (12,000/20 years × 6/12); six months' depreciation from the date of revaluation to 31 March 20X5 would be $400,000 (10,800/13.5 years remaining life × 6/12). Total depreciation is $700,000.

12   B, C

Item A is incorrect as the deferred income method can be used. Item D is incorrect as any repayment is corrected in the current period, not retrospectively.

13   A

Six months' depreciation should be accounted for up to 30 June 20X5, which is $100,000 expense ($10 million/50 years × 6/12).

When the asset is transferred to investment property it should be revalued to the fair value of $11 million. At the date that the asset's use is changed, this gain should be recorded in other comprehensive income and in a revaluation surplus, not in the statement of profit or loss.

From this date, the fair value model is used. No depreciation is accounted for, but the asset will be revalued to fair value, with gains or losses going through the statement of profit or loss. As there is a gain of $500,000 from June 20X5 to December 20X5, this would be included in the statement of profit or loss.

Therefore the total net income will be **$400,000**, being the $500,000 fair value gain less the depreciation expense of $100,000 for the first 6 months of the year.

14 $595,000

The interest can only be capitalised during the period of construction, which is from 1 February. Therefore the interest can be capitalised for 10 months, being from 1 February to 30 November. This gives $625,000 ($7.5 million × 10% × 10/12).

Any temporary investment income earned during this period should be netted off the amount capitalised. The amount earned from 1 February to 1 May is $22,500 ($2 million × 4.5% × 3/12).

Therefore the amount to be capitalised is $625,000 - $30,000 = **$602,500.**

Note that all interest incurred and earned in January is before the construction period and therefore is recorded in the statement of profit or loss.

15 $1,300,000

The income of $300,000 should be taken to the statement of profit or loss, in addition to the fair value gain of $1 million. Costs to sell are ignored. If Croft Co uses the fair value method, no depreciation will be charged on the asset.

16   A

The finance was only available after the year end. Therefore the criteria of recognising an asset were not met, as the resources were not available to complete the project.

Even though the brand is internally generated in the subsidiary's accounts, it can be recognised at fair value for the group. Item C can be recognised as a purchased intangible and item D meets the criteria for being capitalised has development costs.

17   D

Item A cannot be capitalised because it does not meet all the criteria, i.e. it is not viable.

Item B is research and cannot be capitalised.

Item C cannot be capitalised because it does not meet all the criteria, i.e. making a loss.

18   B, C

Key staff cannot be capitalised as firstly they are not controlled by an entity. Secondly, the value that one member of key staff contributes to an entity cannot be measured reliably.

19   A

The costs of $750,000 relate to ten months of the year (up to April 20X5). Therefore per month the costs were $75,000. As the project was confirmed as feasible on 1 January 20X5, the costs can be capitalised from this date. Therefore four months of these costs can be capitalised = $75,000 × 4 = $300,000.

This asset should be amortised when the products go on sale. Therefore one month's amortisation should be charged to 30 June. Amortisation is ($300,000/5) × 1/12 = $5,000. The carrying amount of the asset at 30 June 20X5 is $300,000 – $5,000 = $295,000.

If you chose C you have forgotten to amortise the development costs. If you chose B or D you have either capitalised the full amount or capitalised none of the costs.

20   B

The brand can be measured reliably, so this should be accounted for as a separate intangible on consolidation. The customer list cannot be valued reliably, and so will form part of the overall goodwill calculation. It will be subsumed within the goodwill value.

21   D

	$
Write off to 1 January 20X4 to 28 February 20X4 (2 × $40,000)	80,000
Amortisation 160,000 (i.e. 4 × 40,000)/5 years × 3/12 (March to June)	8,000
	88,000

22   B

A new process may produce benefits (and therefore be recognised as an asset) other than increased revenues, e.g. it may reduce costs.

23   A

In a cash generating unit, no asset should be impaired below its recoverable amount. The valuation of $2.5 million is an indication that the property is not impaired and should therefore be left at $2.3 million.

$2.5 million cannot be chosen as the company uses the cost model. If you chose item C or D then you have impaired the asset.

24   C

The cash generating unit is impaired by $1,180,000, being the difference between the recoverable amount of $4 million and the total carrying values of the assets of $5,180,000. In a cash generating unit, no asset should be impaired below its recoverable amount, meaning that the property and other net assets are not impaired. The impairment is allocated to goodwill first, resulting in the entire $700,000 being written off. This leaves a remaining impairment of $480,000 to be allocated across plant and intangibles.

This should be allocated on a pro-rata basis according to their carrying value. The plant and intangible have a total carrying value of $1,750,000 ($950,000 plant and $800,000 intangible). Therefore the impairment should be allocated to plant as follows:

$950,000/$1,750,000 × $480,000 = $261,000.

The carrying value of plant is therefore $950,000 – $261,000 = $689,000

If you selected D you have chosen the impairment rather than the carrying amount. If you selected A or B you have pro-rated the impairment over the property or other net assets as well as the plant and intangibles.

25 $6,500

The recoverable amount of an asset is the higher of its value in use (being the present value of future cash flows) and fair value less costs to sell. Therefore the recoverable amount is $6,500.

26   A

Goodwill should be written off in full and the remaining loss is allocated pro rata to property plant and equipment and the product patent.

	B/f $	Loss $	Post loss $
Property, plant and equipment	200,000	(45,455)	154,545
Goodwill	50,000	(50,000)	nil
Product patent	20,000	(4,545)	15,455
Net current assets (at NRV)	30,000	nil	30,000
	300,000	(100,000)	200,000

27   D

Although the estimated NRV is lower than it was (due to fire damage), the entity will still make a profit on the inventory and thus it is not an indicator of impairment.

28 $17,785

	$
Cost 1 October 2009	100,000
Depreciation 1 October 2009 to 30 September 2014 (100,000 × 5/10)	(50,000)
Carrying amount	50,000

fair value less costs to sell	value in use
30,000	32,215 (8,500 × 3.79) (is higher)

the recoverable amount is therefore $32,215

	$
Carrying amount	50,000
Recoverable amount	(32,215)
Impairment to statement of profit or loss	17,785

29 $214,600

Is the lower of its carrying amount ($217,000) and recoverable amount ($214,600) at 31 March 2015.

Recoverable amount is the higher of value in use ($214,600) and fair value less (any) costs of disposal ($200,000)).

Carrying amount = $217,000 (248,000 – (248,000 × 12.5%))

Value in use is based on present values = $214,600

30   C

At 30 September 20X4:

Carrying amount = $37.5 million (45,000 – 6,000 b/f – 1,500 for 6 months; no further depreciation when classified as held for sale).

Recoverable amount = $36.8 million ((42,000 × 90%) – 1,000).

Therefore included at $36.8 million (lower of carrying amount and fair value less cost to sell).

31   A

Assets held for sale should be held at the lower of carrying value and fair value less costs to sell. Therefore the asset should be held at $750.

Item B is just the fair value. Item C is the fair value plus the costs to sell, which is incorrect. Item D is the carrying value.

32 C

A sale has to be expected within 12 months, not one month. The others are all criteria which must be met to classify an asset as held for sale.

33

	Shown on the face of the statement of profit or loss	Not shown
Revenue		X
Gross profit		X
Profit after tax	X	

One line should be shown regarding profit from discontinued operations. This line is the profit after tax from the discontinued operation, with a full breakdown of the amount in the notes to the accounts.

34

	Discontinued operation Yes/No
Sector X	No
Sector Y	Yes

Although Sector X is the only operation of Total Co in Country A, it is not a separate major line of geographical operations, as it only contributes 0.5% of Total Co revenue. Therefore Total Co would not report this as a discontinued operation.

Sector Y is a separate major line of business operations, as it contributes a significant amount of Total Co revenue, and produces a different item from the other parts of Total Co. Therefore, Total Co would report Sector Y as a discontinued operation.

35 B

Although disclosing discontinued operations separately may help with business valuation, and understanding the business, the primary reason discontinued operations are separately presented is to enhance the predictive nature of the financial statements. Financial statements are historic, and this is a major limitation of them. Including information about discontinued operations means that the users of the financial statements can use the continuing operations only when predicting the future performance of an entity.

36 A

The property would be depreciated by $25,000 (800,000/16 × 6/12) for six months giving a carrying amount of $775,000 (800,000 − 25,000) before being classified as held-for-sale. This would also be the value at 31 March 2015 as it is no longer depreciated and is lower than its fair value less cost to sell.

37   D

The objectives of financial statements are set out in the IASB *Framework*. Note that providing information about 'changes in the financial position', as well as information about financial position and financial performance, is included in these objectives.

38   B

You should learn the IASB definitions of both assets and liabilities. The definition in the question is in two parts: (1) a liability is a present obligation that has arisen out of a past event, and (2) it is certain or probable that settlement of this obligation will result in an outflow of economic benefits, such as a payment of money. It is also necessary for the amount of the liability to be measured reliably.

39

	Faithful representation	Relevance
Completeness	X	
Predictive value		X
Neutrality	X	

Information that is relevant has predictive or confirmatory value. For information to have faithful representation, it must be complete, neutral and free from error.

40   B, D

It is important to learn that the two fundamental characteristics are relevance and faithful representation.

41

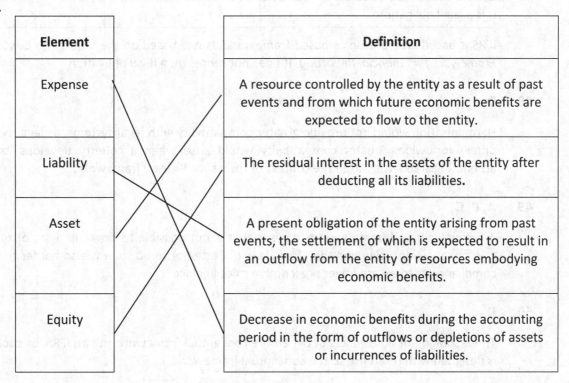

Element	Definition
Expense	A resource controlled by the entity as a result of past events and from which future economic benefits are expected to flow to the entity.
Liability	The residual interest in the assets of the entity after deducting all its liabilities.
Asset	A present obligation of the entity arising from past events, the settlement of which is expected to result in an outflow from the entity of resources embodying economic benefits.
Equity	Decrease in economic benefits during the accounting period in the form of outflows or depletions of assets or incurrences of liabilities.

42   **C**

Relevant information contains information which has predictive and confirmatory value.

43   **D**

Faithful representation means presenting transactions according to their economic substance rather than their legal form. Items A to C all represent incorrect accounting treatments, and item D reflects that a sale and repurchase agreement with a bank may represent a secured loan rather than a sale.

44   **B**

All other definitions include some part of the correct answer, but are incomplete.

45   **A**

There only has to be probable flow of economic benefits, rather than a certain flow. Also, the cost or value must be capable of reliable measurement, or no amount can be put into the financial statements.

46   **D**

Information is relevant if it influences the economic decisions of the users. The other definitions describe good treatment but are not explaining the concept of relevance.

47

	True	False
It is a principles-based framework	X	
It is a legal obligation		X

IFRS is based on a principles-based framework, as it is based on the IASB's *The Conceptual Framework for Financial Reporting.* It does not represent a legal obligation.

48   **D**

Harmonisation would not provide greater compatibility with legal systems, as legal systems differ worldwide. Greater compatibility would arise when a country develops its own accounting standards within the context of their specific legal framework.

49   **A, B, C**

A principles-based framework recognises that is not possible to draw up a set of rules to cover every eventuality and therefore does not attempt to do so. It is also harder to prove compliance as there are fewer prescriptive rules in place.

50   **D**

There should not be conflicts between the conceptual framework and an IFRS, as each IFRS is designed with reference to the conceptual framework.

51   C

Receivables sold without recourse represent a transfer of control to the purchaser, as they now carry the risk of irrecoverable debts. Therefore these should be regarded as a sale.

52   D

The substance is that there is no 'free' finance; its cost, as such, is built into the selling price as this will represent a significant financing component.

53   B

By definition irredeemable preference shares do not have a contractual obligation to be repaid and thus do not meet the definition of a liability; they are therefore classed as equity.

54   B

Historical cost annual depreciation = $90,000 ((500,000 × 90%)/5 years).

After two years carrying amount would be $320,000 (500,000 – (2 × 90,000)).

Current cost annual depreciation = $108,000 ((600,000 × 90%)/5 years).

After two years carrying amount would be $384,000 (600,000 – (2 × 108,000)).

55   A, C

A is an onerous contract and C the provision is still required if there is no intention to sell.

56   D

As the receivable is 'sold' with recourse it must remain as an asset on the statement of financial position; it is not derecognised.

57   D

As it is a new type of transaction, comparability with existing treatments is not relevant.

58   B

Historical cost is the easiest to verify as the cost can be proved back to the original transaction. Fair value is often more difficult to verify as it may involve elements of estimation.

59   C

The prior period error is corrected by restating the comparative amounts for the previous period at their correct value. A note to the accounts should disclose the nature of the error, together with other details.

60   B

Level 3 inputs do include the best information available, but this is not regarded as the most reliable evidence of fair value, as level 1 inputs are likely to be the most reliable evidence.

61   B

A change in the method of inventory valuation would be classified as a change in accounting policy under IAS 8. The allowance for receivables, useful life and depreciation method are all accounting estimates.

62   A, D

A change in accounting policy may be made firstly if this is required by an IFRS (mandatory change). If there is no requirement, an entity can choose to change their accounting policy if they believe a new accounting policy would result in a more reliable and relevant presentation of events and transactions.

Entities cannot change their accounting policies simply to make financial reporting easier, or to try and show a more favourable picture of results.

63

	Can be used	Cannot be used
Historical cost	X	
Present value	X	
Realisable value	X	

All of the given methods can be used.

64   A

In times of rising prices, asset values will be understated, as historical cost will not be a true representation of the asset values. Additionally, the real purchase cost of replacement items will not be incorporated, meaning that profits are overstated.

B and D relate to asset values being overstated, which is incorrect. Unrecognised gains is irrelevant.

65   D

The capital maintenance concept aims to ensure that excess dividends are not paid in times of rising prices, by considering the effects of both inflation and specific price rises.

A, B and C are all key concepts regarding financial statements, but do not cover rising prices.

66

	Change in accounting policy	Change in accounting estimate
Classifying commission earned as revenue in the statement of profit or loss, having previously classified it as other operating income	X	
Revising the remaining useful life of a depreciable asset		X

A change of classification in presentation in financial statements is a change of accounting policy (CAP) under IAS 8.

67   B

Item A is an adjustment when preparing consolidated financial statements. Item C is an accounting estimate, and item D is applying the same policy as previously, with a correction to the figure used.

68   A

IAS 10 defines adjusting events as those providing evidence of conditions existing at the end of the reporting period. In the case of inventories, it may be sales of inventory in this period indicate that the net realisable value of some items of inventory have fallen below their cost and require writing down to their net realisable value as at 30 September 20X4.

69   B

The logs will be classed as inventories. The land will be classed as property, plant and equipment. The development costs will be treated as an intangible asset.

70   B, D, E

IAS 2 states that:

(a)   selling costs cannot be included in inventory cost, therefore item A cannot be included

(b)   general overheads cannot be included (item C)

(c)   overhead costs should be added to inventory cost on the basis of normal capacity of the production facilities, therefore item F cannot be included in cost

(d)   the cost of **factory** management and administration can be included, so that item D can be included in inventory values.

71 $55,800

	Cost	Recoverable amount (Net Realisable Value)	Lower of cost and recoverable amount
Item 1	$24,000	See note 1	$24,000
Item 2	$33,600	$31,800 (note 2)	$31,800
			$55,800

Notes:

(1)   The recoverable amount is not known, but it must be above cost because the contract is expected to produce a high profit margin. The subsequent fall in the cost price to $20,000 is irrelevant for the inventory valuation.

(2)   The recoverable amount is $36,000 minus 50% of $8,400.

72   B

The costs of inventory should include all costs of bringing inventory to its present location and condition, so Mario should include the raw materials cost, import duties, direct labour, subcontracted labour and production overheads in its inventory.

Sales tax would not be included as it is refundable.

Storage costs are specifically excluded from the value of inventory, as they are incurred once the inventory is ready to be sold.

Abnormal wastage costs are excluded from the valuation of inventory per IAS2.

73 $970,000

The normal selling price of damaged inventory is $300,000 (210/70%).

This will now sell for $240,000 (300,000 × 80%), and have a NRV of $180,000 (240 – (240 × 25%)). The expected loss on the inventory is $30,000 (210 cost – 180 NRV) and therefore the inventory should be valued at $970,000 (1,000 – 30).

74

	Accounted for under IAS 41 *Agriculture*	Outside the scope of IAS 41 *Agriculture*
Dairy cattle	X	
Milk	X	
Cheese		X

The cheese will be a product which is the result of processing after harvest, so will be outside the scope of IAS 41.

75   D

Biological assets should be revalued to fair value less point of sale costs at the year end, with the gain or loss being taken to the statement of profit or loss.

If you chose A, you have used the cost model. If you chose B or C, you have not deducted the point of sale costs.

76   C

Rental of excavation equipment $13,500 (18 × 9/12)

Depreciation of finance leased plant $68,000 (340/5 years)

Finance cost $25,000 ((340 – 90) × 10%)

Total $106,500.

77   B

	B/f	Interest 7%	Payment	c/f
	$	$	$	$
31/10/X3	45,000	3,150	(10,975)	37,175
31/10/X4	37,175	2,602	(10,975)	28,802

The figure to the right of the payment in the next year is the non-current liability. Once a payment has been made, $28,802 will still be owed, making this the non-current liability. The current liability will be the difference between the total liability of $37,175 and the non-current liability of $28,802, which is $8,373.

If you selected C, you chose the year end liability rather than the non-current liability. If you selected A, you recorded the payment in advance rather than arrears. If you selected D you recorded the payment in advance and chose the year end liability rather than the non-current liability.

78 $5,000

The expense in relation to an operating lease should be expensed into the statement of profit or loss on a straight-line basis over the lease term. The total amount to be paid is $30,000 (paying $1,000 a month for 3 years, less the first six month rent-free period).

This would be spread across the 3 year lease period, giving an expense of $10,000 a year. As the lease was only entered into six months into the year, six months expense should be recorded. This gives an expense of $5,000. As nothing has been paid by the year end, an accrual of $5,000 would also be shown in the statement of financial position.

79 A

Initial value of lease liability: $100,000 FV – $13760 deposit = $86,240

	Balance b/f	Payment	Subtotal	Interest	Balance c/f
20X3	86,240	(20,000)	66,240	5,299	71,539
20X4	71,539	(20,000)	51,539	4,123	55,662
20X5	55,662	(20,000)	35,662		

The non-current liability is the figure to the right of the payment in the following year, therefore $35,662. The current liability is the total liability of $55,662 less the non-current liability of $35,662, which is $20,000.

The finance cost is the figure in the interest column for 20X4.

If you chose B you have done the entries for year one. If you chose C or D, you have recorded the payments in arrears, not in advance.

80

Statement of profit or loss expense	Statement of financial position
6,667	Accrual

SPL expense = $20,000 total payments/3 years = $6,667

SFP accrual = $6,667 (Expensed $6,667, paid nothing)

81 A

Reverse operating lease treatment – Dr Liability 210,000, Cr RE b/f 210,000

Include depreciation of asset of $127,000 ($635,000/5) – Dr RE b/f 127,000, Cr NCA 127,000

Include finance cost for lease of $77,470 ($635,000 × 12.2%) – Dr RE b/f 77,470, Cr Liability 77,470

This gives a net adjustment of $5,530 to be credited to opening retained earnings.

If you selected B, you have missed the depreciation. If you selected C or D, you have either reversed the whole entry or nothing.

82 $58,000

The asset would initially be capitalised at $87,000. This is then depreciated over six years, being the shorter of the useful life and the lease term. The lease term is taken to be seven years due to the nominal rent in the final two years of the lease.

This would give a depreciation expense of $14,500 a year. After two years, accumulated depreciation would be $29,000 and therefore the carrying amount would be $58,000.

83   C

The asset should be depreciated for six months prior to the disposal, leading to a depreciation expense of $40,000 ($1.6 million/20 years × 6/12). This gives the asset a carrying value of $1,560,000 and means that the profit on disposal is $440,000.

Finally, the rent expense should be expensed into the statement of profit or loss on a straight line basis. As 6 months have elapsed, the expense should be $75,000.

If you chose A or B, you have not depreciated the asset for the first six months. If you chose D, you have applied a full year's depreciation.

84   B

$4,070,000 (19,300 – 15,230)

Workings (in $000)

	$
Fair value 1 October 20X3	25,000
Deposit	(2,000)
	23,000
Interest 10%	2,300
Payment 30 September 20X4	(6,000)
Lease obligation 30 September 20X4	19,300
Interest 10%	1,930
Payment 30 September 20X5	(6,000)
Lease obligation 30 September 20X5	15,230

85   A, C

The lease term needs to be the majority of the useful life, and the present value of the lease payments should be substantially all of the fair value of the asset. Therefore (ii) and (iv) are incorrect.

86 $1,090,000

The asset should be removed at $6 million, with the $7 million recorded in cash and $1 million profit held in deferred income. Then, the asset should be brought back under a finance lease with a fair value of $7 million and 7% interest. Therefore the following items will be included in the statement of profit or loss:

Depreciation: $7 million/10 years = $700,000

Finance cost: $7million × 7% = $490,000

Release of deferred income: $1million/10 years = $100,000.

Therefore the total expense = $700,000 + $490,000 - $100,000 = **$1,090,000.**

87 B

The amount payable each year is based on the coupon rate of 7%, giving an amount of $210,000 payable each year ($3 million × 7%). This should be discounted at the market rate of interest of 9% to find the value of the liability.

Year 1 ($210,000 × 0.914)	191,940
Year 2 ($210,000 × 0.837)	175,770
Year 3 ($3,210,000 × 0.766)	2,458,860
Total present value of debt	**2,826,570**
Equity element	**173,430**

If you chose A, you used the incorrect discount rate. If you chose C you forgot to calculate the repayment of $3 million. If you chose D you have no used split accounting.

88 B

The loan notes should initially be recorded at their net proceeds, being the $100,000 raised less the $3,000 issue costs, giving $97,000. This should then be held at amortised cost, taking the effective rate of interest to the statement of profit or loss. The annual payment will be the coupon rate, which will be 5% × $100,000 = $5,000 a year.

Applying this to an amortised cost table gives $7,981, as shown below.

	B/f	Interest 8%	Payment	c/f
	$	$	$	$
20X4	97,000	7,760	(5,000)	99,760
20X5	99,760	**7,981**		

If you chose C, you have done the calculation you 20X4. If you chose D, you have used 8% of the full $100,000 and done the calculation for 20X4. If you chose A, you have used 8% of the full $100,000

89 A

The business model test must also be passed, which means that the objective is to hold the instrument to collect the cash flows rather than to sell the asset. The others are irrelevant.

90 A

The default position for equity investments is fair value through profit or loss, meaning the investment is revalued each year end, with the gain or loss being taken to the statement of profit or loss.

Fair value through other comprehensive income is the alternative position.

Amortised cost is an alternative treatment for debt instruments.

Net proceeds relates to financial liabilities.

91 $9,500

The investment should be classified as Fair Value through other comprehensive income.

As such, they will initially be valued inclusive of transaction costs.

Therefore, the initial value is 10,000 × $3.50 = $35,000 + $500 = $35,500.

At year-end, these will be revalued to fair value of $4.50 each, therefore 10,000*$4.50 = $45,000.

The gain is therefore $45,000 – $35,500 = $9,500.

92

Gain	Where recorded
18,750	Statement of profit or loss

Financial Assets held for trading will be valued at Fair Value through Profit or Loss. These are therefore valued excluding any transaction costs (which will be expensed to profit or loss).

The initial value of the investment is therefore 15,000 × $6.50 = $97,500

The shares will be revalued to fair value as at year end, and the gain will be taken to profit or loss. The year-end value of the shares is 15,000 × $7.75 = $116,250, giving a gain of $18,750. This is recognised within profit or loss.

93 B

Transaction costs are included when measuring all financial assets and liabilities at amortised costs, and when valuing financial assets valued at fair value through other comprehensive income.

Financial assets valued at fair value through profit or loss are expensed through the profit or loss account on initial valuation and not included in the initial value of the asset.

94 $810,000

Year ended 30 September	Cash flow	Discount rate	Discounted cash flows
	$000	at 8%	$000
2014	500	0.93	465
2015	500	0.86	430
2016	10,500	0.79	8,295
			———
Value of debt component			9,190
Difference – value of equity option component			**810**
			———
Proceeds			10,000
			———

95   **$768,000**

The initial liability should be recorded at the net proceeds of $9.6 million. The finance cost should then be accounted for using the effective rate of interest of 8%. Therefore the finance cost for the year is **$768,000** ($9.6 million × 8%).

96

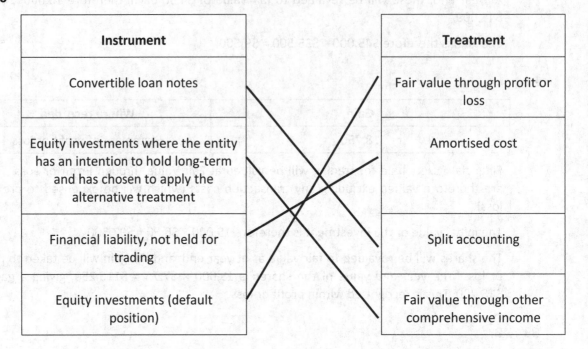

Instrument	Treatment
Convertible loan notes	Fair value through profit or loss
Equity investments where the entity has an intention to hold long-term and has chosen to apply the alternative treatment	Amortised cost
Financial liability, not held for trading	Split accounting
Equity investments (default position)	Fair value through other comprehensive income

97   **D**

Functional currency is defined as the currency of the primary economic environment in which an entity operates.

Answer A is the definition of presentation currency. Answer C is one of the primary ways of determining an entity's functional currency.

98   **A**

Overseas transactions are recorded in the functional currency using the spot rate of exchange. Therefore, the land is initially recorded at $10 million (30m dinars/3). Land is a non-monetary asset and so is not retranslated, meaning that its carrying amount remains as $10 million.

If you selected answer B then you retranslated the land at the closing rate of exchange. If you selected answer C then you translated the land at the average rate of exchange. If you selected answer D then you measured the land at its fair value, despite the fact that it is held using the cost model.

99   **B**

Statement (i) is false. Exchange gains and losses arising on the retranslation of monetary items are recognised in profit or loss in the period.

100 $200,000

The loan should initially be translated into dollars using the spot rate of 6.0.

The repayment of the loan should be translated using the spot rate of 5.0.

The outstanding loan at the reporting date is a monetary item so is retranslated using the closing rate of 5.6

The exchange loss is calculated as follows:

	Dinar (m)	Rate	Dollars (m)
1/1/20X1	12	6.0	2.0
30/11/20X1	(3)	5.0	(0.6)
Foreign exchange loss	–	Bal. fig.	0.2
31/12/20X1	9	5.6	1.6

101 C

The machine is recorded in the functional currency using the spot rate, giving an initial value of $10 million (20m dinars/2).

The machine is then depreciated over its useful life. By the reporting date, the carrying amount will be $9.5 million ($10m × 19/20). The machine is a non-monetary item held under a cost model so is not retranslated at the reporting date.

If you selected answer A then you have translated the depreciation at the closing rate of exchange. If you selected answer B then you have translated depreciation at the average rate of exchange. If you selected answer D then you have retranslated the machine at the closing rate of exchange.

102 D

The sale should be treated as a loan secured against the inventory. The inventory would remain with Mango, and a $500,000 loan would be recorded. This loan would include interest at 10% a year. In year one, $50,000 would therefore be recorded as a finance cost.

Answers A and B treat this as a sale, which is incorrect. Deferred income is not taken to the statement of profit or loss, so item C is incorrect.

103 C

Although the invoiced amount is $180,000, $30,000 of this has not yet been earned and must be deferred until the servicing work has been completed.

104

	$m
Step 1 – Overall	
Price	5
Total cost – incurred to date	(1.6)
– estimated future	(2.4)
	———
Overall profit	1
	———

Step 2 – Progress

Progress = work certified 1.8/total price 5 = 36%

	$m
Step 3 – P/L	
Revenue (36% of 5)	1.8
Cost of sales (36% of 4m total costs)	(1.44)
	———
Profit	0.36
	———

	$m
Step 4 – SOFP	
Costs to date	1.6
Profit to date	0.36
Less: Amount billed	(1.8)
	———
Contract asset	0.16
	———

105

Revenue	Cost of sales
$63 million	$83 million

	$m
Step 1 – Overall	
Price	90
Total cost – incurred to date	(77)
– estimated future	(33)
	———
Overall loss	(20)
	———

Step 2 – Progress

Progress = work certified 63/total price 90 = 70%

	$m
Step 3 – P/L	
Revenue (70% of 90)	63
Cost of sales (70% of 110)	(77)
Cost of sales (provision to recognise full loss)	(6)
	———
FULL loss to be recognised immediately	(20)
	———

106 $89

As the service is not sold separately, the discount cannot simply be applied to this element. Instead, the discount should be allocated to each part of the bundled sale. Applying the discount across each part gives revenue as follows:

Goods	$50	($75 × $100/$150)
Installation	$17	($25 × $100/$150)
Service	$33	($50 × $100/$150)

The revenue in relation to the goods and installation should be recognised on 1 May. As 8 months of the service has been performed (from 1 May to 31 December), then $22 should be recognised ($33 × 8/12).

This gives a total revenue for the year of 50 + 17 + 22 = $89.

107

Step	Correct order
Identify the separate performance obligations within a contract	Identify the contract
Identify the contract	Identify the separate performance obligations within a contract
Determine the transaction price	Determine the transaction price
Recognise revenue when (or as) a performance obligation is satisfied	Allocate the transaction price to the performance obligations in the contract
Allocate the transaction price to the performance obligations in the contract	Recognise revenue when (or as) a performance obligation is satisfied

108 D

	$m
Price	40
Total cost – incurred to date	(16)
– estimated future	(18)
	――
Overall profit	6
	――

Progress = 45%

	$m
Revenue (45% of 40)	18
Cost of sales (45% of total costs of 34)	(15.3)
	――
Overall profit	2.7
	――

Items A and B incorrectly include the full revenue. Item C includes the actual costs to date incorrectly.

109 **$30,000**

Contract price	200,000
Total contract cost (130,000 + 20,000)	(150,000)
Estimated total profit	50,000
Progress 180,000/200,000 = 90%	
Profit earned = 50,000 × 90% =	45,000
Recognised in previous year	(15,000)
Current year profit	30,000

110 **B**

With item B, the sale of the goods has fulfilled a contractual obligation so the revenue in relation to this can be recognised. The service will be recognised over time, so the revenue should be deferred and recognised as the obligation is fulfilled.

For item A, Hatton acts as an agent, so only the commission should be included in revenue.

For item C, any profit or loss on disposal should be taken to the statement of profit or loss. The proceeds should not be included within revenue.

For item D, the $1 million should be initially discounted to present value as there is a significant financing component within the transaction. The revenue would initially be recognised at $826k, with an equivalent receivable. This would then be held at amortised cost with finance income of 10% being earned each year.

111 **$500,000**

	$000
Costs to date	4,500
Loss	(2,000)
Less: Amount billed	(3,000)
Contract liability	(500)

As the contract is loss-making, Sugar should record the full loss immediately.

112 **A**

Using the work certified basis, the progress of this contract is 1,050/1,500= 70%

Therefore 70% of the total contract costs should be recognised, giving 800 × 70% = $560,000

As $240,000 of costs were recognised in the prior year, costs of $560,000 − $240,000 = $320,000 should be recognised in the current year profit or loss statement.

113 A

Contract price	1,000,000
Total contract cost (530,000 + 170,000)	(700,000)
Estimated total profit	300,000

Progress 600,000/1,000,000 = 60%

Revenue (60% × 1,000,000)	600,000
Cost of sales (60% × 700,000)	(420,000)
Profit	180,000
Costs to date	530,000
Profit to date	180,000
Less: Amount billed	(600,000)
Contract liability	110,000

114 D

At 31 March 2015, the deferred consideration of $12,650 would need to be discounted by 10% for one year to $11,500 (effectively deferring a finance cost of $1,150). The total amount credited to profit or loss would be $24,150 (12,650 + 11,500).

115 D

The tax expense in the statement of profit or loss is made up of the current year estimate, the prior year overprovision and the movement in deferred tax. The prior year overprovision must be deducted from the current year expense, and the movement in deferred tax must be added to the current year expense, as the deferred tax liability has increased.

Tax expense = $60,000 – $4,500 + $600 = $56,100

If you chose A, you have deducted the movement in deferred tax, even though the liability has increased. If you chose C you have added the overprovision. If you chose B you have added the overprovision and the closing deferred tax liability.

116

Statement of profit or loss	Statement of financial position
$88,000	$83,000

The tax expense in the statement of profit or loss is made up of the current year estimate and the prior year underprovision. The year end liability in the statement of financial position is made up of the current year estimate only.

Tax expense = $83,000 + $5,000 underprovision from previous year = $88,000

Tax liability = $83,000 year end estimate only.

117 C

Deferred tax provision required	9,000 (30,000 × 30%)
Opening balance per TB	12,000
Reduction in provision	(3,000)

Tax expense:

Current year estimate	15,000
Prior year overprovision	(4,000)
Deferred tax, as above	(3,000)
	─────
Charge for year	8,000
	─────

If you chose A, you have added in the full deferred tax liability. If you chose B you have added the full liability and the overprovision. If you chose D, you have not dealt with the overprovision.

118 A

Deferred taxation increase (23,000 – 16,000) = 7,000

Less tax on revaluation gain	(3,000) recognised as OCI (10,000 × 30%)
	─────
Charge to SPL	4,000
	─────

Tax expense:

Current year estimate	12,000
Prior year overprovision	(7,000)
Deferred tax, as above	4,000
	─────
Charge for year	9,000
	─────

If you chose B, you have used the full deferred tax increase. If you chose C you have added the overprovision. If you chose D you have deducted the deferred tax movement.

119 89.1

EPS = $3,000,000/3,366,667 (W1) = $0.89

(W1) Weighted average number of shares

Step 1 – Theoretical ex-rights price (TERP)

2 shares @ $2 =	$4
1 share @ $1.40 =	$1.40
	─────
3 shares	$5.40

TERP = $5.40/3 = $1.80

Step 2 – Rights fraction = 2/1.8

Step 3 – Weighted average number of shares (WANS)

Date	Number	Fraction of year	Rights fraction	Weighted Average
1 January	2,400,000	3/12	2/1.8	666,667
1 April	3,600,000	9/12		2,700,000
				3,366,667

120 A

EPS = $2,000,000/4,250,000 (W1) = $0.47

(W1) **Weighted average number of shares**

Date	Number	Fraction of year	Bonus fraction	Weighted Average
1 January	3,000,000	5/12	4/3	1,666,667
1 June	4,000,000	4/12		1,333,333
30 September	5,000,000	3/12		1,250,000
				4,250,000

If you chose C or D, you have failed to apply the bonus fraction correctly. If you chose B you have applied the bonus fraction for more than the first 5 months.

121 **$0.76**

The prior year earnings per share figure must be restated by the inverse of the rights fraction that relates to the current year earnings per share calculation.

The current year rights fraction is calculated below.

Step 1 – Theoretical ex-rights price (TERP)

3 shares @ $2.20 =	$6.60
1 share @ $1.40 =	$1.60
4 shares	$8.20

TERP = $8.20/4 = $2.05

Step 2 – Rights fraction

$$\frac{2.20}{2.05}$$

Therefore the restated earnings per share figure is 81c × 2.05/2.20 = $0.76.

122 D

Diluted EPS is calculated as 10,644,000/7,250,000 = $1.47

The earnings adjustment is:	$
Earnings for basic EPS	10,500,000
Plus interest saved (2.5m*8%)	200,000
Less tax (200,000*28%)	(56,000)
Earnings for Diluted EPS	10,644,000

Shares for basic EPS	6,000,000	
Shares issued on conversion	1,250,000	(2,500,000/100)*50
Shares for diluted EPS	7,250,000	

123 C

To calculate diluted earnings per share with an option, you need to work out the number of 'free' shares that will be issued if the options are exercised, and add that to the weighted average number of shares.

If the options are exercised, $3 million will be received ($3 × 1 million options).

At the market value of $5, $3 million would buy 600,000 shares ($3m/$5).

Therefore the cash received is the equivalent of 600,000 shares. As there are 1 million options, this means that 400,000 shares are being issued for free.

Diluted EPS = $2m/(4 million + 400,000) = **$0.46 cents**

124 $2,250,000

The Earnings figure for the EPS calculation is the profit attributable to the parent company shareholders.

125 A, E

Redeemable preference dividends will already have been removed from net profit when arriving at this figure in a profit or loss account. Therefore this adjustment is not necessary. Dividends are simply the cash paid out of the earnings, and are often compared to the earnings per share. All the other items will need to be removed from the overall net profit figure in the profit or loss account.

126

Considered within DEPS	Considered within Basic EPS
The issue during the year of a convertible (to equity shares) loan note	A 1 for 5 rights issue of equity shares during the year at $1.20 when the market price of the equity shares was $2.00
The granting during the year of directors' share options exercisable in three years' time	Equity shares issued during the year as the purchase consideration for the acquisition of a new subsidiary company

127 B

A and D will give the same impression as overall profit for the year. C is incorrect as diluted EPS is no indication of future profit.

128 A

(1,550/((2,500 × 2 + 1,200 see below)

2 million shares at $1.20 = $2.4 million which would buy 800,000 shares at full price of $3. Therefore, dilution element (free shares) is 1,200,000 (2,000 – 800).

129

Legal action against AP	Legal action by AP
Provision	Contingent Asset

The legal action against AP has a probable outflow, so AP should make a provision. The legal action taken by AP is a contingent asset. As it is probable, it should be disclosed in a note. Assets should only be recognised when there is a virtually certain inflow.

130 C

A provision is only required when (i) there is a present obligation arising as a result of a past event, (ii) it is probable that an outflow of resources embodying economic benefits will be required to settle the obligation, and (iii) a reliable estimate can be made of the amount. Only answer C meets all these criteria. Answer A is incorrect because the obligation does not exist at the reporting date and also cannot be reliably measured at present. Answer B is an example of an adjusting event after the reporting date as it provides evidence of conditions existing at the reporting. Answer D is a contingent liability. However, as it is remote, no provision is necessary.

131 C

The warehouse fire is an adjusting event as it occurred before the reporting date. Settlement of the insurance claim should therefore be included in the financial statements.

The other events are non-adjusting as they occurred after the reporting date and do not provide evidence of conditions existing at the reporting date. Issue B is a brand new event, and therefore should not be adjusted. As it is clearly material, the event should be disclosed in the notes to the accounts.

132 $3,500,000

Per IAS 37, the amount payable relates to a past event (the sale of faulty products) and the likelihood of payout is probable (i.e. more likely than not). Hence, the full amount of the payout should be provided for.

133 B

The costs associated with ongoing activities (being the relocation and retraining of employees) should not be provided for.

134 B

Extraction provision at 30 September 20X4 is $2.5 million (250 × 10).

Dismantling provision at 1 October 20X3 is $20.4 million (30,000 × 0.68).

This will increase by an 8% finance cost by 30 September 20X4 = $22,032,000.

Total provision is $24,532,000.

135 B, C

The change in tax rate and the fire will be non-adjusting events as the conditions did not exist at the reporting date.

136

	Adjusting	Non-adjusting
A public announcement in April 2015 of a formal plan to discontinue an operation which had been approved by the board in February 2015.		X
The settlement of an insurance claim for a loss sustained in December 2014.	X	

A board decision to discontinue an operation does not create a liability. A provision can only be made on the announcement of a formal plan (as it then raises a valid expectation that the discontinuance will be carried out). As this announcement occurs during the year ended 31 March 2016, this a non-adjusting event for the year ended 31 March 2015.

The insurance claim was in existence at the year end, so this will be an adjusting event as it provides further evidence of conditions in existence.

137 D

Deferred tax relating to the revaluation of an asset must be provided for even if there is no intention to sell the asset in accordance with IAS 12.

138

	True	False
IAS 10 *Events After the Reporting Period* covers the period from the reporting date to the annual general meeting		X
According to IAS 10 *Events After the Reporting Period*, any non-adjusting event should be disclosed as a note in the financial statements		X

Both are false. IAS 10 covers the period from the reporting date up to the date the financial statements are authorised for issue. Only material non-adjusting events need to be disclosed as notes in the financial statements.

139

There is a present obligation from a past event	No
A reliable estimate can be made	Yes
There is a probable outflow of economic benefits	Yes

Whilst there is an estimate of $500,000 and it is probable that Faubourg Co will make the changes, there is no present obligation at 31 December 20X4.

If Faubourg Co changes its mind and sells the building prior to June 20X5, no obligation would arise. Future obligations are not accounted for as provisions.

140 A, D

Changes in provisions are regarded as changes in accounting estimates so should be accounted for prospectively rather than retrospectively.

Provisions should be recorded at the best estimate, reflecting the amount most likely to be paid out, rather than the highest possible liability.

CONSOLIDATED FINANCIAL STATEMENTS

141

	Consolidated	Not to be consolidated
Beta is a bank and its activity is so different from the engineering activities of the rest of the group that it would be meaningless to consolidate it.	X	
Delta is located in a country where local accounting standards are compulsory and these are not compatible with IFRS used by the rest of the group.	X	
Gamma is located in a country where a military coup has taken place and Petre has lost control of the investment for the foreseeable future.		X

The investment in Gamma no longer meets the definition of a subsidiary (ability to control) and therefore would not be consolidated.

142 A

Is the correct treatment for a bargain purchase (negative goodwill).

143 C

While having the majority of shares may be a situation which leads to control, it does not feature in the definition of control per IFRS 10.

144 D

The deferred consideration needs to initially be discounted to present value on 1 Jan 20X1.

$200,000/1.1^3 = $150,262 on 1 January 20X1.

At 31 December 20X2, the discount will have been unwound for 2 years.

$150,262 × 10% = $15,026 to 31 Dec 20X1, making the liability $165,288 at 31 Dec 20X1.

$165,288 × 10% = $16,529 to 31 Dec 20X2, making the liability **$181,817** at 31 Dec 20X2.

If you chose C, you have not discounted the consideration. If you chose A, you have not unwound the discount. If you chose B, you have only done the first year calculation.

145 $371,000

To work out the net assets at acquisition, the retained earnings at acquisition must be calculated.

The retained earnings at the end of the year are given as $180,000, and there has been a profit of $36,000 for the year.

As Philip has owned Stanley for 3 months, then 3 months of this profit is regarded as post acquisition. Therefore $9,000 has been made since acquisition.

Once this has been worked out, the retained earnings at acquisition can be calculated by deducting the post-acquisition retained earnings of $9,000 from the closing retained earnings of $180,000 to give $171,000.

Net assets at acquisition = $200,000 share capital + $171,000 retained earnings = $371,000.

146 $2,780,000

The cost of investment is worked out as follows:

Shares: 800,000 × ¾ × $3.80 = $2,280,000

Deferred cash = $550,000 × 1/1.1 = $500,000

The professional fees cannot be capitalised as part of the cost of investment. Therefore the total cost of investment is $2,280,000 + $500,000 = **$2,780,000**

147 B

The profit on the $800,000 sale is $160,000 ($800,000 × 25/125).

As 75% of the goods have been sold on to third parties, 25% remain in inventory at the year end. Unrealised profits only arise on goods remaining in inventory at the year end, so the unrealised profit is $40,000.

148 $352,000

The unrealised profit on the non-current asset transfer needs to be removed.

The carrying amount at the year end after the transfer is $32,000 ($40,000 less 1 year's depreciation).

The carrying amount of the asset if it had never been transferred would have been $24,000 ($30,000 less 1 year's depreciation).

Therefore the unrealised profit on the non-current asset is $8,000.

The total PPE is therefore $300,000 + $60,000 − $8,000 = **$352,000.**

149 B, E

The fact that unanimous consent is required would suggest that there is no control over the investee. Preference shares carry no voting rights and therefore are excluded when considering the control held over a company.

150

	Include in cost of investment	Do not include in the cost of investment
An agreement to pay a further $30,000 if the subsidiary company achieves an operating profit of over $100,000 in the first 3 years after acquisition.	X	
Professional fees of $10,000 in connection with the investment		X

Any incidental costs associated with the acquisition should be expensed as incurred. Contingent consideration can all be included as part of the cost of an investment in a subsidiary company.

151 D

All of Paul's revenue and expenses will be time-apportioned from the date of acquisition to the date of consolidation to reflect the period for which these were controlled by Peter.

152 A

The asset has not been sold outside of the group and therefore there is an unrealised profit to adjust for on consolidation.

153

	True	False
It will always be deducted in full from the parent company retained earnings		X
It will be apportioned between the parent company and the non-controlling interest (NCI) when the NCI is valued at fair value	X	

Where the NCI is valued at fair value, the goodwill impairment will be split between the parent and the NCI in accordance with their shareholdings.

154 A

The activities of the subsidiary are irrelevant when making the decision as to whether to produce consolidated financial statements or not.

155 **$160,000**

	$000	
Consideration - shares	100,000	(see below)
Consideration – cash	60,000	

Branch purchased 75% of Leaf's 80 million shares, giving them 60 million shares. Branch issued 2 shares for every 3 purchased, meaning 40 million shares have been issued (60m × 2/3). At a market value of $2.50 each, 40 million shares have a value of $100 million.

156 **$108,000**

NCI % × S's PAT = 20% × $600k = $120k

NCI% × PURP (S selling to P) = 20% × 60k =   ($12k)

Total NCI = $120k – $12k = **$108k**

157 **D**

Cost of sales = $14.7m + $8.7m (9/12 × $11.6m) – $4.3m (I/C sale) + $200k (PURP) = **$19.3m**

The PURP is $2.2m × 10/110 = $200k.

If you chose B, you have not time-apportioned the results. If you chose A you have deducted the PURP rather than adding it. If you chose C, you have missed the PURP.

158 **$970,000**

Operating expenses = $600,000 + $350,000 + $20,000 (FV depreciation) = $970,000

The only adjustments to the statement of profit or loss should be the current year income or expenses. Therefore the prior year fair value depreciation and goodwill impairment are ignored.

159 **B**

The finance costs for the subsidiary must be time apportioned for six months, as A has only owned them for that period of time. Also, the intra-group interest must be split out. The intra-group interest would not have existed in the first half of the year, as the loan was only given to B in July.

The intra-group interest for the second 6 months would have been $20,000 ($500,000 × 8% × 6/12). Without this, B's finance costs would have been $50,000 for the year. Splitting this evenly across the year would mean that $25,000 was incurred in each six month period.

Therefore the total finance costs would be $200,000 + $25,000 = **$225,000.**

160 A

	Impacts the NCI share of profit	Does not impact the NCI share
Goodwill impairment	X	
The parent transferring an item of inventory to the subsidiary for $10,000 greater than its carrying amount, all of which remains in the group at the year end		X
The subsidiary having an item of plant with a fair value of $500,000 above its carrying amount, and a remaining life of 10 years	X	

The parent transferring inventory at a profit would mean that the parent's profits are overstated. This would have no impact on the non-controlling interest.

161 $6,600,000

Consolidated revenue: AB $5.5m+ CD $2.1m – $1m intercompany = $6.6 million

All intercompany sales and cost of sales are removed from the group accounts.

162 B

The dividend would not have been in Allen's statement of profit or loss, so no adjustment to this would be made. The adjustment to remove the dividend would be made in investment income, where Burridge will have recorded the income in its individual financial statements.

The profit needs to be time-apportioned for the six months of ownership, with the $10,000 impairment then deducted.

Share of profit of associate = 30% × $200,000 ($400,000 × 6/12) – $10,000 = **$50,000**

If you chose D, you have not time-apportioned the associate. If you chose C, you have not deducted the impairment.

163 B

Beasant own 30% of Arnie's shares, which is 30,000 shares (30% of Arnie's 100,000 shares).

As Beasant gave 1 share away for every 3 purchased, Beasant gave 10,000 shares away. These had a market value of $4.50 and were therefore worth $45,000.

After that, Beasant must include 30% of Arnie's post acquisition movement in net assets. Arnie has made a post-acquisition loss of $40,000 (net assets at acquisition were $500,000 and net assets at 31 December were $460,000). Therefore Beasant's share of this is a $12,000 loss (30%).

Cost of investment	$45,000
Share of post-acquisition loss	($12,000)
Investment in associate	$33,000

If you chose D, you based the consideration on 30,000 shares rather than 10,000. If you chose C, you have ignored share capital from the net assets movement. If you chose A, you have used the wrong share price for consideration.

164

	Single entity concept	Going concern concept
Removing unrealised profits on group sales	X	
Removing intra-group balances	X	

165

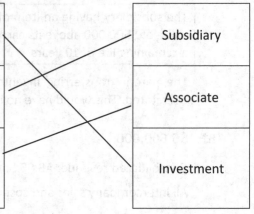

30% of the share capital of Hansen Co. The other 70% is owned by Lawro, another listed company, whose directors make up Hansen's board.	Subsidiary
80% of the share capital of Kennedy Co, whose activities are significantly different from the rest of the Nicol group.	Associate
30% of the share capital of Bruce Co. The Nicol group have appointed 2 of the 5 board members of Bruce Co, with the other board members coming from three other entities.	Investment

Normally 30% would suggest that Nicol have significant influence, making Hansen an associate. However, Lawro having 70% and controlling the entire board would mean that it is unlikely that Nicol have influence and therefore treat it as a trade investment.

166 A

	$
Cost of Investment	5,500,000
Badger % of post-acquisition profits	46,875
30% × (625,000 × 3/12)	
Total	**5,546,875**

167 $325,000

	$
Share of Net Profit: 30% * 1,500,000	450,000
Share of PURP: 30%*[(2m*50%)*30%]	(90,000)
Current Year impairment	(35,000)
Total	**325,000**

168 A

IFRS 10 states that where the reporting date for a parent is different from that of a subsidiary, the subsidiary should prepare additional financial information as of the same date as the financial statements of the parent unless it is impracticable to do so.

If it is impracticable to do so, IFRS 10 allows use of subsidiary financial statements made up to a date of not more than three months earlier or later than the parent's reporting date, with due adjustment for significant transactions or other events between the dates.

The companies do not have to have the same policies in their individual financial statements, but adjustments will be made to prepare the consolidated financial statements using the group policies.

Only the profit relating to goods remaining in the group at year end needs to be adjusted.

169 A, B

Items C and D would signify control.

170 C, D

While the same accounting policies must be used in the consolidated financial statements, the subsidiaries do not have to operate the same policies as the parent. Having different activities is not an acceptable reason for non-consolidation.

171 A

	$000
Cost (240,000 × $6)	1,440
Share of associate's profit (400 × 6/12 × 240/800)	60
Less dividend received (150 × 240/800)	(45)
	1,455

172 $63,800,000

	$000
Viagem	51,200
Greca (26,000 × 9/12)	19,500
Intra-group purchases (800 × 9 months)	(7,200)
URP in inventory (1,500 × 25/125)	300
	63,800

173 C

Market price of Sact's shares at acquisition was $2.50 (3.00 – (3.00 × 20/120)), therefore NCI at acq was $50,000 (100,000 × 20% × $2.50). NCI share of the post-acq profit is $6,000 (40,000 × 9/12 × 20%). Therefore non-controlling interest as at 31 March 2015 is $56,000.

174 C

Germaine only owns 40% of Foll's voting shares so is unlikely to exercise control.

175 $546,000

	$
Wilmslow	450,000
Post acq Zeta ((340 – 200) × 80%)	112,000
URP in inventory (320,000 × ¼ × 25/125)	(16,000)
	546,000

176 C, D

The fair value of deferred consideration is its present value (i.e. discounted). Fair values are applied to the subsidiaries assets, liabilities and contingent liabilities.

While the use of fair value seems to not comply with the historical cost principle, this will effectively form part of the cost of the subsidiary, so the principle is still applied. Depreciation will not increase if the fair value of assets is lower than the current carrying amount. Patents can be recorded as intangibles as they are separable.

177

	True	False
The profit made by a parent on the sale of goods to a subsidiary is only realised when the subsidiary sells the goods to a third party	X	
Eliminating intra-group unrealised profits never affects non-controlling interests		X
The profit element of goods supplied by the parent to an associate and held in year-end inventory must be eliminated in full		X

178 $1,335,000

	$000	
Investment at cost	1,200	
Share of post-acq profit	150	(750 × 8/12 × 30%)
URP in inventory	(15)	(300 × 20/120 × 30%)
	1,335	

179 $98,600,000

The $1 million cash in transit should be treated as received (Dr Cash $1 million, Cr Receivables $1 million). After this, an intra-group balance of $3 million will remain. This is then removed (Dr Payables $3 million, Cr Receivables $3 million).

Therefore consolidated receivables = 64,600 + 38,600 – 1,000 – 3,000 = **$98,600,000**

180

	True	False
If a subsidiary is disposed of on the last day of the reporting period then its assets and liabilities must still be included in the consolidated statement of financial position		X
The gain or loss arising on the disposal of a subsidiary in the financial statements is recorded in other comprehensive income		X

181

Cash consideration of $4.8 million

Deferred cash consideration of $8.3 million

The professional fees cannot be capitalised. The deferred cash should be discounted to present value at the date of acquisition, $10 million/$1.1^2$ = $8.3 million.

182 B

The profit or loss on the disposal is calculated as follows:

Proceeds	10m
Goodwill at disposal	(2m)
Net assets at disposal	(9m)
Non-controlling interest at disposal	3m
	———
Profit on disposal	2m
	———

If you selected answer A you have incorrectly identified it as a loss. If you selected answer C you have added the goodwill instead of deducting it. If you selected answer D you have added the non-controlling interest onto the carrying amount of the subsidiary (rather than deducting it) when calculating the profit or loss on disposal.

183 $6,000,000

The profit arising in the individual financial statements of Wind will be the difference between the proceeds received of $10 million and the purchase price of $6 million.

184 $2,500,000

	$m	$m
Proceeds		9
Goodwill at disposal		(4.6)
Net assets at disposal		(5)
Non-controlling interest at disposal		3.1
		———
Profit on disposal		2.5
		———

185 A

	$m	$m
Proceeds		15
Goodwill at disposal		Nil
Net assets at disposal		(8)
Non-controlling interest:		
At acquisition	2.2	
NCI % of post-acquisition net assets	1.2	
40% × ($8m – $5m)		
NCI % of goodwill impairment (40% × $1m)	(0.4)	
Non-controlling interest at disposal		3
Profit on disposal		10.0

If you selected answer B you have used the non-controlling interest at acquisition when calculating the profit or loss on disposal, instead of the non-controlling interest at disposal. If you selected answer C you have not reduced the non-controlling interest by its share of the goodwill impairment. If you selected answer D you have valued the non-controlling interest at its share of the disposal date net assets.

INTERPRETATION OF FINANCIAL STATEMENTS

186 A

A not-for-profit entity is not likely to have shareholders or 'earnings'.

187 B

A, C and D are all ratios associated with profit. A charity is more likely to be concerned with liquidity rather than the profits made by the entity.

188

	Limitation	Not a limitation
Different ways of calculating certain ratios exist	X	
Accounting policy choices can limit comparability between different companies	X	

189 35

Inventory turnover is six times, so inventory days must be 365/6 = 61 days.

The cash collection period is inventory days, plus receivables days, less payables days.

Therefore the trade payables period is 61 + 42 – 68 = 35 days

190   C, E

A new website selling direct to the public is unlikely to be on credit terms, as payment will be taken on the order.

This should therefore reduce the receivables collection period, as will the new retail units to the public, which will be cash based.

191   C

Return on capital employed is calculated as profit from operations/capital employed. Capital employed consists of debt and equity.

The deferred tax and payables are not included. Therefore the return on capital employed = $240,000/$900,000 = **26.7%**

192   0.87:1

The quick ratio is made up of the current assets excluding inventory divided by the current liabilities = ($80,000 + $10,000)/($70,000 + $34,000) = **0.87:1**

193   A

While the website is new in the year, the additional delivery costs are likely to be incurred every year in the future, meaning it is not a 'one-off' item.

194   C

Delivery costs to customers come after gross profit in the statement of profit or loss, so the increased prices will have no impact on the gross profit margin.

195

	Available to KRL to use	Not available to KRL to use
Details of the overseas country in which the target entity operates	X	
Recent financial statements of the entity	X	
Internal business plans of the takeover target		X

Internal business plans would be internal information for an entity; therefore KRL would not be able to obtain this information publically.

196   A

P/E ratio is seen as a marker of risk, and a high P/E ratio is indicative of a lower perceived risk than a company with a lower P/E ratio. Therefore Marcel is seen as less risky than the sector average.

P/E ratio is also indicative of market confidence, and a high P/E ratio means that high future growth is expected. Therefore, there is more confidence about the future prospects of Marcel than the sector average.

197

	True	False
It acts as a prediction of the future Earnings Per Share figure		X
It discloses that Earnings Per Share could have been higher		X

Diluted EPS is not a prediction of the future EPS figure as firstly there is no forecast made of the earnings figure.

Secondly, if there were a range of conversion terms for a convertible, the terms giving the maximum number of issued shares would always be used in the Diluted EPS calculation, rather than the most likely conversion terms.

Diluted EPS is a warning to shareholders that the EPS calculation could have been lower if the commitments to issue ordinary shares had been issued as shares in the current period.

198 B

The finance cost in the profit or loss account will be based on the effective interest rate, so the charge will be $2.5m × 8% = $200,000.

If the interest cover to be maintained is 9, then the minimum operating profit to be maintained must be $200 × 9 = $1.8m

Option A used the coupon rate of 6% to calculate the finance cost, giving $150k.

Option C used the difference between the effective and coupon rate which is $50k.

Option D includes the transaction costs in the initial value of the loan, when calculating effective interest, giving $220k.

199 5.6

Price Earnings (P/E) Ratio is Current Market Price per share/Earnings Per Share.

The Earnings Per Share (EPS) for Rogers is net profit/number of ordinary shares in issue. The share capital is $1 million. As each share is worth $0.50, there must be 2 million shares in issue.

Therefore, EPS is 1,250/2000 = $0.625, or 62.5c

P/E ratio is therefore 3.50/0.625 = 5.6 times

200 21.4%

The dividend yield is calculated as the Dividend per share/Current share price × 100%.

Dividend per share is Total dividends/Total number of shares

Dividend per share is therefore $1.5m/2m = $0.75, or 75c

The current share price is $3.50

Therefore the dividend yield is 0.75/3.5 × 100% = 21.4%

201 B

ROCE can be sub-divided into net profit × asset turnover.

Alco has a higher net profit, and therefore must be a high end retailer. Its asset turnover is 0.4 times, so it does not use assets intensively to generate a profit.

This would be expected at a high end retailer, as they are not volume driven.

Saleco has a low net profit, and therefore must be a lower end retailer. Its asset turnover is 5 times, so it uses assets intensively to generate a profit.

This would be expected at a lower end retailer, as they are volume driven.

202

	Limitation	Not a limitation
Financial statements often use historic cost, meaning that inflation is not taken into account	X	
Complex items may not fit into any accounting standards and therefore may be omitted from the financial statements		X

While complex items may exist which don't fit easily into an accounting standard, these cannot simply be omitted from the financial statements. IFRS is a principles-based framework, so these would be accounted for using the principles contained within the IASB's *Conceptual Framework for Financial Reporting.*

203 A

Lepchem have not yet made any sales, so any ratio involving profit or revenue is irrelevant. The current ratio will be relevant, as Lepchem may have cash flow problems as they spend cash to develop new pharmaceuticals without any cash receipt until they are successful. This could threaten Lepchem's ability to continue as a going concern.

204 C

	Could be used to assess	Will not be used
The return given to investors		X
The success in achieving the organisation's stated aims	X	
How well costs are being managed	X	

Not-for-profit entities do not exist to make profits, therefore the return given to investors is irrelevant.

205 D

With a property management company, the value in the business is linked to the properties and the income which they can generate. Therefore the revenue and profits generated will be relevant.

However, there will be no real inventory so inventory turnover is unlikely to be a key measure that is used.

206 B, C

Rising costs may be across the industry. If not, it would still mean that Quartile could be compared to the sector, it may mean that Quartile's margins are worse. As the error has been corrected, there will be no issues over comparability this year.

207 51

Year end inventory of six times is 61 days (365/6).

Trade payables period is 42 days (230,000 × 365/2,000,000).

Therefore receivables collection period is 51 days (70 – 61 + 42).

208 B, D

Factoring with recourse means Trent still has the risk of an irrecoverable receivable and therefore would not derecognise the receivable. The cash sales are irrelevant as Trent does not include them within the calculation.

209 D

Is correct as it will increase debt but have no effect on equity.

210 C

Is correct as use of average cost gives a higher cost of sales (and in turn lower operating profit) than FIFO during rising prices.

STATEMENT OF CASH FLOWS

211 A

PPE

B/f	14,400	Disposal (CV)	3,000
Revaluation	2,000	Depreciation	2,500
Provision	4,000		
Additions (balance)	**8,500**	C/f	23,400
	28,900		28,900

212 B

	$
Accrued interest b/f	12,000
Interest per statement of profit or loss	41,000
Less unwinding (this is unpaid, $150k, × 6%)	(9,000)
Accrued interest c/f	(15,000)
Paid	29,000

If you chose A, you have ignored the unwinding of the discount. If you chose C you have made an error between the opening and closing liability. If you chose D you have simply taken the expense for the year.

213 $98,000

Tax liabilities

		B/f (27 + 106)	133
Paid	98	Statement of profit or loss	122
C/f (38 + 119)	157		
	255		255

214 D

Finance costs are added back in the indirect method but are not included in the direct method.

215 A, C

Purchase of investments and purchase of equipment would both be shown within cash flows from investing activities.

216 D

	$
Profit	37,500
Depreciation	2,500
Increase in receivables	(2,000)
Decrease in inventory	3,600
Increase in payables	700
Cash generated from operations	42,300
Purchase of non-current assets	(16,000)
Net increase in cash and cash equivalents	26,300

If you chose A, you have deducted depreciation. If you chose C you have deducted the payables movement. If you chose B, you have added the movement in receivables.

217 D

	Add to profit before tax	Deduct from profit before tax
Decrease in trade receivables	X	
increase in inventories		X
Profit on sale of non-current assets		X
Depreciation	X	

Profit on disposal of non-current assets will be deducted from profit, as it relates to non-cash income. Increases in inventories would be deducted as they have a negative impact on cash flow. Decreases in receivables would have a positive impact on cash flow. Depreciation should be added to profit, as it relates to non-cash expenses.

218 $10,000

There will be an inflow of $30,000 relating to a share issue (being the total movement in share capital and share premium), and a $20,000 outflow on repayment of the debentures. Therefore the overall movement will be a net $10,000 inflow.

219 A

PPE

B/f	180	Disposal (CV)	60
Revaluation	25	Depreciation	20
Paid (balance)	**125**	C/f	250
	———		———
	330		330
	———		———

The amounts to be shown in investing activities will be:

Purchase of PPE: ($125,000) (See working above)

Sale of PPE: $50,000 (Given in question)

This gives a **net outflow of $75,000**

If you chose B or D, you have only accounted for one of the cash flows. If you chose C, you have missed the disposal from your PPE working.

220

Amortisation of government grant	Receipt of grant
	Cash received from grant $300,000 in investing activities
Decrease of 100,000 to cash generated from operations	

The release of government grant should be decreased from cash generated from operations, as this represents non-cash income. The grant received of $300,000 can be calculated using a working, as shown below.

Grant liability

		B/f	900,000
Release to P/L	100,000	**Receipt of grant (Balance)**	**300,000**
C/f	1,100,000		
	———		———
	1,200,000		1,200,000
	———		———

Section 5

ANSWERS TO OBJECTIVE CASE QUESTIONS – SECTION B

CONCEPTUAL FRAMEWORK/INTERNATIONAL FINANCIAL REPORTING STANDARDS

221 $300,000

The engine will be depreciated over the life of 36,000 flight hours. As the aircraft has flown for 1,200 in the first 6 months, the depreciation for the engine will be $9 million × 1,200/36,000 = $300,000.

222 D

Replacement components of complex assets can be capitalised. As the new engine has a life of 36,000 hours, the engine will be depreciated over this life rather than the based on the remaining life of the previous engine 1.

223

	Capitalise	Expense
$3 million repair of engine 2		X
$2 million repainting of the exterior		X

Both costs will be regarded as repairs and maintenance and must be expensed.

224 B

Cabin fittings – at 1 October 20X8 the carrying amount of the cabin fittings is $7.5 million (25,000 − (25,000 × 3.5/5)). The cost of improving the cabin facilities of $4.5 million should be capitalised as it led to enhanced future economic benefits in the form of substantially higher fares.

The cabin fittings would then have a carrying amount of $12 million (7,500 + 4,500) and an unchanged remaining life of 18 months. Thus depreciation for the six months to 31 March 20X9 is $4 million (12,000 × 6/18), giving a carrying amount of $8 million.

If you selected A, you have depreciated the upgrade over 5 years rather than the remaining life. If you selected C, you have not capitalised the upgrade. If you selected D, you have done a full year's depreciation on the upgrade.

---

225 C

Flightline is accounting for the aircraft under the cost model so any loss would be taken directly to the statement of profit or loss.

226 A

As Speculate uses the fair value model for investment properties, the asset should be revalued to fair value before being classed as an investment property. The gain on revaluation should be taken to other comprehensive income, as the asset is being revalued while held as property, plant and equipment.

At 1 October, the carrying amount of the asset is $1,950, being $2 million less 6 months' depreciation. As the fair value at 1 October is $2.3 million, this leads to a $350,000 gain which will be recorded in other comprehensive income.

227 B

Investment properties can be accounted for under the cost or fair value model but not the revaluation model, which applies to property, plant and equipment.

228 $190,000

		$000
Gain on investment properties:	A (2,340 – 2,300)	40
	B (1,650 – 1,500)	150

229 D

In Speculate's consolidated financial statements property B would be accounted for under IAS 16 *Property, Plant and Equipment* and be classified as owner-occupied. The group is regarded as a single entity, and the group use the building. Therefore it will be classed as property under IAS 16 rather than an investment property.

230 B

If Speculate uses the cost model, the asset would be transferred to investment properties at its carrying amount and then depreciated over its remaining life. This would mean that the asset would have a year's depreciation applied to it (6 months while held as property, plant and equipment, 6 months while held as investment properties). Fair values would be irrelevant.

The depreciation would therefore be $2 million/20 years = $100,000, giving a carrying amount of $1.9 million.

If you selected A, you have only accounted for depreciation for 6 months. If you selected C or D, you have applied depreciation to the fair value of the asset.

231 D

Loans are regarded as financial liabilities and should be held at amortised cost.

232   A

Borrowing costs must be capitalised if they are directly attributable to qualifying assets, which are assets that take a substantial time to complete.

233 $125,000

The finance cost of the loan must be calculated using the effective rate of 7.5%, so the total finance cost for the year ended 31 March 20X8 is $750,000 ($10 million × 7.5%). As the loan relates to a qualifying asset, the finance cost (or part of it in this case) can be capitalised in accordance with IAS 23.

Capitalisation commences from when expenditure is being incurred (1 May 20X7) and must cease when the asset is ready for its intended use (28 February 20X8); in this case a 10-month period.

The finance cost to be capitalised = $625,000 ($750,000 × 10/12). The remaining two-months finance costs of $125,000 must be expensed.

234 $625,000

The finance cost to be capitalised = $625,000 ($750,000 × 10/12).

235   B

Temporary investment income earned during the construction period should be netted off the amount capitalised. However, the interest was earned **prior to the period of construction**. Therefore the investment income earned should be taken to the statement of profit or loss as investment income.

236   B

The dismantling costs should be capitalised at the present value of $4 million, with an equivalent liability set up. In addition to this, the discount on the $4 million should be unwound by 8% each year, with the increase being taken to finance costs in the statement of profit or loss.

Therefore the finance cost is $320,000 unwinding of interest ($4 million × 8%).

If you selected A, spread the cost over the life of the asset. If you selected C, you have expensed the full amount. If you selected D, you have discounted the $4 million, despite being told this was already at its present value.

237   A

The $1.2 million government grant should be released over the 5 year life of the asset, meaning that $240,000 will be released to the statement of profit or loss each year. As Shawler only received the grant on 1 October 20X3, only $120,000 should be released to the statement of profit or loss in the year (being the release of 6 months).

Therefore there is a remaining balance of $1,080,000 at the year-end. Of this, $240,000 will be released in the next year. Therefore $840,000 will be shown as a non-current liability.

If you selected B, you have not split the year-end liability into current and non-current. If you selected C, you have released a full year of the grant and then not split the year-end liability. If you selected D, you have split the year-end liability but have released a full year of the grant rather than 6 months.

238 A

The land is initially translated using the spot rate of exchange and so is recognised at $3 million (12m dinar/4).

Land is a non-monetary asset and so is **not** retranslated at the reporting date.

239 B

Training costs cannot be capitalised as it is not possible to restrict the access of others to the economic benefit as staff could leave and take their skills elsewhere.

240 A, B

The deferred income should be removed, with an expense recorded in the statement of profit or loss. No prior year adjustment should be made. The plant cost would only be increased if the grant was accounted for using the netting off method.

241 B, D

Whilst items A and D are necessary for an item to be capitalised as an asset, they are not linked to the characteristic of them being identifiable.

242

	Capitalise	Expense
Training courses for staff		X
Expenditure on processor chip		X

Training courses for staff cannot be capitalised as Darby will not be able to restrict the access of others to the economic benefit. The expenditure on the chip would be classed as research expenditure, which is an expense.

243 $320,000

The amounts incurred from 1 February to 30 April should be expensed, meaning that $300,000 should be expensed. Following this, the costs from 1 May to 30 October should be capitalised, meaning that $600,000 should be capitalised.

This should then be amortised over the 5 year remaining life, giving $120,000 amortisation each year. This should be amortised from 1 November, meaning that 2 months' amortisation should be expensed, giving $20,000.

Therefore the total expense = $300,000 + $20,000 = **$320,000.**

244 C

The development costs will not be subject to an annual impairment review, but will be amortised over the 5 year useful life. The development costs will be held at the carrying value, and will not be revalued each year.

Plant used solely on the development project will result in the depreciation being a directly attributable cost of the project. Therefore any depreciation on the asset will be swept up in the costs to be capitalised and will be taken to the statement of profit or loss as the project is amortised over the 5 year life.

245 D

At the date of the impairment review, the asset had a carrying amount of $450,000 (9/10 × $500,000).

The recoverable amount of the asset is the **higher** of the fair value less costs to sell of $380,000 ($400,000 – $20,000) and the value in use of $480,000. The value in use is therefore $480,000.

The carrying amount of the asset is **lower** than the recoverable amount, so no impairment is charged.

246 B

A is incorrect as the recoverable amount is the higher of the value in use and fair value less costs to sell. C is wrong as it describes fair value, not value in use. D is wrong as impairment losses can be taken to the revaluation surplus if one exists for that asset.

247 A

The plant had a carrying amount of $240,000 on 1 October 20X4. The accident that may have caused impairment occurred on 1 April 20X5 and an impairment test would be done at this date.

The depreciation on the plant from 1 October 20X4 to 1 April 20X5 would be $40,000 (640,000 × 12.5% × 6/12) giving a carrying amount of $200,000 at the date of impairment.

248 B

The recoverable amount of the plant is the higher of its value in use of $150,000 or its fair value less costs to sell. If Wilderness trades in the plant it would receive $180,000 by way of a part exchange, but this is conditional on buying new plant which Wilderness is reluctant to do.

A more realistic amount of the fair value of the plant is its current disposal value of only $20,000. Thus the recoverable amount would be its value in use of $150,000.

249 B

First, the brand must be completely written off.

Writing this off would give a remaining carrying amount of $20 million ($12 million land and $8 million plant) meaning that $5 million must be allocated across the other assets.

Therefore the $5 million should be allocated across the land and the plant on a pro-rata basis according to their carrying amounts.

Impairment to plant = 8,000/20,000 × 5,000 = $2,000. Therefore carrying amount is **$6 million.**

250 A

Annual impairment reviews are required for intangible assets with an indefinite life, intangible assets not yet ready for use, and goodwill.

Other items should have impairment reviews when indications of impairment exist.

251 B

Profit or loss from discontinued operations will consist of the post-tax profit or loss, inclusive of any gains or losses on disposal of assets and any costs associated with the closure of the operation.

This figure should be placed underneath profit from continuing operations, but before other comprehensive income.

252 A

The disposal of outlets in country A represents a separate geographical location and should be treated as a discontinued operation. The change in focus in Country B is not going to be regarded as a separate major line of business, as it is just targeting different customers.

253 D

Depreciation should cease on the date that the asset is held for sale. In this case, this will be 1 January 20X3. Therefore depreciation would be $150,000 ($4 million/20 years × 9/12), giving a carrying amount of $3,850,000.

As the asset is expected to sell for $4 million, the asset should be held at $3,850,000 as the asset should be held at the lower of carrying amount and fair value less costs to sell.

254 A

Costs relating to the ongoing activities of the entity cannot be provided for according to IAS 37 *Provisions, Contingent Liabilities and Contingent Assets*. Therefore only the redundancy costs of $300,000 can be provided for.

255 C

Both events relate to conditions in existence at the reporting date, so both events should be regarded as adjusting events.

256 B, C

Accounting policies should only be changed if required by a new international financial reporting standard or if doing so results in the production of more reliable and relevant information.

257

The change in useful life of the plant will be a change in accounting **estimate** and should be applied **prospectively.**

258 A

A change in accounting policy must be accounted for as if the new policy had always been in place (retrospective application). In this case, for the year ended 30 September 20X9, both the opening and closing inventories would need to be measured at AVCO which would reduce reported profit by $400,000 (($20 million – $18 million) – ($15 million – $13.4 million) – i.e. the movement in the values of the opening and closing inventories).

The other effect of the change will be on the retained earnings brought forward at 1 October 20X8. These will be restated (reduced) by the effect of the reduced inventory value at 30 September 20X8 i.e. $1.6 million ($15 million – $13.4 million). This adjustment would be shown in the statement of changes in equity.

259 $88,000

The inventories should be valued at the lower of cost and net realisable value (NRV). The items have a cost of $100,000 (20,000 at $5). The NRV is $88,000, being the 20,000 units at their net selling price of $44 (being $55 less 20% commission).

260 B

The inventories should be held at the cost of $80,000 as the net realisable value of $150,000 less $20,000 to complete will be higher than the cost. The replacement cost of $50,000 is irrelevant.

261 C

The flock of sheep will be classed as a biological asset and the milk will be classed as agricultural produce. The cheese is produced after processing so will be classed as inventory.

262 B

The cattle will be held at fair value less point of sale costs. Initially the cattle would have been recognised at $95,000, being the $100,000 less 5% selling costs. At 31 March 20X6, it will be valued at $114,000, being $120,000 less 5% selling costs. Therefore a gain of $19,000 will be recorded in the statement of profit or loss.

263 B

Current cost accounting will apply the current cost of the asset less depreciation to date to reflect the age of the asset. As a new asset would cost $300,000, a 4 year old asset under current cost accounting will be $300,000 less 4 years' depreciation, which is $180,000 ($300,000 – 4 × 30,000 (300,000/10 years)).

264 B

This will be a level 2 input, as it is using the price of similar assets without adjustment.

265 A, C

The revaluation will increase equity, therefore affecting the gearing and return on capital employed. The depreciation will also increase. As Schrute charges depreciation to operating expenses, this will affect the net profit margin.

266 C

The lease is for the majority of the useful life of the asset, and the amount paid is substantially all of the fair value of the asset so the lease should be treated as a finance lease, meaning that an asset and liability are recorded.

A is incorrect as it represents the treatment for an operating lease, which would not be appropriate.

B outlines incorrect treatment for interest, which should decrease over the life of the lease as the lease liability decreases.

D is incorrect as the payments reduce the lease liability rather than being treated as prepayments.

267 B, F

If the lease were classed as an operating lease, the payments would be expensed on a straight-line basis over the lease term. Therefore $100,000 would be expensed each year. As Fino only entered into the lease halfway through the year, only $50,000 should be expensed.

Fino has paid $100,000 so $50,000 is regarded as a prepayment.

268 $306,250

The plant would be capitalised at the fair value of $350,000. This would then be depreciated over the four year lease term, giving depreciation of $87,500 a year.

As Fino only entered into the lease halfway through the year, this would give depreciation of $43,750. Therefore the carrying amount would be $350,000 less $43,750, which is $306,250.

269 A

Working:

Cost	350,000
Payment	(100,000)
	————
	250,000
Interest to 30 September 20X7 (6 months at 10%)	12,500

270

	Increase	Decrease
Return on Capital Employed		X
Gearing	X	
Interest cover		X

If the lease was classified as a finance lease, liabilities and finance costs would increase. This means that the capital employed would be higher, therefore decreasing return on capital employed. Gearing would increase due to the increased debt. Interest cover would decrease due to the higher level of finance costs.

271 B

An operating lease should be expensed on a straight line basis over the lease term. As Lotso has been given a 6 month rent-free period, Lotso will pay $450,000 over the 5 year lease term. This gives an annual expense of $90,000 in the statement of profit or loss ($450,000/5 years).

As Lotso has paid $50,000 on 31 December, there will be an accrual of $40,000 in Lotso's statement of financial position.

272 B

	B/f	Interest 6%	Payment	c/f
	$000	$000	$000	$000
20X6	1,263	76	(300)	1,039
20X7	1,039	62	(300)	801

At 31 December 20X6 the total lease liability is $1,039,000. This must be split into current and non-current liabilities. The non-current liability is $801,000, being the amount remaining after the payment in 20X7. Therefore the current liability is $238,000, being the difference between $1,039,000 and $801,000.

If you selected C, you have chosen the non-current liability.

If you selected A, you have calculated the liability as if payments were made in advance rather than arrears.

If you selected D, you have calculated the liability as if payments were made in advance rather than arrears and selected the non-current liability.

273 C

A leased asset would normally be depreciated over the shorter of the lease term and useful life of the asset. However, ownership transfers to Lotso at the end of the lease term, meaning that Lotso will be using the asset for the entire 6 year period. Therefore the asset is depreciated over 6 years. $1,263,000/6 = $210,500 depreciation a year.

Therefore the carrying amount as at 31 December 20X6 is $1,052,500.

274 C

This represents a sale and finance leaseback. The asset will be removed at its carrying amount of $10 million.

The gain on disposal of $1.5 million will be deferred and released over the 20 year lease term. Therefore only $75,000 income will be taken to the statement of profit or loss for the year ended 31 December 20X6.

275 D

In a sale and operating lease, the asset would be removed from the books of the lessee, as the risks and rewards associated with the asset would transfer to the party the asset has been sold to.

For an asset to be treated as a finance lease, the lessee must have the majority of the risks and rewards associated with the asset, signifying control over the asset. The legal ownership of the asset is irrelevant.

276 D

Laidlaw should not 'derecognise' the receivables, but instead treat the $1.8 million cash received from Finease as a current liability (a loan or financing arrangement secured on the receivables).

This is a 'with recourse' factoring arrangement, as Finease can return the receivables to Laidlaw, meaning that Laidlaw carries the risk of these.

277 D, E

This will be regarded as a genuine disposal of property. The property was disposed at fair value, and Laidlaw's option to repurchase will be at fair value.

Therefore the profit on disposal should be recognised, in addition to the rent expense.

278 $810,000

The payments should be discounted at the market rate to find the split of the liability and equity, shown in the working below.

Working

Year ended 30 September	Cash flow	Discount rate at	Discounted cash flows
	$000	8%	$000
20X3	500	0.93	465
20X4	500	0.86	430
20X5	10,500	0.79	8,295
Value of debt component			9,190
Value of equity option component (= balance)			**810**
Total proceeds			10,000

279 D

5% will not be charged to the statement of profit or loss, as the liability element will be held at amortised cost with 8% on the outstanding balance being charged to the statement of profit or loss each year.

280 A

Applying split accounting is essential for faithful representation, otherwise the correct accounting treatment is not being applied. While the disclosures may assist relevance, applying the correct accounting treatment is ensuring the fundamental characteristic of faithful representation is met.

281 D

All three items fall under the description of financial instruments. A financial instrument is a contract that gives rise to a financial asset of one entity and a financial liability or equity instrument of another entity. The convertible loan notes will be split between a financial liability and equity. The loan notes will be a financial liability and the investments will be a financial asset.

282 C

The liability should be held at amortised cost using the effective rate of interest at 10%.

	B/f	Interest 10%	Payment	c/f
	$000	$000	$000	$000
20X5	28,508	2,851	(2,400)	28,959

283 A

The loan notes should initially be recorded at the net proceeds of $9.6 million, being the $10 million received less the $400,000 issue costs. The interest is then expensed at the effective rate of 8%, giving a finance cost of $768,000 ($9.6m × 8%). If you selected B, you have ignored the issue costs. If you selected C, you have added the issue costs. If you selected D, you have ignored the issue costs and expensed 5% rather than the 8% effective interest rate.

284 B

Howard should record the dividend income of $100,000 (10 cents × 1 million shares) as well as the gain in value of $1 million.

285 D

Transaction costs relating to fair value through profit or loss investments should be expensed in the statement of profit or loss.

286 C

The payable should initially by translated at the spot rate of Kr10:$1, giving a payable of $1,000. As payables are a monetary liability, they should be retranslated at the closing rate of Kr8:$1. This gives a closing payable of $1,250. Therefore there is a foreign exchange loss of $250, as it will now cost $250 more to settle the liability.

287 B

The receivable should initially be translated at the spot rate of Kr10:$1, giving a receivable of $6,000. When the cash of Kr 30,000 is received, the foreign currency gain or loss should be recorded.

At the rate of Kr10.5:$1, this will give a value of $2,857. As the Kr 30,000 would have originally been included at $3,000, this gives a loss of $143.

Finally, the year-end balance must be retranslated at the closing rate of Kr8:$1. This gives a closing receivable of $3,750. As this would originally have been included at $3,000, this gives a gain of $750. Therefore the net gain is $750 – $143 = $607.

288 D

Inventory should not be retranslated as it is not a monetary item. Foreign exchange gains will not be included in revenue.

289 A

The tax expense in the statement of profit or loss consists of the current tax estimate and the movement on deferred tax in the year. The closing deferred tax liability is $90,000, being the temporary differences of $360,000 at the tax rate of 25%. This means that the deferred tax liability has decreased by $40,000 in the year. This decrease should be deducted from the current tax estimate of $43,000 to give a total expense of $3,000.

If you selected B, you have added the deferred tax movement.

If you selected C, you have added the tax estimate and the temporary differences together and then multiplied by the tax rate. If you selected D, you have added the deferred tax liability to the tax estimate for the year rather than taking the movement in deferred tax.

290 C

A debit balance represents an under-provision of tax from the prior year. This should be added to the current year's tax expense in the statement of profit or loss.

An under or over provision only arises when the prior year tax estimate is paid so there is no adjustment required to the current year liability.

291 A

Revenue should be recorded by multiplying the contract price by the progress to date. Therefore the revenue to be recorded is $10 million × 80% = $8 million.

If you selected B, you have ignored the progress figure given and calculated progress on the basis of costs to date compared to total contract costs.

If you selected C you have selected the amount billed.

If you selected D you have calculated the profit to be recognised rather than the revenue.

292 D

This is a loss making contract. In this situation, the loss should be recorded in full immediately. Revenue should be based on the progress to date.

Step 1 – Overall	$000
Price	8,000
Total cost – incurred to date	(4,000)
– estimated future	(6,000)
Overall loss	(2,000)

Step 2 – Progress

60%

Step 3 – P/L	$000
Revenue (60% of 8,000)	4,800
Cost of sales (Balancing figure	**(6,800)**
FULL loss to be recognised immediately	(2,000)

293 C

See the workings below

Step 1 – Overall	$000
Contract price	4,000
Total contract cost (500 + 2,000)	(2,500)
Estimated total profit	1,500

Step 2 – Progress = 25%

Step 3 – P/L	
Revenue (25% × 4,000,000)	1,000
Cost of sales (25% × 2,500)	(625)
	375

Step 4 – SOFP	
Costs to date	500
Profit to date	375
Less: Amount billed	(1,000)
Contract liability	(125)

Where the progress and overall profit of a contract are uncertain, revenue must be recognised to the level of recoverable costs. There may be a contract asset based on the amount spent to date compared to the amount billed to the customer.

295 B

IFRS 15 Revenue from Contracts with Customers explains that a change in the method of measuring progress is a change in accounting estimate. Changes in accounting estimate are always applied prospectively.

296 D

The revenue in relation to the installation and the machine itself can be recognised, with the revenue on the service recognised over time as the service is performed. The service will be recognised over the 2 year period. By 31 December 20X7, 2 months of the service has been performed. Therefore $20,000 can be recognised ($240/24 × 2).

Total revenue is therefore $580,000, being the $800,000 less the $220,000 relating to the service which has not yet been earned.

297 A

Discounts should be applied evenly across the components of a sale unless any one element is regularly sold separately at a discount. As Creg does not sell the service and installation separately, and never sells the machinery at a discount, the discount must be applied to each of the three elements.

298 B

Revenue as an agent is made by earning commission. Therefore the revenue on these sales should only be $600,000 (10% of $6 million). As Creg currently has $6 million in revenue, $5.4 million needs to be removed, with $5.4 million also removed from cost of sales.

299 B

The fact that Creg has given the customer a year to pay on such a large amount suggests there is a significant financing component within the sale.

The $1 million received can be recognised in revenue immediately. The remaining $9 million must be discounted to its present value of $8.491 million. This is then unwound over the year.

Therefore total initial revenue = $1,000 + $8,491 = $9,491.

If you selected A, you have ignored the initial $1 million.

If you selected C, you have discounted the whole $10 million.

If you selected D, you have not discounted anything.

300 D

This is not going to represent a real sale as control is not passing to the bank. Creg still maintains responsibility for the upkeep of the goods.

The bank cannot benefit from the price rise as Creg holds the option to repurchase for a price below the expected fair value.

Therefore this will be treated as a $3 million loan. The repayment of $630,000 represents interest of 10% a year over two years on the $3 million.

301 D

(Basic) EPS for the year ended 30 September 20X7 ($15 million/43.25 million × 100)	$0.35	cents

Step 1 – Theoretical ex rights price (TERP)

4 shares at $3.80	15.2
1 share at $2.80	2.8
———	———
5 shares at **$3.60** (TERP)	18

Step 2 – Rights fraction

Market value before issue/TERP = $3.80/$3.60

Step 3 – Weighted average number of shares

36 million × 3/12 × $3.80/$3.60	9.50	million
45 million × 9/12	33.75	million
	———	
	43.25	million

If you selected A, you have simply divided the profit for the year by the number of shares at the start of the year. If you selected B, you have used the inverse of the rights fraction. If you selected C, you have applied the rights fraction for the whole year rather than for the period up to the rights issue.

302 A

Diluted EPS for the year ended 30 September 2009 ($15.6 million/45.75 million × 100)	$0.34

Adjusted earnings

15 million + (10 million × 8% × 75%)	$15.6	million

Adjusted number of shares

43.25 million + (10 million × 25/100)	45.75	million

If you selected B, you have ignored the additional tax that would be payable on the interest saved. If you selected C, you have ignored the additional shares that would be issued. If you selected D, you have ignored the impact to the profit and simply increased the number of shares.

303 C

(Basic) EPS for the year ended 30 September 20X7		
($12 million/43.2 million × 100)		$0.28
Weighted average number of shares		
1 Oct	34 million × 4/12 × 6/5	13.6 million
1 Feb	37 million × 5/12 × 6/5	18.5 million
1 July	44.4 million × 3/12	11.1 million
		─────
		43.2 million
		─────

The bonus fraction should be applied from the start of the year up to the date of the bonus issue. If you selected A, you have added the bonus issue in July to the number of shares in addition to the bonus fraction, effectively double counting the bonus issue. If you selected B, you have missed out the bonus fraction completely. If you selected D you have just added the 3 million market issue without considering the bonus issue.

304 B

Prior year earnings per share figures must be restated when there is a bonus element to a share issue. Rights issues contain a bonus element so Barstead must restate the prior year figure. Dunstan performed a bonus issue so must restate the prior year figure.

305 B

Diluted EPS uses the current year's profit, adjusted for items currently in existence such as options or convertibles. It is not a predictor of future earnings.

306 C

To recognise a provision, it must be **probable** that an outflow of resources will be required.

307 C

A provision is recognised at the best estimate of the expenditure required. For a single obligation, this should be the most likely outcome.

If you selected answer B you have calculated an expected value. This is used when the provision being measured involves a large population of items.

308 $840,000

The provision being measured involves a large population of items, so an expected value must be calculated:

(100,000 × 6% × $100) + (100,000 × 8% × $30) = $840,000

309 A

The employees affected have been told about the restructuring and therefore a constructive obligation exists. The provision must not include any costs related to the ongoing activities of the entity. This means that only the redundancy payments should be provided for.

310 D

A provision should not be recognised for situation 1 because it does not give rise to an obligation. Hermione could change its operations in order to avoid the legal requirement to fit smoke filters.

A provision should not be recognised for situation 2. Future operating losses can be avoided, meaning that no obligation exists.

311 B

Provisions must be made if a legal or constructive obligation exists. The provision will be made at present value and added to the cost of the asset. Over the 10 year period, the asset will be depreciated and the discount on the provision will be unwound.

312 $7,452,000

The provision should be recorded at the present value of $6.9 million initially ($15 million × 0.46). After this, the discount on the provision must be unwound, meaning the provision will increase by 8% a year. Therefore the year-end provision is $6.9 million × 1.08 = $7,452,000.

313

	Adjusting	Non-adjusting
Fire in the warehouse		X
Sale of inventory	X	

The fire will be a non-adjusting event as the condition did not exist at the year end. The sale of inventory will be an adjusting event, as this shows that the net realisable value of the inventory is lower than its cost, meaning that inventory was incorrectly valued at the year end.

314 C

The date of the government announcement of the tax change is beyond the period of consideration in IAS 10. Thus this would be neither an adjusting nor a non-adjusting event. The increase in the deferred tax liability will be provided for in the year to 30 September 20X9. Had the announcement been before 6 November 20X8, it would have been treated as a non-adjusting event requiring disclosure of the nature of the event and an estimate of its financial effect in the notes to the financial statements.

315 A

From Borough's perspective, as a separate entity, the guarantee for Hamlet's loan is a contingent liability of $10 million. As Hamlet is a separate entity, Borough has no liability for the secured amount of $15 million, not even for the potential shortfall for the security of $3 million. The $10 million contingent liability would be disclosed in the notes to Borough's financial statements.

In Borough's consolidated financial statements, the full liability of $25 million would be included in the statement of financial position as part of the group's non-current liabilities – there would be no contingent liability disclosed.

CONSOLIDATED FINANCIAL STATEMENTS

316 B

Share for share exchange: 15,000 × 80% = 12,000 shares acquired × 2/5 = 4,800 Penfold shares issued @ 5.30 = $25,440,000 consideration given for Superted.

Penfold have issued 4,800 shares so 4,800 will be added to share capital with the remaining 20,640,000 added to other components of equity. As Penfold currently has $6,000,000 other components of equity, the total will be $26,640,000.

If you selected C, you have added Superted's other components of equity, and the subsidiary's equity is not included in the consolidated equity.

If you selected A, you have added the entire share consideration.

If you selected D, you have added the entire share consideration and Superted's other components of equity.

317 D

The cash-in-transit must be treated as received. To do this, $2 million will be added to cash and deducted from receivables. This will leave a $6 million intra-group balance, which will then be removed along with the $6 million intra-group payable balance.

Total receivables = 32,400 + 38,000 − 2,000 − 6,000 = $66,400,000.

If you selected A, you have ignored the cash in transit.

If you selected B, you have deducted the cash in transit and nothing else.

If you selected C, you have added the cash in transit.

318 A

The non-controlling interest at acquisition will be $7.2.

Penfold has owned Superted for 6 months so 6 months profit should be included in the consolidated financial statements for the year. Therefore the NCI's share of this will be $2.4 million ($24 million × 6/12 × 20%).

Therefore NCI = $7.2 million + $2.4 million = $9.6 million.

If you selected B, you have not time apportioned the subsidiary's profits.

If you selected C, you have taken the NCI at acquisition.

If you selected D, you have deducted the NCI's share of profit.

319 C

The unrealised profit on the non-current asset transfer needs to be removed.

The carrying amount at the year-end after the transfer is $22.5 million ($25 million less 6 months depreciation).

The carrying amount of the asset if it had never been transferred would have been $18 million ($20 million less 6 months depreciation).

Therefore the unrealised profit on the non-current asset is $4.5 million

The total PPE is therefore $345 million + $141 million – $4.5 million = $481.5 million.

If you selected A, you have added the unrealised profit rather than deducted.

If you selected B you have deducted the initial $5 million profit rather than the unrealised profit at the year end.

If you selected D you have accounted for a full year's depreciation rather than 6 months.

320 C

There is no control or significant influence, as Arnold is controlled by the other investor. Therefore the investment in Arnold will be held as an equity investment, which is a financial instrument.

321 B

The deferred consideration should be discounted to the present value at acquisition. $6 million/1.082 = $5.144 million.

At 31 March 20X5, 6 months have elapsed, so the discount needs to be unwound for 6 months. $5.144 million × 6/12 = $205,000. Therefore the liability at 31 March 20X5 = $5,144 + 205 = $5,349,000.

If you selected A you have not unwound any interest.

If you selected C you have unwound a full year's interest.

If you selected D you have not discounted the consideration.

322 B

Cost of sales = 319,200 + (176,400 × 6/12) – 6,000 (I/G) + 360 (PURP(W1)) = 401,760

(W1) Provision for unrealised profit (PUP)

	$000	
Original profit made:		
Sales	6,000	100%
Cost of sales	(4,800)	80%
Gross profit	1,200	20%

30% remain, so PURP = 1,200 × 30% = 360

If you selected A, you have adjusted for all the profit, rather than the 30% remaining in the group at the year-end. If you selected C you have taken out a full year's sales rather than 6 months. If you selected D you have taken out a full year's sales and adjusted for all the profit rather than the amount remaining in the group.

323 D

Operating expenses = 50,610 + (33,120 × 6/12) + 100 FV depreciation* + 600 impairment = 67,870.

*Fair value depreciation = $4 million/20 years = $200,000 a year × 6/12 = $100,000.

If you selected A, you have added a full year's fair value depreciation. If you selected B, you have deducted the fair value depreciation. If you selected C, you have either time apportioned the impairment or deducted a full year's fair value depreciation.

324 C

Unrealised profits from note (i) would only affect the non-controlling interest if the subsidiary sold goods to the parent, which is not the case. Fair value depreciation (note (ii)) always affects the NCI. Goodwill impairment (note (iii)) will affect the NCI if the NCI is measured at fair value, which it is here.

325 A

A subsidiary's assets, liabilities and contingent liabilities must be included at fair value in the consolidated financial statements. Professional fees associated with the acquisition of a subsidiary cannot be capitalised, regardless of which method is used to measure the non-controlling interest.

326 D

Consolidated retained earnings will consist of 100% of Prunier's retained earnings plus 80% of Sheringham's post acquisition loss, including the fair value depreciation on Sheringham's assets.

	$000
Prunier	11,000
Sheringham ((500) − 40 × 80%)	(432)
	10,568

327 $2,400,000

The other comprehensive income attributable to the parent will be 100% of Prunier's revaluation gain in the year and 80% of Sheringham's post acquisition revaluation gain. Prunier has made a gain of $2 million in the year and Sheringham has made $500,000. Therefore the other comprehensive income attributable to the parent is $2 million plus 80% × $500,000 = $2,400,000.

328

	Recognise	*Not to be recognised*
Sheringham's brand name, which was internally generated so not shown in Sheringham's financial statements but has a fair value of $3 million	X	
A research project in progress, which was one of the main reasons Prunier purchased Sheringham and has a fair value of $2 million	X	
An intangible asset related to an encryption process which has now been deemed illegal. This is included within intangibles at $1.5 million.		X

Internally generated assets and research projects can be recognised within consolidated financial statements if a fair value can be attached to them. The encryption process is now illegal so cannot be recognised as an asset.

329 B

Profit on all sales = 3,000 × 20/120 = $500,000. Anderson has a quarter left, so this is $125,000. As Anderson is an associate, only 30% of this needs to be removed, which is $37,500. If you selected A, you have used margin and not mark-up, and not adjusted for the associate. If you selected C, you have taken all of the unrealised profit, rather than 30%. If you selected D, you have used margin and not mark-up.

330 A

The profit or loss on the disposal is calculated as follows:

	$000
Proceeds	9,000
Goodwill at disposal	(1,000)
Net assets at disposal	(10,600)
Non-controlling interest at disposal	2,500
Loss on disposal	(100)

If you selected B, you have added the goodwill instead of deducting it. If you selected C, you have deducted the non-controlling interest at disposal. If you selected D, you have deducted 80% of the net assets, rather than all of them.

INTERPRETATION OF FINANCIAL STATEMENTS

331   B

B is correct, as follows:

	A $m		B $m
Gross profit = 26% × $160m	41.6	Gross profit = 17% × $300m	51
Operating profit = 9% × $160m	14.4	Operating profit = 11% × $300m	33
Operating expenses	27.2		18

A is incorrect. A's revenue is significantly lower than B's and therefore B is more likely to be benefiting from economies of scale.

C is incorrect. A has higher gearing than B and would therefore be considered a higher risk by lenders. (The low interest rate may however explain why A are using debt finance in the first place.)

D is incorrect. LOP's gross profit margin is higher than both A's and B's and therefore acquisition of either entity is likely to reduce the overall margin of the combined business (unless cost savings can be achieved as a result of the acquisition).

332   A, D

B is incorrect. A has higher gearing than B and therefore reduced capacity for additional borrowings.

C is incorrect. LOP's P/E ratio is higher than B's suggesting that the market is more confident about the future performance of LOP.

E is incorrect. The share price may react positively or negatively, depending on the investor's view of the impact the acquisition will have on LOP.

333   B

A and B may target different customers, but that would not mean that their financial statements are incomparable. It may lead to different margins earned, but comparison could still be made, and would help LOP to assess which type of customer and market they made wish to target.

334   24.5%

	LOP $m		B $m
Gross profit = 28% × $500m	140	Gross profit = 17% × $300m	51

Without the cost savings, LOP and B are making a gross profit of $191 million on revenue of $800 million. If the cost savings of $5 million are taken into account, the gross profit will increase to $196 million. This will give a gross profit margin of **24.5%** (196/800).

335 B

If B has treated the leases incorrectly as operating leases, then B's liabilities will be understated, meaning that gearing would be understated. B would also not have included any finance costs in the statement of profit or loss, meaning the average interest rate expensed will not have included the interest on the finance lease.

336 7.5%

1,500/(15,000 + 3,000 + 2,000) = 1,500/20,000 = 7.5%

337 D

Combined profit from operations = 1,500 – 600 = 900,000.

Combined revenue = 9,400 + 1,200 = 10,600,000.

Operating margin = 900/10,600 = 8.5%.

If you selected C, you have just used Franck's profit. If you selected B, you have added the loss of 600 rather than deducting it. If you selected A, you have just used Franck's revenue rather than the combined revenue.

338 C

Return on capital employed will clearly decrease, as Franck has made a loss. The capital employed will increase, but overall profit will decrease. Duik has a higher level of gearing (4,000/22,800 = 17.5%) compared to Franck (2,000/18,000 = 11%), which means gearing will increase when the two companies are combined.

339 C

Individual company financial statements should not contain errors, and if they do, this is not a problem specific to a company being a subsidiary of another company.

340 C

The upcoming projects is unlikely to be publicly available information, whereas A, B and D can all be assessed from looking at Duik's financial statements for the current or previous periods.

STATEMENT OF CASH FLOWS

341 C

Cooper has used the indirect method. The direct method is an alternative method of calculating cash generated from operations.

Classification by function and nature relate to the way that items are presented in the statement of profit or loss.

342

	$000
Profit from operations	3,500
Depreciation	4,600
Release of government grant	1,400
Profit on disposal of property	(3,700)
Increase in inventories	(400)
Decrease in trade and other receivables	(300)
Increase in trade and other payables	900

The release of government grant is non-cash income, so should be deducted from profit from operations.

The decrease in trade receivables is good for cash so would be added to profit rather than being deducted.

343 A

Property

	Dr		Cr
	$000		$000
b/f	39,500	Depreciation	4,600
		Disposal (Balance)	**5,900**
		c/f	29,000
	39,500		39,500

The carrying amount of the property disposed was $5.9 million. As Cooper made a profit of $3.7 million on disposal, the sale proceeds must have been **$9.6 million.**

If you selected B, you have deducted the profit on disposal rather than adding it.

If you selected C, you have used the profit on disposal.

If you selected D, you have selected the carrying amount disposed rather than the sale proceeds.

344 $3,400,000

Grant deferred income

	Dr		Cr
	$000		$000
		b/f	6,000
Released in year	1,400	**Received (Balance)**	**3,400**
c/f	8,000		
	———		———
	9,400		9,400
	———		———

345 B

A rights issue will mean that cash has been raised, increasing the cash from financing activities. Intangible assets can affect the statement of cash flow if they are purchased as this will lead to an outflow of cash.

346 A

Retained earnings

	Dr		Cr
	$000		$000
		b/f	940
Dividend paid (Balance)	**145**	Revaluation surplus	20
c/f	900	Profit for the year	85
	———		———
	1,045		1,045
	———		———

When the land is disposed, the remaining revaluation surplus will be taken to retained earnings. If you selected B, you have deducted the revaluation surplus. If you selected C, you have taken the movement in retained earnings. If you selected D, you have missed out the revaluation surplus transfer into retained earnings.

347 C

Loan notes

	Dr		Cr
	$000		$000
		b/f	500
Interest paid (Balance)	**25**	Finance cost	40
c/f	515		
	———		———
	540		540
	———		———

The loan notes should be held at amortised cost, with the effective rate of interest being taken to the statement of profit or loss. As these have an effective rate of 8%, $40,000 has been taken to the statement of profit or loss. However, it is only the coupon rate of 5% which has been paid in the year.

348 B

Tax liabilities

	Dr		Cr
	$000		$000
		b/f (40 + 125)	165
Tax paid (Balance)	42	Tax expense	57
c/f (30 + 150)	180		
	–––––		–––––
	222		222
	–––––		–––––

If you selected A, you have calculated the tax paid using only the deferred tax liabilities. If you selected C, you have taken the tax expense. If you selected D, you have only used the current tax payable.

349 B

Dividends received are shown within cash flows from investing activities.

350 D

Finance lease liabilities

	Dr		Cr
	$000		$000
		b/f	310
Total paid (Balance)	100	PPE additions	70
c/f	300	Interest	20
	–––––		–––––
	400		400
	–––––		–––––

The total paid in respect of finance leases is $100,000, as shown above. As $20,000 relates to interest, the amount of the liability repaid must be $80,000.

If you selected A, you have taken the movement in finance lease liabilities.

If you selected B, you have ignored the additions in the year.

If you selected C, you have ignored taken the full amount paid, including interest.

Section 6

ANSWERS TO CONSTRUCTED RESPONSE QUESTIONS – SECTION C

PREPARATION OF SINGLE COMPANY FINANCIAL STATEMENTS

351   LLAMA

(a)   **Llama – Statement of profit or loss – Year ended 30 September 2007**

	$000	$000
Revenue		180,400
Cost of sales (w (i))		(81,700)
Gross profit		98,700
Distribution costs (11,000 + 1,000 depreciation)	(12,000)	
Administrative expenses (12,500 + 1,000 depreciation)	(13,500)	(25,500)
Investment income	2,200	
Gain on fair value of investments (27,100 – 26,500)	600	2,800
Finance costs (w (ii))		(2,400)
Profit before tax		73,600
Income tax expense		
(18,700 – 400 – (11,200 – 10,000) deferred tax)		(17,100)
Profit for the period		56,500
Other comprehensive income		
Loss on revaluation		(3,000)
Total comprehensive income		53,500

(b) Llama – Statement of financial position as at 30 September 2007

	$000	$000
Assets		
Non-current assets		
Property, plant and equipment (w (iii))		228,500
Investments at fair value through profit and loss		27,100
		255,600
Current assets		
Inventory	37,900	
Trade receivables	35,100	73,000
Total assets		328,600
Equity and liabilities		
Equity		
Equity shares of 50 cents each		84,000
Revaluation reserve (14,000 – 3,000 (w (iii)))	11,000	
Retained earnings (56,500 + 25,500)	82,000	93,000
		177,000
Non-current liabilities		
2% loan note (80,000 + 1,600 (w (ii)))	81,600	
Deferred tax (40,000 × 25%)	10,000	91,600
Current liabilities		
Trade payables	34,700	
Bank overdraft	6,600	
Current tax payable	18,700	60,000
Total equity and liabilities		328,600

Workings (monetary figures in brackets are in 000)

(i) Cost of sales:

	$000
Per question	89,200
Plant capitalised (w (iii))	(24,000)
Depreciation (w (iii)) – buildings	3,000
– plant	13,500
	81,700

(ii) The loan has been in issue for six months. The total finance charge should be based on the effective interest rate of 6%. This gives a charge of $2.4 million (80,000 × 6% × 6/12). As the actual interest paid is $800,000 an accrual (added to the carrying amount of the loan) of $1.6 million is required.

(iii)   Non-current assets/depreciation:

Land and buildings:

On 1 October 2006 the value of the buildings was $100 million (130,000 – 30,000 land). The remaining life at this date was 20 years, thus the annual depreciation charge will be $5 million ($3 million to cost of sales and $1 million each to distribution and administration). Prior to the revaluation at 30 September 2007 the carrying amount of the building was $95 million (100,000 – 5,000). With a revalued amount of $92 million, this gives a revaluation deficit of $3 million which should be debited to the revaluation reserve. The carrying amount of land and buildings at 30 September 2007 will be $122 million (92,000 buildings + 30,000 land (unchanged)).

Plant

The existing plant will be depreciated by $12 million ((128,000 – 32,000) × 12½%) and have a carrying amount of $84 million at 30 September 2007.

The plant manufactured for internal use should be capitalised at $24 million (6,000 + 4,000 + 8,000 + 6,000). Depreciation on this will be $1.5 million (24,000 × 12½% × 6/12). This will give a carrying amount of $22.5 million at 30 September 2007. Thus total depreciation for plant is $13.5 million with a carrying amount of $106.5 million (84,000 + 22,500)

	$000
Summarising the carrying amounts:	
Land and buildings	122,000
Plant	106,500
Property, plant and equipment	228,500

Marking scheme		
		Marks
(a)	**Statement of profit or loss**	
	Revenue	½
	Cost of sales	3
	Distribution costs and administrative expenses	2
	Investment income and gain on investment	1½
	Finance costs	1½
	Tax	1½
		10
(b)	**Statement of financial position**	
	Property, plant and equipment	3
	Investments	1
	Current assets	½
	Equity shares	½
	Revaluation surplus	1
	Retained earnings	1
	2% loan notes	1
	Deferred tax	1
	Trade payables and overdraft	½
	Income tax provision	½
		10
Total		**20**

352 CAVERN

(a) **Cavern – Statement of profit or loss and other comprehensive income for the year ended 30 September 2010**

	$000
Revenue	182,500
Cost of sales (w (i))	(137,400)
Gross profit	45,100
Distribution costs	(8,500)
Administrative expenses	(6,500)
Loss on investments (700 – (15,800 – 13,500))	(1,600)
Finance costs (300 + 400 (w (ii)) + 3,060 (w (iii)))	(3,760)
Profit before tax	24,740
Income tax expense (5,600 + 900 – 250 (w (iv)))	(6,250)
Profit for the year	18,490
Other comprehensive income	
Gain on revaluation of land and buildings (w (ii))	800
Total comprehensive income	19,290

(b) **Cavern – Statement of financial position as at 30 September 2010**

	$000	$000
Assets		
Non-current assets		
Property, plant and equipment (41,800 + 51,100 (w (ii)))		92,900
Financial asset investments		13,500
		106,400
Current assets		
Inventory	19,800	
Trade receivables	29,000	
		48,800
Total assets		155,200
Equity and liabilities		
Equity shares of 20 cents each		51,000
Revaluation surplus (7,000 + 800)	7,800	
Retained earnings (6,600 + 18,490	25,090	
		32,890
		83,890

Non-current liabilities

Provision for decontamination costs (4,000 + 400 (w (ii)))	4,400	
8% loan note (w (iii))	31,260	
Deferred tax (w (iv))	3,750	
		39,410

Current liabilities

Trade payables	21,700	
Bank overdraft	4,600	
Current tax payable	5,600	
		31,900

Total equity and liabilities	155,200

Workings (monetary figures in brackets in $'000)

(i)   Cost of sales

Per trial balance	128,500
Depreciation of building (36,000/18 years)	2,000
Depreciation of new plant (14,000/10 years)	1,400
Depreciation of existing plant and equipment ((67,400 – 10,000 – 13,400) × 12.5%)	5,500
	137,400

(ii)   Property, plant and equipment

The new plant of $10 million should be grossed up by the provision for the present value of the estimated future decontamination costs of $4 million to give a gross cost of $14 million. The 'unwinding' of the provision will give rise to a finance cost in the current year of $400,000 (4,000 × 10%) to give a closing provision of $4.4 million.

The gain on revaluation and carrying amount of the land and building will be:

Valuation – 30 September 2009	43,000
Building depreciation (w (i))	(2,000)
Carrying amount before revaluation	41,000
Revaluation – 30 September 2010	41,800
Gain on revaluation	800

The carrying amount of the plant and equipment will be:

New plant (14,000 – 1,400)	12,600
Existing plant and equipment (67,400 – 10,000 – 13,400 – 5,500)	38,500
	51,100

(iii) Loan note

The finance cost of the loan note, at the effective rate of 10% applied to the carrying amount of the loan note of $30.6 million, is $3.06 million. The interest actually paid is $2.4 million. The difference between these amounts of $660,000 (3,060 – 2,400) is added to the carrying amount of the loan note to give $31.26 million (30,600 + 660) for inclusion as a non-current liability in the statement of financial position.

(iv) Deferred tax

Provision required at 30 September 2010 (15,000 × 25%)	3,750
Provision at 1 October 2009	(4,000)
	———
Credit (reduction in provision) to income statement	250
	———

Marking scheme			Marks
(a)	Statement of profit or loss		
	Revenue		1½
	Cost of sales		3
	Distribution costs and administration expenses		½
	Investment income loss		1
	Finance costs		2
	Income tax expense		1½
	Gain on revaluation of land and buildings		½
			———
		Maximum	10
(b)	Statement of financial position		
	Property, plant and equipment		2½
	Financial asset investments		½
	Inventory and trade receivables		½
	Share capital		½
	Retained earnings		1
	Revaluation surplus		1
	Contamination provision		1
	8% loan note		1
	Deferred tax		1
	Trade payables and overdraft		½
	Current tax payable		½
			———
		Maximum	10
Total			20

353 CANDEL *Walk in the footsteps of a top tutor*

(a)   Candel – Revised profit for the year

	$000
Draft profit before tax	59,100
Depreciation (w (iii)) – leasehold property	(2,500)
– plant and equipment	(9,600)
Removal of disposal proceeds	(2,500)
Loss on disposal of plant (4,000 – 2,500)	(1,500)
Amortisation of development costs (w (iii))	(4,000)
Research and development expenses (1,400 + 2,400 (w (iii)))	(3,800)
Removal of legal provision (w (i))	400
Inclusion of provision for legal costs (w (i))	(100)
Finance costs (w (ii)))	(1,200)
Income tax expense (11,400 + (6,000 – 5,800 deferred tax))	(11,600)
	————
Profit for the year	22,700

(b)   Candel – Statement of financial position as at 30 September 2008

Assets	$000	$000
Non-current assets (w (iii))		
Property, plant and equipment (43,000 + 38,400)		81,400
Development costs (w (iii))		14,800
		————
		96,200
Current assets		
Inventory	20,000	
Trade receivables	43,100	63,100
	————	————
Total assets		159,300
		————
Equity and liabilities:		
Equity shares of 25 cents each		50,000
Revaluation surplus (10,000 – 4,500)	5,500	
Retained earnings (18,500 + 22,700)	41,200	46,700
	————	————
		96,700
Non-current liabilities		
Deferred tax	6,000	
8% redeemable preference shares (20,000 + 400 (w (ii)))	20,400	26,400
	————	
Current liabilities		
Trade payables (23,800 – 400 + 100 – re legal action (w (i)))	23,500	
Bank overdraft	1,300	
Current tax payable	11,400	36,200
	————	————
Total equity and liabilities		159,300
		————

Workings (figures in brackets in $000)

(i) Legal case

As it is considered that the outcome of the legal action against Candel is unlikely to succeed (only a 20% chance) it is inappropriate to provide for any damages. The potential damages are an example of a contingent liability which should be disclosed (at $2 million) as a note to the financial statements. Therefore the legal provision of $400,000 should be removed. The unrecoverable legal costs are a liability (the start of the legal action is a past event) and should be provided for in full at $100,000.

(ii) Preference shares

Tutorial note

This requires knowledge of accounting for financial instruments under IAS 32 and IFRS 9.

The finance cost of $1.2 million for the preference shares is based on the effective rate of 12% applied to $20 million issue proceeds of the shares for the six months they have been in issue (20m × 12% × 6/12). The dividend paid of $800,000 is based on the nominal rate of 8%. The additional $400,000 (accrual) is added to the carrying amount of the preference shares in the statement of financial position. As these shares are redeemable they are treated as debt and their dividend is treated as a finance cost.

(iii) Non-current assets:

Leasehold property

Valuation at 1 October 2007	50,000
Depreciation for year (20 year life)	(2,500)
Carrying amount at date of revaluation	47,500
Valuation at 30 September 2008	(43,000)
Revaluation deficit	4,500

Tutorial note

Remember to write off the disposed asset, both cost and b/fwd accumulated depreciation before calculating the current year depreciation charge.

	$000
Plant and equipment per trial balance (76,600 – 24,600)	52,000
Disposal (8,000 – 4,000)	(4,000)
	48,000
Depreciation for year (20%)	(9,600)
Carrying amount at 30 September 2008	38,400

Tutorial note

Remember research costs are to be expensed and development costs are to be capitalised only when the recognition criteria in IAS38 are met. In this question- the directors do not become confident that the project will be successful until 1 April – therefore development costs on the new project in January – March must be expensed.

Capitalised/deferred development costs

Carrying amount at 1 October 2007 (20,000 – 6,000)	14,000
Amortised for year (20,000 × 20%)	(4,000)
Capitalised during year (800 × 6 months)	4,800
Carrying amount at 30 September 2008	14,800

Note: Development costs can only be treated as an asset from the point where they meet the recognition criteria in IAS 38 *Intangible assets*. Thus development costs from 1 April to 30 September 2008 of $4.8 million (800 × 6 months) can be capitalised. These will not be amortised as the project is still in development. The research costs of $1.4 million plus three months' development costs of $2.4 million (800 × 3 months) (i.e. those incurred before the criteria were met) must be expensed.

354 PRICEWELL

(a)   **Pricewell – Statement of profit or loss for the year ended 31 March 2009:**

	$000
Revenue (310,000 + 22,000 (w (i)) – 6,400 (w (ii)))	325,600
Cost of sales (w (iii))	(255,100)
Gross profit	70,500
Distribution costs	(19,500)
Administrative expenses	(27,500)
Finance costs (w (v)))	(1,248)
Profit before tax	22,252
Income tax expense (4,500 + 700 – (8,400 – 5,600 deferred tax)	(2,400)
Profit for the year	19,852

(b)   **Pricewell – Statement of financial position as at 31 March 2009:**

Assets	$000	$000
Non-current assets		
Property, plant and equipment (24,900 + 41,500 w (iv))		66,400
Current assets		
Inventory	28,200	
Trade receivables	33,100	
Contract asset (w (i))	17,100	
Bank	5,500	83,900
Total assets		150,300
Equity and liabilities:		
Equity shares of 50 cents each		40,000
Retained earnings (w (vi))		55,952
		95,952
Non-current liabilities		
Deferred tax	5,600	
Finance lease obligation (w (v))	5,716	
		11,316
Current liabilities		
Trade payables	33,400	
Finance lease obligation (10,848 – 5,716) (w (v)))	5,132	
Current tax payable	4,500	43,032
Total equity and liabilities		150,300

Workings (figures in brackets in $000)

		$000
(i)	**Contract with customer:**	
1	**Overall**	
	Selling price	50,000
	Estimated cost	
	To date	(12,000)
	To complete	(10,000)
	Plant	(8,000)
	Estimated profit	20,000

2   Progress

Work done is agreed at $22 million so the contract is 44% complete (22,000/50,000).

3   Statement of profit or loss

Revenue	22,000
Cost of sales (44% × 30,000 total costs)	(13,200)
Profit to date	8,800

4   Statement of financial position

Property, Plant & Equipment (8,000 less 6 months depreciation)	6,000
Costs to date (12,000 + 2,000 depreciation)	14,000
Profit to date	8,800
Billed to date	(5,700)
Contract asset	17,100

(ii)   Pricewell is acting as an agent (not the principal) for the sales on behalf of Trilby. Therefore the statement of comprehensive income should only include $1.6 million (20% of the sales of $8 million). Therefore $6.4 million (8,000 – 1,600) should be deducted from revenue and cost of sales. It would also be acceptable to show agency sales (of $1.6 million) separately as other income.

(iii)   **Cost of sales**

Per question	234,500
Contract (w (i))	13,200
Agency cost of sales (w (ii))	(6,400)
Depreciation (w (iv))– leasehold property	1,800
– owned plant ((46,800 – 12,800) × 25%)	8,500
– leased plant (20,000 × 25%)	5,000
Surplus on revaluation of leasehold property (w (iv))	(1,500)
	255,100

	$000

(iv) **Non-current assets**

Leasehold property

valuation at 31 March 2008	25,200
depreciation for year (14 year life remaining)	(1,800)
carrying amount at date of revaluation valuation at 31 March 2009	23,400
valuation at 31 March 2009	(24,900)
revaluation surplus (to statement of comprehensive income – see below)	1,500

The $1.5 million revaluation surplus is credited to the statement of comprehensive income as this is the partial reversal of the $2.8 million impairment loss recognised in the statement of comprehensive income in the previous period (i.e. year ended 31 March 2008).

Plant and equipment

– owned (46,800 – 12,800 – 8,500)	25,500
– leased (20,000 – 5,000 – 5,000)	10,000
– contract (8,000 – 2,000 (w (i)))	6,000
Carrying amount at 31 March 2009	41,500

(v) **Finance lease liability**

Balance b/f	Interest 8%	Payment	Balance c/f
15,600	1,248	(6,000)	10,848
10,848	868	(6,000)	5,716

Finance cost:	1,248
Non-current liability:	5,716
Current liability:	5,132

(vi) **Retained earnings**

Balance at 1 April 2008	44,100
Profit for year	19,852
Equity dividend paid	(8,000)
Balance at 31 March 2009	55,952

Marking scheme		
		Marks
(a)	Statement of profit or loss	
	Revenue	2
	Cost of sales	4½
	Distribution costs	½
	Administrative expenses	½
	Finance costs	1
	Income tax expense	1½
		———
	Maximum	10
(b)	Statement of financial position	
	Property, plant and equipment	2
	Inventory	½
	Due on construction contract	2
	Trade receivables and bank	½
	Equity shares	½
	Retained earnings	1
	Deferred tax	1
	Finance lease – non-current liability	½
	Trade payables	½
	Finance lease – current liability	1
	Current tax payable	½
		———
	Maximum	10
		———
Total		**20**

355 SANDOWN

Key answer tips

This question required the preparation of a statement of profit or loss and a statement of financial position and had common adjustments such as tax and non-current assets. Be wary when dealing with the convertible loan this has already been accounted for in 2008 and you are now required to account for the second year of the convertible loan.

(a)   Sandown – Statement of profit or loss for the year ended 30 September 2009

	$000
Revenue (380,000 – 4,000 (w (i)))	376,000
Cost of sales (w (ii))	(265,300)
	———
Gross profit	110,700
Distribution costs	(55,900)
Investment income (1,300 + 2,500 (w (iii)))	3,800
Finance costs (w (iv))	(1,475)
	———
Profit before tax	57,125
Income tax expense (16,200 + 2,100 – 1,500 (w (v)))	(16,800)
	———
Profit for the year	40,325
	———

(b)   Sandown – Statement of financial position as at 30 September 2009

	$000	$000
Assets		
Non-current assets		
Property, plant and equipment (w (vi))		67,500
Intangible – brand (15,000 – 2,500 (w (ii)))		12,500
Investment property (w (iii))		29,000
		109,000
Current assets		90,500
Total assets		199,500
Equity and liabilities		
Equity		
Equity shares of 20 cents each		50,000
Equity option		2,000
Retained earnings (21,260 + 40,325 profit for the year)		61,585
		113,585
Non-current liabilities		
Deferred tax (w (v))	3,900	
Deferred income (w (i))	2,000	
5% convertible loan note (w (iv))	18,915	24,815
Current liabilities		
Trade payables	42,900	
Deferred income (w (i))	2,000	
Current tax payable	16,200	61,100
Total equity and liabilities		199,500

Workings (figures in brackets in $000)

(i)   Where revenue includes an amount for after sales servicing and support costs then a proportion of the revenue should be deferred. The amount deferred should cover the cost and a reasonable profit (in this case a gross profit of 40%) on the services.

As the servicing and support is for three years and the date of the sale was 1 October 2008, revenue relating to two years' servicing and support provision must be deferred: ($1.2 million × 2/0.6) = $4 million. This is shown as $2 million in both current and non-current liabilities.

(ii) **Cost of sales**

Per question		246,800
Depreciation	– building (50,000/50 years – see below)	1,000
	– plant and equipment (42,200 – 19,700) × 40%))	9,000
Amortisation	– brand (1,500 + 2,500 – see below)	4,000
Impairment of brand (see below)		4,500
		———
		265,300
		———

The cost of the building of $50 million (63,000 – 13,000 land) has accumulated depreciation of $8 million at 30 September 2008 which is eight years after its acquisition. Thus the life of the building must be 50 years.

The brand is being amortised at $3 million per annum (30,000/10 years). The impairment occurred half way through the year, thus amortisation of $1.5 million should be charged prior to calculation of the impairment loss. At the date of the impairment review the brand had a carrying amount of $19.5 million (30,000 – (9,000 + 1,500)).

The recoverable amount of the brand is its fair value of $15 million (as this is higher than its value in use of $12 million) giving an impairment loss of $4.5 million (19,500 – 15,000). Amortisation of $2.5 million (15,000/3 years × 6/12) is required for the second-half of the year giving total amortisation of $4 million for the full year.

(iii) The gain on the investment property is shown below

Fair value at 1 October 2008	26,500
Fair value at 30 September 2009	29,000
	———
Gain on investment property	2,500
	———

The investment property is to be reported in the statement of financial position at fair value of $29 million at 30 September 2009 which gives a fair value increase (credited to the statement of profit or loss) of $2.5 million.

(iv) The finance cost of the convertible loan note is based on its effective rate of 8% applied to $18,440,000 carrying amount at 1 October 2008 = $1,475,000 (rounded). The accrual of $475,000 (1,475 – 1,000 interest paid) is added to the carrying amount of the loan note giving a figure of $18,915,000 (18,440 + 475) in the statement of financial position at 30 September 2009.

(v) **Deferred tax**

Credit balance required at 30 September 2009 (13,000 × 30%)	3,900
Balance at 1 October 2008	(5,400)
	———
Credit (reduction in balance) to statement of comprehensive income	1,500
	———

(vi) **Non-current assets**

Freehold property (63,000 – (8,000 + 1,000)) (w (ii))	54,000
Plant and equipment (42,200 – (19,700 + 9,000)) (w (ii))	13,500
	———
Property, plant and equipment	67,500
	———

Examiner's comments

A 'familiar' question requiring candidates to prepare a statement of profit or loss and a statement of financial position. A series of adjustments were required: for deferred revenue, an effective interest rate calculation, basic depreciation, taxation and the impairment and amortisation of a brand.

The ability to produce financial statements from a trial balance seems well understood, but some of the adjustments created difficulties:

- few candidates correctly calculated the amount of revenue to be deferred in relation to a sale (of $16 million) with ongoing service support. Most candidates deferred the whole of the revenue rather than the amount of the support costs (plus appropriate profit) relating to the remaining two years of service support. Some candidates increased revenue rather than defer it and some thought it was an in-substance loan

- many candidates applied the effective rate of interest (8%) to the nominal amount ($20 million) of a convertible loan rather than its carrying amount of $18.44 million. A few candidates made complicated calculations of the split between debt and equity for the loan not realising that it was the second year after its issue and the split had been made a year before

- most candidates got the taxation aspects correct, but there were still some basic errors such as charging the whole of the deferred tax provision to income (rather than the movement) and treating the underpayment of tax in the previous period as a credit

- it was worrying that a number of candidates made basic errors on straight forward depreciation calculations. Some used the straight line method for the plant (not reading the question properly which stated the use of the reducing balance method) and some charged the accumulated depreciation to cost of sales rather than the charge for the period. Amortisation and impairment of the brand caused many problems; not calculating two 6 month charges (before and after the impairment) and not using the (higher) realisable value of the brand as the basis for the impairment charge.

The statement of financial position was generally well answered; most problems were follow-on errors from mistakes made in the statement of profit or loss. Overall, a well-answered question.

---

356 HIGHWOOD

(a) **Highwood – Statement of profit or loss and other comprehensive income for the year ended 31 March 2011**

	$000
Revenue	339,650
Cost of sales (w (i))	(206,950)
Gross profit	132,700
Distribution costs	(27,500)
Administrative expenses (30,700 – 1,300 + 600 allowance (w (iv)))	(30,000)
Finance costs (w (v))	(2,848)
Profit before tax	72,352
Income tax expense (19,400 – 800 + 400 (w (vi)))	(19,000)
Profit for the year	53,352
Other comprehensive income:	
Gain on revaluation of property (w (iii))	15,000
Deferred tax on revaluation (w (iii))	(3,750)
Total comprehensive income	64,602

(b) **Highwood – Statement of changes in equity for the year ended 31 March 2011**

	Share capital	Equity option	Revaluation reserve	Retained earnings	Total equity
	$000	$000	$000	$000	$000
Balance at 1 April 2010 (see below)	6,000	nil	nil	1,400	7,400
8% loan note issue (w (v))		1,524			1,524
Comprehensive income			11,250	53,352	64,602
Balance at 31 March 2011	6,000	1,524	11,250	54,752	73,526

(c)   Highwood – Statement of financial position as at 31 March 2011

Assets	$000	$000
Non-current assets		
Property, plant and equipment (w (ii))		77,500
Current assets		
Inventory (36,000 – 2,700 + 6,000) (w (iii))	39,300	
Trade receivables (47,100 + 10,000 – 600 allowance) (w (iv))	56,500	95,800
Total assets		173,300
Equity and liabilities		
Equity (see answer (b))		
Equity shares of 50 cents each		6,000
Other component of equity – equity option		1,524
Revaluation surplus		11,250
Retained earnings		54,752
		73,526
Non-current liabilities		
Deferred tax (w (iv))	6,750	
8% convertible loan note (28,476 + 448) (w (iii))	28,924	35,674
Current liabilities		
Trade payables	24,500	
Liability to Easyfinance (w (ii))	8,700	
Bank overdraft	11,500	
Current tax payable	19,400	64,100
Total equity and liabilities		173,300

Workings (figures in brackets in $000)

(i) Cost of sales	$000
Per question	207,750
Depreciation – building (w (ii))	2,500
Adjustment/increase to closing inventory (w (iii))	(3,300)
	206,950

(ii)   Freehold property

The revaluation of the property will create an initial revaluation reserve of $15 million (80,000 – (75,000 – 10,000)). $3.75 million of this (25%) will be transferred to deferred tax leaving a net revaluation reserve of $11.25 million. The building valued at $50 million will require a depreciation charge of $2.5 million (50,000/20 years remaining) for the current year. This will leave a carrying amount in the statement of financial position of $77.5 million (80,000 – 2,500).

(iii)   Inventory adjustment

Goods delivered (deduct from closing inventory)	(2,700)
Cost of goods sold (7,800 × 100/130) (add to closing inventory)	6,000
Net increase in closing inventory	3,300

(iv)   Factored receivables

As Highwood still bears the risk of the non-payment of the receivables, the substance of this transaction is a loan. Thus the receivables must remain on Highwood's statement of financial position and the proceeds of the 'sale' treated as a current liability. The difference between the factored receivables (10,000) and the loan received (8,700) of $1.3 million, which has been charged to administrative expenses, should be reversed except for $600,000 which should be treated as an allowance for uncollectible receivables.

(v)   8% convertible loan note

This is a compound financial instrument having a debt (liability) and an equity component. These must be quantified and accounted for separately:

Year ended 31 March	Outflow	10%	Present value
	$000		$000
2011	2,400	0.91	2,184
2012	2,400	0.83	1,992
2013	32,400	0.75	24,300
Liability component			28,476
Equity component (balance)			1,524
Proceeds of issue			30,000

The finance cost for the year will be $2,848,000 (28,476 × 10% rounded). Thus $448,000 (2,848 – 2,400 interest paid) will be added to the carrying amount of the loan note in the statement of financial position.

(vi)   Deferred tax

Credit balance required at 31 March 2011 (27,000 × 25%)	6,750
Revaluation of property (w (i))	(3,750)
Balance at 1 April 2010	(2,600)
Charge to statement of profit or loss	400

			Marks
Marking scheme			

Marking scheme

			Marks
(a)	Statement of profit or loss		
	revenue		½
	cost of sales		3
	distribution costs		½
	administrative expenses		1
	finance costs		1½
	income tax expense		1½
	other comprehensive income		1
		Maximum	9
(b)	Statement of changes in equity		
	opening balances		1
	other component of equity (equity option)		1
	Total comprehensive income (½ each)		1
		Maximum	3
(c)	Statement of financial position		
	property, plant and equipment		1
	inventory		1
	trade receivables		1
	deferred tax		1
	issue of 8% loan note		1½
	liability to Easyfinance		1
	bank overdraft		½
	trade payables		½
	current tax payable		½
		Maximum	8
Total			**20**

357 KEYSTONE

(a)   **Keystone – Statement of profit or loss and other comprehensive income for the year ended 30 September 2011**

	$000	$000
Revenue		377,600
Cost of sales (w (i))		(258,100)
Gross profit		119,500
Distribution costs		(14,200)
Administrative expenses (46,400 – 24,000 dividend (50,000 × 5 × 2.40 × 4%))		(22,400)
Profit from operations		82,900
Investment income		800
Finance costs		(350)
Profit before tax		83,350
Income tax expense (24,300 + 1,800 (w (iii)))		(26,100)
Profit for the year		57,250
Other comprehensive income		
Revaluation of leased property	8,000	
Transfer to deferred tax (w (iii))	(2,400)	5,600
Total comprehensive income for the year		62,850

(b)   **Keystone – Statement of financial position as at 30 September 2011**

	$000	$000
Assets		
Non-current assets		
Property, plant and equipment (w (ii))		78,000
Current assets		
Inventory	56,600	
Trade receivables	31,150	87,750
Total assets		165,750

Equity and liabilities		
Equity shares of 20 cents each		50,000
Revaluation surplus (w (ii))	5,600	
Retained earnings (15,600 + 57,250 – 24,000 dividend paid)	48,850	54,450
		104,450
Non-current liabilities		
Deferred tax (w (iii))		6,900
Current liabilities		
Trade payables	27,800	
Bank overdraft	2,300	
Current tax payable	24,300	54,400
Total equity and liabilities		165,750

Workings (figures in brackets in $000)

(i)	Cost of sales	$000
	Opening inventory	46,700
	Materials (64,000 – 3,000)	61,000
	Production labour (124,000 – 4,000)	120,000
	Factory overheads (80,000 – (4,000 × 75%))	77,000
	Amortisation of leased property (w (ii))	3,000
	Depreciation of plant (1,000 + 6,000 (w (ii)))	7,000
	Closing inventory	(56,600)
		258,100

The cost of the self-constructed plant is $10 million (3,000 + 4,000 + 3,000 for materials, labour and overheads respectively that have also been deducted from the above items in cost of sales). It is not permissible to add a profit margin to self-constructed assets.

(ii) Non-current assets:

The leased property has been amortised at $2.5 million per annum (50,000/20 years). The accumulated amortisation of $10 million therefore represents four years, thus its remaining life at the date of revaluation is 16 years.

	$000
Carrying amount at date of revaluation (50,000 – 10,000)	40,000
Revalued amount	48,000
Gross gain on revaluation	8,000
Transfer to deferred tax (at 30%)	(2,400)
Net gain to revaluation surplus	5,600

The revalued amount of $48 million will be amortised over its remaining life of 16 years at $3 million per annum.

The self-constructed plant will be depreciated for six months by $1 million (10,000 × 20% × 6/12) and have a carrying amount at 30 September 2011 of $9 million. The plant in the trial balance will be depreciated by $6 million ((44,500 − 14,500) × 20%) for the year and have a carrying amount at 30 September 2011 of $24 million.

In summary:

	$000
Leased property (48,000 – 3,000)	45,000
Plant (9,000 + 24,000)	33,000
Property, plant and equipment	78,000

(iii) Deferred tax

Provision required at 30 September 2011 ((15,000 + 8,000) × 30%)	6,900
Provision at 1 October 2010	(2,700)
Increase required	4,200
Transferred from revaluation reserve (w (iv))	(2,400)
Balance: charge to statement of profit or loss	1,800

Marking scheme		
		Marks
(a)	Statement of profit or loss	
	revenue	½
	cost of sales	5½
	distribution costs	½
	administrative expenses	1½
	investment income	1
	finance costs	½
	income tax expense	1½
	other comprehensive income	1
	Maximum	12
(b)	Statement of financial position	
	property, plant and equipment	1
	inventory	½
	trade receivables	½
	equity shares	½
	revaluation surplus	1½
	retained earnings	1½
	deferred tax	1
	trade payables & overdraft	1
	current tax payable	½
	Maximum	8
Total		**20**

358 FRESCO *Online question assistance*

(a) (i) **Fresco – Statement of profit or loss and other comprehensive income for the year ended 31 March 2012**

	$000
Revenue	350,000
Cost of sales (w (i))	(311,000)
Gross profit	**39,000**
Distribution costs	(16,100)
Administrative expenses (26,900 + 3,000 re fraud)	(29,900)
Finance costs (300 + 2,300 (w (iii)))	(2,600)
Loss before tax	**(9,600)**
Income tax relief (2,400 + 200 (w (iv)) – 800)	1,800
Loss for the year	**(7,800)**
Other comprehensive income	
Revaluation of leased property (w (ii))	4,000
Total comprehensive losses	**(3,800)**

(ii) **Fresco – Statement of changes in equity for the year ended 31 March 2012**

	Share capital	Share premium	Revaluation reserve	Retained earnings	Total equity
	$000	$000	$000	$000	$000
Balances at 1 April 2011	45,000	5,000	nil	5,100	55,100
Prior period adjustment (re fraud)				(1,000)	(1,000)
Restated balance				4,100	
Rights share issue (see below)	9,000	4,500			13,500
Total comprehensive losses (see (i) above)			4,000	(7,800)	(3,800)
Transfer to retained earnings			(500)	500	
Balances at 31 March 2012	54,000	9,500	3,500	(3,200)	63,800

The rights issue was 18 million shares (45,000/50 cents each × 1/5) at 75 cents = $13.5 million. This equates to the balance on the suspense account. This should be recorded as $9 million equity shares (18,000 × 50 cents) and $4.5 million share premium (18,000 × (75 cents – 50 cents)).

The discovery of the fraud represents an error part of which is a prior period adjustment ($1 million) in accordance with IAS 8 *Accounting policies, changes in accounting estimates and errors*.

(iii) **Fresco – Statement of financial position as at 31 March 2012**

	$000	$000
Assets		
Non-current assets		
Property, plant and equipment (w (ii))		62,700
Current assets		
Inventory	25,200	
Trade receivables (28,500 – 4,000 re fraud)	24,500	
Current tax refund	2,400	52,100
Total assets		114,800
Equity and liabilities		
Equity (see (ii) above)		
Equity shares of 50 cents each		54,000
Reserves		
Share premium	9,500	
Revaluation	3,500	
Retained earnings	(3,200)	9,800
		63,800
Non-current liabilities		
Finance lease obligation (w (iii))	15,230	
Deferred tax (w (iv))	3,000	18,230
Current liabilities		
Trade payables	27,300	
Finance lease obligation (w (iii)))	4,070	
Bank overdraft	1,400	32,770
Total equity and liabilities		114,800

Workings (figures in brackets are in $000)

		$000
(i)	Cost of sales	
	Per question	298,700
	Amortisation of – leased property (w (ii))	4,500
	Amortisation of – leased plant (w (ii))	5,000
	Depreciation of other plant and equipment ((47,500 – 33,500) × 20%)	2,800
		311,000

(ii)	Non-current assets	
	Carrying amount 1 April 2011 (48,000 – 16,000)	32,000
	Revaluation surplus	4,000
	Revalued amount 1 April 2011	36,000
	Amortisation year to 31 March 2012 (over 8 years)	(4,500)
	Carrying amount 31 March 2012	31,500

$500,000 (4,000/8 years) of the revaluation surplus will be transferred to retained earnings (reported in the statement of changes in equity).

Amortisation for the leased plant for the year ended 31 March 2012 is $5 million (25,000/5 years).

Summarising the carrying amount of property, plant and equipment as at 31 March 2012:

Leased property	31,500
Owned plant (47,500 – 33,500 – 2,800)	11,200
Leased plant (25,000 – 5,000)	20,000
	62,700

(iii) Lease liability:

Balance b/f	Interest	Payment	Balance c/f
23,000	2,300	(6,000)	19,300
19,300	1,930	(6,000)	15,230

Finance cost:	$2,300
Non-current liability:	$15,230
Current liability:	$4,070

(iv) Deferred tax

Provision required at 31 March 2012 (12,000 × 25%)	3,000
Provision at 1 April 2011	(3,200)
Credit (reduction in provision) to statement of profit or loss	200

359 QUINCY

(a) **Quincy – Statement of profit or loss and other comprehensive income for the year ended 30 September 2012**

	$000
Revenue (213,500 – 1,600 (w (i)))	211,900
Cost of sales (w (ii))	(144,300)
Gross profit	67,600
Distribution costs	(12,500)
Administrative expenses (19,000 – 1,000 loan issue costs (w (iv)))	(18,000)
Loss on fair value of equity investments (17,000 – 15,700)	(1,300)
Investment income	400
Finance costs (w (iv))	(1,920)
Profit before tax	33,280
Income tax expense (7,400 + 1,100 – 200 (w (v)))	(8,300)
Profit for the year	25,980

(b) **Quincy – Statement of changes in equity for the year ended 30 September 2012**

	Share capital	Retained earnings	Total equity
	$000	$000	$000
Balance at 1 October 2011	60,000	6,500	68,500
Total comprehensive income		25,980	25,980
Dividend paid (60,000 × 4 × 8 cents)		(19,200)	(19,200)
Balance at 30 September 2012	60,000	13,280	75,280

(c)   Quincy – Statement of financial position as at 30 September 2012

Assets	$000	$000
Non-current assets		
Property, plant and equipment (w (iii)))		42,500
Equity financial asset investments		15,700
		58,200
Current assets		
Inventory	24,800	
Trade receivables	28,500	
Bank	2,900	56,200
Total assets		114,400
Equity and liabilities		
Equity shares of 25 cents each		60,000
Retained earnings		13,280
		73,280
Non-current liabilities		
Deferred tax (w (v))	1,000	
Deferred revenue (w (i))	800	
6% loan note (2014) (w (iv))	24,420	26,220
Current liabilities		
Trade payables	6,700	
Deferred revenue (w (i))	800	
Current tax payable	7,400	14,900
Total equity and liabilities		114,400

Workings (figures in brackets in $000)

(i)   The revenue for the service must be deferred. The deferred revenue must include the normal profit margin (25%) for the deferred work. At 30 September 2012, there are two more years of servicing work, thus $1.6 million ((600 × 2) × 100/75) must be deferred, split between current and non-current liabilities.

(ii)   Cost of sales

	$000
Per trial balance	136,800
Depreciation of plant (w (iii))	7,500
	144,300

(iii)   Plant and equipment:

	$000
Carrying amount as at 1 October 2011 (83,700 – 33,700)	50,000
Depreciation at 15% per annum	(7,500)
Carrying amount as at 30 September 2012	42,500

(iv)   Loan note

The finance cost of the loan note is charged at the effective rate of 8% applied to the carrying amount of the loan. The issue costs of the loan ($1 million) should be deducted from the proceeds of the loan ($25 million) and not treated as an administrative expense. This gives an initial carrying amount of $24 million and a finance cost of $1,920,000 (24,000 × 8%). The interest actually paid is $1.5 million (25,000 × 6%) and the difference between these amounts, of $420,000 (1,920 – 1,500), is accrued and added to the carrying amount of the loan note. This gives $24.42 million (24,000 + 420) for inclusion as a non-current liability in the statement of financial position.

Note: The loan interest paid of $1.5 million plus the dividend paid of $19.2 million (see (b)) equals the $20.7 million shown in the trial balance for these items.

(v)   Deferred tax

	$000
Provision required as at 30 September 2012 (5,000 × 20%)	1,000
Less provision b/f	(1,200)
Credit to statement of profit or loss	200

Marking scheme		Marks
(a)	Statement of profit or loss	
	Revenue	1½
	Cost of sales	1½
	Distribution costs	½
	Administrative expenses	1½
	Loss on investments	1
	Investment income	½
	Finance costs	1½
	Income tax expense	2
	Maximum	10
(b)	Statement of changes in equity	
	Balances b/f	1
	Total comprehensive income	½
	Dividend paid	½
	Maximum	2

(c)			
	Statement of financial position		
	Property, plant and equipment		1
	Equity investments		1
	Inventory		½
	Trade receivables		½
	Bank		½
	Deferred tax		1
	Deferred revenue		1
	6% loan note		1½
	Trade payables		½
	Current tax payable		½
			———
		Maximum	8
			———
Total			**20**
			———

360 ATLAS

(a) (i) **Atlas – Statement of profit or loss and other comprehensive income for the year ended 31 March 2013**

Monetary figures in brackets are in $000

	$000
Revenue (550,000 – 10,000 in substance loan (w(iii))	540,000
Cost of sales (w (i))	(420,600)
	———
Gross profit	119,400
Distribution costs	(21,500)
Administrative expenses (30,900 + 5,400 re directors' bonus of 1% of sales made)	(36,300)
Finance costs (700 + 500 (10,000 × 10% × 6/12 re in substance loan))	(1,200)
	———
Profit before tax	60,400
Income tax expense (27,200 – 1,200 + (9,400 – 6,200) deferred tax)	(29,200)
	———
Profit for the year	31,200
Other comprehensive income	
Revaluation gain on land and buildings (w (ii))	7,000
	———
Total comprehensive income for the year	38,200
	———

(ii) **Atlas – Statement of financial position as at 31 March 2013**

	$000	$000
Assets		
Non-current assets		
Property, plant and equipment (44,500 + 52,800 (w (ii)))		97,300
Current assets		
Inventory (43,700 + 7,000 re in substance loan (w(iii))	50,700	
Trade receivables	42,200	92,900
Plant held for sale (w (ii))		3,600
Total assets		193,800
Equity and liabilities		
Equity		
Equity shares of 50 cents each		50,000
Revaluation surplus	7,000	
Retained earnings (11,200 + 31,200	42,400	49,400
		99,400
Non-current liabilities		
In substance loan from Xpede (10,000 + 500 accrued interest (w(iii))	10,500	
Deferred tax	9,400	19,900
Current liabilities		
Trade payables	35,100	
Income tax	27,200	
Accrued directors' bonus	5,400	
Bank overdraft	6,800	74,500
Total equity and liabilities		193,800

Workings (figures in brackets are in $000)

	$000
(i) Cost of sales	
Per question	411,500
Closing inventory re in substance loan (w (iii)	(7,000)
Depreciation of buildings (w (ii))	2,500
Depreciation of plant and equipment (w (ii))	13,600
	420,600

(ii)   Non-current assets

Land and buildings

The gain on revaluation and carrying amount of the land and buildings will be:

	$000
Carrying amount at 1 April 2012 (60,000 – 20,000)	40,000
Revaluation at that date (12,000 + 35,000)	47,000
Gain on revaluation	7,000
Buildings depreciation (35,000/14 years)	(2,500)
Carrying amount of land and buildings at 31 March 2013 (47,000 – 2,500)	44,500

Plant

The plant held for sale should be shown separately and not be depreciated after 1 October 2012.

Other plant	
Carrying amount at 1 April 2012 (94,500 – 24,500)	70,000
Plant held for sale (9,000 – 5,000)	(4,000)
	66,000
Depreciation for year ended 31 March 2013 (20% reducing balance)	(13,200)
Carrying amount at 31 March 2013	52,800

Plant held for sale:	
At 1 April 2012 (from above)	4,000
Depreciation to date of reclassification (4,000 × 20% × 6/12)	(400)
Carrying amount at 1 October 2012	3,600
Total depreciation of plant for year ended 31 March 2013 (13,200 + 400)	13,600

As the fair value of the plant held for sale at 1 October 2012 is $4.2 million, it should continue to be carried at its (lower) carrying amount (and no longer depreciated).

(iii)   The transaction with Xpede will not be recognised as a sale. The presence of the option suggests that control of the goods has not passed to Xpede. Therefore this transaction will be recognised as a financial liability, with interest of 10% accruing each year.

As the transaction occurred partway through the year, 6 months interest ($500k) should be included within finance costs and added to the liability.

As this is not a sale, the goods should be recorded back into inventory at the cost of $7 million. This should also be deducted from cost of sales.

			Marks
(a)	(i)	Statement of profit or loss and other comprehensive income	
		revenue	1
		cost of sales	3
		distribution costs	½
		administrative expenses	1
		finance costs	1
		income tax	1½
		other comprehensive income	1
		Maximum	9
	(ii)	Statement of financial position	
		property, plant and equipment	2½
		inventory	1
		trade receivables	½
		plant held for sale (at 3,600)	1
		retained earnings	1
		revaluation surplus	1
		in substance loan	1
		deferred tax	1
		trade payables	½
		current tax	½
		directors' bonus	½
		bank overdraft	½
		Maximum	11
Total			**20**

Marking scheme

361 MOBY

(a) **Moby – Statement of profit or loss and other comprehensive income for the year ended 30 September 2013**

	$000
Revenue (227,800 + 10,000 contract with customer (w (i)))	237,800
Cost of sales (w (ii))	(181,900)
Gross profit	55,900
Administrative expenses (29,850 – 150 disallowed provision – see below)	(29,700)
Profit from operations	26,200
Finance costs (4,000 loan + 2,930 lease (w (iv)))	(6,930)
Profit before tax	19,270
Income tax expense (3,400 – 2,000 (w (v)))	(1,400)
Profit for the year	17,870

Other comprehensive income

Items which will not be reclassified to profit or loss:

Gain on revaluation of land and buildings (w (iii))	4,400
Deferred tax on gain (4,400 × 25%)	(1,100)
Total other comprehensive income for the year	3,300
Total comprehensive income for the year	21,170

(b)   Moby – Statement of financial position as at 30 September 2013

Assets	$000	$000
Non-current assets		
Property, plant and equipment (w (iii))		73,000
Current assets		
Inventory	56,600	
Trade receivables	38,500	
Contract asset (w (i))	6,000	101,100
Total assets		174,100
Equity and liabilities		
Equity shares of 20 cents each		27,000
Revaluation surplus	3,300	
Retained earnings (19,800 + 17,870)	37,670	40,970
		67,970
Non-current liabilities		
Lease obligation (w (iv))	16,133	
Deferred tax (w (v))	7,100	
Loan note (40,000 × 1.1)	44,000	67,233
Current liabilities		
Lease obligation (23,030 – 16,133 (w (iv)))	6,897	
Trade payables	21,300	
Bank overdraft	7,300	
Current tax payable	3,400	38,897
Total equity and liabilities		174,100

Workings (monetary figures in brackets in $000)

(i) Contract with customer:

	$000	$000
Step 1 – Overall		
Total contract revenue		25,000
Costs incurred to date	14,000	
Estimated costs to complete	6,000	(20,000)
Total contract profit		5,000

Step 2 – Progress

Percentage of completion is 40% (10,000/25,000)

Step 3 – Statement of profit or loss

Revenue	10,000
Cost of sales (40% × 20,000 total costs)	(8,000)
Profit for year	2,000

Step 4 – Statement of financial position

Costs to date	14,000
Profit to date	2,000
Billed to date	(10,000)
Contract asset	6,000

(ii) Cost of sales:

	$000
Per question	164,500
Contract with customer (w(i))	8,000
Depreciation of building (w (iii))	2,400
Depreciation of leased plant (w (iii))	7,000
	181,900

(iii) Non-current assets:

	$000	$000
Land and building		
Carrying amount 1 October 2012 (60,000 – 10,000)		50,000
Revalued land	16,000	
Revalued building	38,400	54,400
Revaluation gain		4,400
Depreciation for year (38,400/16 years)		(2,400)
Carrying amount at 30 September 2013 (54,400 – 2,400)		52,000
Leased plant		
Carrying amount 1 October 2012 (35,000 – 7,000)		28,000
Depreciation for year (35,000/5 years)		(7,000)
Carrying amount at 30 September 2013		21,000
Carrying amount of property, plant and equipment at 30 September 2013: (52,000 + 42,000 + 21,000)		115,000

(iv) Lease obligation:

	$000
Liability at 1 October 2012	29,300
Interest at 10% for year ended 30 September 2013	2,930
Rental payment 30 September 2013	(9,200)
Liability at 30 September 2013	23,030
Interest at 10% for year ended 30 September 2014	2,303
Rental payment 30 September 2014	(9,200)
Liability at 30 September 2014	16,133

(v)   Deferred tax:

	$000	$000
Provision b/f at 1 October 2012		(8,000)
Provision c/f required at 30 September 2013		
Taxable differences: per question	24,000	
on revaluation of land and buildings	4,400	
	28,400	
	× 25%	7,100
Net reduction in provision		(900)
Charged to other comprehensive income on revaluation gain (4,400 × 25%)		(1,100)
Credit to profit or loss		2,000

Marking scheme		
		Marks
(a)	Statement of profit or loss and other comprehensive income	
	revenue	1½
	cost of sales	2½
	operating expenses	1
	finance costs	1½
	income tax expense	1½
	gain on revaluation of land and buildings	1
	deferred tax on gain	1
	Maximum	10
(b)	Statement of financial position	
	property, plant and equipment	1½
	inventory	½
	amount due on contract	1
	trade receivables	½
	equity shares	½
	revaluation surplus	½
	retained earnings	½
	non-current lease obligation	1
	deferred tax	1
	loan note	1
	current lease obligation	½
	bank overdraft	½
	trade payables	½
	current tax payable	½
	Maximum	10
Total		**20**

362 XTOL

(a) **Xtol – Statement of profit or loss for the year ended 31 March 2014**

	$000
Revenue (490,000 – 20,000 agency sales (w (i)))	470,000
Cost of sales (w (i))	(289,600)
Gross profit	180,400
Distribution costs	(33,500)
Administrative expenses	(36,800)
Other operating income – agency sales	2,000
Finance costs (900 overdraft + 3,676 (w (ii)))	(4,576)
Profit before tax	107,524
Income tax expense (28,000 + 3,200 + 3,700 (w (iii)))	(34,900)
Profit for the year	72,624

(b) **Xtol – Statement of financial position as at 31 March 2014**

	$000	$000
Non-current assets		
Property, plant and equipment (75,000 + 155,500 – 57,500)		173,000
Current assets		
Inventory	61,000	
Trade receivables	63,000	124,000
Total assets		297,000
Equity and liabilities		
Equity shares of $1 each		66,000
Share premium		15,000
Other component of equity – equity option		4,050
Retained earnings (15,200 + 72,624 profit for year)		87,824
		172,874
Non-current liabilities		
Deferred tax	8,300	
5% convertible loan note (w (ii))	47,126	55,426
Current liabilities		
Trade payables (32,200 + 3,000 re Francais (w (i)))	35,200	
Bank overdraft	5,500	
Current tax payable	28,000	68,700
Total equity and liabilities		297,000

(c) **Basic earnings per share for the year ended 31 March 2014**

Profit per statement of profit or loss	$72.624 million
Weighted average number of shares (w (iv))	66.255 million
Earnings per share	$1.17

Workings (figures in brackets in $000)

(i) **Cost of sales (including the effect of agency sales on cost of sales and trade payables)**

	$000
Cost of sales per question	290,600
Remove agency costs	(15,000)
Depreciation of plant and equipment ((155,500 – 43,500) × 12½%)	14,000
	———
	289,600
	———

The agency sales should be removed from revenue (debit $20 million) and their 'cost' from cost of sales (credit $15 million). Instead, Xtol should report the commission earned of $2 million (credit) as other operating income (or as revenue would be acceptable). This leaves a net amount of $3 million ((20,000 – 15,000) – 2,000) owing to Francais as a trade payable.

(ii) **5% convertible loan note**

The convertible loan note is a compound financial instrument having a debt and an equity component which must be accounted for separately:

Year ended 31 March	outflow	8%	present value
	$000		$000
2014	2,500	0.93	2,325
2015	2,500	0.86	2,150
2016	52,500	0.79	41,475
			———
Debt component			45,950
Equity component (= balance)			4,050
			———
Proceeds of issue			50,000
			———

The finance cost for the year will be $3,676,000 (45,950 × 8%) and the carrying amount of the loan as at 31 March 2014 will be $47,126,000 (45,950 + (3,676 – 2,500)).

(iii) **Deferred tax**

	$000
Provision at 31 March 2014	8,300
Balance at 1 April 2013	(4,600)
	———
Charge to statement of profit or loss	3,700
	———

(iv)   Earnings per share

Step 1 – Theoretical ex-rights price (TERP)

5 shares @ $2.50 =	$12.50
1 share @ $1.60 =	$1.60
	————
6 shares	$14.10

TERP = $14.10/6 = $2.35

Step 2 – Rights fraction = 2.50/2.35

Step 3 – Weighted average number of shares (WANS)

Date	Number	Fraction of year	Rights fraction	Weighted Average
1 April	55,000,000	6/12	2.5/2.35	29,255,319
1 October	66,000,000	6/12		33,000,000
				————
				62,255,319
				————

There are 66 million shares at 31 March 2014. This is after the 1 for 5 rights issue. Therefore anyone who held 5 shares at the start of the year now has 6 shares. Therefore the opening number of shares would be 55 million (66 million × 5/6).

Marking scheme			
			Marks
(a)	Statement of profit or loss		
	revenue		1
	cost of sales		1½
	distribution costs		½
	administrative expenses		½
	operating income agency sales		½
	finance costs		1½
	income tax expense		1½
		Maximum	**7**
(b)	Statement of financial position		
	property, plant and equipment		½
	inventory		½
	trade receivables		½
	deferred tax		½
	share capita/share premium		½
	Retained earnings		½
	Convertible option – Equity component		1
	5% loan note		1½
	trade payables		1½
	bank overdraft		½
	current tax		½
		Maximum	**8**
(c)	Calculation of opening shares		1
	Calculation of TERP		1
	Application of fraction to first 6 months only		1
	Time apportionment		1
	Use of own profit from P/L		1
			———
Total			**20**
			———

363 WELLMAY

(a) **Statement of profit or loss and other comprehensive income year ended 31 March 2007**

	$000	$000
Revenue (4,200 – 500 (w (i)))		3,700
Cost of sales (w (ii))		(2,500)
Gross profit		1,200
Operating expenses		(470)
Investment property – rental income	20	
– fair value loss (400 –375)	(25)	(5)
Finance costs (w (iii))		(113)
Profit before tax		612
Income tax (360 + 30 (w (v)))		(390)
Profit for the period		222

Statement of changes in equity – year ended 31 March 2007

	Equity shares $000	Equity option $000	Revaluation reserve $000	Retained earnings $000	Total $000
Balances at 1 April 2006	1,200		350	2,215	4,165
Equity conversion option (w (iv))		40			40
Revaluation of factory (w (vi))			190		190
Profit for the period				222	297
Balances at 31 March 2007	1,200	40	540	2,437	4,292

Statement of financial position as at 31 March 2007

	$000	$000
Non-current assets		
Property, plant and equipment (w (vi))		4,390
Investment property (w (vi))		375
		4,765
Current assets (1,400 + 200 inventory (w (i)))		1,600
Total assets		6,365
Equity and liabilities (see statement of changes in equity above)		
Equity shares of 50 cents each		1,200
Equity option (w (iv))		40
		1,240

Reserves:		
Revaluation reserve	540	
Retained earnings	2,437	2,977
		4,217
Non-current liabilities		
Deferred tax (w (v))	210	
8% Convertible loan note ((560 + 8) (w (iv)))	568	778
Current liabilities	820	
Loan from Westwood (500 + 50 accrued interest (w (i)))	550	1,370
Total equity and liabilities		6,365

(b) Diluted earnings per share (DEPS) acts as a warning to the shareholders, and should be shown alongside basic earnings per share (EPS). Diluted earnings per share shows how the current EPS figure could fall in the future based on items that are currently in existence, such as convertible loans or options.

This can aid the predictive nature of financial statements as shareholders are given information that could potentially occur in the future. This increases the relevance of the financial statements and provides information which could affect the decisions taken by the users.

In the scenario, Wellmay has convertible loans in issue, and the DEPS figure will be calculated by looking at two items. Firstly, Wellmay's profit will increase if the loans are converted as there will no longer be the finance cost in the statement of profit or loss. As interest is tax deductible, the increase in earnings will consist of the interest saved less and additional tax payable on the profits.

The second item is that the number of shares will increase. From the scenario, it can be calculated that an additional 300,000 shares will be issued ($600k × 100/200).

The additional earnings are added to the current profit, with the additional shares added to the current number of shares for the calculation of diluted EPS.

Workings (All figures in $000)

(i) The 'sale' to Westwood is, in substance, a secured loan, as the repurchase agreement suggests control has not passed in relation to the goods. The repurchase price is the cost of sale plus compound interest at 10% for two years. The correct accounting treatment is to reverse the sale with the goods going back into inventory and the 'proceeds' treated as a loan with accrued interest of 10% ($50,000) for the current year.

(ii) **Cost of sales**

From draft financial statements	2,700
Sale of goods added back to inventory (see above)	(200)
	2,500

(iii) **Finance costs**

From draft financial statements	55
Additional accrued interest on convertible loan (w (iv))	8
Finance cost on in-substance loan (500 × 10%)	50
	113

(iv) **Convertible loan**

This is a compound financial instrument that contains an element of debt and an element of equity (the option to convert). IAS 32 *Financial instruments: disclosure and presentation* requires that the substance of such instruments should be applied to the reporting of them. The value of the debt element is calculated by discounting the future cash flows (at 10%). The residue of the issue proceeds is recorded as the value of the equity option.

	Cash flows	Factor at 10%	Present value $000
Year 1 interest	48	0.91	43.6
Year 2 interest	48	0.83	39.8
Year 3 interest	48	0.75	36.0
Year 4 interest, redemption premium and capital	648	0.68	440.6
Total value of debt component			560.0
Proceeds of the issue			600.0
Equity component (residual amount)			40.0

For the year ended 31 March 2007, the interest cost for the convertible loan in the statement of comprehensive income should be increased from $48,000 to $56,000 (10% × 560) by accruing $8,000, which should be added to the carrying amount of the debt.

(v) **Taxation**

The required deferred tax balance is $210,000 (600 × 35%), the current balance is $180,000, and thus a further transfer of $30,000 (via the statement of comprehensive income) is required.

(vi) **Properties**

The fair value model in IAS 40 Investment property requires the loss of $25,000 on the fair value of investment properties to be reported in the statement of comprehensive income. This differs from revaluations of other properties. IAS 16 Property, plant and equipment requires surpluses and deficits to be recorded as movements in equity (a revaluation reserve). After depreciation of $40,000 for the year ended 31 March 2007, the factory (used by Wellmay) would have a carrying amount of $1,160,000 (1,200 – 40). The valuation of $1,350,000 at 31 March 2007 would give a further revaluation surplus of $190,000 (1,350 – 1,160) and a carrying amount of property, plant and equipment of $4,390,000 (4,200 + 190) at that date.

364 DUNE

Key answer tips

This question contained many of the usual adjustments that you would expect with a published accounts question such as depreciation and tax adjustments. You were also expected to demonstrate your knowledge of accounting for held for sale assets and financial assets and liabilities in this time-consuming question.

(a)   Dune – Statement of profit or loss for the year ended 31 March 2010

	$000
Revenue (400,000	400,000
Cost of sales (w (i))	(306,100)
Gross profit	93,900
Distribution costs	(26,400)
Administrative expenses (34,200 – 500 loan note issue costs)	(33,700)
Investment income	1,200
Profit (gain) on investments at fair value through profit or loss (28,000 – 26,500)	1,500
Finance costs (200 + 1,950 (w (iii)))	(2,150)
Profit before tax	34,350
Income tax expense (12,000 – 1,400 – 1,800 (w (iv)))	(8,800)
Profit for the year	25,550

Dune – Statement of financial position as at 31 March 2010

	$000	$000
Assets		
Non-current assets		
Property, plant and equipment (w (v))		37,400
Investments at fair value through profit or loss		28,000
		65,400
Current assets		
Inventory	48,000	
Trade receivables	40,700	
Bank	15,500	104,200
Non-current assets held for sale (w (ii))		33,500
Total assets		203,100

Equity and liabilities

Equity

Equity shares of $1 each	40,000
Other components of equity	20,000
Retained earnings (38,400 + 25,550 – 10,000 dividend paid)	53,950
	113,950

Non-current liabilities

Deferred tax (w (iv))	4,200	
5% loan notes (2012) (w (iii))	20,450	24,650

Current liabilities

Trade payables	52,000	
Accrued loan note interest (w (iii))	500	
Current tax payable	12,000	64,500
Total equity and liabilities		203,100

(b)   Earnings per share:

EPS = $25,550,000/36,594,595 (w (vi)) = $0.70

Re-stated 2009 EPS = 68c × (0.74/0.82) = $0.61

Workings (figures in brackets in $000)

(i)   Cost of sales

	$000
Per question	294,000
Depreciation of leasehold property (see below)	1,500
Impairment of leasehold property (see below)	4,000
Depreciation of plant and equipment ((67,500 – 23,500) × 15%)	6,600
	306,100

(ii)   The leasehold property must be classed as a non-current asset held for sale from 1 October 2009 at its fair value less costs to sell. It must be depreciated for six months up to this date (after which depreciation ceases). This is calculated at $1.5 million (45,000/15 years × 6/12). Its carrying amount at 1 October 2009 is therefore $37.5 million (45,000 – (6,000 + 1,500)).

Its fair value less cost to sell at this date is $33.5 million ((40,000 × 85%) – 500). It is therefore impaired by $4 million (37,500 – 33,500).

(iii)   The finance cost of the loan note, at the effective rate of 10% applied to the correct carrying amount of the loan note of $19.5 million is, $1.95 million (the issue costs must be deducted from the proceeds of the loan note; they are not an administrative expense). The interest actually paid is $500,000 (20,000 × 5% × 6/12); however, a further $500,000 needs to be accrued as a current liability (as it will be paid soon). The difference between the total finance cost of $1.95 million and the $1 million interest payable is added to the carrying amount of the loan note to give $20.45 million (19,500 + 950) for inclusion as a non-current liability in the statement of financial position.

(iv)   **Deferred tax**

Provision required at 31 March 2010 (14,000 × 30%)	4,200
Provision at 1 April 2009	(6,000)
	———
Credit (reduction in provision) to statement of profit or loss	1,800
	———

(v)   **Property, plant and equipment**

Property, plant and equipment (67,500 − 23,500 − 6,600)	37,400

(vi)   **Weighted average number of shares**

Step 1 – Theoretical ex-rights price (TERP)

4 shares @ $0.82 =	$3.28
1 share @ $0.42 =	$0.42
	———
5 shares	$3.70
	———

TERP = $3.70/5 = $0.74

Step 2 – Rights fraction = 0.82/0.74

Step 3 – Weighted average number of shares (WANS)

Date	Number	Fraction of year	Rights fraction	Weighted Average
1 April	32,000,000	9/12	0.82/0.74	26,594,595
1 January	40,000,000	3/12		10,000,000
				———————
				36,594,595
				———————

Based on 40 million shares in issue at 31 March 2010, a rights issue of 1 for 4 on 1 January 2010 would have resulted in the issue of 8 million new shares (40 million − (40 million × 4/5)). Therefore there would have been 32 million shares at the start of the year.

Marking scheme

		Marks
(a)	**Statement of profit or loss**	
	revenue	½
	cost of sales	2
	distribution costs	½
	administrative expenses	1
	investment income	½
	gain on investments	½
	finance costs	1½
	income tax expense	2
	Maximum	7½
	Statement of financial position	
	property, plant and equipment	½
	investments	½
	inventory	½
	trade receivables	½
	bank	½
	non-current asset held for sale	1
	equity shares	½
	retained earnings (1 for dividend)	1
	deferred tax	1
	5% loan note	1
	trade payables	½
	accrued loan note interest	½
	current tax payable	½
	Maximum	7½
(b)	Number of shares at start of year	1
	TERP	1
	Application of rights fraction and time apportionment	1
	Use of own profit	1
	Restatement of prior year	1
Total		**20**

Examiner's comments

This was a question of preparing financial statements from a trial balance with various adjustments required. These involved the dealing with the use of the effective interest rate for a loan, a fair value investment, an impairment of a leasehold property (including presenting it as 'held for sale'), and accounting for taxation. The most common errors were:

- loan: the issue costs were often ignored and calculating the finance charge at the nominal rate of 5% instead of the effective rate of 10%. Omission of accrued interest from current liabilities or including it at the incorrect amount

- leasehold property: a failure to depreciate it up to the date it became 'held for sale'; not calculating the subsequent impairment loss and most candidates continuing to show it as a non-current (rather than a current) asset

- there were many errors in the treatment of the taxation, including: debiting (should be credited) the over provision of the previous year's tax; treating the closing provision (rather than the movement) of deferred tax as the charge in the statement of profit or loss; and confusion over SOFP entries.

365 KANDY *Online question assistance*

(a) **Kandy – Schedule of retained earnings of Kandy as at 30 September 2014**

	$000
Retained earnings per trial balance	19,500
Adjustments re:	
Note (i)	
Add back issue costs of loan note (w (i))	1,000
Loan finance costs (29,000 × 9% (w (i)))	(2,610)
Note (ii)	
Depreciation of buildings (w (ii))	(2,600)
Depreciation of plant and equipment (w (ii))	(3,000)
Note (iii)	
Income tax expense (w (iii))	(800)
Property rental (1,000 + 1,000/4 years)	(1,250)
Adjusted retained earnings	10,240

(b) **Kandy – Statement of financial position as at 30 September 2014**

Assets	$000	$000
Non-current assets		
Property, plant and equipment (44,400 + 21,000 (w (ii)))		65,400
Lease premium (w (iv))		500
Current assets (per trial balance plus 250 lease premium (w (iv))		68,950
Total assets		134,850
Equity and liabilities		
Equity		
Equity shares of $1 each		40,000
Revaluation surplus (12,000 – 2,400 (w (ii) and (iii)))	9,600	
Retained earnings (from (a))	10,240	19,840
		59,840
Non-current liabilities		
Deferred tax (w (iii))	4,400	
6% loan note (w (i))	29,810	34,210
Current liabilities		
Per trial balance	38,400	
Current tax payable	2,400	40,800
Total equity and liabilities		134,850

Workings (monetary figures in brackets in $000)

(i) **Loan note**

The issue costs should be deducted from the proceeds of the loan note and not charged as an expense. The finance cost of the loan note, at the effective rate of 9% applied to the carrying amount of the loan note of $29 million (30,000 – 1,000), is $2,610,000. The interest actually paid is $1.8 million. The difference between these amounts of $810,000 (2,610 – 1,800) is added to the carrying amount of the loan note to give $29,810,000 (29,000 + 810) for inclusion as a non-current liability in the statement of financial position.

(ii) **Non-current assets**

Land and buildings

The gain on revaluation and carrying amount of the land and buildings will be:

	$000
Carrying amount at 1 October 2013 (55,000 – 20,000)	35,000
Revaluation at that date (8,000 + 39,000)	47,000
Gain on revaluation	12,000
Buildings depreciation for the year ended 30 September 2014 (39,000/15 years)	(2,600)
Carrying amount at 30 September 2014 (47,000 – 2,600)	44,400

	$000
Plant and equipment	
Carrying amount at 1 October 2013 (58,500 – 34,500)	24,000
Depreciation for year ended 30 September 2014 (121/2% reducing balance)	(3,000)
Carrying amount at 30 September 2014	21,000

(iii) **Taxation**

Income tax expense

Provision for year ended 30 September 2014	2,400
Less over-provision in previous year	(1,100)
Deferred tax (see below)	(500)
	800

Deferred tax

Provision required at 30 September 2014 ((10,000 + 12,000) × 20%)	4,400
Provision at 1 October 2013	(2,500)

Movement in provision	1,900
Charge to revaluation of land and buildings (12,000 × 20%)	(2,400)
Balance – credit to profit or loss	(500)

(iv) Operating lease

The operating lease should be expensed into the statement of profit or loss on a straight line basis over the lease term. Therefore $1 million should be expensed for the annual rental. In addition to this, the lease premium should also be expensed over the lease term. This means that an additional $250,000 is expensed each year. As the whole $1 million has been paid, there is a $750,000 prepayment as at 30 September 20X4. Of this, $500,000 will be held as a non-current asset, with $250,000 held within current assets.

Marking scheme		Marks
(a)	Schedule of retained earnings as at 30 September 2014	
	retained earnings per trial balance	½
	issue costs	1
	loan finance costs	1½
	depreciation charges	2
	income tax expense	2
	Operating lease	2
	Maximum	9
(b)	Statement of financial position	
	property, plant and equipment	2
	Operating lease	1
	current assets	1½
	equity shares	½
	revaluation surplus	2
	deferred tax	1
	6% loan note	1½
	current liabilities (per trial balance)	½
	current tax payable	1
	Maximum	11
Total		**20**

366 CLARION

(a)   **Clarion – Statement of profit or loss for the year ended 31 March 2015**

	$000
Revenue	132,000
Cost of sales (w (i))	(105,300)
Gross profit	26,700
Distribution costs	(7,400)
Administrative expenses	(8,000)
Finance costs (w (ii))	(2,790)
Investment income (w (iii))	1,000
Profit before tax	9,510
Income tax expense (3,500 – 400 + 300 (w (iv)))	(3,400)
Profit for the year	6,110

(b)   **Clarion – Statement of financial position as at 31 March 2015**

Assets	$000	$000
Non-current assets		
Property, plant and equipment (85,000 – 19,000 – 17,000)		49,000
Investments through profit or loss		6,500
		55,500
Current assets		
Inventory	11,700	
Trade receivables	20,500	32,200
Total assets		87,700
Equity and liabilities		
Equity		
Equity shares of $1 each		35,000
Retained earnings (4,700 + 6,110)		10,810
		45,810
Non-current liabilities		
8% loan notes	15,000	
Deferred tax (w (iv))	3,000	
Environmental provision (4,000 + 320 (w (ii)))	4,320	
Finance lease obligation (w (v))	3,747	26,067
Current liabilities		
Trade payables	9,400	
Finance lease obligation (4,770 – 3,747 (w (v)))	1,023	
Bank overdraft	1,900	
Current tax payable	3,500	15,823
Total equity and liabilities		87,700

(c)   **Clarion – Extracts from the statement of cash flows for the year ended 31 March 2015**

	$000
Cash flows from investing activities	
Purchase of plant and equipment	(14,000)
Sale of investments	1,600
Cash flows from financing activities	
Redemption of loan notes (w (vii))	(5,000)
Repayment of finance lease (2,300 + (1,500 – 570))	(3,230)

Workings (figures in brackets in $000)

(i)

	$000
Cost of sales (per question)	88,300
Depreciation of plant and equipment (85,000 × 20%)	17,000
	———
	105,300

(ii)   **Finance costs**

8% loan notes (800 trial balance + 800 suspense account (w (vi)))	1,600
Finance lease (w (v))	570
Bank interest	300
Environmental provision (4,000 × 8%)	320
	———
	2,790

(iii)   **Investment income**

Dividends received and profit on sale	500
Gains on fair value (6,500 – 6,000)	500
	———
	1,000

(iv)   **Deferred tax**

Provision required as at 31 March 2015 (12,000 × 25%)	3,000
Balance at 1 April 2014	(2,700)
	———
Charge to profit or loss	300

(v)   **Leased plant/finance lease obligation**

Fair value of plant/initial obligation	8,000
Less deposit	(2,300)
	———
	5,700
Interest at 10% to 31 March 2015	570
Less first annual payment	(1,500)
	———
Liability at 31 March 2015	4,770
Interest at 10% to 31 March 2016	477
Less second annual payment	(1,500)
	———
Liability at 31 March 2016 (therefore non-current liability)	3,747

(vi)   Elimination of suspense account

	$000
Cash cost of loan note redemption (20,000 × 25%)	5,000
Six months' interest on loan note (20,000 × 8% × 6/12)	800
	5,800

Marking scheme		
		Marks
(a)	Statement of profit or loss	
	revenue	½
	cost of sales	2
	distribution costs	½
	administrative expenses	½
	investment income	1½
	finance costs	1½
	income tax expense	1½
		8
(b)	Statement of financial position	
	property, plant and equipment	1
	investments through profit or loss	½
	unamortised lease premium	1
	Inventory and receivables	½
	share capital	½
	retained earnings	½
	8% loan notes	1
	deferred tax	1
	environmental provision	½
	non-current lease obligation	½
	trade payables and overdraft	½
	current lease obligation	1
	current tax payable	½
		9
(c)	Purchase of property, plant and equipment	½
	Sale of investments	½
	Redemption of loan notes	½
	Repayment of finance lease	1½
Total		20

367 MOSTON *Walk in the footsteps of a top tutor*

(a)   **Moston – Statement of profit or loss and other comprehensive income for the year ended 30 June 2015**

	$000
Revenue (113,500 – 3,000 see below)	110,500
Cost of sales (w (i))	(95,700)
Gross profit	14,800
Distribution costs	(3,600)
Administrative expenses (6,800 – 500 loan note issue costs)	(6,300)
Investment income	300
Gain on financial asset equity investments (9,600 – 8,800)	800
Finance costs (w (ii))	(1,710)
Profit before tax	4,290
Income tax expense (1,200 + 800)	(2,000)
Profit for the year	2,290
Other comprehensive income	
Items that will not be reclassified to profit or loss	
Gain on revaluation of property (29,000 – (28,500 – 1,900) w (i))	2,400
Total comprehensive income for the year	4,690

Tutorial note

The 'sale' of the maturing goods is a $3 million loan in substance, carrying 10% interest per annum. This is a loan as the option is almost certain to be exercised. This means control of the goods has not passed over from Moston. Therefore the $3 million should be removed from revenue and included as a loan.

(b)   **Moston – Statement of changes in equity for the year ended 30 June 2015**

	Share capital	Other components of equity	Revaluation surplus	Retained earnings	Total equity
	$000	$000	$000	$000	$000
Balance at 1 July 2014	20,000	2,300	3,000	6,200	31,500
Share issue	10,000	7,000			17,000
Total comprehensive income for the year			2,400	2,290	4,690
Dividends paid (20,000 × 20 cents)				(4,000)	(4,000)
Balance at 30 June 2015	30,000	9,300	5,400	4,490	49,190

(c)   **Moston – Statement of cash flows for the year ended 30 June 2015**

	$000
Cash flows from investing activities	
Capitalised development costs	(3,200)
Cash flows from financing activities	
Shares issued	17,000
Dividends paid	(4,000)
Loan notes issued	19,500

Tutorial note

It is crucial that you know what each section of the statement of cash flows contains so that you are able to produce extracts if required. This is likely to contain a number of figures given to you in the question, such as the loan notes and shares issued so there is scope to pick up some simpler marks here.

Workings (monetary figures in brackets in $000)

(i)   Cost of sales

	$000
Per trial balance	88,500
Goods re in-substance loan	(2,000)
Depreciation of property (28,500/15 years)	1,900
Depreciation of plant and equipment ((27,100 – 9,100) × 15%)	2,700
Research and development expenses (see below)	4,600
	95,700

Tutorial note

Development costs can only be capitalised from the date the directors became confident that the new product would be commercially successful, which is 1 May. Research of $3 million (3 months at $1 million per month) from January to March and April's costs of $1.6 million should be expensed. This leaves $3.2 million (2 months at $1.6 million per month) to be capitalised at the year end.

(ii)   Loan interest

	$000
5% loan note ((20,000 – 500) × 8% see below)	1,560
In-substance loan (3,000 × 10% × 6/12)	150
	1,710

The 5% loan note issue costs should not be charged to administrative expenses, but deducted from the proceeds of the loan.

PAPER F7: FINANCIAL REPORTING

368 MINSTER *Online question assistance*

Key answer tips

The question asks you to analyse the performance of the company from the statement of cash flows you have prepared and the financial statements given. There is therefore no need to calculate any ratios.

(a) **Statement of cash flows of Minster for the Year ended 30 September 20X6:**

	$000	$000
Cash flows from operating activities		
Profit before tax		142
Adjustments for:		
Depreciation of property, plant and equipment	255	
Amortization of software (180 – 135)	45	300
		————
Investment income		(20)
Finance costs		40
		————
		462
Working capital adjustments		
Decrease in trade receivables (380 – 270)	110	
Increase in amounts due from construction contracts (80 – 55)	(25)	
Decrease in inventories (510 – 480)	30	
Decrease in trade payables (555 – 350)	(205)	(90)
		————
Cash generated from operations		372
Interest paid (40 – (150 × 8%) re unwinding of environmental provision)		(28)
Income taxes paid (w (ii))		(54)
		————
Net cash from operating activities		290
Cash flows from investing activities		
Purchase of – property, plant and equipment (w (i))	(410)	
– software	(180)	
– investments (150 – (15 + 125))	(10)	
Investment income received (20 – 15 gain on investments)	5	
		————
Net cash used in investing activities		(595)

KAPLAN PUBLISHING

Cash flows from financing activities
Proceeds from issue of equity shares (w (iii))   265
Proceeds from issue of 9% loan note   120
Dividends paid (500 × 4 × 5 cents)   (100)

Net cash from financing activities   285

Net decrease in cash and cash equivalents   (20)
Cash and cash equivalents at beginning of period (40 – 35)   (5)

Cash and cash equivalents at end of period   (25)

Note: Interest paid may be presented under financing activities and dividends paid may be presented under operating activities.

Workings (T-account format) (in $000)

(W1) **Property, plant and equipment**

	Dr $000		Cr $000
b/f	940		
Provision	150		
Revaluation	35	Depreciation	255
Cash additions (Balancing fig)	**410**		
		c/f	1,280
	1,535		1,535

(W2) **Tax liabilities**

	Dr $000		Cr $000
		b/f (50 + 25)	75
		SPorL charge	57
Cash paid (bal fig)	**54**		
c/f (60 + 18)	78		
	132		132

Workings (Columnar format) (in $000)

(i)   Property, plant and equipment:

Carrying amount b/f	940
Non-cash environmental provision	150
Revaluation	35
Depreciation for period	(255)
Carrying amount c/f	(1,280)
Difference is cash acquisitions	(410)

(ii)   Taxation:

Tax provision b/f	(50)
Deferred tax b/f	(25)
Statement of comprehensive income charge	(57)
Tax provision c/f	60
Deferred tax c/f	18
Difference is cash paid	(54)

(iii)   Equity shares

Balance b/f	(300)
Bonus issue (1 for 4)	(75)
Balance c/f	500
Difference is cash issue	125

Share premium	
Balance b/f	(85)
Bonus issue (1 for 4)	75
Balance c/f	150
Difference is cash issue	140

Therefore the total proceeds of cash issue of shares are $265,000 (125 + 140).

(b) **Comment on Minster's cash flows from investing and financing activities**

Investing activities:

The statement of cash flows shows considerable investment in non-current assets, in particular $410,000 in property, plant and equipment. These acquisitions represent an increase of 44% of the carrying amount of the property, plant and equipment as at the beginning of the year. As there are no disposals, the increase in investment must represent an increase in capacity rather than the replacement of old assets. Assuming that this investment has been made wisely, this should bode well for the future (most analysts would prefer to see increased investment rather than contraction in operating assets). An unusual feature of the required treatment of environmental provisions is that the investment in non-current assets as portrayed by the statement of cash flows appears less than if statement of financial position figures are used. The statement of financial position at 30 September 20X6 includes $150,000 of non-current assets (the discounted cost of the environmental provision), which does not appear in the cash flow figures as it is not a cash 'cost'. A further consequence is that the 'unwinding' of the discounting of the provision causes a financing expense in the statement of profit or loss which is not matched in the statement of cash flows as the unwinding is not a cash flow. Many commentators have criticized the required treatment of environmental provisions because they cause financing expenses which are not (immediate) cash costs and no 'loans' have been taken out. Viewed in this light, it may be that the information in the statement of cash flows is more useful than that in the statement of profit or loss and statement of financial position.

Financing activities:

The increase in investing activities (before investment income) of $600,000 has been largely funded by an issue of shares at $265,000 and raising a 9% $120,000 loan note. This indicates that the company's shareholders appear reasonably pleased with the company's past performance (or they would not be very willing to purchase further shares). The interest rate of the loan at 9% seems quite high, and virtually equal to the company's overall return on capital employed of 9.1% (162/(1,660 + 120)). Provided current profit levels are maintained, it should not reduce overall returns to shareholders.

Summary

The above analysis shows that Minster has invested substantially in new non-current assets suggesting expansion. To finance this, the company appears to have no difficulty in attracting further long-term funding. It may be that the new investment is a change in the nature of the company's activities (e.g. mining) which has different working capital characteristics. The company has good operating cash flow generation and the slight deterioration in short term net cash balance should only be temporary.

369 TABBA *Walk in the footsteps of a top tutor*

Key answer tips

The statement of cash flows has the usual standard calculations but take care with the government grant and finance leases which both have balances in both current and non-current liabilities.

(a) **Statement of cash flows of Tabba for the year ended 30 September 20X5:**

Cash flows from operating activities	$000	$000
Profit before tax	50	
Adjustments for:		
Depreciation (W1)	2,200	
Amortization of government grant (W3)	(250)	
Profit on sale of factory (W1)	(4,600)	
Increase in insurance claim provision (1,500 – 1,200)	(300)	
Interest receivable	(40)	
Interest expense	260	
	(2,680)	
Working capital adjustments:		
Increase in inventories (2,550 – 1,850)	(700)	
Increase in trade receivables (3,100 – 2,600)	(500)	
Increase in trade payables (4,050 – 2,950)	1,100	
Cash outflow from operations	(2,780)	
Interest paid	(260)	
Income taxes paid (W4)	(1,350)	
Net cash outflow used in operating activities		(4,390)
Cash flows from investing activities		
Sale of factory	12,000	
Purchase of non-current assets (W1)	(2,900)	
Receipt of government grant (from question)	950	
Interest received	40	
Net cash from investing activities		10,090

Cash flows from financing activities

Issue of 6% loan notes	800
Redemption of 10% loan notes	(4,000)
Repayment of finance leases (W2)	(1,100)
Net cash used in financing activities	(4,300)
Net increase in cash and cash equivalents	1,400
Cash and cash equivalents at beginning of period	(550)
Cash and cash equivalents at end of period	850

Note: Interest paid may also be presented as a financing activity and interest received as an operating cash flow.

Workings ($000)

(W1) **Non-current assets – Cost**

	Dr			Cr
	$000			$000
b/f	20,200			
Finance lease additions	1,500	Disposals		8,600
Cash additions (Balancing fig)	**2,900**			
		c/f		16,000
	————			————
	24,600			24,600
	————			————

(W1b) **Non-current assets – Accumulated depreciation**

	Dr			Cr
	$000			$000
		b/f		4,400
Disposal	1,200	**Charge for year (Bal. Fig)**		**2,200**
c/f	5,400			
	————			————
	6,600			6,600
	————			————

(W2) Finance lease liabilities

	Dr $000		Cr $000
		b/f (800 + 1,700)	2,500
Repaid	**1,100**	New assets to PPE	1,500
c/f (900 + 2,000)	2,900		
	_____		_____
	4,000		4,000
	_____		_____

(W3) Government grants

	Dr $000		Cr $000
		b/f (400 + 900)	1,300
Amortisation in P/L (bal fig)	**250**	New grants	950
c/f (600 + 1,400)	2,000		
	_____		_____
	2,250		2,250
	_____		_____

(W4) Tax liabilities

	Dr $000		Cr $000
		b/f (1,200 + 500)	1,700
SPorL credit	50		
Cash paid (bal fig)	**1,350**		
c/f (100 + 200)	300		
	_____		_____
	1,700		1,700
	_____		_____

(W5) Retained earnings

	Dr $000		Cr $000
		b/f	850
		Profit per SPorL	100
		Transfer from revaluation reserve	1,600
c/f	2,550		
	_____		_____
	2,550		2,550
	_____		_____

Workings

(W1) **Non-current assets:**

Cost/valuation b/f	20,200
New finance leases (from question)	1,500
Disposals	(8,600)
Acquisitions – balancing figure	2,900
Cost/valuation c/f	16,000
Depreciation b/f	4,400
Disposal	(1,200)
Depreciation c/f	(5,400)
Charge for year – balancing figure	(2,200)
Sale of factory:	
Carrying amount	7,400
Proceeds (from question)	(12,000)
Profit on sale	(4,600)

(W2) **Finance lease obligations:**

Balance b/f	– current	800
	– over 1 year	1,700
New leases (from question)		1,500
Balance c/f	– current	(900)
	– over 1 year	(2,000)
Cash repayments – balancing figure		1,100

(W3) **Government grant:**

Balance b/f	– current	400
	– over 1 year	900
Grants received in year (from question)		950
Balance c/f	– current	(600)
	– over 1 year	(1,400)
Difference – amortization credited to statement of comprehensive income		250

(W4) Taxation:

Current provision b/f	1,200
Deferred tax b/f	500
Tax credit in statement of comprehensive income	(50)
Current provision c/f	(100)
Deferred tax c/f	(200)
Tax paid – balancing figure	1,350

(W5) Reconciliation of retained earnings

Balance b/f	850
Transfer from revaluation reserve	1,600
Profit for period	100
Balance c/f	2,550

(b) There is a huge net cash outflow from operating activities of $4,390,000 despite Tabba reporting a modest operating profit of $270,000. More detailed analysis of this difference reveals some worrying concerns for the future. Many companies experience higher operating cash flows than the underlying operating profit mainly due to depreciation charges being added back to profits to arrive at the cash flows. This is certainly true in Tabba's case, where operating profits have been 'improved' by $2.2 million during the year in terms of the underlying cash flows.

However, the major reconciling difference is the profit on the sale of Tabba's factory of $4.6 million. This amount has been credited in the statement of profit or loss and has dramatically distorted the profit from operations. If the sale and leaseback of the factory had not taken place, Tabba's would show losses of $4.33 million (4,600 – 270 ignoring any possible tax effects). When Tabba publishes its financial statements this profit will almost certainly require separate disclosure which should make the effects of the transaction more transparent to the users of the financial statements. A further indication of poor operating profits is that they have been boosted by $300,000 due to an increase in the insurance claim provision (again this is not a cash flow) and $250,000 release of government grants.

Another relevant point is that there has been a very small increase in working capital of $100,000 (700 + 500 – 1,100). However, underlying this is the fact that both inventories and trade receivables are showing substantial increases (despite the profit deterioration), which may indicate the presence of bad debts or obsolete inventories, and trade payables have also increased substantially (by $1.1 million) which may be a symptom of liquidity problems prior to the sale of the factory.

370 COALTOWN *Walk in the footsteps of a top tutor*

Key answer tips

This proved to be a relatively straightforward statement of cash flow. Watch out for the disposal, Coaltown has an unexpected COST associated with disposal that will represent a cash outflow rather than an inflow.

Coaltown – Statement of cash flows for the year ended 31 March 2009:

Note: Figures in brackets in $000

		$000
Cash flows from operating activities		
Profit before tax		10,200
Adjustments for:		
depreciation of non-current assets (W1)	6,000	
loss on disposal of displays (W1)	1,500	
Interest expense		600
Increase in warranty provision (1,000 – 180)		820
increase in inventory (5,200 – 4,400)		(800)
increase in receivables (7,800 – 2,800)		(5,000)
Decrease in payables (4,500 – 4,200)		(300)
Negligence claim previously provided		(120)
Cash generated from operations		12,900
Interest paid		(600)
Income tax paid (W2)		(5,500)
Net cash from operating activities		6,800
Cash flows from investing activities (W1)		
Purchase of non-current assets	(20,500)	
Disposal cost of non-current assets	(500)	
Net cash used in investing activities		(21,000)
		(14,200)
Cash flows from financing activities		
Issue of equity shares (10,500 capital (W5)l + 4,00 premium (W6))	14,500	
Issue of 10% loan notes	1,000	
Convertible loan repaid	(1,600)	
Equity dividends paid (W4)	(4,000)	
Net cash from financing activities		9,900
Net decrease in cash and cash equivalents		(4,300)
Cash and cash equivalents at beginning of period		700
Cash and cash equivalents at end of period		(3,600)

Workings $000

(W1) Non-current assets
Cost
Balance b/f ... 80,000
Revaluation (5,000 – 2,000 depreciation) ... 3,000
Disposal ... (10,000)
Balance c/f ... (93,500)

Cash flow for acquisitions ... 20,500

Depreciation
Balance b/f ... 48,000
Revaluation ... (2,000)
Disposal ... (9,000)
Balance c/f ... (43,000)

Difference – charge for year ... 6,000

Disposal of displays
Cost ... 10,000
Depreciation ... (9,000)
Cost of disposal ... 500

Loss on disposal ... 1,500

(W2) Income tax paid: $000
Provision b/f ... (5,300)
Statement of profit or loss tax charge ... (3,200)
Provision c/f ... 3,000

Difference – cash paid ... (5,500)

(W3) Revaluation surplus: $000
Balance b/f ... 2,500
Gain on revaluation ... 5,000
Balance c/f ... (6,500)

Difference – reserves transfer to retained earnings ... (1,000)

(W4) Retained earnings: $000
Balance b/f ... 15,800
Profit for year ... 7,000
Reserves transfer from revaluation surplus (W3) ... 1,000
Balance c/f ... (19,800)

Difference – dividend paid ... (4,000)

(W5)	Share capital:	$000
	Balance b/f	6,000
	Loan note converted to shares (see below)	100
	Balance c/f	(16,600)
	Difference – shares issued	10,500

(W6)	Other components of equity	$000
	Balance b/f	500
	Loan note converted to shares (see below)	300
	Balance c/f	4,800
	Difference – shares issued	4,000

Therefore the total cash from share issue = 10,500 + 4,000 = $14,500.

Note:

The $2 million convertible has 20% of it converted into shares. As each holder choosing conversion gets 25 shares for every $100 held, the entries for this will be:

Dr Convertible loan $400,000

Cr Share Capital $100,000 ($400,000 × 25/100)

Cr Other components of equity $300,000

The remaining 80% has been repaid, and the double entries for this would be:

Dr Convertible loan $1,600,000

Cr Cash $1,600,000

Workings – T account format

(W1a) **Non-current assets – Cost**

	Dr		Cr
	$000		$000
b/f	80,000		
Revaluation	3,000	Disposals	10,000
Cash additions (Balancing fig)	**20,500**		
		c/f	93,500
	103,500		103,500

(W1b) **Non-current assets – Accumulated depreciation**

	Dr $000		Cr $000
Revaluation	2,000	b/f	48,000
Disposal	9,000	**Charge for year (Bal. Fig)**	**6,000**
c/f	43,000		
	54,000		54,000

Note: The disposal had a carrying amount of $1m at disposal (cost $10m, accumulated depreciation $9m), and cost $500k to dispose, making a loss on disposal of $1,500k.

(W2) **Tax Liabilities**

	Dr $000		Cr $000
		b/f	5,300
Tax paid (bal fig)	**5,500**	Charge from P/L	3,200
c/f	3,000		
	8,500		8,500

(W3) **Revaluation surplus**

	Dr $000		Cr $000
		b/f	2,500
Retained earnings (bal fig)	**1,000**	PPE	5,000
c/f	6,500		
	7,500		7,500

(W4) **Retained earnings**

	Dr $000		Cr $000
		b/f	15,800
Dividend paid	**4,000**	Profit for the year	7,000
c/f	19,800	Revaluation surplus	1,000
	23,800		23,800

(W5) Share capital

	Dr			Cr
	$000			$000
		b/f		6,000
		Convertible (see note under (W6) in columnar format		100
c/f	16,600	**Shares issued**		**10,500**
	16,600			16,600

(W6) Other components of equity

	Dr			Cr
	$000			$000
		b/f		500
		Convertible (see note under (W6) in columnar format		300
c/f	4,800	**Shares issued**		**4,000**
	4,800			4,800

Marking scheme	Marks
Profit from operations (PBT + finance costs)	1
Depreciation charge	2
Loss on disposal	1
Warranty adjustment	1
Negligence claim	1
Working capital items	1.5
Finance costs	1
Income tax paid	1
Purchase of non-current assets	2
Disposal cost of non-current assets	1
Issue of equity shares	2
Convertible repaid	1
Issue of 10% loan note	1
Dividend paid	2
Cash and cash equivalents b/f and c/f, movement	1.5
Total	**20**

371 MONTY

Monty – Statement of cash flows for the year ended 31 March 2013:

(Note: Figures in brackets are in $000)

	$000	$000
Cash flows from operating activities:		
Profit before tax		3,000
Adjustments for:		
depreciation of non-current assets		900
amortisation of non-current assets		200
release of government grant		(25)
finance costs		400
decrease in inventories (3,800 – 3,300)		500
increase in receivables (2,950 – 2,200)		(750)
increase in payables (2,650 – 2,100)		550
		———
Cash generated from operations		4,775
Finance costs paid (w (vi))		(320)
Income tax paid (w (i))		(425)
		———
Net cash from operating activities		4,030
Cash flows from investing activities:		
Purchase of property, plant and equipment (w (ii))	(700)	
Deferred development expenditure (1,000 + 200)	(1,200)	
Receipt of government grant (w (v))	150	
	———	
Net cash used in investing activities		(1,750)
Cash flows from financing activities:		
Repayment of finance lease obligations (w (iii))	(1,050)	
Equity dividend paid (w (iv))	(550)	
	———	
Net cash used in financing activities		(1,600)
		———
Net increase in cash and cash equivalents		680
Cash and cash equivalents at beginning of period		1,300
		———
Cash and cash equivalents at end of period		1,980
		———

Workings (columnar format) $000

(i)   Income tax paid

	$000
Provision b/f – current	(725)
– deferred	(800)
Tax charge	(1,000)
Transfer from revaluation reserve	(650)
Provision c/f – current	1,250
– deferred	1,500
Balance – cash paid	(425)

(ii)   Property, plant and equipment

Balance b/f	10,700
Revaluation	2,000
New finance lease	1,500
Depreciation	(900)
Balance c/f	(14,000)
Balance – cash purchases	(700)

(iii)   Finance leases

Balances b/f – current	(600)
– non-current	(900)
New finance lease	(1,500)
Balances c/f – current	750
– non-current	1,200
Balance cash repayment	(1,050)

(iv)   Equity dividend

	$000
Retained earnings b/f	1,750
Profit for the year	2,000
Retained earnings c/f	(3,200)
Balance – dividend paid	(550)

(v)   Government grant

	$000
Liabilities b/f (100 + 25)	125
Released to statement of profit or loss in the year	(25)
Liabilities c/f	(250)
Balance – receipt of government grant	150

(vi)   Finance costs

As the loan notes are repayable at a premium, the effective rate of interest of 10% will be expensed to the statement of profit or loss each year. However, it is only the amount paid (the coupon rate of 8%) which will be taken to the statement of cash flows.

Loan notes	$000
Balance b/f	4,000
Statement of profit or loss expense	400
Liabilities c/f	(4,080)
	———
Balance – interest paid	(320)
	———

Workings – T account format

(i) Tax Liabilities

	Dr		Cr
	$000		$000
		b/f (725 + 800)	1,525
Tax paid (bal fig)	425	Charge from P/L	1,000
c/f (1,250 + 1,500)	2,750	Transfer from reval reserve	650
	———		———
	3,175		3,175
	———		———

(ii) Property, plant and equipment

	Dr		Cr
	$000		$000
b/f	10,700		
Revaluation	2,000	Depreciation	900
Finance lease additions	1,500		
Cash additions (Balancing fig)	700		
		c/f	14,000
	———		———
	14,900		14,900
	———		———

(iii) Finance lease liabilities

	Dr		Cr
	$000		$000
		b/f (600 + 900)	1,500
Liabilities repaid	1,050	New leases (PPE)	1,500
c/f (750 + 1,200)	1,950		
	———		———
	3,000		3,000
	———		———

(iv) Retained earnings

	Dr $000		Cr $000
		b/f	1,750
Dividend paid (bal fig)	**550**	Charge from P/L	2,000
c/f	3,200		
	3,750		3,750

(v) Government grants

	Dr $000		Cr $000
		b/f (100 + 25)	125
Release of grant	25	**Receipt of grant (bal fig)**	**150**
c/f (200 + 50)	250		
	275		275

(vi) Loan note

	Dr $000		Cr $000
		b/f	4,000
Interest paid (bal fig)	**320**	Interest expensed	400
c/f	4,080		
	4,400		4,400

Marking scheme	
	Marks
Profit from operations (PBT + finance costs)	1
Depreciation	1
Amortisation	1
Release of grant	1
Working capital items	1½
Interest paid	2
Tax paid	2
Purchase of PPE	3
Development costs	1
Grant received	2
Finance lease repaid	2
Dividends paid	1
Movement in cash	1½
Total	**20**

372 KINGDOM

(a) **Kingdom – Statement of cash flows for the year ended 30 September 2013:**

	$000	$000
Cash flows from operating activities:		
Profit before tax		2,400
Adjustments for:		
depreciation of property, plant and equipment		1,500
loss on sale of property, plant and equipment (2,300 – 1,800)		500
finance costs		600
investment properties – rentals received		(350)
– fair value changes		700
		5,350
decrease in inventory (3,100 – 2,300)		800
decrease in receivables (3,400 – 3,000)		400
increase in payables (4,200 – 3,900)		300
Cash generated from operations		6,850
Interest paid (600 – 100 + 50)		(550)
Income tax paid (w (i))		(1,950)
Net cash from operating activities		4,350
Cash flows from investing activities:		
Purchase of property, plant and equipment (w (ii))	(5,000)	
Sale of property, plant and equipment	1,800	
Purchase of investment property	(1,400)	
Investment property rentals received	350	
Net cash used in investing activities		(4,250)
Cash flows from financing activities:		
Issue of equity shares (17,200 – 15,000)	2,200	
Equity dividends paid (w (iii))	(2,800)	
Net cash used in financing activities		(600)
Net decrease in cash and cash equivalents		(500)
Cash and cash equivalents at beginning of period		300
Cash and cash equivalents at end of period		(200)

Workings – columnar format

		$000
(i)	Income tax:	
	Provision b/f	(1,850)
	Profit or loss charge	(600)
	Provision c/f	500
		————
	Tax paid (= balance)	(1,950)
		————
(ii)	Property, plant and equipment:	
	Balance b/f	(25,200)
	Depreciation	1,500
	Revaluation (downwards)	1,300
	Disposal (at carrying amount)	2,300
	Transfer from investment properties	(1,600)
	Balance c/f	26,700
		————
	Acquired during year (= balance)	(5,000)
		————
(iii)	Equity dividends:	
	Retained earnings b/f	8,700
	Profit for the year	1,800
	Retained earnings c/f	(7,700)
		————
	Dividends paid (= balance)	2,800
		————

Note: For tutorial purposes the reconciliation of the investment properties is:

	$000
Balance b/f	5,000
Acquired during year (from question)	1,400
Loss in fair value	(700)
Transfer to property, plant and equipment	(1,600)
	————
Balance c/f	4,100
	————

Workings – T account format

(W1) **Tax liabilities**

	Dr		Cr
	$000		$000
		b/f	1,850
Tax paid (bal fig)	1,950	Charge from P/L	600
c/f	500		
	————		————
	2,450		2,450
	————		————

(W2) Property, plant and equipment

	Dr $000		Cr $000
b/f	25,200	Revaluation	1,300
Transfer from investment properties	1,600	Depreciation	1,500
		Disposal	2,300
Cash additions (Balancing fig)	**5,000**		
		c/f	26,700
	31,800		31,800

(W3) Retained earnings

	Dr $000		Cr $000
		b/f	8,700
Dividend paid (bal fig)	**2,800**	Profit from P/L	1,800
c/f	7,700		
	10,500		10,500

(W4) Investment properties

	Dr $000		Cr $000
b/f	5,000	Transfer to PPE	1,600
Additions	1,400	FV loss	700
		c/f	4,100
	6,400		6,400

(b) The fall in the company's profit before tax can be analysed in three elements: changes at the gross profit level; the effect of overheads; and the relative performance of the investment properties. The absolute effect on profit before tax of these elements are reductions of $1·4 million (15,000 − 13,600), $2·25 million (10,250 − 8,000) and $1·25 million (900 + 350) respectively, amounting to $4·9 million in total. Many companies would consider returns on investment properties as not being part of operating activities; however, these returns do impact on profit before tax.

Gross profit

Despite slightly higher revenue, gross profit fell by $1·4 million. This is attributable to a fall in the gross profit margin (down from 34·1% to 30·3%). Applying the stated 8% rise in the cost of sales, last year's cost of sales of $29 million would translate to an equivalent figure of $31·32 million in the current year which is almost the same as the actual figure ($31·3 million). This implies that the production activity/volume of sales has remained the same as last year. As the increase in revenue in the current year is only 2%, the decline in gross profitability has been caused by failing to pass on to customers the percentage increase in the cost of sales. This may be due to management's slow response to rising prices and/or to competitive pressures in the market.

Although there has been a purchase of new plant of $5 million (from the statement of cash flows), it would seem that this is a replacement of the $2·3 million of plant sold during the year. This is supported by the stagnation in the (apparent) volume of sales. The replacement of plant has probably led to slightly higher depreciation charges.

Operating costs/overheads

The administrative expenses and distribution costs are the main culprit of the fall in profit before tax as these are $2·25 million (or 28%) higher than last year. Even if they too have increased 8%, due to rising prices, they are still much higher than would have been expected, which implies a lack of cost control of these overheads.

Performance of investment properties

The final element of the fall in profit before tax is due to declining returns on the investment properties. This has two elements. First, a reduction in rentals received which may be due to the change in properties under rental (one transferred to owner-occupation and one newly let property) and/or a measure of falling rentals generally. The second element is clearer: there has been a decrease in the fair values of the properties in the current year compared to a rise in their fair values in the previous year. The fall in investment properties mirrors a fall in the value of the company's other properties within property, plant and equipment (down $1·3 million), which suggests problems in the commercial property market.

Marking scheme	
	Marks
Profit from operations (PBT + finance costs – investment income)	2
Depreciation/loss on sale	1
Working capital items	1½
Interest paid	1
Tax paid	1½
Purchase of PPE	3
Sale of PPE	½
Purchase of investment property	1
Investment property rentals	1
Share issue	½
Dividends paid	1
Movement in cash	1
(b) One per point made	5 max
Total	**20**

BUSINESS COMBINATIONS

373 PREMIER *Walk in the footsteps of a top tutor*

Key answer tip

Remember the statement of profit or loss is for a period, so the results of the subsidiary must be time apportioned to reflect the post-acquisition period but in the statement of financial position, the subsidiary's results must not be time apportioned.

(a) **Consolidated statement of profit or loss and other comprehensive income for the year ended 30 September 2010**

	$000
Revenue (92,500 + (45,000 × 4/12) – 4,000 intra-group sales)	103,500
Cost of sales (W6)	(78,850)
Gross profit	24,650
Other expenses (12,000 + (5,100 × 4/12))	(13,700)
Profit for the year	10,950
Other comprehensive income:	
Gain on FVTOCI investments	300
Total other comprehensive income for the year	300
Total comprehensive income	11,250
Profit for year attributable to:	
Equity holders of the parent	10,760
Non-controlling interest (W7)	190
	10,950
Total comprehensive income attributable to:	
Equity holders of the parent (10,760 + 300 + 500)	11,060
Non-controlling interest (from above)	190
	11,250

(b) **Consolidated statement of financial position as at 30 September 2010.**

	$000
Non-current assets	
Property, plant and equipment	38,250
(25,500 + 13,900 – 1,200 (FV adj) + 50 (FV adj))	
Goodwill (W3)	9,300
Investments (1,800 – 800 (consideration) + 300 (gain on FVTOCI))	1,300
	48,850
Current assets (12,500 + 2,400 +130 – 130 (cash in transit) – 350 (intra-group) – 400 (W2))	14,150
	63,000
Equity	
Equity shares of $1 each ((12,000 + 2,400 (W3))	14,400
Share premium (W3)	9,600
Other equity reserve (500 + 300 (gain on FVTOCI))	800
Retained earnings (W5)	13,060
	39,860
Non-controlling interest (W4)	3,690
	43,550
Current liabilities (15,000 + 6,800 – 350 intra group balance)	21,450
	63,000

Tutorial note

FVOCI investment gains are shown in other comprehensive income at the foot of the SPLOCI

Workings in $000

(W1) Group structure

Premier

| 1 June 2010 (4/12)   80%

Sanford

(W2) **Net assets**

	At acquisition	At reporting date	Post acq
Share capital	5,000	5,000	–
Retained earnings (4,500 – (3900 × 4/12))	3,200	4,500	1,300
Property fair value	(1,200)	(1,200)	–
Depreciation reduction (below)		50	50
PURP (below)		(400)	(400)
	7,000	7,950	950
	W3		W4/W5

The unrealised profit (PURP) in inventory is calculated as $2 million × 25/125 = $400,000

The depreciation reduction is calculated as $1,200/8 years × 4/12 = $50,000.

Tutorial note

The fair value adjustment for property is a downwards fair value adjustment and therefore should be deducted from W2 and non-current assets. The reduction in depreciation should be added back in W2 and added back to non-current assets.

(W3) **Goodwill**

Parent holding (investment) at fair value:	
Shares ((5,000 × 80%) × 3/5 × $5)	12,000
Cash	800
NCI value at acquisition	3,500
	16,300
Less: Fair value of net assets at acquisition (W2)	(7,000)
Goodwill on acquisition	9,300

Tutorial note

The 2.4 million shares (5,000 × 80% × 3/5) issued by Premier at $5 each would be recorded as share capital of $2.4 million and share premium of $9.6 million.

(W4) **Non-controlling interest (SOFP)**

NCI value at acquisition	3,500
NCI share of post-acquisition reserves	190
(7,950 – 7,000 (W2)) × 20%	
	3,690

(W5) **Consolidated retained earnings**

Premier	12,300
Post-acquisition in Sanford post acquisition reserves	
(7,950 – 7,000 (W2)) × 80%	760
	13,060

(W6) **Cost of sales**

Premier	70,500
Sanford (36,000 × 4/12)	12,000
Intra-group purchases	(4,000)
PURP in inventory (w2)	400
Reduction of depreciation charge (w6)	(50)
	78,850

(W7) **NCI (in SPL):**

NCI share of subsidiary profit (20% × (3,900 × 4/12)	260
Less: 20% PURP (20% × 400)	(80)
Add: 20% × reduction in depreciation (20% × 50)	10
	190

Marking scheme			
			Marks
(a)	Statement of profit or loss:		
	Revenue		1
	Cost of sales		2
	Other expenses		½
	Other comprehensive income – gain on investments		½
	NCI split of profit for the year		1½
	NCI split of total comprehensive income		½
		Maximum	6
(b)	Statement of financial position:		
	Property, plant and equipment		2
	Goodwill		3
	Investments		1
	Current assets		2
	Equity shares		1
	Share premium		1
	Other equity reserve		½
	Retained earnings		1½
	Non-controlling interest		1
	Current liabilities		1
		Maximum	14
Total			**20**

374 PARENTIS

(a) **Consolidated statement of financial position of Parentis as at 31 March 2007**

	$ million	$ million
Non-current assets		
Property, plant and equipment (640 + 340 + 40 FV adj – 2 FV depn)		1,018
Intellectual property (30 – 30)		
Goodwill (W3)		170
		1,188
Current assets (160 + 70 – 2 PURP + 10 intellectual property receivable)		238
Total assets		1,426
Equity and liabilities		
Equity shares 25c each (W3)		375
Reserves:		
Share Premium (W3)	150	
Retained earnings (W5)	291	441
		786
Non-controlling interest (W4)		124
Total equity		
		940
Non-current liabilities		
10% loan notes (120 + 20)		140
Current liabilities		
Current liabilities (200 + 80)	280	
Cash consideration due 1 April 2007 (60 + 6 interest)	66	346
Total equity and liabilities		1,426

Workings (All workings are in $ milliion)

(W1) **Group structure**

Parentis

1 April 20X6   75%

Offspring

(W2) **Net assets**

	At acquisition	At reporting date	Post acq
Share capital	200	200	–
Retained earnings	120	140	20
Fair value adjustment	40	40	–
Fair value depreciation		(2)	(2)
Intellectual property w/off		(30)	(30)
Compensation receivable		10	10
PURP		(2)	(2)
	———	———	———
	360	356	(4)
	———	———	———
	W3		W4/W5

(W3) **Goodwill**

Tutorial note

The acquisition of 600 million shares represents 75% of Offspring's 800 million shares ($200m/25c). The share exchange of 300 million (i.e. 1 for 2) at $0.75 each will result in an increase in equity share capital of $75 million (the nominal value) and create a share premium balance of $150 million (i.e. $0.50 premium on 300 million shares).

Parent holding (investment) at fair value:

Share exchange ((600 × 1 / 2) × $0.75)	225
10% loan notes (see below)	120
Cash (600 × $0.11/1.1 i.e. discounted at 10%)	60
	———
	405
NCI value at acquisition (given)	125
	———
	530
Less:	
Fair value of net assets at acquisition (W2)	(360)
	———
Goodwill on acquisition	170
	———

(W4) **Non-controlling interest**

NCI value at acquisition	125
NCI share of post-acquisition reserves	(1)
(25% × ($356 – 360) (W2))	
	———
	124
	———

(W5) **Retained earnings**

Parentis	300
Unwinding of the discount (60 × 10%)	(6)
75% Offspring post-acquisition reserves (75% × ($356 – 360) (W2))	(3)
	291

375 PLATEAU *Walk in the footsteps of a top tutor*

Key answer tip

Part (a) required the preparation of a statement of financial position that is relatively straightforward. Ensure that you do not include the associate on a line-by-line basis and equity account instead. One of the complications in this question is a negative fair value adjustment.

(a) **Consolidated statement of financial position of Plateau as at 30 September 2007**

	$000	$000
Assets		
Non-current assets:		
Property, plant and equipment (18,400 + 10,400)		28,800
Goodwill (W3)		6,000
Investments – associate (W6)		10,500
– other (fair value through profit or loss)		9,000
		54,300
Current assets		
Inventory (6,900 + 6,200 – 300 PURP) (W7)	12,800	
Trade receivables (2,800 + 1,300 – 400 cash in transit – 700 intra-group)	3,000	
Cash (400 + 200 + 400 cash in transit	1,000	16,800
Total assets		71,100
Equity		
Equity shares of $1 each (10,000 + 1,500) (W3)		11,500
Reserves:		
Share premium (W3)	7,500	
Retained earnings (W5)	30,700	38,200
		49,700
Non-controlling interest (W4)		3,900
Total equity		53,600

Non-current liabilities

7% Loan notes (5,000 + 1,000)   6,000

Current liabilities (8,000 + 4,200 – 700 intra group)   11,500

Total equity and liabilities   71,100

Workings

(W1) **Group structure**

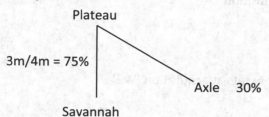

Plateau

3m/4m = 75%

Axle   30%

Savannah

Savannah was acquired on 1 October 2006 and so have been held for 1 year.

(W2) **Net assets of Savannah**

Tutorial note

A net asset working really helps.

	At acquisition	At reporting date	Post acq
	$000	$000	$000
Share capital	4,000	4,000	
Retained earnings	6,500	8,900	2,400
Fair value adjustment	(500)	–	500
PURP on inventory (W7)		(300)	(300)
	10,000	12,600	2,600
	W3		W4/W5

Tutorial note

The fair value adjustment does not need recording at the reporting date since Savannah had written the asset down in their books after acquisition. It should have been written down at acquisition and hence the adjustment is required at this date.

(W3) Goodwill

	$000
Parent holding (investment) at fair value:	
Share exchange((3,000 × ½) × $6)	9,000
Cash (3,000 × $1.25)	3,750
	─────
	12,750
NCI value at acquisition	3,250
	─────
	16,000
Less:	
Fair value of net assets at acquisition (W2)	(10,000)
	─────
	6,000
	─────

Tutorial note

The share consideration given on the acquisition of Savannah has not been recorded. Therefore share capital should be increased by (3,000 × ½ × $1) $1,500 and share premium should be increased by (3,000 × ½ × $5) $7,500.

(W4) Non-controlling interest

	$000
NCI value at acquisition	3,250
NCI share of post-acquisition reserves ((12,600 − 10,000) × 25% (W2))	650
	─────
	3,900
	─────

(W5) Consolidated reserves

	$000
Plateau (16,000 + 9,250)	25,250
Acquisition costs to be expensed	(500)
Fair value through profit or loss investments (9,000 − 6,500)	2,500
Savannah (75% × (12,600 − 10,000))	1,950
Axle (W6)	1,500
	─────
	30,700
	─────

(W6) **Investment in Associate**

	$000
Cost of investment (30% × 4,000 × $7.50)	9,000
Post-acquisition profits (30% × 5,000)	1,500
	10,500

(W7) **Provision for unrealised profit on inventory**

Profit on sale = 50/150 × 2,700 = 900,000

Profit in inventory = 1/3 × 900 = 300,000

Examiner's comments

The main areas where candidates went wrong were:

In **part (a)**

— most candidates incorrectly deducted a $500,000 reduction in the fair value of the land from the property, plant and equipment. This effectively double counted the fall in value as the question clearly stated that the land had already been written down in the post-acquisition period. The point of the information is that the fall in the value of the land should have been treated as an adjustment between pre and post-acquisition profits (affecting goodwill).

— some confusion existed over the value of the associate with many simply showing it in the statement of financial position at cost rather than using equity accounting. A very small minority proportionally consolidated the associate (some even proportionately consolidated the subsidiary).

— many candidates did correctly calculate the unrealised profit on inventory but did not always eliminate it from retained earnings.

— surprisingly, many candidates failed to adjust share capital and premium for the share issue relating to the acquisition.

— generally candidates scored well in the calculation of retained earnings, but the most common errors were not adjusting the subsidiary's post acquisition profit for the revaluation of land (mentioned earlier) and not including the gain on investments (often incorrectly shown as a revaluation reserve).

---

376 PATRONIC *Walk in the footsteps of a top tutor*

Key answer tip

Part (a) requires the calculation of the purchase consideration, testing the commonly examined areas of share exchanges and deferred cash payments. Part (b) requires the preparation of a consolidated statement of profit or loss – be careful to ensure that you pro-rate the subsidiaries results to take into account that they have only been a subsidiary for eight months.

(a)   Cost of control in Sardonic:

	$000	$000
Parent holding (investment) at fair value:		
Share exchange (18,000 × 2/3 × $5.75)		69,000
Deferred payment ((18,000 × 2.42) × $1/1.1^2$)		36,000
		105,000

Tutorial note

The acquisition of 18 million out of a total of 24 million equity shares is a 75% interest.

(b)   Patronic Group

Consolidated statement of profit or loss for the year ended 31 March 2008

	$000
Revenue (150,000 + (78,000 × 8/12) − (1,250 × 8 months intra group))	192,000
Cost of sales (W1)	(119,100)
Gross profit	72,900
Distribution costs (7,400 + (3,000 × 8/12))	(9,400)
Administrative expenses (12,500 + (6,000 × 8/12))	(16,500)
Finance costs (W2)	(5,000)
Impairment of goodwill	(2,000)
Share of profit from associate (6,000 × 30%)	1,800
Profit before tax	41,800
Income tax expense (10,400 + (3,600 × 8/12))	(12,800)
Profit for the year	29,000

Attributable to:

Equity holders of the parent	27,400
Non-controlling interest (W3)	1,600
	29,000

Workings

(W1) **Cost of sales**

	$000	$000
Patronic		94,000
Sardonic (51,000 × 8/12)		34,000
Intra group purchases (1,250 × 8 months)		(10,000)
Additional depreciation: plant (2,400/4 years × 8/12)	400	
Property (per question)	200	600
Unrealised profit in inventories (3,000 × 20/120)		500
		119,100

Tutorial note:

For both sales revenues and cost of sales, only the post acquisition intra group trading should be eliminated.

(W2) **Finance costs**

	$000
Patronic per question	2,000
Unwinding interest – deferred consideration (36,000 × 10% × 8/12)	2,400
Sardonic (900 × 8/12)	600
	5,000

(W3) **Non-controlling interest**

NCI share of S's post acquisition profit (13,500 × 8/12 × 25%)	2,250
Less NCI share of FV depreciation (600 (W1) × 25%)	(150)
Less NCI share of impairment (2,000 × 25%)	(500)
	1,600

Examiner's comments

The main areas where candidates went wrong were:

In **part (a)** – cost of investment

— most candidates correctly calculated the share exchange consideration, but failed to discount (for two years) the deferred cash consideration correctly.

Part (b) – consolidated statement of profit or loss

— a surprisingly common error was not time apportioning (for 8 months) the subsidiary's results, instead a full year's results were often included. This is a fundamental error showing a lack of understanding of the principle that a subsidiary's results are only included the consolidated accounts from date it becomes a member of the group. A small minority of candidates proportionally consolidated, rather than equity accounted, the associate (some even proportionately consolidated the subsidiary), however this error is now becoming much less common.

— many candidates did not correctly eliminate the intra-group trading; either no adjustment at all or eliminating pre-acquisition trading as well.

— the unrealised profit in inventory was often calculated as a gross profit percentage, whereas the question stated it was a mark-up was on cost. It was also common for this adjustment to be deducted from cost of sales rather than added.

— impairment/amortisation of goodwill was often omitted.

— the finance cost relating to the unwinding of the deferred consideration was omitted by most candidates.

— the calculation of the non-controlling interest (now called non-controlling interest) was sometimes ignored or did not take account the post-acquisition additional depreciation adjustment or time apportionment.

Marking scheme		
		Marks
(a)	Goodwill of Sardonic:	
	consideration	3
(b)	Statement of profit or loss:	
	revenue	2
	cost of sales	5
	distribution costs and administrative expenses	1
	finance costs	2
	impairment of goodwill	1
	share of associate's profit	2
	income tax	1
	Parent's share	1
	Non-controlling interest	2
	Maximum	**17**
Total		**20**

377 PEDANTIC

(a)   **Consolidated statement of profit or loss for the year ended 30 September 2008**

	$000
Revenue (85,000 + (42,000 × 6/12) – 8,000 intra-group sales)	98,000
Cost of sales (W8)	(72,000)
Gross profit	26,000
Operating expenses (8,300 + (5,600 × 6/12) + 1,000 impairment))	(12,100)
Profit before tax	13,900
Income tax expense (4,700 + (1,400 × 6/12))	(5,400)
Profit for the year	8,500
Attributable to:	
Equity holders of the parent	8,700
Non-controlling interest (W9)	(200)
	8,500

(b)   **Consolidated statement of financial position as at 30 September 2008**

Non-current assets	
Property, plant and equipment	
(40,600 + 12,600 + 2,000 – 200 depreciation adjustment (W2))	55,000
Goodwill (W3)	3,500
	58,500
Current assets (W7)	21,400
Total assets	79,900
Equity and liabilities	
Equity shares of $1 each (10, 000 + 1,600 (W3))	11,600
Share premium (W3)	8,000
Retained earnings (W5)	35,100
	54,700
Non-controlling interest (W4)	5,700
Total equity	60,400
Non-current liabilities	
10% loan notes (4,000 + 3,000)	7,000
Current liabilities (8,200 + 4,700 – 400 intra-group balance)	12,500
Total equity and liabilities	79,900

Workings

(W1) Group structure

Pedantic

60%

Sophistic

Investments occurred on 1 April 2008 so has been held for 6 months.

(W2) Net assets of Sophistic

	At acquisition	At reporting date	Post acq
	$000	$000	$000
Share capital	4,000	4,000	–
Retained earnings	5,000	6,500	1,500
Fair value adjustment:			
Plant	2,000	2,000	–
Depreciation (2,000 / 5 years) × 6 months		(200)	(200)
PURP on inventory (W6)		(800)	(800)
	11,000	11,500	500

(W3) Goodwill

	$000
Parent holding (investment) at fair value:	
Share exchange ((4,000 × 60%) × 2/3 × $6)	9,600
NCI value at acquisition (given)	5,900
Less: Fair value of net assets at acquisition (W2)	(11,000)
	4,500
Less impairment	(1,000)
Goodwill as at 30 September 2008	3,500

(W4) Non-controlling interest (SOFP)

	$000
NCI value at acquisition	5,900
NCI share of post acquisition reserves (500 × 40%)	200
NCI share of impairment (1,000 × 40%)	(400)
	5,700

(W5) **Consolidated reserves**

	$000
Pedantic	35,400
Sophistic (60% × (11,500 – 11,000))	300
Pedantic share of impairment (1,000 × 60%)	(600)
	35,100

(W6) **Provision for unrealised profit on inventory**

The unrealised profit (PURP) in inventory is calculated as ($8 million – $5.2 million) × 40/140 = $800,000.

(W7) **Current assets**

	$000
Pedantic	16,000
Sophistic	6,600
PURP in inventory	(800)
Cash in transit	200
Intra-group balance	(600)
	21,400

(W8) **Cost of sales**

	$000
Pedantic	63,000
Sophistic (32,000 × 6/12)	16,000
Intra-group sales	(8,000)
PURP in inventory	800
Additional depreciation (2,000/5 years × 6/12)	200
	72,000

(W9) **Non-controlling interest (SPL)**

NCI share of S's post acquisition profit (3,000 × 6/12 × 40%)	600
Less NCI share of FV depreciation (200 (W8) × 40%)	(80)
Less NCI share of PURP (800 × 40%)	(320)
Less NCI share of impairment (1,000 × 40%)	(400)
	(200)

378 PANDAR *Walk in the footsteps of a top tutor*

(a)   Carrying amount of investment in Ambra at 30 September 2009

	$000
Cost (40 million × 40% × $2)	32,000
Share of post-acquisition losses (5,000 × 40% × 6/12)	(1,000)
Impairment charge	(3,000)
Unrealised profit (6,000 × 20 × ½ × 40%)	(240)
	27,760

(b)   Pandar Group

Consolidated statement of profit or loss for the year ended 30 September 2009

	$000	$000
Revenue (210,000 + (150,000 × 6/12) – 15,000 intra-group sales)		270,000
Cost of sales (w (W1))		(162,500)
Gross profit		107,500
Distribution costs (11,200 + (7,000 × 6/12))		(14,700)
Administrative expenses (18,300 + (9,000 × 6/12) + 2,000 impairment)		(24,800)
Investment income (W2)		1,100
Finance costs (W3)		(2,300)
Share of loss from associate (5,000 × 40% × 6/12)	(1,000)	
Impairment of investment in associate	(3,000)	
Unrealised profit in associate (see (a))	(240)	(4,240)
Profit before tax		62,560
Income tax expense (15,000 + (10,000 × 6/12))		(20,000)
Profit for the year		42,560
Attributable to:		
Owners of the parent		41,160
Non-controlling interest (W4)		1,400
		42,800

Workings (figures in brackets in $000)

(W1) **Cost of sales**

	$000
Pandar	126,000
Salva (100,000 × 6/12)	50,000
Intra-group purchases	(15,000)
Additional depreciation: plant (5,000/5 years × 6/12)	500
Unrealised profit in inventories (15,000/3 × 20%)	1,000
	162,500

Tutorial note

As the registration of the domain name is renewable indefinitely (at only a nominal cost) it will not be amortised.

(W2) **Investment income**

	$000
Per statement of comprehensive income	9,500
Intra-group interest (50,000 × 8% × 6/12)	(2,000)
Intra-group dividend (8,000 × 80%)	(6,400)
	1,100

(W3) **Finance costs**

	$000
Pandar	1,800
Salva post-acquisition ((3,000 – 2,000) × 6/12 + 2,000)	2,500
Intra-group interest (W2)	(2,000)
	2,300

Tutorial note

The interest on the loan note is $2 million ($50 million × 8% × 6/12). This is in Salva's profit in the post-acquisition period. Thus Salva's profit of $21 million has a split of $11.5 million pre-acquisition ((21 million + 2 million interest) × 6/12) and $9.5 million post-acquisition.

(W4) **Non-controlling interest**

	$000
NCI % × Salva's post-acquisition profit (20% × 9,500 see tutorial note above)	1,900
Less: NCI % × FV depreciation (20% × 500 (W1))	(100)
Less: NCI % × impairment (20% × 2,000 (W1))	(400)
	1,400

Marking scheme		Marks
(a)	Carrying amount of Ambra	
	Cost	1.0
	share of post-acquisition losses	1.0
	Unrealised profit	1.0
	impairment charge	1.0
	Maximum	4.0
(b)	Statement of comprehensive income:	
	Revenue	1.5
	cost of sales	3.0
	distribution costs and administrative expenses	0.5
	Administrative expenses	1.5
	investment income	2.5
	finance costs	1.5
	share of associate's losses and impairment charge	1.5
	income tax	1.0
	non-controlling interests	3.0
	Maximum	16.0
Total		**20**

Examiner's comments

The main areas where candidates made errors were:

In **part (a)** calculation of associate:

- the calculation of the carrying amount of the associate was also very good, often gaining full marks. The main problems were not apportioning (by 6/12) the losses in the year of acquisition and not applying the 40% group holding percentage. Some treated the losses as profits.

The consolidated statement of profit or loss (b). Again well-prepared candidates gained good marks with most understanding the general principles. The main errors were with the more complex adjustments:

- a full year's additional depreciation of the plant was charged, but it should have been only for the post-acquisition period of six months
- many candidates incorrectly amortised the domain name; its registration was renewable indefinitely at negligible cost so it should not have been amortised
- surprisingly a number of candidates incorrectly calculated the PURP on inventory by treating the gross profit of 20% as if it were a mark up on cost of 20%
- the elimination of intra-group dividend was often ignored or the full $8 million was eliminated instead
- often the trading and impairment losses of the associate were ignored in preparing the statement of comprehensive income
- the non-controlling interest was frequently ignored and where it was calculated, many forgot to adjust for the additional depreciation on the fair value of the plant.

Despite the above, this was the best answered question and many candidates gained good marks.

379 PICANT

Key answer tips

Part (a) required the preparation of a statement of financial position that is relatively straightforward. Ensure that you do not include the associate on a line-by-line basis and equity account instead. One of the complications in this question is the contingent consideration. The contingent consideration should be accounted for at the acquisition date regardless of its probability providing it can be reliably measured. The fair value of the consideration has then changed at the year end. Under IFRS 3 the change in the consideration is taken via group retained earnings and the goodwill calculation is not adjusted for.

(a)   **Consolidated statement of financial position of Picant as at 31 March 2010**

	$000	$000
Non-current assets:		
Property, plant and equipment (37,500 + 24,500 + 2,000 FV adj – 100 FV depn)		63,900
Goodwill (16,000 – 3,800 (W3))		12,200
Investment in associate (W6))		13,200
		89,300
Current assets		
Inventory (10,000 + 9,000 + 1,800 GIT – 600 PURP (W7)))	20,200	
Trade receivables (6,500 + 1,500 – 3,400 intra-group (W7))	4,600	24,800
Total assets		114,100
Equity and liabilities		
Equity attributable to owners of the parent		
Equity shares of $1 each		25,000
Share premium	19,800	
Retained earnings (W5))	27,500	47,300
		72,300
Non-controlling interest (W4))		8,400
Total equity		80,700
Non-current liabilities		
7% loan notes (14,500 + 2,000)		16,500
Current liabilities		
Contingent consideration	2,700	
Other current liabilities (8,300 + 7,500 – 1,600 intra-group (W7))	14,200	16,900
Total equity and liabilities		114,100

Workings (all figures in $ million)

(W1) Group structure

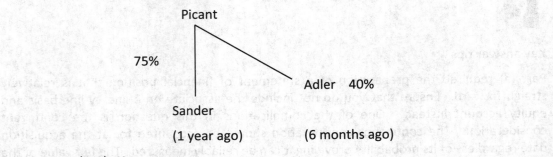

Picant

75%

Adler   40%

Sander

(1 year ago)   (6 months ago)

(W2) Net assets

	At acquisition	At reporting date	Post acq
	$000	$000	$000
Share capital	8,000	8,000	–
Retained earnings	16,500	17,500	1,000
Fair value adjustment:			
Factory	2,000	2,000	–
Fair value depreciation		(100)	(100)
Software w/off	(500)		500
	26,000	27,400	1,400
	W3		W4/W5

(W3) Goodwill

Parent holding (investment) at fair value

	$000
– Share exchange (8,000 × 75% × 3/2 × $3.20)	28,800
– Contingent consideration	4,200
	33,000
NCI value at acquisition (8,000 × 25% × $4.50)	9,000
	42,000
Less:	
Fair value of net assets at acquisition (W2)	(26,000)
Goodwill on acquisition	16,000
Impairment	(3,800)
	12,200

(W4) **Non-controlling interest**

	$000
NCI value at acquisition (W3)	9,000
NCI share of post-acquisition reserves ((27,400 – 26,000) × 25% (W2))	350
NCI share of impairment (3,800 × 25%)	(950)
	8,400

(W5) **Group retained earnings**

	$000
Picant's retained earnings	27,200
Sanders post-acquisition profits ((27,400 – 26,000) × 75% (W2))	1,050
Group share of impairment (3,800 × 75%)	(2,850)
Adler's post-acquisition profits (6,000 × 6/12 × 40%)	1,200
PURP in inventories (1,800 × 50/150)	(600)
Gain from reduction of contingent consideration (4,200 – 2,700 see below)	1,500
	27,500

(W6) **Investment in associate**

	$000
Investment at cost:	
Cash consideration (5,000 × 40% × $4)	8,000
7% loan notes (5,000 × 40% × $100/50)	4,000
	12,000
Adler's post-acquisition profits (6,000 × 6/12 × 40%)	1,200
	13,200

(W7) **Goods in transit and unrealised profit (PURP)**

The intra-group current accounts differ by the goods-in-transit sales of $1.8 million on which Picant made a profit of $600,000 (1,800 × 50/150). Thus inventory must be increased by $1.2 million (its cost), $600,000 is eliminated from Picant's profit, $3.4 million is deducted from trade receivables and $1.6 million (3,400 – 1,800) is deducted from trade payables (other current liabilities).

(b) An associate is defined by IAS 28 *Investments in Associates and Joint Ventures* as an investment over which an investor has significant influence. There are several indicators of significant influence, but the most important are usually considered to be a holding of 20% or more of the voting shares and board representation. Therefore it was reasonable to assume that the investment in Adler (at 31 March 2010) represented an associate and was correctly accounted for under the equity accounting method.

The current position (from May 2010) is that although Picant still owns 30% of Adler's shares, Adler has become a subsidiary of Spekulate as it has acquired 60% of Adler's shares. Adler is now under the control of Spekulate (part of the definition of being a subsidiary), therefore it is difficult to see how Picant can now exert significant influence over Adler. The fact that Picant has lost its seat on Adler's board seems to reinforce this point. In these circumstances the investment in Adler falls to be treated under IFRS 9 *Financial Instruments*. It will cease to be equity accounted from the date of loss of significant influence. Its carrying amount at that date will be its initial recognition value under IFRS 9 (fair value) and thereafter it will be accounted for in accordance with IFRS 9.

380 PRODIGAL

(i) **Prodigal – Consolidated statement of profit or loss and other comprehensive income for the year ended 31 March 2011**

	$000
Revenue (450,000 + (240,000 × 6/12) – 40,000 intra-group sales)	530,000
Cost of sales (W1)	(278,800)
Gross profit	251,200
Distribution costs (23,600 + (12,000 × 6/12))	(29,600)
Administrative expenses (27,000 + (23,000 × 6/12))	(38,500)
Finance costs (1,500 + (1,200 × 6/12))	(2,100)
Profit before tax	181,000
Income tax expense (48,000 + (27,800 × 6/12))	(61,900)
Profit for the year	119,100
Other comprehensive income	
Gain on revaluation of land (2,500 + 1,000)	3,500
Total comprehensive income	122,600
Profit attributable to:	
Owners of the parent	111,600
Non-controlling interest (W2)	7,500
	119,100
Total comprehensive income attributable to:	
Owners of the parent	114,850
Non-controlling interest (W2)	7,750
	122,600

(ii) **Prodigal – Equity section of the consolidated statement of financial position as at 31 March 2011**

	$000
Equity attributable to owners of the parent	
Revaluation surplus (land) (W6)	11,650
Retained earnings (W5)	201,600
	———
	213,250
Non-controlling interest (W4)	107,750
	———
Total equity	321,000
	———

Workings

(W1) **Cost of sales**

	$000
Prodigal	260,000
Sentinel (110,000 × 6/12)	55,000
Intra-group purchases	(40,000)
Unrealised profit on sale of plant	1,000
Depreciation adjustment on sale of plant (1,000/2½ years × 6/12)	(200)
Unrealised profit in inventory (12,000 × 10,000/40,000)	3,000
	———
	278,800
	———

(W2) **NCI (SPL)**

	$000
NCI % ×S's post-acquisition profit (25% × (66,000 × 6/12))	8,250
Less: NCI % × PURP	(750)
	———
	7,500
	———
NCI (Total comprehensive income)	
As above	7,500
Other comprehensive income (1,000 × 25%)	250
	———
	7,750
	———

(W3) Net assets

	At acquisition $000	At reporting date $000	Post acq $000
Retained earnings	158,000	191,000	33,000
Revaluation surplus	–	1,000	1,000 (W6)
PURP	–	(3,000)	(3,000)
	158,000	189,000	31,000

Note: Only the post-acquisition impact on retained earnings should go to the group retained earnings. This will be the 33,000 post acquisition profits less the 3,000 PURP. Therefore P's share of post-acquisition retained earnings = 75% × 30,000 = 22,500

(W4) Non-controlling interest

	$000
NCI value at acquisition (note (iv))	100,000
NCI share of post-acquisition reserves (31,000 × 25% (W3))	7,750
	107,750

(W5) Group retained earnings

	$000
Prodigal's retained earnings (90,000 b/f + 89,900 profit for yr)	179,900
Sentinel's post-acquisition profits (30,000 (W3) × 75%)	22,500
NCA PURP	(800)
	201,600

(W6) Revaluation surplus

	$000
Prodigal's revaluation surplus (8,400 + 2,500 gain in year)	10,900
Sentinel's post-acquisition surplus (1,000 (W3) × 75%)	750
	11,650

Alternative workings for the equity section:

Prodigal – Equity section

	$000
Equity attributable to owners of the parent	
Revaluation surplus (land) (8,400 + 2,500 + (1,000 × 75%))	11,650
Retained earnings (see below)	201,600
	213,250
Non-controlling interest (see below)	107,700
Total equity	321,000

Retained earnings

	$000
Prodigal at 1 April 2010	90,000
Per statement of profit or loss	111,600
	201,600

NCI

	$000
At acquisition	100,000
Per statement of profit or loss	7,750
	107,750

		Marking scheme		Marks
(a)	(i)	Statement of profit or loss and other comprehensive income		
		Revenue		2
		Cost of sales		5
		Distribution costs and administrative expenses		1
		Finance costs		1
		Income tax expense		1
		Non-controlling interest in profit for year		2
		Other comprehensive income		1
		Non-controlling interest in other comprehensive income		2
			Maximum	15
	(ii)	Consolidated equity		
		Revaluation surplus		1½
		Retained earnings		2
		Non-controlling interest		1½
			Maximum	5
Total				20

381 PALADIN

Consolidated statement of financial position of Paladin as at 30 September 2011

	$000
Assets	
Non-current assets:	
Property, plant and equipment (40,000 + 31,000 + 4,000 FV − 1,000 FV dep'n)	74,000
Intangible assets	
– goodwill (W3)	15,000
– other intangibles (7,500 + 3,000 FV − 500 FV amor'n)	10,000
Investment in associate (W6)	7,700
	106,700
Current assets (22,000 + 13,700 − 600 URP (W7)	35,100
Total assets	141,800
Equity and liabilities	
Equity attributable to owners of the parent	
Equity shares of $1 each	50,000
Retained earnings (W5)	35,200
	85,200
Non-controlling interest (W4)	7,900
Total equity	93,100
Non-current liabilities	
Deferred tax (15,000 + 8,000)	23,000
Current liabilities (11,600 + 8,700 + 5,400 deferred consideration)	25,700
Total equity and liabilities	141,800

Workings

(W1) **Group structure**

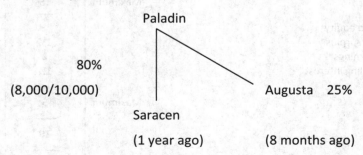

(W2) Net assets

	At acquisition	At reporting date	Post acq
	$000	$000	$000
Share capital	10,000	10,000	–
Retained earnings	12,000	18,000	6,000
Fair value adjustment to plant	4,000	4,000	–
Fair value depreciation (4,000/4 years)		(1,000)	(1,000)
Fair value adjustment to intangible	3,000	3,000	–
Fair value amortisation (3,000/6 years)		(500)	(500)
	29,000	33,500	4,500
	W3		W4/W5

(W3) Goodwill

	$000
Immediate cash	32,000
Deferred consideration (5,400 × 100/108)	5,000
NCI at acquisition (2,000 shares owned × $3.50)	7,000
Less: Fair value of net assets at acquisition (W2)	(29,000)
Goodwill on acquisition	15,000

(W4) Non-controlling interest

	$000
Fair value on acquisition (W3)	7,000
Post-acquisition profits (4,500 (w (2) × 20%)	900
	7,900

(W5) Group retained earnings

	$000
Paladin's retained earnings (25,700 + 9,200)	34,900
Saracen's post-acquisition profits (4,500 (W2) × 80%)	3,600
Augusta's post-acquisition profits (W6)	200
Augusta's impairment loss	(2,500)
PURP (W7)	(600)
Finance cost of deferred consideration (5,000 × 8%)	(400)
	35,200

(W6) Investment in associate

	$000
Cash consideration	10,000
Share of post-acquisition profits (1,200 × 8/12 × 25%)	200
Impairment loss	(2,500)
	7,700

(W7) PURP

The PURP in Saracen's inventory is $600,000 (2,600 × 30/130).

Marking scheme	
	Marks
Property, plant and equipment	2
Goodwill	5
Other intangibles	1½
Investment in associate	1½
Current assets	1½
Equity shares	½
Retained earnings	5
Non-controlling interest	1
Deferred tax	½
Current liabilities	1½
Total	**20**

382 PYRAMID *Online question assistance*

Pyramid – Consolidated statement of financial position as at 31 March 2012

	$000	$000
Assets		
Non-current assets:		
Property, plant and equipment (38,100 + 28,500 + 3,000 fair value – 600 depreciation)		69,000
Goodwill (W3)		7,400
– fair value equity investments		2,800
		79,200
Current assets		
Inventory (13,900 + 10,400 + 1,500 GIT (W8) – 500 PURP (W7))	25,300	
Trade receivables (11,400 + 5,500 – 1,200 CIT – 3,200 intra group (W 8))	12,500	
Bank (9,400 + 600 + 1,200 CIT (W8))	11,200	49,000
Total assets		128,200
Equity and liabilities		
Equity attributable to owners of the parent		
Equity shares of $1 each		25,000
Reserves:		
Share premium	17,600	
Retained earnings (W5)	35,780	53,380
		78,380
Non-controlling interest (W4)		8,480
Total equity		86,860
Non-current liabilities (16,500 + 4,000 + 1,000 deferred tax)		21,500
Current liabilities		
Deferred consideration (6,400 + 640 unwinding of discount (W5))	7,040	
Other current liabilities (9,500 + 5,000 + 1,500 GIT – 3,200 intra group (W8)	12,800	19,840
Total equity and liabilities		128,200

Workings

(W1) Group structure

```
                    Pyramid
                       |
      80%              |
                       |
                    Square
                  (1 year ago)
```

(W2) Net assets

	At acquisition	At reporting date	Post acq
	$000	$000	$000
Share capital	10,000	10,000	–
Retained earnings	18,000	26,000	8,000
Fair value adjustment	3,000	3,000	–
Fair value depreciation		(600)	(600)
Fair value adj deferred tax	(1,000)	(1,000)	–
	———	———	———
	30,000	37,400	7,400
	———	———	———
	W3		W4/W5

(W3) Goodwill

	$000
Shares	24,000
Deferred consideration (8,000 × 88c × 1/1.1)	6,400
	———
	30,400
NCI at acquisition (2,000 shares owned × $3.50)	7,000
	———
	37,400
Less:	
Fair value of net assets at acquisition (W2)	(30,000)
	———
Goodwill on acquisition	7,400
	———

(W4) Non-controlling interest

	$000
Fair value on acquisition (W3)	7,000
Post-acquisition profits (7,400 (W2) × 20%)	1,480
	———
	8,480
	———

(W5) **Group retained earnings**

	$000
Pyramid's retained earnings (16,200 + 14,000)	30,200
Square's post-acquisition profits (7,400 (W2) × 80%)	5,920
Gain on equity investments (2,800 – 2,000)	800
PURP (W7)	(500)
Finance cost of deferred consideration (6,400 × 10%)	(640)
	35,780

(W6) **PURP**

The PURP in inventory is $500,000 (1,500 × 50/150).

(W7) **Intra-group current accounts**

The goods-in-transit and cash-in-transit need to be dealt with first.

Goods in transit: Dr Inventory 1,500, Cr Payables 1,500

Cash in transit: Dr Cash 1,200, Cr Receivables 1,200

This leaves $3,200 in receivables/payables, which can now be cancelled down.

Marking scheme	
	Marks
Statement of financial position:	
Property, plant and equipment	2
Goodwill	4½
Other equity investments	1
Inventory	1½
Receivables	1½
Bank	1
Share capital and share premium	½
Retained earnings	3½
Non-controlling interest	1
Non-current liabilities	1
Deferred consideration	1
Other current liabilities	1½
Total	**20**

383 VIAGEM

(a) **Viagem: Consolidated goodwill on acquisition of Greca as at 1 January 2012**

	$000	$000
Investment at cost		
Shares (10,000 × 90% × 2/3 × $6.50)		39,000
Deferred consideration (9,000 × $1.76/1.1)		14,400
Non-controlling interest (10,000 × 10% × $2.50)		2,500
		55,900
Net assets (based on equity) of Greca as at 1 January 2012		
Equity shares	10,000	
Retained earnings b/f at 1 October 2011	35,000	
Earnings 1 October 2011 to acquisition (6,200 × 3/12)	1,550	
Fair value adjustments: plant	1,800	
contingent liability recognised	(450)	
Net assets at date of acquisition		(47,900)
Consolidated goodwill		8,000

(b) **Viagem: Consolidated statement of profit or loss for year ended 30 September 2012**

	$000
Revenue (64,600 + (38,000 × 9/12) − 7,200 intra-group sales)	85,900
Cost of sales (w1)	(64,250)
Gross profit	21,650
Distribution costs (1,600 + (1,800 × 9/12))	(2,950)
Administrative expenses (3,800 + (2,400 × 9/12) + 2,000 goodwill impairment)	(7,600)
Income from associate (2,000 × 40% based on underlying earnings)	800
Finance costs (420 + (14,400 × 10% × 9/12 re deferred consideration))	(1,500)
Profit before tax	10,400
Income tax expense (2,800 + (1,600 × 9/12))	(4,000)
Profit for the year	6,400
Profit for year attributable to:	
Equity holders of the parent	6,180
Non-controlling interest (W2)	220
	6,400

Workings

(W1) **Cost of sales**

	$000
Viagem	51,200
Greca (26,000 × 9/12)	19,500
Intra-group purchases (800 × 9 months)	(7,200)
PURP in inventory (1,500 × 25/125)	300
Additional depreciation (1,800/3 years × 9/12)	450
	64,250

(W2) **NCI**

	$000
NCI % × S's post-acquisition profit (10% × (6,200 × 9/12))	465
Less: NCI % × FV depreciation (10% × 450)	(45)
Less: NCI % × impairment (10% × 2,000)	(200)
	220

	Marking scheme		Marks
(a)	Consolidated goodwill:		
	consideration	– share exchange	1½
		– deferred	1½
		– NCI	1
	net assets	– equity	½
		– retained at acquisition	1
		– fair value adjustments	1½
		Maximum	7
(b)	Consolidated statement of profit or loss		
	Revenue		1½
	Cost of sales		3½
	Distribution costs		½
	Administrative expenses		1½
	Income from associate		1½
	Finance costs		2
	Income tax		½
	NCI		2
		Maximum	13
Total			**20**

384 PARADIGM *Online question assistance*

(a)   **Paradigm – Consolidated statement of financial position as at 31 March 2013**

	$000	$000
Assets		
Non-current assets:		
Property, plant and equipment (47,400 + 25,500 – 3,000 fair value + 500 depreciation)		70,400
Goodwill (W3)		8,500
Financial asset: equity investments (7,100 + 3,900)		11,000
		89,900
Current assets		
Inventory (20,400 + 8,400 – 600 PURP (W6)	28,200	
Trade receivables (14,800 + 9,000)	23,800	
Bank (2,100)	2,100	54,100
Total assets		144,000
Equity and liabilities		
Equity attributable to owners of the parent		
Equity shares of $1 each (40,000 + 6,000 (W3)		46,000
Share premium (W3)		6,000
Retained earnings (W5)		33,925
Non-controlling interest (W4)		8,800
Total equity		94,725
10% loan notes (8,000 + 1,500 (W3)		9,500
Current liabilities		
Trade payables (17,600 + 13,000 + 75 interest (W7))	30,675	
Bank overdraft	9,100	39,775
Total equity and liabilities		144,000

Workings

(W1) **Group structure**

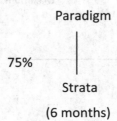

(W2) Net assets

	At acquisition	At reporting date	Post acq
	$000	$000	$000
Share capital	20,000	20,000	–
Retained earnings	(6,000)	4,000	10,000
Fair value adjustment	(3,000)	(3,000)	–
Fair value depreciation (3,000 × 6/36 months)		500	500
Gain on equity investment		700	700
	_____	_____	_____
	11,000	22,200	11,200
	_____	_____	_____

(W3) Goodwill

	$000
Share exchange ((20,000 × 75%) × 2/5 × $2)	12,000
10% loan notes (15,000 × 100/1,000)	1,500
Non-controlling interest (20,000 × 25% × $1.20)	6,000
Less: Fair value of net assets at acquisition (W2)	(11,000)
	_____
Goodwill on acquisition	8,500
	_____

The market value of the shares issued of $12 million would be recorded: $6 million share capital and $6 million share premium as the shares have a nominal value of $1 each and their issue value was $2 each.

(W4) Non-controlling interest

	$000
Fair value on acquisition (W3)	6,000
Post-acquisition profits (11,200 (W2) × 25%)	2,800
	_____
	8,800
	_____

(W5) Group retained earnings

	$000
Paradigm's retained earnings (19,200 + 7,400)	26,600
Strata's post-acquisition profit (11,200 (W2) × 75%)	8,400
PURP in inventory (W6)	(600)
Loss on equity investments (7,500 – 7,100)	(400)
Interest on unrecorded loan notes (W7)	(75)
	_____
Total	33,925
	_____

(W6) **PURP**

Strata's inventory (from Paradigm) at 31 March 2013 is $4.6 million (one month's supply). At a mark-up on cost of 15%, there would be $600,000 of URP (4,600 × 15/115) in the inventory.

(W7) **Interest**

Paradigm must accrue for the interest on the loan notes issued to Strata's previous owners. This is 1,500 × 10% × 6/12 = 75.

(b) IFRS 3 *Business Combinations* requires the purchase consideration for an acquired entity to be allocated to the fair value of the assets, liabilities and contingent liabilities acquired (henceforth referred to as net assets) with any residue being allocated to goodwill. This also means that those net assets will be recorded at fair value in the consolidated statement of financial position. This is entirely consistent with the way other net assets are recorded when first transacted (i.e. the initial cost of an asset is normally its fair value). The ensures that individual assets and liabilities are correctly valued in the consolidated statement of financial position. Whilst this may sound obvious, consider what would happen if say a property had a carrying amount of $5 million, but a fair value of $7 million at the date it was acquired. If the carrying amount rather than the fair value was used in the consolidation it would mean that tangible assets (property, plant and equipment) would be understated by $2 million and intangible assets (goodwill) would be overstated by the same amount.

There could also be a 'knock on' effect with incorrect depreciation charges in the years following an acquisition and incorrect calculation of any goodwill impairment. Thus the use of carrying amounts rather than fair values would not give a 'faithful representation' as required by the Framework.

The assistant's comment regarding the inconsistency of value models in the consolidated statement of financial position is a fair point, but it is really a deficiency of the historical cost concept rather than a flawed consolidation technique. Indeed the fair values of the subsidiary's net assets are the historical costs to the parent. To overcome much of the inconsistency, there would be nothing to prevent the parent company from applying the revaluation model to its property, plant and equipment.

Marking scheme	
	Marks
Property, plant and equipment	1½
Goodwill	3½
Equity investments	1
Inventory	½
Receivables	½
Bank	½
Equity shares	1
Share premium	½
Retained earnings	2½
Non-controlling interest	1½
10% loan notes	1
Trade payables	½
Bank overdraft	½
(b) One mark per point made	5
	–––
Total	**20**
	–––

385 POLESTAR

(a) **Consolidated statement of profit or loss for the year ended 30 September 2013**

	$000
Revenue (110,000 + (66,000 × 6/12) – (4,000 + 9,000 intra-group sales))	130,000
Cost of sales (W6)	(109,300)
Gross profit	20,700
Operating expenses (8,500 + (4,400 × 6/12) – 3,400 negative goodwill (W3)	(7,300)
Decrease in contingent consideration (1,800 – 1,500)	300
Profit before tax	13,700
Income tax expense (3,500 – (1,000 × 6/12))	(3,000)
Profit for the year	10,700
Profit for year attributable to:	
Equity holders of the parent	11,450
Non-controlling interest losses (W7)	(750)
	10,700

(b) **Consolidated statement of financial position as at 30 September 2013**

	$000
Assets	
Non-current assets	
Property, plant and equipment (41,000 + 21,000 + 2,000 FV – 100 depn)	63,900
Investments (13,500 – (13,500 cash consideration))	-
	63,900
Current assets (19,000 + 4,800 – 600 PURP)	23,200
Total assets	87,100

Equity and liabilities

Equity attributable to owners of the parent

Equity shares of 50 cents each	30,000
Retained earnings (W5)	29,950
	59,950
Non-controlling interest (W4)	2,850
Total equity	62,800
Current liabilities	
Contingent consideration	1,500
Other (15,000 + 7,800)	22,800
Total equity and liabilities	87,100

Workings

(W1) **Group structure**

<pre>
            Polestar
              |
   75% |
              |
           Southstar
          (6 months)
</pre>

(W2) **Net assets**

	At acquisition	At reporting date	Post acq
	$000	$000	$000
Share capital	6,000	6,000	–
Retained earnings	14,300	12,000	(2,300)
Fair value adjustment	2,000	2,000	–
Fair value depreciation (2,000/ 10 years × 6/12)		(100)	(100)
PURP		(600)	(600)
	22,300	19,300	(3,000)
	W3		W4/W5

(W3) **Goodwill**

		$000
Cash consideration (6,000/0.5 × 75% × 1.50)		13,500
Contingent consideration		1,800
Non-controlling interest		3,600
		18,900
Less:		
Fair value of net assets at acquisition (W2)		(22,300)
Gain on bargain purchase		(3,400)

(W4) **Non-controlling interest**

	$000
Fair value on acquisition (W3)	3,600
Post-acquisition losses ((3000) (W2) × 25%)	(750)
	2,850

(W5) **Group retained earnings**

	$000
Polestar's retained earnings	28,500
Southstar's post-acquisition losses((3,000) (W2) × 75%)	(2,250)
Change in contingent consideration	300
Gain on bargain purchase (w3)	3,400
	29,950

(W6) **Cost of sales**

	$000
Polestar	88,000
Southstar (67,200 × 6/12)	33,600
Intra-group purchases (4,000 + 9,000)	(13,000)
PURP in inventory (see below)	600
Additional depreciation on leased property (2,000/ 10 years × 6/12)	100
	109,300

The profit on the sale of the goods back to Polestar is $3.6 million (9,000 – (4,000 + 1,400)). Therefore the unrealised profit in the inventory of $1.5 million at 30 September 2013 is $600,000 (3,600 × 1,500/9,000).

(W7) NCI (SPL)

	$000
NCI % × S's post-acquisition loss (25% × ((4,600) × 6/12))	(575)
Less: NCI % × PURP (25% × 600)	(150)
Less: NCI % × FV depreciation (25% × 100)	(25)
	———
	(750)
	———

Note: IFRS 3 Business Combinations says negative goodwill should be credited to the acquirer, thus none of it relates to the non-controlling interests.

Marking scheme		Marks
(a)	Consolidated statement of profit or loss	
	revenue	1½
	cost of sales	3
	Operating expenses – other than negative goodwill	½
	– negative goodwill finance costs	3½
	decrease in contingent consideration	½
	income tax expense	½
	non-controlling interest	1½
		———
	Maximum	11
		———
(b)	Consolidated statement of financial position	
	property, plant and equipment	1½
	current assets	1½
	equity shares	½
	retained earnings	3
	non-controlling interest	1
	contingent consideration	1
	other current liabilities	½
		———
	Maximum	9
		———
Total		**20**
		———

386 PENKETH

(a) Goodwill

	$000
Deferred consideration (1.54 × 90,000 × 1/1.10)	126,000
Non-controlling interest (1.25 × 60,000)	75,000
Less: Fair value of net assets at acquisition (w (i))	(196,000)
	———
Goodwill on acquisition	5,000
	———

Penketh – Consolidated statement of profit or loss and other comprehensive income for the year ended 31 March 2014

	$000
Revenue (620,000 + (310,000 × 6/12) – 20,000 intra-group sales)	755,000
Cost of sales (w (ii))	(457,300)
Gross profit	297,700
Distribution costs (40,000 + (20,000 × 6/12))	(50,000)
Administrative expenses (36,000 + (25,000 × 6/12) + (5,000/5 × 6/12))	(49,000)
Investment income (5,000 + (1,600 × 6/12))	5,800
Finance costs (2,000 + (5,600 × 6/12) + (126,000 × 10% × 6/12 re deferred consideration))	(11,100)
Profit before tax	193,400
Income tax expense (45,000 + (31,000 × 6/12))	(60,500)
Profit for the year	132,900
Other comprehensive income	
Loss on revaluation of land (2,200 – (3,000 – 2,000) gain for Sphere)	(1,200)
Total comprehensive income for the year	131,700
Profit attributable to:	
Owners of the parent	117,700
Non-controlling interest (w (ii))	15,200
	132,900
Total comprehensive income attributable to:	
Owners of the parent	116,100
Non-controlling interest (w (iii))	15,600
	131,700

Workings

(i)   Net assets of Sphere at acquisition

	$000
Share capital	75,000
Retained earnings (70,000 b/f + 40,000 pre acquisition)	110,000
Fair value adjustment plant	6,000
Fair value adjustment customer relationships	5,000
	196,000

(ii)   Cost of sales

	$000
Penketh	400,000
Sphere (150,000 × 6/12)	75,000
Intra-group purchases	(20,000)
Additional depreciation of plant (6,000/2 years × 6/12)	1,500
Unrealised profit in inventory (20,000 × 1/5 × 25/125)	800
	457,300

(iii)   Non-controlling interest in profit for the year:

	$000
NCI % × Sphere's profit (80,000 × 6/12)	16,000
NCI% × FV depreciation (1,500 × 40%)	(600)
NCI% × FV amortisation (500 × 40%)	(200)
	15,200

Non-controlling interest in total comprehensive income:

	$000
Non-controlling interest in statement of profit or loss (above)	15,200
Other comprehensive income ((3,000 − 2,000) × 40%)	400
	15,600

Marking scheme	
	Marks
Goodwil	
Consideration paid	1
NCI at acquisition	1
Net assets at acquisition (½ share capital, 1½ RE, 1 FV adjustments)	3
Consolidated statement of profit or loss and other comprehensive income	
Revenue	2
Cost of sales	3
Distribution costs	½
Administrative expenses	1½
Investment income	1
Finance costs	1½
Income tax expense	1
Other comprehensive income	1½
Non-controlling interest in profit for year	2
Non-controlling interest in other comprehensive income	1
Total	**20**

387 PLASTIK

(a) **Plastik**

Consolidated statement of profit or loss and other comprehensive income for the year ended 30 September 2014

	$000
Revenue (62,600 + (30,000 × 9/12) – (300 × 9 months intra-group sales))	82,400
Cost of sales (45,800 + (24,000 × 9/12) – 2,700 intra-group sales + 120 PURP (W7) + 100 FV dep'n)	(61,320)
Finance costs (200 + 135 (w (5)))	(335)

(b) **Plastik – Consolidated statement of financial position as at 30 September 2014**

Assets

Non-current assets	$000
Property, plant and equipment (18,700 + 13,900 + 4,000 FV – 100 FV dep'n + 600 revaluation)	37,100
Intangible asset: goodwill (W3)	5,700
	42,800
Current assets (9,000 + 4,000 – 120 PURP (W6) – 400 cash in transit - 800 intra-group	11,680
Total assets	54,480

Equity and liabilities

Equity shares of $1 each ((10, 000 + 4,800)	14,800
Other component of equity (share premium)	9,600
Revaluation surplus (2,000 + (600 × 80%))	2,480
Retained earnings (W5)	7,165
Non-controlling interest (W4)	4,900
Total equity	38,945

Non-current liabilities	
10% loan notes (2,500 + 1,000 – 1,000 intra-group)	2,500

Current liabilities	
Trade payables (7,900 + 4,400 – 400 cash in transit — 800 intra-group)	11,100
Deferred consideration (1,800 + 135 W5)	1,935
	13,035
Total equity and liabilities	54,480

Workings (note figure in brackets are in $000)

(W1) **Group structure**

Plastik

80% – owned for 9 months |

Subtrak

(W2) **Net assets**

	At acquisition	At reporting date	Post acq
	$000	$000	$000
Share capital	9,000	9,000	–
Retained earnings	2,000	3,500	1,500
Fair value adjustment	4,000	4,000	–
Fair value depreciation		(100)	(100)
	15,000	16,400	1,400
	W3		W4/W5

(W3) **Goodwill**

	$000
Shares (9,000 × 80% × 2/3 × $3)	14,400
Deferred consideration (9,000 × 80% × $0.275 × 1/1.1)	1,800
Non-controlling interest (9,000 × 20% × $2.50)	4,500
Less: Fair value of net assets at acquisition (W2)	(15,000)
Goodwill on acquisition	5,700

The 4.8 million shares issued by Plastik would go to share capital of $4.8 million (4,800 × $1) and share premium of $9.6 million (4,800 × $2).

(W4) **Non-controlling interest (SOFP)**

	$000
At date of acquisition (See (W3)	4,500
NCI % × S post acquisition (20% × 1,400)	280
NCI % × S post acquisition revaluation (20% × 600)	120
	4,900

(W5) **Group retained earnings**

	$000
Plastik's retained earnings	6,300
Subtrak's post acquisition (1,400 (W2) × 80%)	1,120
Unwinding discount on deferred consideration (1,800 × 10% × 9/12)	(135)
PURP	(120)
	7,165

(W6) **Provision for unrealised profit (PURP)**

	$000	%
Sale	600	125
Cost	480	(100)
Profit	120	25

Marking scheme		
		Marks
(a)	Consolidated statement of profit or loss and other comprehensive income:	
	revenue	1½
	cost of sales	2½
	finance costs	1
	Maximum	5
(b)	Consolidated statement of financial position:	
	property, plant and equipment	2
	goodwill	2
	current assets	2
	equity shares	1
	other component of equity (share premium)	1
	revaluation surplus	1
	retained earnings	1½
	non-controlling interest	1
	10% loan notes	1
	current liabilities	1½
	deferred consideration	1
	Maximum	15
Total		20

388 BYCOMB

(a) **Bycomb: Goodwill on acquisition of Cyclip as at 1 July 2014**

	$000	$000
Investment at cost:		
Shares (12,000 × 80% × 2/3 × $3.00)		19,200
Deferred consideration (12,000 × 80% × $1.54/1.1)		13,440
Non-controlling interest (12,000 × 20% × $2.50)		6,000
		———
		38,640
Net assets at date of acquisition (w (i))		(26,845)
		———
Consolidated goodwill		11,795
		———

Note: The profit for the year for Cyclip would be increased by $100,000 due to interest capitalised, in accordance with IAS 23 Borrowing Costs. Alternatively, this could have been calculated as: 2400 × 3/12 + 25. As the interest to be capitalised has accrued evenly throughout the year, $25,000 would relate to pre-acquisition profits and $75,000 to post-acquisition profits.

(b) **Bycomb: Extracts from consolidated statement of profit or loss for the year ended 31 March 2015**

		$000
(i)	Revenue (24,200 + (10,800 × 9/12) – 3,000 intra-group sales)	29,300
(ii)	Cost of sales (w (i))	(20,830)
(iii)	Finance costs (w (ii))	(1,558)
(iv)	Profit for year attributable to non-controlling interest (1,015 × 20% (w (iv)))	203

(c) IFRS 3 allows (as an option) a non-controlling interest to be valued at its proportionate share of the acquired subsidiary's identifiable net assets; this carries forward the only allowed method in the previous version of this Standard. Its effect on the statement of financial position is that the resulting carrying amount of purchased goodwill only relates to the parent's element of such goodwill and as a consequence the non-controlling interest does not reflect its share of the subsidiary's goodwill. Some commentators feel this is an anomaly as the principle of a consolidated statement of financial position is that it should disclose the whole of the subsidiary's assets that are under the control of the parent (not just the parent's share). This principle is applied to all of a subsidiary's other identifiable assets, so why not goodwill?

Any impairment of goodwill under this method would only be charged against the parent's interest, as the non-controlling interest's share of goodwill is not included in the consolidated financial statements.

The second (new) method of valuing the non-controlling interest at its fair value would (normally) increase the value of the goodwill calculated on acquisition. This increase reflects the non-controlling interest's ownership of the subsidiary's goodwill and has the effect of 'grossing up' the goodwill and the non-controlling interests in the statement of financial position (by the same amount). It is argued that this method reflects the whole of the subsidiary's goodwill/premium on acquisition and is thus consistent with the principles of consolidation.

Under this method any impairment of the subsidiary's goodwill is charged to both the controlling (parent's share) and non-controlling interests in proportion to their holding of shares in the subsidiary.

Workings

(i)   Net assets of Sphere at acquisition

	$000
Share capital	12,000
Retained earnings b/f	13,500
Earnings 1 April to acquisition:	
(2,400 + 100 × 3/12) – see note below	625
Fair value adjustment plant	720
	————
	26,845
	————

(ii)   Cost of sales

Bycomb	17,800
Cyclip (6,800 × 9/12)	5,100
Intra-group purchases	(3,000)
URP in inventory (420 × 20/120)	70
Impairment of goodwill per question	500
Additional depreciation of plant (720 × 9/18 months)	360
	————
	20,830
	————

(iii) Finance costs

Bycomb per question	400
Unwinding of deferred consideration (13,440 × 10% × 9/12)	1,008
Cyclip ((300 – 100 see below) × 9/12)	150
	————
	1,558
	————

The interest capitalised in accordance with IAS 23 of $100,000 would reduce the finance costs of Cyclip for consolidation purposes.

(iv)   Post-acquisition profit of Cyclip

Profit plus interest capitalised and time apportioned ((2,400 + 100) × 9/12) – see note below	1,875
Impairment of goodwill (per question)	(500)
Additional depreciation of plant (w (i))	(360)
	———
	1,015
	———

(v)   Alternative working for NCI shared of profit:

NCI share of profit ((2,400 + 100) × 9/12 × 20%)	375
NCI share of impairment (500 × 20%)	(100)
NCI share of FVI depreciation of plant (360 × 20%)	(72)
	———
	203
	———

Note: This could also have been calculated as (2,400 × 9/12) + 75 (see 1(a) above).

Marking scheme			Marks
(a)		Goodwill at acquisition	6
			———
(b)	(i)	Revenue	1
	(ii)	Cost of sales	3
	(iii)	Finance costs	2½
	(iv)	Profit or loss attributable to non-controlling interests.	2½
			———
			9
			———
(c)		One mark per point made	5
			———
Total			20
			———

KAPLAN PUBLISHING

389 PALISTAR

Palistar – Consolidated statement of financial position as at 30 June 2015

	$000
Non-current assets:	
Property, plant and equipment (55,000 + 28,600)	83,600
Goodwill (w (i))	3,000
Game rights (12,000 – 1,200 (w (iv)))	10,800
Financial asset equity investments (13,200 + 7,900)	21,100
	———
	118,500
Current assets	
Inventory (17,000 + 15,400 + 800 GIT –- 600 URP (W6))	32,600
Trade receivables (14,300 + 10,500 – 2,400 intra-group)	22,400
Bank (2,200 + 1,600)	3,800
	———
	58,800
	———
Total assets	177,300
	———
Equity and liabilities	
Equity attributable to owners of the parent	
Equity shares of $1 each (20,000 + 6,000 (W3))	26,000
Other component of equity (share premium) (4,000 + 18,000 (W3))	22,000
Retained earnings (W5))	52,425
	———
	100,425
Non-controlling interest (W4))	15,675
	———
Total equity	116,100
Current liabilities	
Deferred consideration (18,000 + 900 finance cost (W5))	18,900
Other current liabilities (25,800 + 18,100 –- (2,400 intra-group – 800 GIT))	42,300
	———
	61,200
	———
Total equity and liabilities	177,300
	———

Workings (figures in brackets are in $000)

(W1) Group structure

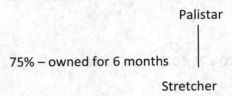

Palistar

75% – owned for 6 months

Stretcher

(W2) Net assets

	At acquisition	At reporting date	Post acq
	$000	$000	$000
Share capital	20,000	20,000	–
Retained earnings (below)	18,000	24,000	6,000
Fair value adjustment	12,000	10,800	(1,200)
Fair value investments	1,000	1,900	900
	51,000	56,700	5,700
	W3		W4/W5

Stretcher makes 60% of its profit in the period from 1 June. Therefore the post acquisition retained earnings is $6 million (60% × $10 million), making the retained earnings at acquisition $18 million ($24 million less $6 million).

(W3) Goodwill in Stretcher

	$000	$000
Controlling interest		
Share exchange (20,000 × 75% × 2/5) = (6,000 × $4.00)		24,000
Deferred consideration (20,000 × 75% × $1.32/1.1)		18,000
Non-controlling interest (20,000 × 25% × $3.00)		15,000
		57,000
Net assets at acquisition		(51,000)
Goodwill on acquisition		6,000
Impairment		(3,000)
Goodwill at 30 June 2015		3,000

The shares issued by Palistar (6 million at $4 – see above) would be recorded as share capital of $6 million (6,000 × $1.00) and share premium in other components of equity of $18 million (6,000 × $3.00).

(W4) **Non-controlling interest**

	$000
Fair value on acquisition (w (i))	15,000
Post-acquisition profit (5,700 × 25% (W2))	1,425
NCI share of impairment (3,000 × 25%)	(750)
	————
	15,675
	————

(W5) **Consolidated retained earnings:**

	$000
Palistar's retained earnings (26,200 + 24,000)	50,200
Stretcher's adjusted post-acquisition profit (5,700 (W2) × 75%)	4,275
Palistar's share of impairment (3,000 × 75%)	(2,250)
Finance cost on deferred consideration (18,000 × 10% × 6/12)	(900)
URP in inventory (w (iii))	(600)
Gain on equity investments (13,200 – 11,500)	1,700
	————
	52,425
	————

(W6) The inventory of Stretcher at 30 June 2015 (adjusted for goods-in-transit (GIT) sale of $800,000) is $2.6 million (1,800 + 800). The unrealised profit (URP) on this will be $600,000 (2,600 × 30/130).

Marking scheme	
	Marks
Consolidated statement of financial position:	
property, plant and equipment	½
goodwill	5
game rights	1
financial asset investments	1
inventory	2
receivables	1
bank	½
equity shares	1
other component of equity	1
retained earnings	4
non-controlling interest	1
deferred consideration	1
other current liabilities	1
	———
Total	**20**
	———

ANALYSING FINANCIAL STATEMENTS

390 HARDY *Walk in the footsteps of a top tutor*

Key answer tips

This question requires an appraisal of a company that is experiencing problems as a result of a global recession, so do not be surprised when some profitability ratios produce negative results. A weak answer will simply refer to ratio movements as having increased or decreased, whereas a strong answer will refer to improvements or deteriorations in the ratios and will aim to relate it to the scenario provided by the examiner.

Note: references to 2009 and 2010 should be taken as being to the years ended 30 September 2009 and 2010 respectively.

Profitability:

Statement of profit or loss performance:

Hardy's statement of profit or loss results dramatically show the effects of the downturn in the global economy; revenues are down by 18% (6,500/36,000 × 100), gross profit has fallen by 60% and a healthy after tax profit of $3.5 million has reversed to a loss of $2.1 million. These are reflected in the profit (loss) margin ratios shown in the appendix (the 'as reported' figures for 2010). This in turn has led to a 15.2% return on equity being reversed to a negative return of 11.9%. However, a closer analysis shows that the results are not quite as bad as they seem. The downturn has directly caused several additional costs in 2010: employee severance, property impairments and losses on investments (as quantified in the appendix). These are probably all non-recurring costs and could therefore justifiably be excluded from the 2010 results to assess the company's 'underlying' performance. If this is done the results of Hardy for 2010 appear to be much better than on first sight, although still not as good as those reported for 2009. A gross margin of 27.8% in 2009 has fallen to only 23.1% (rather than the reported margin of 13.6%) and the profit for period has fallen from $3.5 million (9.7%) to only $2.3 million (7.8%). It should also be noted that as well as the fall in the value of the investments, the related investment income has also shown a sharp decline which has contributed to lower profits in 2010.

Given the economic climate in 2010 these are probably reasonably good results and may justify the Chairman's comments. It should be noted that the cost saving measures which have helped to mitigate the impact of the downturn could have some unwelcome effects should trading conditions improve; it may not be easy to re-hire employees and a lack of advertising may cause a loss of market share.

Statement of financial position:

Perhaps the most obvious aspect of the statement of financial position is the fall in value ($8.5 million) of the non-current assets, most of which is accounted for by losses of $6 million and $1.6 million respectively on the properties and investments. Ironically, because these falls are reflected in equity, this has mitigated the fall in the return of the equity (from 15.2% to 13.1% underlying) and contributed to a perhaps unexpected improvement in asset turnover from 1.6 times to 1.7 times.

Liquidity:

Despite the downturn, Hardy's liquidity ratios now seem at acceptable levels (though they should be compared to manufacturing industry norms) compared to the low ratios in 2009. The bank balance has improved by $1.1 million. This has been helped by a successful rights issue (this is in itself a sign of shareholder support and confidence in the future) raising $2 million and keeping customer's credit period under control. Some of the proceeds of the rights issue appear to have been used to reduce the bank loan which is sensible as its financing costs have increased considerably in 2010. Looking at the movement on retained earnings (6,500 – 2,100 – 3,600) it can be seen that the company paid a dividend of $800,000 during 2010. Although this is only half the dividend per share paid in 2009, it may seem unwise given the losses and the need for the rights issue. A counter view is that the payment of the dividend may be seen as a sign of confidence of a future recovery. It should also be mentioned that the worst of the costs caused by the downturn (specifically the property and investments losses) are not cash costs and have therefore not affected liquidity.

The increase in the inventory and work-in-progress holding period and the trade receivables collection period being almost unchanged appear to contradict the declining sales activity and should be investigated. Although there is insufficient information to calculate the trade payables credit period as there is no analysis of the cost of sales figures, it appears that Hardy has received extended credit which, unless it had been agreed with the suppliers, has the potential to lead to problems obtaining future supplies of goods on credit.

Gearing:

On the reported figures debt to equity shows a modest increase due to statement of profit or loss losses and the reduction of the revaluation reserve, but this has been mitigated by the repayment of part of the loan and the rights issue.

Conclusion:

Although Hardy's results have been adversely affected by the global economic situation, its underlying performance is not as bad as first impressions might suggest and supports the Chairman's comments. The company still retains a relatively strong statement of financial position and liquidity position which will help significantly should market conditions improve. Indeed the impairment of property and investments may well reverse in future. It would be a useful exercise to compare Hardy's performance during this difficult time to that of its competitors – it may well be that its 2010 results were relatively very good by comparison.

Appendix:

An important aspect of assessing the performance of Hardy for 2010 (especially in comparison with 2009) is to identify the impact that several 'one off' charges have had on the results of 2010. These charges are $1.3 million redundancy costs and a $1.5 million (6,000 – 4,500 previous surplus) property impairment, both included in cost of sales and a $1.6 million loss on the market value of investments, included in administrative expenses. Thus in calculating the 'underlying' figures for 2010 (below) the adjusted cost of sales is $22.7 million (25,500 – 1,300 – 1,500) and the administrative expenses are $3.3 million (4,900 – 1,600). These adjustments feed through to give an underlying gross profit of $6.8 million (4,000 + 1,300 + 1,500) and an underlying profit for the year of $2.3 million (–2,100 + 1,300 + 1,500 + 1,600).

Note: it is not appropriate to revise Hardy's equity (upwards) for the one-off losses when calculating equity based underlying figures, as the losses will be a continuing part of equity (unless they reverse) even if/when future earnings recover.

	2010 underlying	2010 as reported	2009
Gross profit % (6,800/29,500 × 100)	23.1%	13.6%	27.8%
Profit (loss) for period % (2,300/29,500 × 100)	7.8%	(7.1)%	9.7%
Return on equity (2,300/17,600 × 100)	13.1%	(11.9)%	15.2%
Net asset (taken as equity) turnover (29,500/17,600)	1.7 times	same	1.6 times
Debt to equity (4,000/17,600)	22.7%	same	21.7%
Current ratio (6,200:3,400)	1.8:1	same	1.0:1
Quick ratio (4,000:3,400)	1.2:1	same	0.6:1
Receivables collection (in days) (2,200/29,500 × 365)	27 days	same	28 days
Inventory and work-in-progress holding period (2,200/25,500 × 365)	31 days	same	27 days

Note: the figures for the calculation of the 2010 'underlying' ratios have been given; those of 2010 'as reported' and 2009 are based on equivalent figures from the summarised financial statements provided.

Alternative ratios/calculations are acceptable, for example net asset turnover could be calculated using total assets less current liabilities.

Marking scheme	
	Marks
Comments – 1 mark per valid point, up to	13
Ratio calculations – up to	7
	——
Total	**20**
	——

391 PINTO

(a) Comments on the cash management of Pinto

Operating cash flows:

Pinto's operating cash inflows at $940,000 (prior to investment income, finance costs and taxation) are considerably higher than the equivalent profit before investment income, finance costs and tax of $430,000. This shows a satisfactory cash generating ability and is more than sufficient to cover finance costs, taxation (see later) and dividends. The major reasons for the cash flows being higher than the operating profit are due to the (non-cash) increases in the depreciation and warranty provisions. Working capital changes are relatively neutral; a large increase in inventory appears to be being financed by a substantial increase in trade payables and a modest reduction in trade receivables. The reduction in trade receivables is perhaps surprising as other indicators point to an increase in operating capacity which has not been matched with an increase in trade receivables. This could be indicative of good control over the cash management of the trade receivables (or a disappointing sales performance).

An unusual feature of the cash flow is that Pinto has received a tax refund of $60,000 during the current year. This would indicate that in the previous year Pinto was making losses (hence obtaining tax relief). Whilst the current year's profit performance is an obvious improvement, it should be noted that next year's cash flows are likely to suffer a tax payment as a consequence.

Investing activities:

There has been a dramatic investment/increase in property, plant and equipment. The carrying amount at 31 March 2008 is substantially higher than a year earlier. It is difficult to be sure whether this represents an increase in operating capacity or is the replacement of the plant disposed of. (The voluntary disclosure encouraged by IAS 7 *Statement of cash flows* would help to assess this issue more accurately). However, judging by the level of the increase and the (apparent) overall improvement in profit position, it seems likely that there has been a successful increase in capacity. It is not unusual for there to be a time lag before increased investment reaches its full beneficial effect and in this context it could be speculated that the investment occurred early in the accounting year (because its effect is already making an impact) and that future periods may show even greater improvements.

The investment property is showing a good return, generating rental income of $40,000 in the year.

Financing activities:

It would appear that Pinto's financial structure has changed during the year. Debt of $400,000 has been redeemed (for $420,000) and there has been a share issue raising $1 million. The company is now nil geared compared to modest gearing at the end of the previous year. The share issue has covered the cost of redemption and contributed to the investment in property, plant and equipment. The remainder of the finance for the property, plant and equipment has come from the very healthy operating cash flows. If ROCE is higher than the finance cost of the loan note at 6% (nominal) it may call into question the wisdom of the early redemption especially given the penalty cost (which has been classified within financing activities) of the redemption.

Cash position:

The overall effect of the year's cash flows is that they have improved the company's cash position dramatically. A sizeable overdraft of $120,000, which may have been a consequence of the (likely) losses in the previous year, has been reversed to a modest bank balance of $10,000 even after the payment of a $150,000 dividend.

Summary

The above analysis indicates that Pinto has invested substantially in renewing and/or increasing its property, plant and equipment. This has been financed largely by operating cash flows, and appears to have brought a dramatic turnaround in the company's fortunes. All the indications are that the future financial position and performance will continue to improve.

(b)   The accruals/matching concept applied in preparing a statement of profit or loss has the effect of smoothing cash flows for reporting purposes. This practice arose because interpreting 'raw' cash flows can be very difficult and the accruals process has the advantage of helping users to understand the underlying performance of a company. For example if an item of plant with an estimated life of five years is purchased for $100,000, then in the statement of cash flows for the five year period there would be an outflow in year 1 of the full $100,000 and no further outflows for the next four years. Contrast this with the statement of profit or loss where by applying the accruals principle, depreciation of the plant would give a charge of $20,000 per annum (assuming straight-line depreciation). Many would see this example as an advantage of a statement of profit or loss, but it is important to realise that profit is affected by many items requiring judgements. This has led to accusations of profit manipulation or creative accounting, hence the disillusionment of the usefulness of the statement of profit or loss.

Another example of the difficulty in interpreting cash flows is that counter-intuitively a decrease in overall cash flows is not always a bad thing (it may represent an investment in increasing capacity which would bode well for the future), nor is an increase in cash flows necessarily a good thing (this may be from the sale of non-current assets because of the need to raise cash urgently).

The advantages of cash flows are:

–   it is difficult to manipulate cash flows, they are real and possess the characteristic of objectivity (as opposed to profits affected by judgements).

–   cash flows are an easy concept for users to understand, indeed many users misinterpret statement of profit or loss items as being cash flows.

–   cash flows help to assess a company's liquidity, solvency and financial adaptability. Healthy liquidity is vital to a company's going concern.

–   many business investment decisions and company valuations are based on projected cash flows.

–   the 'quality' of a company's profit is said to be confirmed by closely correlated cash flows. Some analysts take the view that if a company shows a healthy profit from operations, but has low or negative operating cash flows, there is a suspicion of profit manipulation or creative accounting.

392 HARBIN *Walk in the footsteps of a top tutor*

Key answer tip

Be aware that the examiner specifically asks you to draw your attention to the chief executives report and the purchase of Fatima – if you do not discuss this at all you will be limited in the overall marks that you can achieve. You may choose to calculate further ratios to support your analysis (marks would be awarded where relevant). The highlighted words are key phrases that markers are looking for.

Note: Figures in the calculations of the ratios are in $million

(a)

	2007	Workings
Return on year end capital employed	11.2%	24/(114 + 100) × 100
Current ratio	0.86	38,000/44,000
Closing inventory holding period	46 days	25/200 × 365
Trade receivables' collection period	19 days	13/250 × 365
Gearing	46.7%	100/214 × 100

Analysis of the comparative financial performance and position of Harbin for the year ended 30 September 2007. **Note:** References to 2007 and 2006 should be taken as the years ended 30 September 2007 and 2006.

(b)   Introduction

The figures relating to the comparative performance of Harbin 'highlighted' in the Chief Executive's report may be factually correct, but they take a rather biased and one dimensional view. They focus entirely on the performance as reflected in the statement of comprehensive income without reference to other measures of performance (notably the ROCE); nor is there any reference to the purchase of Fatima at the beginning of the year which has had a favourable effect on profit for 2007. Due to this purchase, it is not consistent to compare Harbin's statement of comprehensive income results in 2007 directly with those of 2006 because it does not match like with like. Immediately before the $100 million purchase of Fatima, the carrying amount of the net assets of Harbin was $112 million. Thus the investment represented an increase of nearly 90% of Harbin's existing capital employed. The following analysis of performance will consider the position as shown in the reported financial statements (based on the ratios required by part (a) of the question) and then go on to consider the impact the purchase has had on this analysis.

Profitability

The ROCE is often considered to be the primary measure of operating performance, because it relates the profit made by an entity (return) to the capital (or net assets) invested in generating those profits. On this basis the ROCE in 2007 of 11.2% represents a 58% improvement (i.e. 4.1% on 7.1%) on the ROCE of 7.1% in 2006. Given there were no disposals of non-current assets, the ROCE on Fatima's net assets is 18.9% (22m/100m + 16.5m). **Note:** The net assets of Fatima at the year end would have increased by profit after tax of $16.5 million (i.e. 22m × 75% (at a tax rate of 25%)). Put another way, without the contribution of $22 million to profit before tax,

Harbin's 'underlying' profit would have been a loss of $6 million which would give a negative ROCE. The principal reasons for the beneficial impact of Fatima's purchase is that its profit margins at 42.9% gross and 31.4% net (before tax) are far superior to the profit margins of the combined business at 20% and 6.4% respectively. It should be observed that the other contributing factor to the ROCE is the net asset turnover and in this respect Fatima's is actually inferior at 0.6 times (70m/116.5m) to that of the combined business of 1.2 times.

It could be argued that the finance costs should be allocated against Fatima's results as the proceeds of the loan note appear to be the funding for the purchase of Fatima. Even if this is accepted, Fatima's results still far exceed those of the existing business.

Thus the Chief Executive's report, already criticised for focussing on the statement of comprehensive income alone, is still highly misleading. Without the purchase of Fatima, underlying sales revenue would be flat at $180 million and the gross margin would be down to 11.1% (20m/180m) from 16.7% resulting in a loss before tax of $6 million. This sales performance is particularly poor given it is likely that there must have been an increase in spending on property plant and equipment beyond that related to the purchase of Fatima's net assets as the increase in property, plant and equipment is $120 million (after depreciation).

Liquidity

The company's liquidity position as measured by the current ratio has deteriorated dramatically during the period. A relatively healthy 2.5:1 is now only 0.9:1 which is rather less than what one would expect from the quick ratio (which excludes inventory) and is a matter of serious concern. A consideration of the component elements of the current ratio suggests that increases in the inventory holding period and trade payables payment period have largely offset each other. There is a small increase in the collection period for trade receivables (up from 16 days to 19 days) which would actually improve the current ratio. This ratio appears unrealistically low, it is very difficult to collect credit sales so quickly and may be indicative of factoring some of the receivables, or a proportion of the sales being cash sales. Factoring is sometimes seen as a consequence of declining liquidity, although if this assumption is correct it does also appear to have been present in the previous year. The changes in the above three ratios do not explain the dramatic deterioration in the current ratio, the real culprit is the cash position, Harbin has gone from having a bank balance of $14 million in 2006 to showing short-term bank borrowings of $17 million in 2007.

A statement of cash flow would give a better appreciation of the movement in the bank/short term borrowing position.

It is not possible to assess, in isolation, the impact of the purchase of Fatima on the liquidity of the company.

Dividends

A dividend of 10 cents per share in 2007 amounts to $10 million (100m × 10 cents), thus the dividend in 2006 would have been $8 million (the dividend in 2007 is 25% up on 2006). It may be that the increase in the reported profits led the Board to pay a 25% increased dividend, but the dividend cover is only 1.2 times (12m/10m) in 2007 which is very low. In 2006 the cover was only 0.75 times (6m/8m) meaning previous years' reserves were used to facilitate the dividend. The low retained earnings indicate that Harbin has historically paid a high proportion of its profits as dividends, however in times of declining liquidity, it is difficult to justify such high dividends.

Gearing

The company has gone from a position of nil gearing (i.e. no long-term borrowings) in 2006 to a relatively high gearing of 46.7% in 2007. This has been caused by the issue of the $100 million 8% loan note which would appear to be the source of the funding for the $100 million purchase of Fatima's net assets. At the time the loan note was issued, Harbin's ROCE was 7.1%, slightly less than the finance cost of the loan note. In 2007 the ROCE has increased to 11.2%, thus the manner of the funding has had a beneficial effect on the returns to the equity holders of Harbin. However, it should be noted that high gearing does not come without risk; any future downturn in the results of Harbin would expose the equity holders to much lower proportionate returns and continued poor liquidity may mean payment of the loan interest could present a problem. Harbin's gearing and liquidity position would have looked far better had some of the acquisition been funded by an issue of equity shares.

Conclusion

There is no doubt that the purchase of Fatima has been a great success and appears to have been a wise move on the part of the management of Harbin. However, it has disguised a serious deterioration of the underlying performance and position of Harbin's existing activities which the Chief Executive's report may be trying to hide. It may be that the acquisition was part of an overall plan to diversify out of what has become existing loss making activities. If such a transition can continue, then the worrying aspects of poor liquidity and high gearing may be overcome.

Marking scheme		Marks
(a)	One mark per required ratio	5
(b)	For consideration of Chief Executive's report	3
	Remaining issues 1 mark per valid point	12
Total		**20**

393 GREENWOOD

Note: IFRS 5 uses the term discontinued operation. The answer below also uses this term, but it should be realised that the assets of the discontinued operation are classed as held for sale and not yet sold. In some literature this may be described as a *discontinuing* operation.

Profitability/utilisation of assets

An important feature of the company's performance in the year to 31 March 2007 is to evaluate the effect of the discontinued operation. When using an entity's recent results as a basis for assessing how the entity may perform in the future, emphasis should be placed on the results from continuing operations as it is these that will form the basis of future results. For this reason most of the ratios calculated in the appendix are based on the results from continuing operations and ratio calculations involving net assets/capital employed generally exclude the value of the assets held for sale.

On this basis, it can be seen that the overall efficiency of Greenwood (measured by its ROCE) has declined considerably from 33.5% to 29.7% (a fall of 11.3%). The fall in the asset turnover (from 1.89 to 1.67 times) appears to be mostly responsible for the overall decline in efficiency. In effect the company's assets are generating less sales per $ invested in them. The other contributing factors to overall profitability are the company's profit margins. Greenwood has achieved an impressive increase in headline sales revenues of nearly 30% (6.3m on 21.2m) whilst being able to maintain its gross profit margin at around 29% (no significant change from 2006). This has led to a substantial increase in gross profit, but this has been eroded by an increase in operating expenses. As a percentage of sales, operating expenses were 10.5% in 2007 compared to 11.6% in 2006 (they appear to be more of a variable than a fixed cost). This has led to a modest improvement in the profit before interest and tax margin which has partially offset the deteriorating asset utilisation.

The decision to sell the activities which are classified as a discontinued operation is likely to improve the overall profitability of the company. In the year ended 31 March 2006 the discontinued operation made a modest pre tax profit of $450,000 (this would represent a return of around 7% on the activity's assets of $6.3 million).This poor return acted to reduce the company's overall profitability (the continuing operations yielded a return of 33.5%). The performance of the discontinued operation continued to deteriorate in the year ended 31 March 2007 making a pre tax operating loss of $1.4 million which creates a negative return on the relevant assets. Despite incurring losses on the measurement to fair value of the discontinued operation's assets, it seems the decision will benefit the company in the future as the discontinued operation showed no sign of recovery.

Liquidity and solvency

Superficially the current ratio of 2.11 in 2007 seems reasonable, but the improvement from the alarming current ratio in 2006 of 0.97 is more illusory than real. The ratio in the year ended 31 March 2007 has been distorted (improved) by the inclusion of assets of the discontinued operation under the heading of 'held for sale'. These have been included at fair value less cost to sell (being lower than their cost – a requirement of IFRS 5). Thus the carrying amount should be a realistic expectation of the net sale proceeds, but it is not clear whether the sale will be cash (they may be exchanged for shares or other assets) or how Greenwood intends to use the disposal proceeds. What can be deduced is that without the assets held for sale being classified as current, the company's liquidity ratio would be much worse than at present (at below 1 for both years). Against an expected norm of 1, quick ratios (acid test) calculated on the normal basis of excluding inventory (and in this case the assets held for sale) show an alarming position; a poor figure of 0.62 in 2006 has further deteriorated in 2007 to 0.44. Without the proceeds from the sale of the discontinued operation (assuming they will be for cash) it is difficult to see how Greenwood would pay its payables (and tax liability), given a year end overdraft of $1,150,000.

Further analysis of the current ratios shows some interesting changes during the year. Despite its large overdraft Greenwood appears to be settling its trade payables quicker than in 2006. At 68 days in 2006 this was rather a long time and the reduction in credit period may be at the insistence of suppliers – not a good sign. Perhaps to relieve liquidity pressure, the company appears to be pushing its customers to settle early. It may be that this has been achieved by the offer of early settlement discounts, if so the cost of this would have impacted on profit. Despite holding a higher amount of inventory at 31 March 2007 (than in 2006), the company has increased its inventory turnover; given that margins have been held, this reflects an improved performance.

Gearing

The additional borrowing of $3 million in loan notes (perhaps due to liquidity pressure) has resulted in an increase in gearing from 28.6% to 35.6% and a consequent increase in finance costs. Despite the increase in finance costs the borrowing is acting in the shareholders' favour as the overall return on capital employed (at 29.7%) is well in excess of the 5% interest cost.

Summary

Overall the company's performance has deteriorated in the year ended 31 March 2007. Management's action in respect of the discontinued operation is a welcome measure to try to halt the decline, but more needs to be done. The company's liquidity position is giving cause for serious concern and without the prospect of realising $6 million from the assets held for sale it would be difficult to envisage any easing of the company's liquidity pressures.

Appendix

	2007		2006
ROCE: continuing operations (4,500 + 400)/(14,500 + 8,000 − 6,000))	29.7%	(3,500 + 250)/(12,500 + 5,000 − 6,300)	33.5%

The return has been taken as the profit before interest (on loan notes only) and tax from continuing operations. The capital employed is the normal equity plus loan capital (as at the year end), but less the value of the assets held for sale. This is because the assets held for sale have not contributed to the return from continuing operations.

	2007		2006
Gross profit percentage (8,000/27,500)	29.1%	(6,200/21,200)	29.2%
Operating expense percentage of sales revenue (2,900/27,500)	10.5%	(2,450/21,200)	11.6%
Profit before interest and tax margin (5,100/27,500)	18.5%	(3,750/21,200)	17.7%
Asset turnover (27,500/16,500)	1.67	(21,200/11,200)	1.89
Current ratio (9,500:4,500)	2.11	(3,700:3,800)	0.97
Current ratio (excluding held for sale) (3,500:4,500)	0.77	Not applicable	
Quick ratio (excluding held for sale) (2,000:4,500)	0.44	(2,350:3,800)	0.62
Inventory (closing) turnover (19,500/1,500)	13.0	(15,000/1,350)	11.1
Receivables (in days) (2,000/27,500) × 365	26.5	(2,300/21,200) × 365	39.6
Payables/cost of sales (in days) (2,400/19,500) × 365	44.9	(2,800/15,000) × 365	68.1
Gearing (8,000/8,000 + 14,500)	35.6%	(5,000/5,000 + 12,500)	28.6%

394 VICTULAR *Walk in the footsteps of a top tutor*

Key answer tips

This style of question is naturally time consuming – ensure you answer all parts of the question and do not spend too much time calculating ratios. Part (c) offers easy marks and is independent of the rest of the question – try doing part (c) first to ensure you do not miss out on such easy marks. When interpreting the results in part (b) be wary of making generalisations – you must ensure that you relate it to the information given in the question. Presentation is also crucial in part (b) the marker cannot award you any marks if they cannot read what you have written.

(a) **Equivalent ratios from the financial statements of Merlot (workings in $000)**

Return on year end capital employed (ROCE)	20.9%	(1,400 + 590)/(2,800 + 3,200 + 500 + 3,000) × 100
Pre tax return on equity (ROE)	50%	1,400/2,800 × 100
Net asset turnover	2.3 times	20,500/(14,800 – 5,700)
Gross profit margin	12.2%	2,500/20,500 × 100
Operating profit margin	9.8%	2,000/20,500 × 100
Current ratio	1.3:1	7,300/5,700
Closing inventory holding period	73 days	3,600/18,000 × 365
Trade receivables' collection period	66 days	3,700/20,500 × 365
Trade payables' payment period	77 days	3,800/18,000 × 365
Gearing	71%	(3,200 + 500 + 3,000)/ 9,500 × 100
Interest cover	3.3 times	2,000/600
Dividend cover	1.4 times	1,000/700

As per the question, Merlot's obligations under finance leases (3,200 + 500) have been treated as debt when calculating the ROCE and gearing ratios.

(b) **Assessment of the relative performance and financial position of Grappa and Merlot for the year ended 30 September 2008**

Introduction

This report is based on the draft financial statements supplied and the ratios shown in (a) above. Although covering many aspects of performance and financial position, the report has been approached from the point of view of a prospective acquisition of the entire equity of one of the two companies.

Profitability

The ROCE of 20.9% of Merlot is far superior to the 14.8% return achieved by Grappa. ROCE is traditionally seen as a measure of management's overall efficiency in the use of the finance/assets at its disposal. More detailed analysis reveals that Merlot's superior performance is due to its efficiency in the use of its net assets; it achieved a net asset turnover of 2.3 times compared to only 1.2 times for Grappa. Put another way, Merlot makes sales of $2.30 per $1 invested in net assets compared to sales of only $1.20 per $1 invested for Grappa. The other element contributing to the ROCE is profit margins. In this area Merlot's overall performance is slightly inferior to that of Grappa, gross profit margins are almost identical, but Grappa's operating profit margin is 10.5% compared to Merlot's 9.8%. In this situation, where one company's ROCE is superior to another's it is useful to look behind the figures and consider possible reasons for the superiority other than the obvious one of greater efficiency on Merlot's part.

A major component of the ROCE is normally the carrying amount of the non-current assets. Consideration of these in this case reveals some interesting issues. Merlot does not own its premises whereas Grappa does. Such a situation would not necessarily give a ROCE advantage to either company as the increase in capital employed of a company owning its factory would be compensated by a higher return due to not having a rental expense (and *vice versa*). If Merlot's rental cost, as a percentage of the value of the related factory, was less than its overall ROCE, then it would be contributing to its higher ROCE. There is insufficient information to determine this. Another relevant point may be that Merlot's owned plant is nearing the end of its useful life (carrying amount is only 22% of its cost) and the company seems to be replacing owned plant with leased plant. Again this does not necessarily give Merlot an advantage, but the finance cost of the leased assets at only 7.5% is much lower than the overall ROCE (of either company) and therefore this does help to improve Merlot's ROCE. The other important issue within the composition of the ROCE is the valuation basis of the companies' non-current assets. From the question, it appears that Grappa's factory is at current value (there is a property revaluation reserve) and note (ii) of the question indicates the use of historical cost for plant. The use of current value for the factory (as opposed to historical cost) will be adversely impacting on Grappa's ROCE. Merlot does not suffer this deterioration as it does not own its factory.

The ROCE measures the overall efficiency of management; however, as Victular is considering buying the equity of one of the two companies, it would be useful to consider the return on equity (ROE) – as this is what Victular is buying. The ratios calculated are based on pre-tax profits; this takes into account finance costs, but does not cause taxation issues to distort the comparison. Clearly Merlot's ROE at 50% is far superior to Grappa's 19.1%. Again the issue of the revaluation of Grappa's factory is making this ratio appear comparatively worse (than it would be if there had not been a revaluation). In these circumstances it would be more meaningful if the ROE was calculated based on the asking price of each company (which has not been disclosed) as this would effectively be the carrying amount of the relevant equity for Victular.

Gearing

From the gearing ratio it can be seen that 71% of Merlot's assets are financed by borrowings (39% is attributable to Merlot's policy of leasing its plant). This is very high in absolute terms and double Grappa's level of gearing. The effect of gearing means that all of the profit after finance costs is attributable to the equity even though (in Merlot's case) the equity represents only 29% of the financing of the net assets. Whilst this may seem advantageous to the equity shareholders of Merlot, it does not come without risk. The interest cover of Merlot is only 3.3 times whereas that of Grappa is 6 times. Merlot's low interest cover is a direct consequence of its high gearing and it makes profits vulnerable to relatively small changes in operating activity. For example, small reductions in sales, profit margins or small increases in operating expenses could result in losses and mean that interest charges would not be covered.

Another observation is that Grappa has been able to take advantage of the receipt of government grants; Merlot has not. This may be due to Grappa purchasing its plant (which may then be eligible for grants) whereas Merlot leases its plant. It may be that the lessor has received any grants available on the purchase of the plant and passed some of this benefit on to Merlot via lower lease finance costs (at 7.5% per annum, this is considerably lower than Merlot has to pay on its 10% loan notes).

Liquidity

Both companies have relatively low liquid ratios of 1.2 and 1.3 for Grappa and Merlot respectively, although at least Grappa has $600,000 in the bank whereas Merlot has a $1.2 million overdraft. In this respect Merlot's policy of high dividend payouts (leading to a low dividend cover and low retained earnings) is very questionable. Looking in more depth, both companies have similar inventory days; Merlot collects its receivables one week earlier than Grappa (perhaps its credit control procedures are more active due to its large overdraft), and of notable difference is that Grappa receives (or takes) a lot longer credit period from its suppliers (108 days compared to 77 days). This may be a reflection of Grappa being able to negotiate better credit terms because it has a higher credit rating.

Summary

Although both companies may operate in a similar industry and have similar profits after tax, they would represent very different purchases. Merlot's sales revenues are over 70% more than those of Grappa, it is financed by high levels of debt, it rents rather than owns property and it chooses to lease rather than buy its replacement plant. Also its remaining owned plant is nearing the end of its life. Its replacement will either require a cash injection if it is to be purchased (Merlot's overdraft of $1.2 million already requires serious attention) or create even higher levels of gearing if it continues its policy of leasing. In short although Merlot's overall return seems more attractive than that of Grappa, it would represent a much more risky investment. Ultimately the investment decision may be determined by Victular's attitude to risk, possible synergies with its existing business activities, and not least, by the asking price for each investment (which has not been disclosed to us).

(c)   The generally recognised potential problems of using ratios for comparison purposes are:

- inconsistent definitions of ratios

- financial statements may have been deliberately manipulated (creative accounting)

- different companies may adopt different accounting policies (e.g. use of historical costs compared to current values)

- different managerial policies (e.g. different companies offer customers different payment terms)

- statement of financial position figures may not be representative of average values throughout the year (this can be caused by seasonal trading or a large acquisition of non-current assets near the year end)

- the impact of price changes over time/distortion caused by inflation.

When deciding whether to purchase a company, Victular should consider the following additional useful information:

- in this case the analysis has been made on the draft financial statements; these may be unreliable or change when being finalised. Audited financial statements would add credibility and reliance to the analysis (assuming they receive an unmodified Auditors' Report)

- forward looking information such as profit and financial position forecasts, capital expenditure and cash budgets and the level of orders on the books.

- the current (fair) values of assets being acquired

- the level of risk within a business. Highly profitable companies may also be highly risky, whereas a less profitable company may have more stable 'quality' earnings

- not least would be the expected price to acquire a company. It may be that a poorer performing business may be a more attractive purchase because it is relatively cheaper and may offer more opportunity for improving efficiencies and profit growth.

395 QUARTILE

(a) Below are the specified ratios for Quartile and (for comparison) those of the business sector average:

		Quartile	Sector average
Return on year-end capital employed			
	$((3,400 + 800)/(26,600 + 8,000) \times 100)$	12.1%	16.8%
Net asset turnover	$(56,000/34,600)$	1.6 times	1.4 times
Gross profit margin	$(14,000/56,000 \times 100)$	25%	35%
Operating profit margin	$(4,200/56,000 \times 100)$	7.5%	12%
Current ratio	$(11,200{:}7,200)$	1.6:1	1.25:1
Average inventory (8,300 + 10,200/2) = 9,250) turnover			
	$(42,000/9,250)$	4.5 times	3 times
Trade payables' payment period	$(5,400/43,900 \times 365)$	45 days	64 days
Debt to equity	$(8,000/26,600 \times 100)$	30%	38%

(b) **Assessment of comparative performance**

Profitability

The primary measure of profitability is the return on capital employed (ROCE) and this shows that Quartile's 12.1% is considerably underperforming the sector average of 16.8%. Measured as a percentage, this underperformance is 28% ((16.8 – 12.1)/16.8). The main cause of this seems to be a much lower gross profit margin (25% compared to 35%). A possible explanation for this is that Quartile is deliberately charging a lower mark-up in order to increase its sales by undercutting the market. There is supporting evidence for this in that Quartile's average inventory turnover at 4.5 times is 50% better than the sector average of three times. An alternative explanation could be that Quartile has had to cut its margins due to poor sales which have had a knock-on effect of having to write down closing inventory.

Quartile's lower gross profit percentage has fed through to contribute to a lower operating profit margin at 7.5% compared to the sector average of 12%. However, from the above figures, it can be deduced that Quartile's operating costs at 17.5% (25% – 7.5%) of revenue appear to be better controlled than the sector average operating costs of 23% (35% – 12%) of revenue. This may indicate that Quartile has a different classification of costs between cost of sales and operating costs than the companies in the sector average or that other companies may be spending more on advertising/selling commissions in order to support their higher margins.

The other component of ROCE is asset utilisation (measured by net asset turnover). If Quartile's business strategy is indeed to generate more sales to compensate for lower profit margins, a higher net asset turnover would be expected. At 1.6 times, Quartile's net asset turnover is only marginally better than the sector average of 1.4 times. Whilst this may indicate that Quartile's strategy was a poor choice, the ratio could be partly distorted by the property revaluation and also by whether the deferred development expenditure should be included within net assets for this purpose, as the net revenues expected from the development have yet to come on stream. If these two aspects were adjusted for, Quartile's net asset turnover would be 2.1 times (56,000/(34,600 – 5,000 – 3,000)) which is 50% better than the sector average.

In summary, Quartile's overall profitability is below that of its rival companies due to considerably lower profit margins, although this has been partly offset by generating proportionately more sales from its assets.

Liquidity

As measured by the current ratio, Quartile has a higher level of cover for its current liabilities than the sector average (1.6:1 compared to 1.25:1). Quartile's figure is nearer the 'norm' of expected liquidity ratios, often quoted as between 1.5 and 2:1, with the sector average (at 1.25:1) appearing worryingly low. The problem of this 'norm' is that it is generally accepted that it relates to manufacturing companies rather than retail companies, as applies to Quartile (and presumably also to the sector average). In particular, retail companies have very little, if any, trade receivables as is the case with Quartile. This makes a big difference to the current ratio and makes the calculation of a quick ratio largely irrelevant. Consequently, retail companies operate comfortably with much lower current ratios as their inventory is turned directly into cash. Thus, if anything, Quartile has a higher current ratio than might be expected. As Quartile has relatively low inventory levels (deduced from high inventory turnover figures), this means it must also have relatively low levels of trade payables (which can be confirmed from the calculated ratios). The low payables period of 45 days may be an indication of suppliers being cautious with the credit period they extend to Quartile, but there is no real evidence of this (e.g. the company is not struggling with an overdraft). In short, Quartile does not appear to have any liquidity issues.

Gearing

Quartile's debt to equity at 30% is lower than the sector average of 38%. Although the loan note interest rate of 10% might appear quite high, it is lower than the ROCE of 12.1% (which means shareholders are benefiting from the borrowings) and the interest cover of 5.25 times ((3,400 + 800)/800) is acceptable. Quartile also has sufficient tangible assets to give more than adequate security on the borrowings, therefore there appear to be no adverse issues in relation to gearing.

Conclusion

Quartile may be right to be concerned about its declining profitability. From the above analysis, it seems that Quartile may be addressing the wrong market (low margins with high volumes). The information provided about its rival companies would appear to suggest that the current market appears to favour a strategy of higher margins (probably associated with better quality and more expensive goods) as being more profitable. In other aspects of the appraisal, Quartile is doing well compared to other companies in its sector.

396 BENGAL

Note: references to 2011 and 2010 refer to the periods ending 31 March 2011 and 2010 respectively.

It is understandable that the shareholder's observations would cause concern. A large increase in sales revenue has not led to a proportionate increase in profit. To assess why this has happened requires consideration of several factors that could potentially explain the results.

Perhaps the most obvious would be that the company has increased its sales by discounting prices (cutting profit margins). Interpreting the ratios rules out this possible explanation as the gross profit margin has in fact increased in 2011 (up from 40% to 42%).

Another potential cause of the disappointing profit could be overheads (distribution costs and administrative expenses) getting out of control, perhaps due to higher advertising costs or more generous incentives to sales staff. Again, when these expenses are expressed as a percentage of sales, this does not explain the disparity in profit as the ratio has remained at approximately 19%.

What is evident is that there has been a very large increase in finance costs which is illustrated by the interest cover deteriorating from 36 times to only 9 times.

The other 'culprit' is the taxation expense: expressed as a percentage of pre-tax accounting profit, the effective rate of tax has gone from 28.6% in 2010 to 42.9% in 2011. There are a number of factors that can affect a period's effective tax rate (including under- or over-provisions from the previous year), but judging from the figures involved, it would seem likely that either there was a material adjustment from an under-provision of tax in 2010 or there has been a considerable increase in the rate levied by the taxation authority.

As an illustration of the effect, if the same effective tax rate in 2010 had applied in 2011, the after-tax profit would have been $3,749,000 (5,250 × (100% − 28.6%) rounded) and, using this figure, the percentage increase in profit would be 50% ((3,749 − 2,500)/2,500 × 100) which is slightly higher than the percentage increase in revenue.

Thus an increase in the tax rate and increases in finance costs due to much higher borrowings more than account for the disappointing profit commented upon by the concerned shareholder.

The other significant observation in comparing 2011 with 2010 is that the company has almost certainty acquired another business. The increased expenditure on property, plant and equipment of $6,740,000 and the newly acquired intangibles (probably goodwill) of $6.2 million are not likely to be attributable to organic or internal growth.

Indeed the decrease in the bank balance of $4.2 million and the issue of $7 million loan notes closely match the increase in non-current assets. This implies that the acquisition has been financed by cash resources (which the company looks to have been building up) and issuing debt (no equity was issued).

It may be that these assets were part of the acquisition of a new business and are 'surplus to requirements', hence they have been made available for sale.

They are likely to be valued at their 'fair value less cost to sell' and the prospect of their sale should be highly probable (normally within one year). That said, if the assets are not sold in the near future, it would call into question the acceptability of the company's current ratio which may cause short-term liquidity problems.

In summary, although reported performance has deteriorated, it may be that future results will benefit from the current year's investment and show considerable improvement. Perhaps some equity should have been issued to lower the company's finance costs and if the dividend of $750,000 had been suspended for a year there would be a better liquid position.

Appendix

Calculation of ratios (figures in $000):	2011	2010
Gross profit margin (10,700/25,500 × 100)	42.0%	40.0 %
Operating expenses % (4,800/25,500 × 100)	18.8%	19.1%
Interest cover ((5,250 + 650)/650)	9 times	36 times
Effective rate of tax (2,250/5,250)	42.9%	28.6%
Net profit (before tax) margin (5,250/25,500 × 100)	20.6%	20.3%

The figures for the calculation of 2011's ratios are given in brackets; the figures for 2010 are derived from the equivalent figures.

397 WOODBANK *Online question assistance*

(a)   Note: Figures in the calculations of the ratios are in $million

	2014 Excluding Shaw	2013	2014
Return on capital employed (ROCE) (profit before interest and tax/year-end total assets less current liabilities)	13% (13/100)	10.5%	12.0%
Net asset (equal to capital employed) turnover	1.2 times (120/100)	1.16 times	1.0 times
Gross profit margin	20% (24/120)	22.0%	22.0%
Profit before interest and tax margin	10.8% (13/120)	9.1%	12.0%
Current ratio	–	1.7:1	1.08:1
Gearing (debt/(debt + equity))	–	5.3%	36.7%

(b)   **Analysis of the comparative financial performance and position of Woodbank for the year ended 31 March 2014**

Introduction

When comparing a company's current performance and position with the previous year (or years), using trend analysis, it is necessary to take into account the effect of any circumstances which may create an inconsistency in the comparison. In the case of Woodbank, the purchase of Shaw is an example of such an inconsistency.

2014's figures include, for a three-month period, the operating results of Shaw, and Woodbank's statement of financial position includes all of Shaw's net assets (including goodwill) together with the additional 10% loan notes used to finance the purchase of Shaw. None of these items were included in the 2013 financial statements.

The net assets of Shaw when purchased were $50 million, which represents one third of Woodbank's net assets (capital employed) as at 31 March 2014; thus it represents a major investment for Woodbank and any analysis necessitates careful consideration of its impact.

Profitability

ROCE is considered by many analysts to be the most important profitability ratio. A ROCE of 12.0% in 2014, compared to 10.5% in 2013, represents a creditable 14.3% (12.0 – 10.5)/10.5) improvement in profitability.

When ROCE is calculated excluding the contribution from Shaw, at 13.0%, it shows an even more favourable performance. Although this comparison (13.0% from 10.5%) is valid, it would seem to imply that the purchase of Shaw has had a detrimental effect on Woodbank's ROCE.

However, caution is needed when interpreting this information as ROCE compares the return (profit for a period) to the capital employed (equivalent to net assets at a single point in time).

In the case of Woodbank, the statement of profit or loss only includes three months' results from Shaw whereas the statement of financial position includes all of Shaw's net assets; this is a form of inconsistency.

It would be fair to speculate that in future years, when a full year's results from Shaw are reported, the ROCE effect of Shaw will be favourable.

Indeed, assuming a continuation of Shaw's current level of performance, profit in a full year could be $20 million. On an investment of $50 million, this represents a ROCE of 40% (based on the initial capital employed) which is much higher than Woodbank's pre-existing business.

The cause of the improvement in ROCE is revealed by consideration of the secondary profitability ratios: asset turnover and profit margins. For Woodbank this reveals a complicated picture.

Woodbank's results, as reported, show that it is the increase in the profit before interest and tax margin (12.0% from 9.1%) which is responsible for the improvement in ROCE, as the asset turnover has actually decreased (1.0 times from 1.16 times) and gross profit is exactly the same in both years (at 22.0%).

When the effect of the purchase of Shaw is excluded the position changes; the overall improvement in ROCE (13.0% from 10.5%) is caused by both an increase in profit margin (at the before interest and tax level, at 10.8% from 9.1 %), despite a fall in gross profit (20.0% from 22.0%) and a very slight improvement in asset turnover (1.2 times from 1.16 times). This means that the purchase of Shaw has improved Woodbank's overall profit margins, but caused a fall in asset turnover.

Again, as with the ROCE, this is misleading because the calculation of asset turnover only includes three months' revenue from Shaw, but all of its net assets; when a full year of Shaw's results are reported, asset turnover will be much improved (assuming its three-months performance is continued).

Liquidity

The company's liquidity position, as measured by the current ratio, has fallen considerably in 2014 and is a cause for concern.

At 1.67:1 in 2013, it was within the acceptable range (normally between 1.5:1 and 2.0:1); however, the 2014 ratio of 1.08:1 is very low, indeed it is more like what would be expected for the quick ratio (acid test).

Without needing to calculate the component ratios of the current ratio (for inventory, receivables and payables), it can be seen from the statements of financial position that the main causes of the deterioration in the liquidity position are the reduction in the cash (bank) position and the dramatic increase in trade payables. The bank balance has fallen by $4.5 million (5,000 – 500) and the trade payables have increased by $8 million.

An analysis of the movement in the retained earnings shows that Woodbank paid a dividend of $5.5 million (10,000 + 10,500 – 15,000) or 6.88 cents per share. It could be argued that during a period of expansion, with demands on cash flow, dividends could be suspended or heavily curtailed.

Had no dividend been paid, the 2014 bank balance would be $6.0 million and the current ratio would have been 1.3:1 ((27,000 + 5,500):25,000). This would be still on the low side, but much more reassuring to credit suppliers than the reported ratio of 1.08:1.

Gearing

The company has gone from a position of very modest gearing at 5.3% in 2013 to 36.7% in 2014. This has largely been caused by the issue of the additional 10% loan notes to finance the purchase of Shaw.

Arguably, it might have been better if some of the finance had been raised from a share issue, but the level of gearing is still acceptable and the financing cost of 10% should be more than covered by the prospect of future high returns from Shaw, thus benefiting shareholders overall.

Conclusion

The overall operating performance of Woodbank has improved during the period (although the gross profit margin on sales other than those made by Shaw has fallen) and this should be even more marked next year when a full year's results from Shaw will be reported (assuming that Shaw can maintain its current performance). The changes in the financial position, particularly liquidity, are less favourable and call into question the current dividend policy. Gearing has increased substantially, due to the financing of the purchase of Shaw; however, it is still acceptable and has benefited shareholders. It is interesting to note that of the $50 million purchase price, $30 million of this is represented by goodwill. Although this may seem high, Shaw is certainly delivering in terms of generating revenue with good profit margins.

(c) Below are a number of issues/items of information in relation to the acquisition of Shaw which would be useful in producing a better analysis of Woodbank.

- did the acquisition of Shaw include any consideration payable dependent on Shaw's results? If so, this should be recorded as a liability at its fair value.

- Shaw's statement of financial position would be useful. This would be useful in assessing the working capital cycle of Shaw compared to Woodbank, as the Woodbank group has a low cash balance as at 31 March 2014.

- Shaw's statement of cash flows would be useful (as would the statement of cash flow for Woodbank). This would help assess the reasons for the significant fall in cash during the year.

- Any one-off costs associated with the acquisition of Shaw, such as professional fees. These will have been expensed and will have affected the profit margins in the year.

- Whether there are any potential savings to be made following the acquisition of Shaw, such as reduction in staff costs or shared properties. These may involve one-off costs such as redundancies or lease termination costs but could lead to improved margins in future periods.

- The nature of Shaw's business should be looked at in comparison to Woodbank. It will be useful to know if Shaw was a competitor of Woodbank, or maybe a supplier of goods to Woodbank. This would help with further analysis regarding market share or the potential future cost of goods if Shaw was either of these.

- A breakdown of Shaw's major customers would be useful, to see if any have left following the change of ownership in Shaw.

Marking scheme		Marks
	Maximum	*Marks*
(a)	1 mark per ratio	4
(b)	1 mark per relevant point to maximum	12
(c)	1 mark per relevant point to maximum	4
Total		**20**

398 HYDAN

(a) For comparison

	Hydan adjusted	Hydan as reported	Sector average
Return on equity (ROE)	21.7%	47.1%	22.0%
Net asset turnover	1.75 times	2.36 times	1.67 times
Gross profit margin	28.6%	35.7%	30.0%
Net profit margin	9.3%	20.0%	12.0%

Hydan's adjusted ratios:

On the assumption that after the purchase of Hydan, the favourable effects of the transactions with other companies owned by the family would not occur, the following adjustments to the statement of profit or loss should be made:

	$000
Cost of sales (45,000/0.9)	50,000
Directors' remuneration	2,500
Loan interest (10% × 10,000)	1,000

These adjustments would give a revised statement of profit or loss:

Revenue	70,000
Cost of sales	(50,000)
Gross profit	20,000
Operating costs	(7,000)
Directors' remuneration	(2,500)
Loan interest	(1,000)
Profit before tax	9,500
Income tax expense	(3,000)
Profit for the year	6,500

In the statement of financial position:

Equity would be the purchase price of Hydan (per question)	30,000
The commercial loan (replacing the directors' loan) would now be debt	10,000

From these figures the adjusted ratios above are calculated as:

Return on equity	((6,500 /30,000) × 100)	21.7%
Net asset turnover	(70,000/(30,000 + 10,000))	1.75 times
Gross profit margin	((20,000)/70,000) × 100)	28.6%
Net profit margin	((6,500/70,000) × 100)	9.30%

(b) An analysis of Hydan's ratios based on the financial statements provided reveals a strong position, particularly in relation to profitability when compared to other businesses in this retail sector. Hydan has a very high ROE which is a product of higher-than-average profit margins (at both the gross and net profit level) and a significantly higher net asset turnover. Thus, on the face of it, Hydan is managing to achieve higher prices (or reduced cost of sales), has better control of overheads and is using its net assets more efficiently in terms of generating revenue.

However, when adjustments are made for the effects of its favourable transactions with other companies owned by the family, the position changes somewhat. The effect of purchasing its inventory from another family owned supplier at favourable market prices means that its reported gross profit percentage of 35.7% is flattered; had these purchases been made at market prices, it would fall to 28.6% which is below the sector average of 30.0%. The effects of the favourable inventory purchases carry through to net profit. Based on Xpand's estimate of future directors' remuneration, it would seem the existing directors of Hydan are not charging commercial rates for their remuneration. When Xpand replaces the board of Hydan, it will have to increase directors' remuneration by $1.5 million. Additionally, when the interest free directors' loans are replaced with a commercial loan, with interest at 10% per annum, this would reduce net profit by a further $1 million. The accumulation of these adjustments means that the ROE which Xpand should expect would be 21.7% (rather than the reported 47.1%) which is almost exactly in line with the sector average of 22.0%.

In a similar vein, when the asset turnover is calculated based on the equity purchase price and the commercial loan (equating to net assets), it falls from 2.36 times to 1.75 times which is above, but much closer to, the sector average of 1.67 times. In summary, Hydan's adjusted results would still be slightly ahead of the sector averages in most areas and may well justify the anticipated purchase price of $30 million; however, Hydan will be nowhere near the excellently performing company suggested by the reported figures and Xpand needs to exercise a degree of caution in its negotiations.

(c) The consolidated financial statements of Lodan are of little value when trying to assess the performance and financial position of its subsidiary, Hydan. Therefore the main source of information on which to base any investment decision would be Hydan's own entity financial statements. However, where a company is part of a group, there is the potential for the financial statements (of a subsidiary) to have been subject to the influence of related party transactions. In the case of Hydan, there has been a considerable amount of post-acquisition trading with Lodan and, because of the related party relationship, it appears that this trading is not at arm's length (i.e. not at commercial rates).

There may be other aspects of the relationship where Lodan gives Hydan a benefit that may not have happened had Hydan not been part of the group, e.g. access to technology/research, cheap finance.

The operations of Hydan may now be centralised and run by Lodan. If Lodan doesn't allocate some of these costs to Hydan then Hydan's expenses will be understated. It could also be difficult for a purchaser to assess whether additional property would be required if Hydan share this with other group entities.

The main concern is that any information about the 'benefits' Lodan may have passed on to Hydan through related party transactions is difficult to obtain from published sources. It may be that Lodan would deliberately 'flatter' Hydan's financial statements specifically in order to obtain a high sale price and a prospective purchaser would not necessarily be able to determine that this had happened from either the consolidated or entity financial statements. There are suggestions of this in the fact that Hydan's directors are not charging market rates for their remuneration and are giving interest-free loans.

Marking scheme		
		Marks
(a)	1½ marks per ratio	6
(b)	1 mark per valid point. A good answer must emphasise the different interpretation when using adjusted figures	
		9
Total		**15**

399 YOGI

Note: References to 2015 and 2014 refer to the periods ended 31 March 2015 and 2014 respectively.

(a) **Calculation of equivalent ratios (figures in $000):**

	(i) 2014 *excluding division*	*(ii) 2015* *as reported*	*2014* *per question*
Gross profit margin ((20,000 – 8,000)/(50,000 – 18,000) × 100)	37.5%	33.3%	40.0%
Operating profit margin ((11,800 – 5,800)/32,000 × 100)	18.8%	10.3%	23.6%
Return on capital employed (ROCE) ((11,800 – 5,800)/(29,200 – 7,200 – 7,000 see below) × 100)	40.0%	21.8%	53.6%
Net asset turnover (32,000/15,000)	2.13 times	2.12 times	2.27 times

Note: The capital employed in the division sold at 31 March 2014 was $7 million ($8 million sale proceeds less $1 million profit on sale).

The figures for the calculations of 2014's adjusted ratios (i.e. excluding the effects of the sale of the division) are given in brackets; the figures for 2015 are derived from the equivalent figures in the question, however, the operating profit margin and ROCE calculations exclude the profit from the sale of the division (as stated in the requirement) as it is a 'one off' item.

(b) The most relevant comparison is the 2015 results (excluding the profit on disposal of the division) with the results of 2014 (excluding the results of the division), otherwise like is not being compared with like.

Profitability

Although comparative sales have increased (excluding the effect of the sale of the division) by $4 million (36,000 —— 32,000), equivalent to 12.5%, the gross profit margin has fallen considerably (from 37.5% in 2014 down to 33.3% in 2015) and this deterioration has been compounded by the sale of the division, which was the most profitable part of the business (which earned a gross profit margin of 44.4% (8/18)). The deterioration of the operating profit margin (from 18.8% in 2014 down to 10.3% in 2015) is largely due to poor gross profit margins, but operating expenses are proportionately higher (as a percentage of sales) in 2015 (23.0% compared to 18.8%) which has further reduced profitability. This is due to higher administrative expenses (as distribution costs have fallen), perhaps relating to the sale of the division.

Yogi's performance as measured by ROCE has deteriorated dramatically from 40.0% in 2014 (as adjusted) to only 21.8% in 2015. As the net asset turnover has remained broadly the same at 2.1 times (rounded), it is the fall in the operating profit which is responsible for the overall deterioration in performance. Whilst it is true that Yogi has sold the most profitable part of its business, this does not explain why the 2015 results have deteriorated so much (by definition the adjusted 2014 figures exclude the favourable results of the division). Consequently, Yogi's management need to investigate why profit margins have fallen in 2015; it may be that customers of the sold division also bought (more profitable) goods from Yogi's remaining business and they have taken their custom to the new owners of the division; or it may be related to external issues which are also being experienced by other companies such as an economic recession. A study of industry sector average ratios could reveal this.

Other issues

It is very questionable to have offered shareholders such a high dividend (half of the disposal proceeds) to persuade them to vote for the disposal. At $4 million (4,000 + 3,000 − 3,000, i.e. the movement on retained earnings or 10 million shares at 40 cents) the dividend represents double the profit for the year of $2 million (3,000 − 1,000) if the gain on the disposal is excluded. Another effect of the disposal is that Yogi appears to have used the other $4 million (after paying the dividend) from the disposal proceeds to pay down half of the 10% loan notes. This has reduced finance costs and interest cover; interestingly, however, as the finance cost at 10% is much lower than the 2015 ROCE of 21.8%, it will have had a detrimental effect on overall profit available to shareholders.

Summary

In retrospect, it may have been unwise for Yogi to sell the most profitable part of its business at what appears to be a very low price. It has coincided with a remarkable deterioration in profitability (not solely due to the sale) and the proceeds of the disposal have not been used to replace capacity or improve long-term prospects. By returning a substantial proportion of the sale proceeds to shareholders, it represents a downsizing of the business.

(c) Although the sports club is a not-for-profit organisation, the request for a loan is a commercial activity that should be decided on according to similar criteria as would be used for other profit-orientated entities.

The main aspect of granting a loan is how secure the loan would be. To this extent a form of capital gearing ratio should be calculated; say existing long-term borrowings to net assets (i.e. total assets less current liabilities). Clearly if this ratio is high, further borrowing would be at an increased risk. The secondary aspect is to measure the sports club's ability to repay the interest (and ultimately the principal) on the loan. This may be determined from information in the statement of comprehensive income. A form of interest cover should be calculated; say the excess of income over expenditure (broadly the equivalent of profit) compared to (the forecast) interest payments. The higher this ratio the less risk of interest default. The calculations would be made for all four years to ascertain any trends that may indicate a deterioration or improvement in these ratios. As with other profit-oriented entities the nature and trend of the income should be investigated: for example, are the club's sources of income increasing or decreasing, does the reported income contain 'one-off' donations (which may not be recurring) etc? Also matters such as the market value of, and existing prior charges against, any assets intended to be used as security for the loan would be relevant to the lender's decision-making process. It may also be possible that the sports club's governing body (perhaps the trustees) may be willing to give a personal guarantee for the loan.

Marking scheme			
			Marks
(a)	(i) and (ii)	Gross profit margin	1
		Operating profit margin	1½
		Return on capital employed	1½
		Net asset turnover	1
			5
(b)		1 mark per point (a good answer must consider the effect of the sale of the division)	10
(b)		1 mark per point	5
Total			20

400 XPAND

(a) **Missing ratios for Kovert:**

	Kovert
Return on year-end capital employed (ROCE) (4,900/(5,600 + 9,200 + 1,000 x 100)	31.0%
Profit margin (before interest and tax) (4,900/40,000 × 100)	12.3%
Trade payables' payment period (2,100/32,800 x 365)	23 days
Gearing (debt/(debt + equity)) (10,200/15,800 x 100)	64.6%

(b)   **Assessment of the comparative performance and financial position of Kandid and Kovert for the year ended 30 September 2015**

Introduction

This assessment of the two companies will look at the areas of profitability, liquidity and gearing with reference to some differences which may make the comparison of the reported figures potentially invalid.

Profitability

ROCE is usually considered as the most important measure of profitability and is often described as a measure of management's overall efficiency in the use of the assets at its disposal. The ROCE of 62.5% of Kandid is far superior (more than double) to the 31.0% return achieved by Kovert. This superior return of Kandid can be analysed into its component parts of profit margin and asset turnover and in both of these areas Kandid's performance is better than that of Kovert. Kandid is generating $3.30 for every dollar invested, compared to only $2.50 per dollar invested in Kovert and earning a profit margin of 19.0% compared to just 12.3% by Kovert. Additionally, Kandid's gross profit margin at 24% is a third (6%/18%) higher than the 18% of Kovert. This may be (at least in part) due to marketing policy; Kovert may be deliberately charging lower selling prices in order to generate greater revenue. This is evidenced by Kovert's turnover of $40 million compared to only $25 million for Kandid. The superior gross margin of Kandid continues into the operating profit level indicating that Kandid has better control of its overheads.

There are, however, a number of areas relating to the capital employed which may bring this superiority into question. Kandid has deducted the receipt of a government grant directly from the carrying amount of the related plant (this is allowed but is rather unusual). Normally, plant is shown gross (less accumulated depreciation) and related government grants are shown as a (separate) deferred credit. It also appears that Kandid rents its property whereas Kovert has purchased its property (and indeed revalued it which has increased its capital employed). Kandid also holds proportionately less inventory and receivables than Kovert. Whilst these factors may not necessarily result in a higher profit for Kandid (e.g. property rental may be higher than the equivalent depreciation of property), they would act to give Kandid lower net assets (and thus lower capital employed) and, in turn, a higher ROCE than Kovert.

Bearing in mind these differences, it may be more helpful if Xpand were to calculate a return on its potential equity investment (ROE) of $12 million as this would be more relevant should it acquire either of the companies. Using profit after tax, Kandid's ROE would be 30% (3,600/12,000 × 100) whereas Kovert's ROE would be 25% (3,000/12,000). This still supports Kandid's superior return, but this introduces further differences. Both companies have $5 million in loan notes; however, the interest rate on Kandid's loan is only 5% compared to 10% for Kovert, presumably this reflects the difference in the credit worthiness of the two companies which is something that Xpand should take note of. There also appears to be a favourable tax discrepancy with Kandid paying a nominal rate of tax on its profit of 20% compared with 25% paid by Kovert. This may be due to be adjustments relating to previous years' profits or other tax issues. If Kandid had a comparable (to Kovert) finance cost and tax rate, its ROE would be nearer that of Kovert.

Liquidity

The given ratios show that both companies have healthy liquidity positions. Kandid's current ratio is slightly higher (perhaps too high) than Kovert's. This seems to be down to holding more cash (than Kovert) as it has better inventory and receivables control (their payable periods are very similar); though arguably the current finance lease obligation of Kovert should not be included in this ratio for comparative purposes. The individual components of the current ratio could suggest that Kovert holds a greater range of inventory (perhaps this helps it to achieve more sales) and the relatively high receivables collection period could be indicative of an uncollectible customer balance which should have been written off or may just be due to poor credit control.

Gearing

At around 65%, both companies are highly geared. The relatively low equity, particularly retained earnings, may be due to the companies having a policy of paying most of their earnings as dividends. Kovert's high gearing is in part due to its policy of using finance leases to acquire its plant. Xpand should be aware that, for both companies, the $5 million loans are due for repayment in the near future which will represent a substantial further cash outlay on top of the purchase price it may pay.

Summary

Although both companies operate in a same industry sector and have a similar level of after-tax profits, and indeed have the same indicative valuation, they would represent very different investments. Kovert's revenue is over 60% (15,000/25,000 × 100) higher than that of Kandid, it is financed by high levels of debt (loans and finance leases), and it also owns, rather than rents, its property. Another point of note is that Kovert's plant is 80% depreciated and will need replacement in the near future (with consequent financing implications). Ultimately, the investment decision may be determined by Xpand's attitude to risk and how well each investment would fit in with existing activities and management structure.

(c) Basing an investment decision solely on one year's summarised financial statements is fraught with danger. Below are a number of issues/items of information which Xpand may wish to seek answers to before making an offer.

General:

- in addition to using different strategies (e.g. buying property or renting it, targeting low mark-up/high volume sales), the two companies may use different accounting policies

- the availability of non-published forward looking information such as profit forecasts, capital commitments and the size of orders on the books (providing this information should not be unreasonable if the shareholders are receptive to a takeover)

- is either company established (mature) or a relatively young and growing company (more risk, but potentially more reward)?

Specific:

- as noted above, the owned assets of Kovert are nearing the end of their useful life; will these need replacing soon, or have they already been replaced by the leased assets?

- how much of the profit is due to the reputation or contacts of the current management and would they continue in their role after a takeover (and indeed would Xpand want this or would it prefer to use its own managers)?

- the fair value of the assets, compared to their carrying amounts, which will impact on the calculation of goodwill.

Marking scheme		Marks
(a)	1 mark per ratio	4
(b)	1 mark per value point up to	12
(c)	1 mark per valid point up to	4
Total		**20**

401 SCHRUTE

Ratios for Schrute for the year ended 30 September 20X3

			20X2
Gross profit margin	51.1%	(44,000/94,000) × 100	59.1%
Operating profit margin	1.3%	(1,200/94,000) × 100	8.5%
Return on Capital Employed	2.5%	(1,200/(86,010+2,000) × 100	7.4%
Current ratio	3.2:1	(29,110/9,100)	4.6:1
Inventory turnover period	52 days	(6,500/46,000) × 365	60 days
Receivables collection period	68 days	(22,000/94,000) × 365	83 days

Performance

Revenue and expenses have all increased during the year, due to the acquisition of Howard, the new subsidiary. Howard would have contributed a full year's results to 20X3 that would not have been included within 20X4.

Whilst revenue has increased significantly, it can be seen that higher expenses have meant that the Schrute group has made less profit than in previous years.

It is also worth noting that the new hotel was only opened in March, so a full year's revenue has not yet been generated by the hotel.

The gross profit margin has fallen. It may well be that the hotel business generates much lower margins than the farming side of things. It may also be that the hotel had to offer low room rates to attract new business as it was set up, or to bring customers back with special offers following the poor feedback. As the hotel establishes itself, the need to cut prices will hopefully not be a common issue.

The improvement in online feedback should lead to increased future bookings, so it may be that the new hotel generates a significantly improved return in the next year.

The operating profit margin has also deteriorated in the year. In addition to this fall, there is a significant one-off $4.5 million income relating to the disposal of investments, which shows a false position.

Without this gain on disposal, Schrute would have made a worrying loss from operations of $3.3 million. Analysing this further, it can be seen that the reason for the loss would be due to a significant increase in administrative expenses, which would be $30.1 million if the investment disposal is ignored.

Some of these expenses may be linked to the acquisition of Howard, such as professional fees, which will not be incurred in future years. There may also be some redundancy costs included if Schrute has merged administrative departments with Howard such as human resources.

A number of expenses are likely to be linked to the new hotel project in the year.

A large amount of these administrative expenses will hopefully relate to set up costs for the hotel and can be regarded as one-off expenses. Schrute has undertaken a significant marketing campaign to reverse their reputation.

Whilst these could be classed as one-off expenses, there will be many expenses included that will remain high in future periods. Staff numbers will have increased due to the hotel, and costs such as heating, lighting, and repairs will continue to be incurred each year.

There has not been a significant increase in distribution costs in the year. This could suggest that Schrute Farms have done significantly less business from the farming side of the business, or that the Howard has extremely low distribution costs.

While the distribution costs may have been saved, it is questionable whether it is wise to have diversified to avoid the impact of fuel prices. Howard appears to have smaller margins, and will incur significant heating and lighting costs, which are likely to rise in a similar manner to fuel costs.

The return on capital employed (ROCE) has also deteriorated in the year. This would actually be negative if the gain on investments had not been included, as Schrute would have been loss making.

As well as making less profit, the capital employed by Schrute has also increased significantly. New shares have been bought by the Schrute family, and a new loan has been taken out. All of this seems to have been due to the acquisition of Howard, which hasn't had a full year to generate profits.

It actually appears that Howard is a loss-making entity, as the non-controlling interest share of the profit is negative. This could mean that the rest of the Schrute group has remained profitable, with Howard generating a loss.

It could also be that there has been a significant impairment in the goodwill of Howard since acquisition. If Schrute uses the fair value method for valuing the non-controlling interest, the non-controlling interest will have an allocation of the impairment.

It may well be that in 20X4 the performance improves significantly as the new hotel has a full year's operation in the results and many of the set up costs will not be included.

Cash flow

The cash balance has fallen to $0.6 million. it should be noted that Schrute has undertaken a number of activities to raise cash in the year. Investments were sold for $15.5 million, $19 million was raised from a share issue and $20 million has been raised from debt finance. It seems that the vast majority of these funds were spent on the acquisition of Howard and the new hotel.

Looking at the other areas and their impact on cash flow, it can be seen that receivable days have decreased significantly in the year. With no indication of changes in customer terms for the farms, it is likely that this is the effect of Howard being largely cash based and having a positive impact on cash flow.

The inventory turnover period has reduced, which is likely to be due to Howard not having the same level of inventory, as inventory in a hotel may be limited to food and drink. A period of 51 days still seems potentially high for a company involved in the farming industry, and the inventory should be investigated to ensure that none of the produce has perished.

There has been the receipt of a $20 million loan in the year. It is unclear whether that is further investment from the Schrute family, or with an external source.

Conclusion

It is difficult to judge the success of the business as a whole in this transitional year. There are concerns over the acquisition of Howard. Whilst the revenue has increased significantly, Howard appears to have made a loss and put pressure onto the cash flow of the Schrute group.

The individual results of Howard need to be obtained for a more meaningful comparison to be made. From this, the performance of the new hotel could be judged further.

402 PITCARN

(a) **Ratios for the year ended 31 March 20X6:**

Gross profit margin	30%	(28,200/96,000) × 100
Operating margin	6%	(5,600/96,000) × 100
Interest cover	2.9 times	(5,600/(1,900)

In producing the consolidated information, Sitor must be added in for the year, with adjustments made to remove the intra-group sale, rent, interest and dividend.

	20X6 $000
Revenue (86,000 + 16,000 – 8,000 intra-group)	94,000
Cost of sales (63,400 + 10,400 – 8,000 intra-group)	(65,800)
Gross profit	28,200
Other income (3,400 – 300 rent - 1,000 dividend – 500 interest)	1,600
Operating expenses (21,300 + 3,200 – 300 rent)	(24,200)
Profit from operations	5,600
Finance costs (1,500 + 900 – 500 intra-group)	(1,900)

(b) Looking at the figures calculated for the Pitcarn group, it seems that performance has deteriorated in terms of revenue, margins and interest cover.

This would suggest that the disposal of Sitor is a mistake, as the group appear to be performing worse without Sitor than when Sitor was included as a subsidiary.

Looking at Sitor's individual results appears to confirm this, as Sitor has profit margins which are higher than the rest of the group, both in terms of gross and operating margin.

A closer examination of Sitor's results highlights an issue to be aware of. Half of Sitor's revenue is made by selling to Pitcarn, and this is done at an extremely high margin of 45%. This is much higher than the margin of 35% made overall, and means that the other half of Sitor's sales must be made at a margin of 25%. This means that the external sales of Sitor are actually made at a lower gross margin than the rest of the group.

It is possible that Pitcarn deliberately purchased goods from Sitor at an inflated price in order to demonstrate a stronger performance in Sitor in order to achieve a good selling price.

While this allowed, it highlights the problem with analysing a company's performance on its individual financial statements if it is part of a group, as prices can be manipulated within the group to artificially inflate the performance of one part.

A similar fear arises in respect of the operating margin. Sitor uses Pitcarn's properties, and is paying a lower rate than the market rate of rent. This will again artificially inflate the margin made by Sitor, as Pitcarn bear the majority of the property costs without recharging an accurate rate of rent.

It appears that Pitcarn have suffered lower margins in order to make the margins look better in Sitor by paying a high price for goods and not charging a market rate of rent. Pitcarn has taken a further $1.5 million cash out of Sitor during the year, through the receipt of a $1 million dividend and $500,000 interest. The loan agreement should be investigated further in order to assess if the interest charged was at market rates or not.

Following the disposal of Sitor, Pitcarn will lose at least $1.3 million of income through no longer obtaining a dividend or rent from the properties. For a more detailed analysis of future prospects, it will be important to speak to Pitcarn regarding the excess office space and whether there are plans to utilise it themselves or to rent it to a third party. The loan agreement with Sitor should also be examined to see if this will change following the sale. It may be that the interest rate increases now Sitor is no longer in the group, or the loan may need repaying by the new Sitor owners.

The one area where Sitor underperformed relative to the rest of the Pitcarn group is in terms of interest cover, with profits able to cover interest less times. Again, a review of the loan agreement with Pitcarn will be able to assess if this interest rate is at market rate, as Pitcarn may be charging a higher rate of interest than market rates in exchange for the cheaper rent and higher priced goods.

Examination should also be made as to whether Pitcarn will still need Sitor to supply goods. If so, supplies may be harder to obtain now that Sitor is no longer in the group.

Overall, the sale of Sitor appears to be a reasonable move. Whilst Sitor does appear to be making good profits, when the goods and rent with Pitcarn are adjusted to market values it is likely that Sitor would not be making significant profits. As long as Pitcarn is not reliant on Sitor as a supplier, this seems to be a reasonable move and one which may free up space in the premises to pursue more lucrative options.

(c) **Gain/loss on disposal:**

	$000
Proceeds	25,000
Goodwill at disposal (W1)	(5,000)
Net assets at disposal (10,000 share capital + 7,000 retained earnings)	(17,000)
Non-controlling interest at disposal (W2)	1,800
Profit on disposal	**4,800**

(W1) Goodwill:

	$000
Consideration	17,000
NCI at acquisition	1,000
Less: Net assets at acquisition (10,000 share capital + 3,000 retained earnings	(13,000)
Goodwill at acquisition	5,000

(W2) Non-Controlling Interest at disposal

	$000
NCI at acquisition	1,000
NCI share of Sitor's post acquisition retained earnings (20% × (7,000 – 3,000))	800
Non-Controlling Interest at disposal	1,800

FUNDAMENTALS LEVEL – SKILLS MODULE

Financial Reporting

Specimen Exam applicable from September 2016

Paper F7

Time allowed

Reading and planning: 15 minutes

Writing: 3 hours

This question paper is divided into three sections:

Section A – ALL 15 questions are compulsory and MUST be attempted

Section B – ALL 15 questions are compulsory and MUST be attempted

Section C – BOTH questions are compulsory and MUST be attempted

Do NOT open this question paper until instructed by the supervisor.

During reading and planning time only the question paper may be annotated. You must NOT write in your answer booklet until instructed by the supervisor.

Do NOT record any of your answers on the question paper.

This question paper must not be removed from the examination hall.

The Association of Chartered Certificate Accountants

SECTION A – Objective test (OT) questions

1   **Which of the following should be capitalised in the initial carrying amount of an item of plant?**

(1)   Cost of transporting the plant to the factory.

(2)   Cost of installing a new power supply required to operate the plant.

(3)   Cost of a three-year plant maintenance agreement.

(4)   Cost of a three-week training course for staff to operate the plant.

A   (1) and (3)

B   (1) and (2)

C   (2) and (4)

D   (3) and (4)

2   When a parent is evaluating the assets of a potential subsidiary, certain intangible assets can be recognised separately from goodwill, even though they have not been recognised in the subsidiary's own statement of financial position.

Which of the following is an example of an intangible asset of the subsidiary which may be recognised separately from goodwill when preparing consolidated financial statements?

A   A new research project which the subsidiary has correctly expensed to profit or loss but the directors of the parent have reliably assessed to have a substantial fair value.

B   A global advertising campaign which was concluded in the previous financial year and from which benefits are expected to flow in the future.

C   A contingent asset of the subsidiary from which the parent believes a flow of future economic benefits is possible.

D   A customer list which the directors are unable to value reliably.

3   On 1 October 20X4, Flash Co acquired an item of plant under a five-year finance lease agreement. The plant had a cash purchase cost of $25m. The agreement had an implicit finance cost of 10% per annum and required an immediate deposit of $2m and annual rentals of $6m paid on 30 September each year for five years.

What is the current liability for the leased plant in Flash Co's statement of financial position as at 30 September 20X5?

A $19,300,000

B $4,070,000

C $5,000,000

D $3,850,000

4 Financial statements represent transactions in words and numbers. To be useful, financial information must represent faithfully these transactions in terms of how they are reported.

Which of the following accounting treatments would be an example of faithful representation?

A Charging the rental payments for an item of plant to the statement of profit or loss where the rental agreement meets the criteria for a finance lease.

B Including a convertible loan note in equity on the basis that the holders are likely to choose the equity option on conversion.

C Treating redeemable preference shares as part of equity in the statement of financial position.

D Derecognising factored trade receivables sold without recourse to the seller.

5 On 1 October 20X4, Kalatra Co commenced drilling for oil from an undersea oilfield. Kalatra Co is required to dismantle the drilling equipment at the end of its five-year licence. This has an estimated cost of $30m on 30 September 20X9. Kalatra Co's cost of capital is 8% per annum and $1 in five years' time has a present value of 68 cents.

What is the provision which Kalatra Co would report in its statement of financial position as at 30 September 20X5 in respect of its oil operations?

A $32,400,000

B $22,032,000

C $20,400,000

D $1,632,000

6 When a single entity makes purchases or sales in a foreign currency, it will be necessary to translate the transactions into its functional currency before the transactions can be included in its financial records.

In accordance with IAS 21 The Effect of Changes in Foreign Currency Exchange Rates, which of the following foreign currency exchange rates may be used to translate the foreign currency purchases and sales?

(1) The rate which existed on the day that the purchase or sale took place.

(2) The rate which existed at the beginning of the accounting period.

(3) An average rate for the year, provided there have been no significant fluctuations throughout the year.

(4) The rate which existed at the end of the accounting period.

A (2) and (4)

B (1) only

C (3) only

D (1) and (3)

7   On 1 October 20X4, Hoy Co had $2.5 million of equity share capital (shares of 50 cents each) in issue.

No new shares were issued during the year ended 30 September 20X5, but on that date there were outstanding share options which had a dilutive effect equivalent to issuing 1.2 million shares for no consideration.

Hoy's profit after tax for the year ended 30 September 20X5 was $1,550,000.

In accordance with IAS 33 Earnings Per Share, what is Hoy's diluted earnings per share for the year ended 30 September 20X5?

    A $0.25

    B $0.41

    C $0.31

    D $0.42

8   Fork Co owns an 80% investment in Spoon Co which it purchased several years ago. The goodwill on acquisition was valued at $1,674,000 and there has been no impairment of that goodwill since the date of acquisition.

On 30 September 20X4, Fork Co disposed of its entire investment in Spoon Co, details of which are as follows:

	$000
Sales proceeds of Fork Co's entire investment in Spoon Co	5,580
Cost of Fork Co's entire investment in Spoon Co	3,720

Immediately before the disposal, the consolidated financial statements of Fork Co included the following amounts in respect of Spoon Co:

	$000
Carrying amount of the net assets (excluding goodwill)	4,464
Carrying amount of the non-controlling interests	900

What is the profit/loss on disposal (before tax) which will be recorded in Fork Co's CONSOLIDATED statement of profit or loss for the year ended 30 September 20X4?

    A $1,860,000 profit

    B $2,016,000 profit

    C $342,000 profit

    D $558,000 loss

9 Consolidated financial statements are presented on the basis that the companies within the group are treated as if they are a single economic entity.

Which of the following are requirements of preparing consolidated financial statements?

(1) All subsidiaries must adopt the accounting policies of the parent in their individual financial statements.

(2) Subsidiaries with activities which are substantially different to the activities of other members of the group should not be consolidated.

(3) All entity financial statements within a group should normally be prepared to the same accounting year end prior to consolidation.

(4) Unrealised profits within the group must be eliminated from the consolidated financial statements.

A   (1) and (3)

B   (2) and (4)

C   (3) and (4)

D   (1) and (2)

10 A parent company sells goods to its 80% owned subsidiary during the financial year, some of which remains in inventory at the year end.

What is the adjustment required in the consolidated statement of financial position to eliminate any unrealised profit in inventory?

A	Debit	Group retained earnings
	Credit	Inventory
B	Debit	Group retained earnings
	Debit	Non-controlling interest
	Credit	Inventory
C	Debit	Inventory
	Credit	Group retained earnings
D	Debit	Inventory
	Credit	Group retained earnings
	Credit	Non-controlling interest

11 Caddy Co acquired 240,000 of Ambel Co's 800,000 equity shares for $6 per share on 1 October 20X4. Ambel Co's profit after tax for the year ended 30 September 20X5 was $400,000 and it paid an equity dividend on 20 September 20X5 of $150,000.

On the assumption that Ambel Co is an associate of Caddy Co, what would be the carrying amount of the investment in Ambel Co in the consolidated statement of financial position of Caddy Co as at 30 September 20X5?

A $1,560,000

B $1,395,000

C $1,515,000

D $1,690,000

12 Quartile Co is in the jewellery retail business which can be assumed to be highly seasonal. For the year ended 30 September 20X5, Quartile Co assessed its operating performance by comparing selected accounting ratios with those of its business sector average as provided by an agency. Assume that the business sector used by the agency is a meaningful representation of Quartile Co's business.

Which of the following circumstances may invalidate the comparison of Quartile Co's ratios with those of the sector average?

(1)   In the current year, Quartile Co has experienced significant rising costs for its purchases.

(2)   The sector average figures are compiled from companies whose year ends are between 1 July 20X5 and 30 September 20X5.

(3)   Quartile Co does not revalue its properties, but is aware that other entities in this sector do.

(4)   During the year, Quartile Co discovered an error relating to the inventory count at 30 September 20X4. This error was correctly accounted for in the financial statements for the current year ended 30 September 20X5.

A   (1) and (3)

B   (2) and (4)

C   (2) and (3)

D   (1) and (4)

13 **Which of the following criticisms does NOT apply to historical cost financial statements during a period of rising prices?**

A   They are difficult to verify because transactions could have happened many years ago

B   They contain mixed values; some items are at current values and some are at out of date values

C   They understate assets and overstate profit

D   They overstate gearing in the statement of financial position

14 The following information has been taken or calculated from Fowler's financial statements for the year ended 30 September 20X5:

Cash cycle at 30 September 20X5	70 days
Inventory turnover	six times
Year-end trade payables at 30 September 20X5	$230,000
Credit purchases for the year ended 30 September 20X5	$2 million
Cost of sales for the year ended 30 September 20X5	$1.8 million

What is Fowler's trade receivables collection period as at 30 September 20X5?

A   106 days

B   89 days

C   56 days

D   51 days

15 On 1 October 20X4, Pyramid Co acquired 80% of Square Co's 9 million equity shares. At the date of acquisition, Square Co had an item of plant which had a fair value of $3m in excess of its carrying amount. At the date of acquisition it had a useful life of five years. Pyramid Co's policy is to value non-controlling interests at fair value at the date of acquisition. For this purpose, Square Co's shares had a value of $3.50 each at that date. In the year ended 30 September 20X5, Square Co reported a profit of $8m.

At what amount should the non-controlling interests in Square Co be valued in the consolidated statement of financial position of the Pyramid group as at 30 September 20X5?

A $26,680,000

B $7,900,000

C $7,780,000

D $12,220,000

SECTION B – OT cases

The following scenario relates to questions 16–20.

Telepath Co has a year end of 30 September and owns an item of plant which it uses to produce and package pharmaceuticals. The plant cost $750,000 on 1 October 20X0 and, at that date, had an estimated useful life of five years. A review of the plant on 1 April 20X3 concluded that the plant would last for a further three and a half years and that its fair value was $560,000.

Telepath Co adopts the policy of revaluing its non-current assets to their fair value but does not make an annual transfer from the revaluation surplus to retained earnings to represent the additional depreciation charged due to the revaluation.

On 30 September 20X3, Telepath Co was informed by a major customer that it would no longer be placing orders with Telepath Co. As a result, Telepath revised its estimates that net cash inflows earned from the plant for the next three years would be:

Year ended 30 September:

	$
20X4	220,000
20X5	180,000
20X6	200,000

Telepath Co's cost of capital is 10% which results in the following discount factors:

Value of $1 at 30 September:

20X4	0.91
20X5	0.83
20X6	0.75

Telepath Co also owns Rilda Co, a 100% subsidiary, which is treated as a cash generating unit. On 30 September 20X3, there was an impairment to Rilda's assets of $3,500,000. The carrying amount of the assets of Rilda Co immediately before the impairment were:

	$
Goodwill	2,000,000
Factory building	4,000,000
Plant	3,500,000
Receivables and cash (at recoverable amount)	2,500,000
	————
	12,000,000
	————

16 In accordance with IAS 36 Impairment of Assets, which of the following explains the impairment of an asset and how to calculate its recoverable amount?

A An asset is impaired when the carrying amount exceeds its recoverable amount and the recoverable amount is the higher of its fair value less costs of disposal and its value in use.

B An asset is impaired when the recoverable amount exceeds its carrying amount and the recoverable amount is the lower of its fair value less costs of disposal and its value in use.

C An asset is impaired when the recoverable amount exceeds its carrying amount and the recoverable amount is the higher of its fair value less costs of disposal and its value in use.

D An asset is impaired when the carrying amount exceeds its recoverable amount and the recoverable amount is the lower of its fair value less costs of disposal and its value in use.

17 Prior to considering any impairment, what is the carrying amount of Telepath Co's plant and the balance on the revaluation surplus at 30 September 20X3?

	Plant carrying amount	Revaluation surplus
	$000	$000
A	480	nil
B	300	185
C	480	185
D	300	nil

18 What is the value in use of Telepath Co's plant as at 30 September 20X3?

A $600,000

B $450,000

C $499,600

D $nil

19 Which of the following are TRUE in accordance with IAS 36 Impairment of Assets?

(1) A cash generating unit is the smallest identifiable group of assets for which individual cash flows can be identified and measured.

(2) When considering the impairment of a cash generating unit, the calculation of the carrying amount and the recoverable amount does not need to be based on exactly the same group of net assets.

(3) When it is not possible to calculate the recoverable amount of a single asset, then that of its cash generating unit should be measured instead.

A (1) only

B (2) and (3)

C (3) only

D (1) and (3)

20 What is the carrying amount of Rilda Co's plant at 30 September 20X3 after the impairment loss has been correctly allocated to its assets?

A $2,479,000

B $2,800,000

C $2,211,000

D $3,500,000

The following scenario relates to questions 21–25.

At a board meeting in June 20X3, Neutron Co's directors made the decision to close down one of its factories by 30 September 20X3 and market both the building and the plant for sale. The decision had been made public, was communicated to all affected parties and was fully implemented by 30 September 20X3.

The directors of Neutron Co have provided the following information relating to the closure:

Of the factory's 250 employees, 50 will be retrained and deployed to other subsidiaries within the Neutron group during the year ended 30 September 20X4 at a cost of $125,000. The remainder accepted redundancy at an average cost of $5,000 each.

The factory's plant had a carrying amount of $2.2 million, but is only expected to sell for $500,000, incurring $50,000 of selling costs. The factory itself is expected to sell for a profit of $1.2 million.

The company also rented a number of machines in the factory under operating leases which have an average of three years to run after 30 September 20X3. The present value of these future lease payments at 30 September 20X3 was $1 million, however, the lessor has stated that they will accept $850,000 if paid on 30 October 20X3 as a full settlement.

Penalty payments, due to the non-completion of supply contracts, are estimated to be $200,000, 50% of which is expected to be recovered from Neutron Co's insurers.

21 Which of the following must exist for an operation to be classified as a discontinued operation in accordance with IFRS 5 Non-current Assets Held for Sale and Discontinued Operations?

(1)   The operation represents a separate major line of business or geographical area.

(2)   The operation is a subsidiary.

(3)   The operation has been sold or is held for sale.

(4)   The operation is considered not to be capable of making a future profit following a period of losses.

A   (2) and (4)

B   (3) and (4)

C   (1) and (3)

D   (1) and (2)

22   IFRS 5 Non-current Assets Held for Sale and Discontinued Operations prescribes the recognition criteria for non-current assets held for sale. For an asset or a disposal group to be classified as held for sale, the sale must be highly probable.

Which of the following must apply for the sale to be considered highly probable?

(1)   A buyer must have been located.

(2)   The asset must be marketed at a reasonable price.

(3)   Management must be committed to a plan to sell the asset.

(4)   The sale must be expected to take place within the next six months.

A   (2) and (3)

B   (3) and (4)

C   (1) and (4)

D   (1) and (2)

23   **What is the employee cost associated with the closure and sale of Neutron Co's factory which should be charged to profit or loss for the year ended 30 September 20X3?**

A $125,000

B $1,250,000

C $1,125,000

D $1,000,000

24   **What is the profit or loss on discontinued operations relating to property, plant and equipment for the year ended 30 September 20X3?**

A $1.75 million loss

B $1.75 million profit

C $550,000 loss

D $550,000 profit

25   **In respect of the operating leases and penalty payments, what provision is required in the statement of financial position of Neutron Co as at 30 September 20X3?**

A $950,000

B $1,200,000

C $1,050,000

D $1,100,000

The following scenario relates to questions 26–30.

Speculate Co is preparing its financial statements for the year ended 30 September 20X3. The following issues are relevant:

1   Financial assets

Shareholding A – a long-term investment in 10,000 of the equity shares of another company. These shares were acquired on 1 October 20X2 at a cost of $3.50 each. Transaction costs of 1% of the purchase price were incurred. On 30 September 20X3 the fair value of these shares is $4.50 each.

Shareholding B – a short-term speculative investment in 2,000 of the equity shares of another company. These shares were acquired on 1 December 20X2 at a cost of $2.50 each. Transaction costs of 1% of the purchase price were incurred. On 30 September 20X3 the fair value of these shares is $3.00 each.

Where possible, Speculate Co makes an irrevocable election for the fair value movements on financial assets to be reported in other comprehensive income.

2   Taxation

The existing debit balance on the current tax account of $2.4m represents the over/under provision of the tax liability for the year ended 30 September 20X2. A provision of $28m is required for income tax for the year ended 30 September 20X3. The existing credit balance on the deferred tax account is $2.5m and the provision required at 30 September 20X3 is $4.4m.

3   Revenue

On 1 October 20X2, Speculate Co sold one of its products for $10 million. As part of the sale agreement, Speculate Co is committed to the ongoing servicing of the product until 30 September 20X5 (i.e. three years after the sale). The sale value of this service has been included in the selling price of $10 million. The estimated cost to Speculate Co of the servicing is $600,000 per annum and Speculate Co's gross profit margin on this type of servicing is 25%. Ignore discounting.

---

26   Which of the following meet the definition of a financial asset in accordance with IFRS 9 Financial Instruments?

(1)   An equity instrument of another entity.

(2)   A contract to exchange financial instruments with another entity under conditions which are potentially favourable.

(3)   A contract to exchange financial instruments with another entity under conditions which are potentially unfavourable.

(4)   Cash.

A   (1) and (2) only

B   (1), (2) and (4)

C   (1), (3) and (4)

D   (4) only

27 In respect of the financial assets of Speculate Co, what amount will be included in other comprehensive income for the year ended 30 September 20X3?

A $9,650

B $10,650

C $10,000

D $nil

28 What is the total amount which will be charged to the statement of profit or loss for the year ended 30 September 20X3 in respect of taxation?

A $28,000,000

B $30,400,000

C $32,300,000

D $29,900,000

29 What is the amount of deferred income which Speculate Co should recognise in its statement of financial position as at 30 September 20X3 relating to the contract for the supply and servicing of products?

A $1.2 million

B $1.6 million

C $600,000

D $1.5 million

30 Which of the following are TRUE in respect of the income which Speculate Co has deferred at 30 September 20X3?

(1) The deferred income will be split evenly between the current and non-current liabilities in Speculate Co's statement of financial position as at 30 September 20X3.

(2) The costs associated with the deferred income of Speculate Co should be recognised in the statement of profit or loss at the same time as the revenue is recognised.

(3) The deferred income can only be recognised as revenue by Speculate Co when there is a signed written contract of service with its customer.

(4) When recognising the revenue associated with the service contract of Speculate Co, the stage of its completion is irrelevant.

A (1) and (2)

B (3) and (4)

C (2) and (3)

D (1) and (4)

SECTION C – Constructed response (long questions)

1 KANDY

After preparing a draft statement of profit or loss for the year ended 30 September 20X5 and adding the current year's draft profit (before any adjustments required by notes (i) to (iii) below) to retained earnings, the summarised trial balance of Kandy Co as at 30 September 20X5 is:

	$000	$000
Equity shares of $1 each		20,000
Retained earnings as at 30 September 20X5		15,500
Proceeds of 6% loan note (note (i))		30,000
Investment properties at fair value (note (ii))	20,000	
Land ($5 million) and buildings – at cost (note (ii))	35,000	
Plant and equipment – at cost (note (ii))	58,500	
Accumulated depreciation at 1 October 20X4: buildings		20,000
plant and equipment		34,500
Current assets	68,700	
Current liabilities		43,400
Deferred tax (notes (ii) and (iii))		2,500
Interest paid (note (i))	1,800	
Current tax (note (iii))		1,100
Suspense account (note (ii))		17,000
	———	———
	184,000	184,000
	———	———

The following notes are relevant:

(i) The loan note was issued on 1 October 20X4 and incurred issue costs of $1 million which were charged to profit or loss. Interest of $1.8 million ($30 million at 6%) was paid on 30 September 20X5. The loan is redeemable on 30 September 20X9 at a substantial premium which gives an effective interest rate of 9% per annum. No other repayments are due until 30 September 20X9.

(ii) Non-current assets:

On 1 October 20X4, Kandy owned two investment properties. The first property had a carrying amount of $15 million and was sold on 1 December 20X4 for $17 million. The disposal proceeds have been credited to a suspense account in the trial balance above. On 31 December 20X4, the second property became owner occupied and so was transferred to land and buildings at its fair value of $6 million. Its remaining useful life on 31 December 20X4 was considered to be 20 years. Ignore any deferred tax implications of this fair value.

The price of property has increased significantly in recent years and so the directors decided to revalue the land and buildings. The directors accepted the report of an independent surveyor who, on 1 October 20X4, valued the land at $8 million and the buildings at $39 million on that date. This revaluation specifically excludes the transferred investment property described above. The remaining life of these buildings at 1 October 20X4 was 15 years. Kandy does not make an annual transfer to retained profits to reflect the realisation of the revaluation gain; however, the revaluation will give rise to a deferred tax liability. The income tax rate applicable to Kandy is 20%.

Plant and equipment is depreciated at 12½% per annum using the reducing balance method.

No depreciation has yet been charged on any non-current asset for the year ended 30 September 20X5.

(iii) A provision of $2.4 million is required for income tax on the profit for the year to 30 September 20X5. The balance on current tax in the trial balance is the under/over provision of tax for the previous year. In addition to the temporary differences relating to the information in note (ii), Kandy has further taxable temporary differences of $10 million as at 30 September 20X5.

Required:

(a) **Prepare a schedule of adjustments required to the retained earnings of Kandy Co as at 30 September 20X5 as a result of the information in notes (i) to (iii) above.**

(8 marks)

(b) **Prepare the statement of financial position of Kandy Co as at 30 September 20X5.**

Note: The notes to the statement of financial position are not required.

(9 marks)

(c) **Prepare the extracts from Kandy Co's statement of cash flows for operating and investing activities for the year ended 30 September 20X5 which relate to property, plant and equipment.**

(3 marks)

(Total: 20 marks)

2 TANGIER

The summarised consolidated financial statements for the year ended 30 September 20X5 (and the comparative figures) for the Tangier group are shown below.

Consolidated statements of profit or loss for the year ended 30 September:

	20X5	20X4
	$m	$m
Revenue	2,700	1,820
Cost of sales	(1,890)	(1,092)
Gross profit	810	728
Administrative expense	(345)	(200)
Distribution costs	(230)	(130)
Finance costs	(40)	(5)
Profit before taxation	195	393
Income tax expense	(60)	(113)
Profit for the year	135	280

Consolidated statements of financial position as at 30 September:

	20X5 $m	20X5 $m	20X4 $m	20X4 $m
Non-current assets				
Property, plant and equipment		680		310
Intangible asset: manufacturing licences		300		100
goodwill		230		200
		1,210		610
Current assets				
Inventory	200		110	
Trade receivables	195		75	
Bank	nil	395	120	305
Total assets		1,605		915
Equity and liabilities				
Equity shares of $1 each		330		250
Other components of equity		100		nil
Retained earnings		375		295
		805		545
Non-current liabilities				
5% secured loan notes	100		100	
10% secured loan notes	300	400	nil	100
Current liabilities				
Bank overdraft	110		nil	
Trade payables	210		160	
Current tax payable	80	400	110	270
Total equity and liabilities		1,605		915

At 1 October 20X4, the Tangier group consisted of the parent, Tangier Co, and two wholly owned subsidiaries which had been owned for many years. On 1 January 20X5, Tangier Co purchased a third 100% owned investment in a subsidiary called Raremetal Co. The consideration paid for Raremetal Co was a combination of cash and shares. The cash payment was partly funded by the issue of 10% loan notes. On 1 January 20X5, Tangier Co also won a tender for a new contract to supply aircraft engines which Tangier Co manufactures under a recently acquired long-term licence. Raremetal Co was purchased with a view to securing the supply of specialised materials used in the manufacture of these engines. The bidding process had been very competitive and Tangier Co had to increase its manufacturing capacity to fulfil the contract.

Required:

(a)   Comment on how the new contract and the purchase of Raremetal Co may have affected the comparability of the consolidated financial statements of Tangier Co for the years ended 30 September 20X4 and 20X5.   **(5 marks)**

(b)   Calculate appropriate ratios and comment on Tangier Co's profitability and gearing. Your analysis should identify instances where the new contract and the purchase of Raremetal Co have limited the usefulness of the ratios and your analysis.

   Note: Your ratios should be based on the consolidated financial statements provided and you should not attempt to adjust for the effects of the new contract or the consolidation. Working capital and liquidity ratios are not required.   **(12 marks)**

(c)   Explain what further information you might require to make your analysis more meaningful.   **(3 marks)**

                                                                    (Total: 20 marks)

SECTION A – Answers to Objective Test (OT) questions

1   B

2   A

3   B

25,000 – 2,000 = 23,000 + 2,300 (10% int) – 6,000 (pmt) = 19,300

19,300 + 1,930 (10% int) – 6,000 (pmt) = 15,230

Current liability = 19,300 – 15,230 = $4,070

4   D

5   B

Dismantling provision at 1 October 20X4 is $20.4 million (30,000 × 0.68) discounted

This will increase by an 8% finance cost by 30 September 20X5 = $22,032,000

6   D

7   A

(1,550/(2,500 × 2 + 1,200)) = $0.25

8   C

		$000
Sales proceeds		5,580
Net assets at disposal	4,464	
Goodwill at disposal	1,674	
Less: carrying value of NCI	(900)	(5,238)
		342

9   C

10   A

11   C

	$000
Cost (240,000 × $6)	1,440
Share of associate's profit (400 × 240/800)	120
Less dividend received (150 × 240/800)	(45)
	1,515

12   C

13   A

14   D

Inventory turnover is 61 days (365/6).

Trade payables period is 42 days (230,000 × 365/2 million).

Therefore, receivables collection period is 51 days (70 – 61 + 42).

15   C

	$000
FV NCI at 1 October 14 (9000 × 20% × $3.50)	6,300
Post-acquisition profit (8000 – (3000/5)) = 7,400 at 20%	1,480
	7,780

SECTION B – Answers to OT cases

16   A

17   C

Annual depreciation prior to the revaluation is $150,000 (750/5). At the date of revaluation (1 April 20X3), the carrying amount is $375,000 (750 – (150 × 2.5 yrs)). Revalued to $560,000 with a remaining life of 3.5 years results in a depreciation charge of $160,000 per annum which means $80,000 for six months. The carrying amount at 30 September 20X3 is therefore $480,000 (560 – 80). Alternative calculation: $560,000 – ($560,000/3.5 × 6/12) = $480,000.

The revaluation surplus has a balance of $185,000 (560,000 – 375,000).

18   C

		Cash flow	Discount factor at 10%	Present value
		$000		$000
Year ended:	30 September 20X4	220	0.91	200.2
	30 September 20X5	180	0.83	149.4
	30 September 20X6	200	0.75	150.0
				————
				499.6
				————

19   D

20   B

	Carrying amount before	Impairment loss	Carrying amount after
	$000	$000	$000
Goodwill	2,000	2,000	Nil
Property	4,000	800	3,200
Plant	3,500	700	2,800
Cash and receivables	2,500	Nil	2,500
	————	————	————
	12,000	3,500	8,500
	————	————	————

21   C

22   A

23 D

200 employees at $5,000 = $1,000,000 redundancy costs. The retraining costs are a future cost.

24 A

Impairment loss on plant is $1,750,000 (2,200,000 – (500,000 – 50,000)).

25 C

Onerous contract $850,000 + penalty payments $200,000 = $1,050,000. The possible insurance receipt should be ignored as there is no certainty that it would be received and it would not be netted off against the provision anyway.

26 B

27 A

Shareholding A is not held for trading as an election made – FVTOCI.

Shareholding B is held for trading and so FVTPL (transaction costs are not included in carrying amount).

Cost of shareholding A is 10,000 × $3.50 × 1.01 = $35,350.

FV at 30 September 20X3 10,000 × $4.50 = $45,000.

Gain = 45,000 – 35,350 = $9,650.

28 C

	$000
DT provision required at 30 September 20X3	4,400
DT Provision at 1 October 20X2	(2,500)
	1,900
Write off of the overprovision for the year ended 30 September 20X2	2,400
Income tax for the year ended 30 September 20X3	28,000
Charge for the year ended 30 September 20X3	32,300

29 B

At 30 September 20X3 there are two more years of servicing work, thus $1.6 million ((600,000 × 2) × 100/75) must be treated as deferred income.

30 A

SECTION C – Constructed response (long questions)

1   KANDY

(a)   Kandy Co – Schedule of retained earnings of Kandy as at 30 September 20X5

	$000
Retained earnings per trial balance	15,500
Adjustments re:	
Note (i)	
Add back issue costs of loan note (w (i))	1,000
Loan finance costs (29,000 × 9% (w (i)))	(2,610)
Note (ii)	
Gain on disposal of investment property (17,000 – 15,000)	2,000
Gain on revaluation of investment property prior to transfer (6,000 – 5,000)	1,000
Depreciation of buildings (w (ii))	(2,825)
Depreciation of plant and equipment (w (ii))	(3,000)
Note (iii)	
Income tax expense (w (iii))	(800)
Adjusted retained earnings	10,265

(b)   Kandy Co – Statement of financial position as at 30 September 20X5

	$000	$000
Assets		
Non-current assets		
Property, plant and equipment (50,175 + 21,000 (w (ii)))		71,175
Current assets (per trial balance)		68,700
Total assets		139,875
Equity and liabilities		
Equity		
Equity shares of $1 each		20,000
Revaluation surplus (32,000 – 6,400 (w (ii) and (iii)))	25,600	
Retained earnings (from (a))	10,265	35,865
		55,865

Non-current liabilities		
Deferred tax (w (iii))	8,400	
6% loan note (w (i))	29,810	38,210
Current liabilities		
Per trial balance	43,400	
Current tax payable	2,400	45,800
Total equity and liabilities		139,875

Workings (monetary figures in brackets in $000)

(i) **Loan note**

The issue costs should be deducted from the proceeds of the loan note and not charged as an expense. The finance cost of the loan note, at the effective rate of 9% applied to the carrying amount of the loan note of $29 million (30,000 – 1,000), is $2,610,000. The interest actually paid is $1.8 million. The difference between these amounts of $810,000 (2,610 – 1,800) is added to the carrying amount of the loan note to give $29,810,000 (29,000 + 810) for inclusion as a non-current liability in the statement of financial position.

(ii) **Non-current assets**

Land and buildings

The gain on revaluation and carrying amount of the land and buildings will be:

	$000
Carrying amount at 1 October 20X4 (35,000 – 20,000)	15,000
Revaluation at that date (8,000 + 39,000)	47,000
Gain on revaluation	32,000
Buildings depreciation for the year ended 30 September 20X5:	
Land and buildings existing at 1 October 20X4 (39,000/15 years)	2,600
Transferred investment property (6,000/20 × 9/12)	225
	2,825
Carrying amount at 30 September 20X5 (47,000 + 6,000 – 2,825)	50,175

Plant and equipment

	$000
Carrying amount at 1 October 20X4 (58,500 – 34,500)	24,000
Depreciation for year ended 30 September 20X5 (12½% reducing balance)	(3,000)
Carrying amount at 30 September 20X5	21,000

(iii) **Taxation**

Income tax expense

	$000
Provision for year ended 30 September 20X5	2,400
Less over provision in previous year	(1,100)
Deferred tax (see below)	(500)
	800

Deferred tax

	$000
Provision required at 30 September 20X5 ((10,000 + 32,000) × 20%)	8,400
Provision at 1 October 20X4	(2,500)
Movement in provision	5,900
Charge to revaluation of land and buildings (32,000 × 20%)	(6,400)
Balance – credit to profit or loss	(500)

(c)

	$000
Cash flows from operating activities:	
Add back depreciation	5,825
Deduct gain on revaluation of investment property	(1,000)
Deduct gain on disposal of investment property	(2,000)
Cash flows from investing activities:	
Investment property disposal proceeds	17,000

		Marking scheme	Marks
(a)		**Schedule of retained earnings as at 30 September 20X4**	
		Retained earnings per trial balance	½
		Issue costs	1
		Loan finance costs	1
		Gains on investment properties	1
		Depreciation charges	3
		Income tax expense	1½
(b)		**Statement of financial position**	
		Property, plant and equipment	2
		Current assets	½
		Equity shares	½
		Revaluation surplus	2
		Deferred tax	1
		6% loan note	1½
		Current liabilities (per trial balance)	½
		Current tax payable	1
(c)		**Extracts from the statement of cash flows**	
		Cash flows from operating activities:	
		Add back depreciation	1
		Less gain on revaluation of investment property	½
		Less gain on disposal of investment property	½
		Cash flows from investing activities:	
		Investment property disposal proceeds	1
	Total		**20**

2 TANGIER

(a) **Note: References to '20X5' are in respect of the year ended 30 September 20X5 and '20X4' refers to the year ended 30 September 20X4.**

The key matter to note is that the ratios for 20X4 and 20X5 will not be directly comparable because two significant events, the acquisition of Raremetal Co and securing the new contract, have occurred between these dates. This means that the underlying financial statements are not directly comparable. For example, the 20X4 statement of profit or loss (SOPL) will not include the results of Raremetal Co or the effect of the new contract. However, the 20X5 SOPL will contain nine months of the results of Raremetal Co (although intra-group transactions will have been eliminated) and nine months of the effects of the new contract (which may have resulted in either a net profit or loss). Likewise, the 20X4 statement of financial position does not contain any of Raremetal Co's assets and liabilities, whereas that of 20X5 contains all of the net assets of Raremetal Co and the cost of the new licence. This does not mean that comparisons between the two years are not worthwhile, just that they need to be treated with caution. For some ratios, it may be necessary to exclude all of the subsidiaries from the analysis and use the single entity financial statements of Tangier Co as a basis for comparison with the performance of previous years. Similarly, it may still be possible to compare some of the ratios of the Tangier group with those of other groups in the same sector although not all groups will have experienced similar acquisitions.

Assuming there has been no impairment of goodwill, the investment in Raremetal Co has resulted in additional goodwill of $30 million which means that the investment has cost more than the carrying amount of Raremetal Co's net assets. Although there is no indication of the precise cost, it is known to have been achieved by a combination of a share exchange (hence the $180 million new issue of shares) and a cash element (funded from the proceeds of the loan issue and the decrease in the bank balance). Any intra-group sales have been eliminated on consolidation and it is not possible to determine in which individual company any profit on these intra-group sales will be reported; it is therefore difficult to measure any benefits of the investment. Indeed, the benefit of the investment might not be a financial one but merely to secure the supply of raw materials. It would be useful to establish the cost of the investment and the profit (if any) contributed by Raremetal Co so that an assessment of the benefit of the investment might be made.

(b)   **Relevant ratios:**

	20X5	20X4
Gross profit margin % (810/2,700 × 100)	30.0%	40.0%
Operating profit margin (235/2,700 × 100)	8.7%	21.9%
ROCE (235/(805 + 400))	19.5%	61.7%
Non-current asset turnover (2,700/1,210)	2.23 times	2.98 times
Debt/equity (400/805)	49.7%	18.3%
Interest cover (235/40)	5.9 times	79.6 times

All of the issues identified in part (a) make a comparison of ratios difficult and, if more information was available, then some adjustments may be required. For example, if it is established that the investment is not generating any benefits, then it might be argued that the inclusion of the goodwill in the ROCE and non-current asset turnover is unjustified (it may be impaired and should be written off). Goodwill has not been excluded from any of the following ratios.

The increase in revenues of 48.4% (880/1,820 × 100) in 20X5 will be partly due to the consolidation of Raremetal Co and the revenues associated with the new contract. Yet, despite these increased revenues, the company has suffered a dramatic fall in its profitability. This has been caused by a combination of a falling gross profit margin (from 40% in 20X4 to only 30% in 20X5) and markedly higher operating overheads (operating profit margin has fallen from 21.9% in 20X4 to 8.7% in 20X5). Again, it is important to note that some of these costs will be attributable to the consolidation of Raremetal Co and some to the new contract. It could be speculated that the 73% increase in administrative expenses may be due to one-off costs associated with the tendering process (consultancy fees, etc) and the acquisition of Raremetal Co and the 77% increase in higher distribution costs could be due to additional freight/packing/insurance cost of the engines, delivery distances may also be longer (even to foreign countries) (although some of the increase in distribution costs may also be due to consolidation).

This is all reflected in the ROCE falling from an impressive 61.7% in 20X4 to only 19.5% in 20X5 (though even this figure is respectable). The fall in the ROCE is attributable to a dramatic fall in profit margin at operating level (from 21.9% in 20X4 to only 8.7% in 20X5) which has been compounded by a reduction in the non-current asset turnover, with only $2.23 being generated from every $1 invested in non-current assets in 20X5 (from $2.98 in 20X4).

The information in the question points strongly to the possibility (even probability) that the new contract may be responsible for much of the deterioration in Tangier Co's operating performance. For example, it is likely that the new contract may account for some of the increased revenue; however, the bidding process was 'very competitive' which may imply that Tangier Co had to cut its prices (and therefore its profit margin) in order to win the contract.

The costs of fulfilling the contract have also been heavy: investment in property, plant and equipment has increased by $370 million (at carrying amount), representing an increase of 61% (no doubt some of this increase will be due to the acquisition of Raremetal Co). The increase in licence costs to manufacture the new engines has cost $200 million plus any amortisation and there is also the additional goodwill of $30 million.

An eight-fold increase in finance cost caused by the increased borrowing at double the interest rate of the borrowing in 20X4 and (presumably) some overdraft interest has led to the dramatic fall in the company's interest cover (from 79.6 in 20X4 to only 5.9 in 20X5). The finance cost of the new $300 million 10% loan notes to partly fund the investment in Raremetal Co and other non-current assets has also increased debt/equity (one form of gearing measure) from 18.3% in 20X4 to 49.7% in 20X5 despite also issuing $180 million in new equity shares. At this level, particularly in view of its large increase from 20X4, it may give debt holders (and others) cause for concern as there is increased risk for all Tangier Co's lenders. If it could be demonstrated that the overdraft could not be cleared for some time, this would be an argument for including it in the calculation of debt/equity, making the 20X5 gearing level even worse. It is also apparent from the movement in the retained earnings that Tangier Co paid a dividend during 20X5 of $55 million (295,000 + 135,000 – 375,000) which may be a questionable policy when the company is raising additional finance through borrowings and contributes substantially to Tangier Co's overdraft.

Overall, the acquisition of Raremetal Co to secure supplies appears to have been an expensive strategy, perhaps a less expensive one might have been to enter into a long-term supply contract with Raremetal Co.

(c) Further information which would be useful to obtain would therefore include:

   (i)   The cost of the investment in Raremetal Co, the carrying amount of the assets acquired and whether Tangier Co has carried out a goodwill impairment test as required under IFRS.

   (ii) The benefits generated from the investment; for example, Raremetal Co's individual financial statements and details of sales to external customers (not all of these benefits will be measurable in financial terms).

   (iii) The above two pieces of information would demonstrate whether the investment in Raremetal Co had been worthwhile.

   (iv) The amount of intra-group sales made during the year and those expected to be made in the short to medium term.

   (v)   The pricing strategy agreed with Raremetal Co so that the effects on the profits reported in the individual financial statements of Raremetal Co and Tangier Co can be more readily determined.

   (vi) More information is needed to establish if the new contract has been detrimental to Tangier Co's performance. The contract was won sometime between 1 October 20X4 and 1 January 20X5 and there is no information of when production/sales started, but clearly there has not been a full year's revenue from the contract. Also there is no information on the length or total value of the contract.

	Marking scheme	
		Marks
(a)	**Analysis of results**	
	A like for like comparison taking account of the consolidation and the contract	5
(b)	Up to 5 marks for ratio calculations	5
	Profitability	4½
	Gearing and interest cover	2½
(c)	**Additional information**	
	Any three of the six suggestions provided	3
Total		**20**